Living Weapons

A VOLUME IN THE SERIES

Cornell Studies in Security Affairs

edited by Robert J. Art, Robert Jervis, and Stephen M. Walt

A list of titles in this series is available at www.cornellpress.cornell.edu.

LIVING WEAPONS

Biological Warfare
and International Security

GREGORY D. KOBLENTZ

CORNELL UNIVERSITY PRESS
ITHACA AND LONDON

First published 2009 by Cornell University Press
First printing, Cornell Paperbacks, 2011

Printed in the United States of America

Library of Congress Cataloging-in-Publication Data

Koblentz, Gregory D., 1974–
    Living weapons : biological warfare and international security
/ Gregory D. Koblentz.
        p. cm.—(Cornell studies in security affairs)
    Includes bibliographical references and index.
    ISBN 978-0-8014-4768-6 (cloth : alk. paper)
    ISBN 978-0-8014-7752-2 (pbk. : alk. paper)
1. Biological weapons.   2. Biological warfare.
3. Bioterrorism.   4. Security, International.   I. Title.
II. Series: Cornell studies in security affairs.

UG447.8.K637   2009
358'.38—dc22   2009005497

Cornell University Press strives to use environmentally responsible
suppliers and materials to the fullest extent possible in the publishing of
its books. Such materials include vegetable-based, low-VOC inks and
acid-free papers that are recycled, totally chlorine-free, or partly composed
of nonwood fibers. For further information, visit our website at
www.cornellpress.cornell.edu.

Cloth printing   10 9 8 7 6 5 4 3 2 1
Paperback printing   10 9 8 7 6 5 4 3 2 1

For Linda and Kai

CONTENTS

ACKNOWLEDGMENTS

This book would not have been possible without the help of many colleagues, friends, and family members. I thank Stephen Van Evera for his inspiration, support, and mentoring. I also learned a great deal from Harvey Sapolsky, Thomas Christensen, Sandy Weiner, Barry Posen, Ken Oye, and Geoffrey Forden.

I also thank Robert Art, Alexander Downes, Linda Fu, Martin Furmanski, Gene Godbold, Jeanne Guillemin, Kendall Hoyt, Judith Koblentz, Joel Koblentz, Milton Leitenberg, Sean Lynn-Jones, Alan Pearson, Julian Perry Robinson, Elizabeth Stanley, Seth Stern, Jonathan B. Tucker, John Ellis van Courtland Moon, Margaret Sloane, and Kathleen Vogel for carefully reading previous drafts and providing excellent feedback. I am also grateful for comments from the participants in seminars at the Massachusetts Institute for Technology's Security Studies Program, Harvard University's Olin Institute for Strategic Studies, the Fourth Annual New Faces Conference at the Triangle Institute for Security Studies, and Georgetown University's Program in Science, Technology and International Affairs. I am indebted to Matthew Meselson, John Moon, and Jack McGeorge for generously providing access to their archives and sharing their encyclopedic knowledge of biological weapons.

My colleagues in the Department of Public and International Affairs and the Biodefense Graduate Program at George Mason University, especially Robert Dudley, Frances Harbour, Sonia Ben Ouagrham-Gormley, and Robert Baker, have been tremendously helpful and supportive. I have also benefited enormously from stimulating discussions with my colleagues in the Scientists Working Group on Biological and Chemical Weapons at the Center for Arms Control and Non-Proliferation. I would also like to acknowledge the generous financial support of the MacArthur Foundation, Carnegie Corporation, and the John Anson Kittredge Educational Fund.

Finally, I would like to thank my loving wife, Linda Fu, whose encouragement and support sustained me throughout the entire process.

ACRONYMS AND SCIENTIFIC TERMS

B. anthracis	*Bacillus anthracis* (anthrax)
B. melitensis	*Brucella melitensis* (brucellosis)
B. mallei	*Burkholderia mallei* (glanders)
B. pseudomallei	*Burkholderia pseudomallei* (melioidosis)
BND	Bundesnachrichtendienst (Federal Intelligence Service, Germany)
Bt	*Bacillus thuringiensis*
BW	biological weapon(s)
BWC	Biological Weapons Convention—formally, the Convention on the Prohibition of the Development, Production, and Stockpiling of Bacteriological (Biological) and Toxin Weapons and on their Destruction (1972)
C. psittaci	*Chlamydia psittaci* (psittacosis)
C. botulinum	*Clostridium botulinum* (botulism)
C. perfringens	*Clostridium perfringens* (gas gangrene)
C. burnetii	*Coxiella burnetii* (Q fever)
CBM	confidence-building measure

CBW	chemical and biological weapons
CDC	Centers for Disease Control and Prevention
CEDC	Chemical Engineering Design Center (Iraq)
CMC	Coordinating Management Committee (South Africa)
CW	chemical weapon(s)
CWC	Chemical Weapons Convention—formally, Convention on the Prohibition of the Development, Production, Stockpiling and Use of Chemical Weapons and on their Destruction (1993)
CIA	Central Intelligence Agency
DCI	Director of Central Intelligence
DIA	Defense Intelligence Agency
DNI	Director of National Intelligence
DOD	Department of Defense
F. tularensis	*Francisella tularensis* (tularemia)
FDA	Food and Drug Administration
FFCD	Full, Final, and Complete Disclosure
FBI	Federal Bureau of Investigation
GRU	Glavnoye Razvedyvatelnoye Upravlenie (Main Intelligence Administration, USSR/Russia)
HHS	Department of Health and Human Services
HUMINT	intelligence from human sources
IAEA	International Atomic Energy Agency
IIS	Iraqi Intelligence Service (Mukhabarat)
INC	Iraqi National Congress
ISG	Iraq Survey Group
ISU	Implementation Support Unit of the BWC
KGB	Komitet Gosudarstvennoi Bezopasnosti (State Security Committee, USSR)
NARA	National Archives and Records Administration
NATO	North Atlantic Treaty Organization
NBACC	National Biodefense Analysis and Countermeasures Center
NIE	National Intelligence Estimate
NIH	National Institutes of Health
NSA	National Security Archives
NSABB	National Science Advisory Board for Biosecurity
OMV	ongoing monitoring and verification
OTA	Office of Technology Assessment
R. prowazekii	*Rickettsia prowazekii* (typhus)
RRL	Roodeplaat Research Laboratory (South Africa)
S. Typhimurium	*Salmonella* Typhimurium (salmonellosis)

S. Typhi	*Salmonella* Typhi (typhoid fever)
SADF	South African Defense Force
SCP	single-cell protein
SIPRI	Stockholm International Peace Research Institute
SIS	Secret Intelligence Service (United Kingdom; also known as MI6)
SNIE	Special National Intelligence Estimate
Spp.	species
SSCI	Senate Select Committee on Intelligence
T. indica	*Tilletia indica* (wheat cover smut fungus)
TRC	Truth and Reconciliation Commission (South Africa)
TRC	Technical Research Center (Iraq)
TSMID	Technical and Scientific Materials Import Division (Iraq)
USAMRIID	United States Army Medical Research Institute of Infectious Diseases
UNSC	United Nations Security Council
UNSCOM	United Nations Special Commission
UNMOVIC	United Nations Monitoring, Verification, and Inspection Commission
VEE	Venezuelan equine encephalitis
VEREX	Ad Hoc Group of Government Experts to Identify and Examine Verification Measures from a Scientific and Technical Standpoint
V. cholerae	*Vibrio cholera* (cholera)
variola	smallpox virus
WHO	World Health Organization
WINPAC	Weapons Intelligence, Nonproliferation, and Arms Control (CIA)
WMD	weapon(s) of mass destruction
Y. pestis	*Yersinia pestis* (plague)

Living Weapons

INTRODUCTION

The Threat of Biological Weapons

On February 5, 2003, Secretary of State Colin Powell issued a dire warning to the United Nations Security Council in an effort to convince the international community that Iraq possessed weapons of mass destruction (WMD) in violation of Security Council resolutions. He stated: "There can be no doubt that Saddam Hussein has biological weapons and the capability to rapidly produce more, many more. And he has the ability to dispense these lethal poisons and diseases in ways that can cause massive death and destruction."[1] Powell's presentation to the Security Council, drawing on previously classified intelligence on Iraq's WMD programs, was the George W. Bush administration's most forceful attempt to portray Iraq as a threat to international security and to rally international support for the use of force to overthrow Saddam Hussein.

Powell turned first to the threat posed by Iraq's biological warfare program. He began by holding up a small vial of powder that represented the amount of *B. anthracis* spores that had disrupted the United States Postal Service and U.S.

---

1. Secretary of State Colin Powell, "Remarks to the United Nations Security Council," New York City, February 5, 2003, http://www.state.gov/secretary/former/powell/remarks/2003/17300.htm.

Senate in October 2001. He then compared the teaspoon of material used in the anthrax letter attacks with the thousands of liters of *B. anthracis* that Iraq had admitted to producing but had failed to account for to UN inspectors. According to Powell, "one of the most worrisome things that emerges from the thick intelligence file we have on Iraq's biological weapons" is Iraq's development of a fleet of truck- and rail-mounted biological agent production facilities.[2] Powell then presented the Security Council with detailed diagrams of the Iraqi mobile biological production facilities and described at length the eyewitness accounts on which this information was based. With George Tenet, director of the Central Intelligence Agency, seated directly behind him, Powell reassured his colleagues on the Security Council that "every statement I make today is backed up by sources, solid sources. These are not assertions. What we're giving you are facts and conclusions based on solid intelligence."[3]

As we know now, these conclusions were not based on solid intelligence. In fact, after the March 2003 U.S.-led invasion of Iraq, investigation of Iraq's WMD programs has shown that every single U.S. allegation regarding Iraqi biological weapon (BW) activities was wrong. According to the bipartisan Commission on the Intelligence Capabilities of the United States Regarding Weapons of Mass Destruction (also known as the Silberman-Robb Commission), this failure to properly assess Iraq's BW capabilities and intentions was "one of the most painful errors" committed by the intelligence community before the war.[4] How could the U.S. intelligence community, the largest and most sophisticated in the world, have been so wrong?

Although the severity of this intelligence failure was a shock, intelligence agencies have a long track record of either underestimating or overestimating their adversaries' BW capabilities and intentions. BW programs are notoriously hard intelligence targets. The United States also encountered serious problems assessing the Iraqi BW program before the 1991 Gulf War and the Soviet BW program throughout the cold war. One of my objectives in this book is to describe the challenges in collecting and analyzing intelligence on biological weapons, to determine the reasons for successes and failures in the Iraq and Soviet cases, and to provide recommendations on how to prevent such intelligence failures in the future.

Intelligence, however, is just one line of defense against biological weapons. Understanding the threat posed by biological weapons and how to counter these weapons requires the analysis of other areas of international security, including

---

2. Ibid.
3. Ibid.
4. The Commission on the Intelligence Capabilities of the United States Regarding Weapons of Mass Destruction, *Report to the President* (Washington, DC: GPO, 2005), 48.

arms control, deterrence, civilian-military relations, and terrorism. My larger purpose in this book is to examine the international security implications of biological weapons, to enhance our understanding of the unique challenges posed by these weapons, and to offer recommendations on how to reduce the dangers posed by biological weapons.

The proliferation of biological weapons (BW) to states or terrorists is one of the most pressing security issues of the twenty-first century.[5] At a time when the United States enjoys overwhelming conventional military superiority, biological weapons may be one of the more attractive means of waging asymmetric warfare by less powerful states hoping to challenge the status quo. Therefore, it is important to understand the strategic consequences of the proliferation of biological weapons and how effective traditional security strategies such as arms control and deterrence are at containing this threat. In addition, in this book I examine the challenges posed by BW programs for civilian oversight and management and the prospect of obtaining timely and accurate intelligence on the BW capabilities and intentions of other states.

Terrorist groups whose objectives are to cause mass casualties or mass disruption are the second threat to international security. The catastrophic terrorist attacks on September 11, 2001, demonstrated the desire and ability of some terrorist groups to cause massive casualties and the vulnerability of the United States to such attacks. Shortly after the September 11 attacks, the United States was the victim of biological terrorism when letters filled with a dry powder of *Bacillus anthracis,* the bacterium that causes the disease anthrax, were sent to media outlets and two U.S. senators. The 2001 anthrax letter attacks killed five people, sickened another seventeen, forced thousands more to take antibiotics as a precaution, and contaminated dozens of private and government buildings. The anthrax letters also disrupted the United States Postal Service, caused nationwide anxiety about the safety of the mail, and temporarily shut down the U.S. Senate. The anthrax letter attacks reinforced the nation's vulnerability to terrorism following 9/11 and illustrated the potential impact that even a small BW attack could have. Although the current level of terrorist BW capabilities are limited, advances in technology and the emergence of more violent groups pose long-term risks.

The dangers posed by biological weapons are heightened by advances in the life sciences and biotechnology that can be exploited to develop new or improved biological weapons. The Soviet Union's extensive efforts to apply advanced biotechnologies to biological warfare established that this risk is not a theoretical

---

5. Gregory Koblentz, "Pathogens as Weapons: The International Security Implications of Biological Warfare," *International Security* 28, no. 3 (2003/4): 84–122.

concern. Breakthroughs in the life sciences, such as the sequencing of the human genome in 2001, the synthesis of poliovirus in 2002, and the 2005 resurrection of the virus that caused the 1918 influenza pandemic, have heightened fears that humanity's ability to create and manipulate life is outpacing our capability to prevent this technology from being used for hostile purposes.

Despite the growing awareness of the threat posed by biological weapons, the history of biological warfare and the unique security challenges posed by biological weapons remain unfamiliar to much of the public, academia, and government. Biological weapons are the least well understood of the WMD that also include nuclear and chemical weapons. The Nobel Prize winner in Economics Thomas Schelling has observed that "the tendency in our planning is to confuse the unfamiliar with the improbable. The contingency we have not considered seriously looks strange; what looks strange is thought improbable; what is improbable need not be considered seriously."[6]

During the cold war, the focus of security scholars on nuclear weapons was understandable. The destructive power of nuclear weapons had been established with horrific results during World War II, and postwar advances generated even more powerful weapons. Nuclear weapons formed the core of the superpowers' strategic arsenals and were integral to maintaining the "balance of terror" between them. In addition, these weapons were deployed or under development in zones of potential conflict stretching from Europe to the Middle East to Asia. Thus, the study of nuclear weapons and proliferation offered multiple opportunities for original research and valuable contributions to the theoretical and empirical literatures.

In contrast, biological weapons have never been used openly on the battlefield and their development has always been conducted under the strictest secrecy. In addition, in 1969 the United States abandoned its offensive BW program, and in 1972 biological weapons became the first class of weapons to be completely outlawed by an international treaty, the Biological Weapons Convention (BWC). Thereafter, biological weapons, never high on the list of priorities of scholars, slipped even lower. Biological weapons, however, did not disappear with the signing of the BWC.

The international security implications of the biotechnology revolution and the spread of biological weapons began receiving increased attention in the 1990s following revelations about the Soviet and Iraqi BW programs, continued advances in the life sciences, and the emergence of more lethal terrorist groups interested in WMD. This renewed attention, however, has not always translated

6. Thomas Schelling, foreword to *Pearl Harbor: Warning and Decision* by Roberta Wohlstetter (Stanford: Stanford University Press, 1962), vii.

into a greater understanding of the dangers posed by biological weapons. Government officials and academics frequently lump biological weapons together with nuclear and chemical weapons under the category of WMD or discuss the "chem-bio" threat.

The use of terms such as WMD and "chem-bio" has hindered our understanding of the international security implications of biological weapons. The widespread use of these labels has obscured important differences between these different weapons and the strategic consequences of their proliferation. Unlike nuclear and chemical weapons, biological weapons are composed of, or derived from, living organisms. This unique characteristic of biological weapons is at the heart of many of the security challenges posed by them. The diversity of pathogenic microorganisms and toxins that can be used as weapons provides the attacker with flexibility in planning its attack. The sheer number of potential biological warfare agents complicates the task of the defender. The ability of pathogens to replicate themselves inside a host enables an attacker to use only a small amount of a biological weapon to inflict mass casualties. The overlap between the equipment, knowledge, and materials required to develop biological weapons and to conduct civilian biomedical research or develop biological defenses limits the effectiveness of arms control and verification measures and complicates intelligence collection and analysis.

The study of biological weapons reveals a number of paradoxes and dilemmas. Biological weapons are widely feared, yet rarely used. Biological weapons were the first weapon prohibited by an international treaty, yet the proliferation of these weapons increased after they were banned in 1972. Biological weapons are frequently called "the poor man's atomic bomb," yet they cannot provide the same deterrent capability as nuclear weapons. One of my goals in this book is to explain the underlying principles of these apparent paradoxes.

Policymakers seeking to reduce the dangers posed by biological weapons face two powerful dilemmas. The most important is the multiuse dilemma: the skills, materials, and technology needed to produce biological weapons are also necessary to develop defenses against them and to conduct civilian activities such as biomedical research and pharmaceutical production. Most analyses of biotechnology refer to it as dual-use, since it has both civilian and military applications. In this book, the term "multiuse" is used to highlight the distinct but overlapping applications of biotechnology in civilian, defensive, and offensive domains. The old distinction between military and civilian applications of biology and biotechnology has become more blurred in recent years as more civilian institutions become engaged in defensive research and military organizations become more interested in applying biotechnology in the areas of energy, materials science, logistics, medicine, and electronics. The growing importance of biotechnology to economic development, the global diffusion of this technology, and the growth of national biodefense programs heightens this multiuse dilemma.

A second dilemma facing policymakers is that both legitimate users of biotechnology and those who would use it to develop weapons seek to hide their activities behind a wall of secrecy. While states with illegal BW programs have strong normative, legal, and strategic incentives to shield their activities from outside scrutiny, private actors and governments also use secrecy to protect proprietary and national security information. As a result, there is a constant tension between transparency and secrecy. Although transparency is widely regarded as crucial to scientific progress, the foundation for effective arms control verification, and a means for states to reassure others about their peaceful intentions, the desire for secrecy is driven by equally strong concerns regarding commercial competition, governmental anxiety about revealing vulnerabilities or intelligence capabilities, and apprehension that biological research could be misused for hostile purposes. A common thread throughout this book is the way in which secrecy can be a hydra-headed source of destabilizing effects: it impedes verification, undermines deterrence, hinders civilian oversight, and complicates threat assessments.

Biological weapons possess a number of characteristics that cause them to exert a destabilizing influence on international security. They pose unique challenges from the perspectives of arms control, deterrence, civil-military relations, and intelligence. It is difficult to verify that biotechnology is not being misused for hostile purposes, to exercise effective oversight over BW programs, and to obtain accurate assessments of a state's BW capabilities and intentions. Each of these challenges to international security is discussed in the following chapters.

Chapter 1 provides a brief history of biological warfare and describes the most important characteristics of biological weapons. Because of the diversity and potency of BW agents, the ease with which they can be used to conduct surprise attacks, and the difficulties inherent in defending against a BW attack, an attacker using biological weapons has a significant advantage over a defender. While biological weapons have limited utility as battlefield weapons, they can serve as a force multiplier for conventional military operations, especially at the operational level of combat. Although biological weapons can be as lethal as nuclear weapons, they possess characteristics that make them unsuitable for serving as a strategic deterrent. Despite the rare use of biological weapons in modern times, there are troubling indications that the normative, operational, and political constraints that have inhibited the use of BW may be eroding.

Chapter 2 examines the challenges in verifying that biotechnology is not being used for hostile purposes. Obstacles to verification include the multiuse applications of biotechnology, the overlap between offensive and defensive BW programs, the need for secrecy to protect commercial and national security information, and the lack of unique identifying characteristics of offensive BW programs. This chapter describes the origins and evolution of the 1972 Biological Weapons Convention (BWC), the first international treaty to prohibit an entire class of weapons. Notably, unlike other WMD nonproliferation treaties, the BWC contains no verification mechanism.

The experience of the United Nations Special Commission (UNSCOM) in Iraq provides a fascinating case study in biological arms control verification. UNSCOM was the most intrusive biological arms control regime ever devised, and yet the commission took several years to uncover Iraq's past production of BW agents. In fact, UNSCOM would probably not have learned of the full extent of Iraq's BW production, weaponization, and deployment of biological weapons if not for the defection of a senior Iraqi official in 1995. Although UNSCOM scored some limited achievements in the field of BW verification, its experience is not easily generalizable to a multilateral organization responsible for verifying the BWC. Unfortunately, the political and technical constraints that have hindered the development of an effective verification regime for the BWC are enduring and likely to remain so in the near future.

Chapter 3 examines how the intense secrecy that shrouds BW programs impedes civilian control of these programs. States are compelled to adopt strict secrecy for their BW programs for normative, legal, and strategic reasons. The compartmentalization of knowledge necessary for secrecy allows BW organizations to increase their autonomy and evade accountability. This lack of effective oversight can lead to flawed decision making, violation of international obligations, corruption, and the proliferation of BW technology or materials to other states and to terrorists. This chapter examines how Soviet, Russian, and South African BW program managers exploited the secrecy developed to protect their BW programs from external threats to shield their organizations from attempts by domestic civilian leaders to rollback or terminate their programs.

Chapter 4 analyzes why states tend to have flawed assessments of the BW capabilities and intentions of their adversaries. The combination of intense secrecy; the difficulty in distinguishing between civilian, defense, and offensive activities; and the importance and opacity of intentions for making threat assessments makes BW programs among the hardest targets from an intelligence perspective. Poor intelligence complicates efforts to develop and deploy defenses, engage in diplomacy, conduct inspections, and undertake military operations. In addition, misleading intelligence can give rise to a security dilemma or provoke a state to take unnecessary military action. This chapter evaluates U.S. assessments of the Soviet and Iraqi BW programs and describes the hurdles to developing accurate intelligence concerning these threats.

Chapter 5 examines the threat posed by biological terrorism. This chapter provides a brief history of biological terrorism and a framework for assessing the threat posed by biological weapons in the hands of nonstate actors. In addition, it evaluates the threat posed by al Qaeda and state-sponsored biological terrorism as well as the challenges faced by law enforcement and intelligence agencies in detecting the BW efforts of nonstate actors.

The concluding chapter offers six policy prescriptions for countering the growing danger posed by biological weapons: (1) strengthen defenses against natural and man-made diseases, (2) increase the transparency of defensive and multiuse biological activities, (3) improve intelligence and forensic capabilities, (4) enhance cooperative nonproliferation programs, (5) revitalize the Biological Weapons Convention, and (6) reinforce the norm against the development and use of these weapons. There is no single measure that will be able to eliminate the threat posed by biological weapons. Managing the threat posed by biological weapons requires a network of national and international measures to prevent, deter, prepare for, and respond to BW threats. Building and sustaining this network will be one of the primary security challenges for the twenty-first century.

1

OFFENSE, DEFENSE, AND DETERRENCE

Biological warfare is the use of microorganisms, toxins derived from living organisms, or bioregulators to deliberately cause the death or illness of humans, plants, or animals.[1] Biological weapons are unique among the instruments of warfare because they are composed of, or derived from, living organisms. This feature of biological weapons has several important implications for their use in warfare and their impact on international security.

Disease-causing microorganisms such as bacteria, viruses, and fungi are called pathogens. Pathogens require a human, plant, or animal host in order to multiply and cause disease. Because these organisms are self-reproducing, a small dose can initiate an infection. Once a pathogen infects a host, its effects are determined by a complex interaction between the microorganism and the host's immune system. The time between infection and the onset of disease symptoms is called the incubation period, and it can last for days or weeks. If the disease is transmissible from person to person, a small number of infections could spark an epidemic.

---

1. Microorganisms, toxins, and bioregulators will be referred to collectively as biological agents or BW agents.

Since toxins and bioregulators are nonliving molecules that do not replicate in the body, the initial exposure dose is what causes the illness. This means that toxins tend to be faster acting than pathogens, causing effects within hours or at most a day or two. Their effects are still slower than some chemical weapons, such as nerve agents, which can kill victims within minutes. Toxins can be derived from a variety of sources such as plants (ricin from the castor bean), animals (saxitoxin from shellfish), fungi (aflatoxin from *Aspergillus flavus*), or bacteria (botulinum toxin from *Clostridium botulinum*). The number of toxins that are highly lethal and easily obtainable in large quantities, however, is far more limited than the number of pathogens with these attributes.

Bioregulators are a relatively recent addition to the traditional definition of biological weapons as being pathogens and toxins. Bioregulators are chemicals normally produced in the human body that control communication between cells and that play a crucial role in governing the nervous, endocrine, and immune systems. Neurotransmitters such as serotonin and endorphins are responsible for communication between cells in the nervous system. Hormones such as insulin and epinephrine are used to communicate between organs in the endocrine and cardiovascular systems. Cytokines such as interleukins play a role in modulating the immune system. Small imbalances in the level of bioregulators can have dramatic effects on cognition, emotion, and physiological processes.[2]

Biological weapons, whether pathogens, toxins, or bioregulators, are selective in their targets. They affect only living things and do not damage or destroy vehicles, buildings, or machinery. Most biological agents are fragile creatures. These agents require special measures to stay alive or stable during production, storage, delivery, and dissemination. Most of these agents will die if exposed to sunlight or extremes of temperature or humidity. Thus, the use of biological agents as weapons is fraught with uncertainties.

A History of Biological Warfare

The history of biological warfare can be divided into four eras: (1) pre–germ theory, (2) applied microbiology, (3) industrial microbiology and aerobiology, and (4) molecular biology and biotechnology.[3] These eras roughly correspond to

---

2. See Malcolm Dando, *The New Biological Weapons: Threat, Proliferation, and Control* (Boulder, CO: Lynne Reinner, 2001).

3. The organization of this section was inspired by similar typologies developed by Erhard Geissler, Malcolm Dando, and Raymond Zilinskas. For a more in-depth examination of the history of biological warfare, see Erhard Geissler and John Ellis van Courtland Moon, eds., *Biological and Toxin Weapons: Research, Development and Use from the Middle Ages to 1945* (Oxford: Oxford University Press, 1999); Mark

developments in science and technology in the field of microbiology that successively yielded more capable generations of biological weapons. The four eras of biological warfare are tied to changes in the ability of scientists to identify and isolate pathogens, modify them to yield desired properties, produce larger quantities of a wider range of agents, and more effectively weaponize and disseminate these agents. This evolution is not only a description of the past but is also a warning about the potential misuse of advanced biotechnologies for hostile purposes in the future. This framework applies to both state and terrorist efforts to develop BW capabilities. The history of biological terrorism is related in chapter 5.

Pre–Germ Theory

Biological warfare has been practiced since ancient times, though the number of actual attacks is small. Disease was particularly common and deadly during war. Throughout this era, naturally occurring diseases commonly killed more soldiers than the enemy, and thus they had a significant impact on military conflicts.[4] The natural impact of disease on military campaigns probably motivated early attempts to harness disease as a weapon. Although military forces did not know what caused disease until the development of the germ theory in the late 1800s, they could easily identify sources of disease such as dead bodies.

Armies engaged in biological warfare by contaminating water supplies using toxic plants or dead animals, catapulting infected corpses into fortified areas, giving infected materials to the enemy, and by sending people infected with contagious disease into the enemy's camp. These tactics relied on the use of fomites (a physical object that serves to transmit an infectious agent) or vectors (a living organism such as a human or insect that transmits disease) as crude munitions. The history of Greek and Roman warfare is replete with references to the use of toxic plants and dead animals to contaminate water supplies.[5] In 1346 Mongols reportedly catapulted corpses infected with *Yersinia pestis* (the bacterium that causes plague) into the besieged city of Kaffa in the Crimea. In 1763, during the French and Indian War, beleaguered British soldiers at Fort Pitt gave blankets contaminated with variola (the virus that causes smallpox) to hostile Native American tribes. During the American Revolution, British forces may

---

Wheelis, Lajos Rózsa, and Malcolm Dando, eds., *Deadly Cultures: Biological Weapons since 1945* (Cambridge: Harvard University Press, 2006); and Jeanne Guillemin, *Biological Weapons: From the Invention of State-Sponsored Programs to Contemporary Bioterrorism* (New York: Columbia University Press, 2005).

4. William H. McNeill, *Plagues and People* (New York: Anchor Books, 1998), 288–89; and Jared Diamond, *Guns, Germs and Steel: The Fates of Human Societies* (New York: WW Norton, 1999), 195–214.

5. Adrienne Mayor, *Greek Fire, Poison Arrow, and Scorpion Bombs: Biological and Chemical Warfare in the Ancient World* (Woodstock, NY: Overlook, 2003), 99–118.

have tried to infect the Continental Army with smallpox by sending infected individuals behind enemy lines. Given the prevalence of these diseases at the time and the lack of authoritative records, it is difficult to determine if any of these attacks was successful.[6]

Applied Microbiology

The second era in biological warfare was enabled by the development of germ theory, which identified microorganisms as the causative agent of disease. As a result of experimental breakthroughs, scientists in the late 1800s were able to identify several bacteria as the causes of specific diseases and developed the ability to grow bacteria artificially. Pathogens selected, produced, and employed as weapons during this era were almost exclusively bacteria, in that at this time these were the only pathogens that could be isolated and grown in laboratories. Dissemination of biological agents remained limited to fomites and vectors.

Defenses against disease and biological weapons also improved markedly during this era. Once germ theory was widely accepted, it became possible to block disease transmission by improving sanitation and hygiene. Applied microbiology also led to the creation of vaccines to prevent a number of common diseases. The discovery of penicillin provided physicians for the first time with the means to cure a range of bacterial diseases.

During World War I, Germany applied this knowledge in an extensive sabotage campaign to infect cavalry and draft animals being shipped from neutral countries to the Allies.[7] In response to the horrors of chemical warfare during World War I, the use of chemical and biological weapons was banned in 1925 under the Geneva Protocol. Because the Geneva Protocol did not prohibit the development of chemical and biological weapons and most of the signatories reserved the right to retaliate with these weapons if they were attacked first, most of the great powers had offensive and defensive BW programs by the beginning of World War II.[8] Japan's BW program was the largest of its kind during this era.

---

6. Mark Wheelis, "Biological Warfare before 1914," in *Biological and Toxin Weapons,* ed. Geissler and Moon, 8–34.

7. German agents infected animals bound from Argentina, Norway, Romania, Spain, and the United States with *B. anthracis* and *B. mallei.* Although German officials believed this campaign to have been successful in infecting large numbers of animals, these results have not been independently confirmed. Mark Wheelis, "Biological Sabotage in World War I," in *Biological and Toxin Weapons,* ed. Geissler and Moon, 35–62.

8. The one major exception was Germany. Although Germany pioneered deadly advances in chemical warfare, Hitler forbade the development of biological weapons in the 1940s. Erhard Geissler, "Biological Warfare Activities in Germany, 1923–1945," in *Biological and Toxin Weapons,* ed. Geissler and Moon, 91–126.

Japan embarked on an aggressive BW program in 1931 under the leadership of the military scientist Ishii Shiro.[9] Research was conducted primarily in China and included gruesome experiments on thousands of prisoners. Despite the scope of their research and the amount of resources invested in it, the Japanese could not overcome important scientific and technical hurdles. They were able to produce hundreds of kilograms of BW agents, but their production methods were crude and inefficient. Japan also failed to develop an effective munition to disseminate BW agents. Instead, they were forced to rely on fomites, vectors such as fleas infected with *Y. pestis,* and contamination of food and water supplies to spread disease. Japan first used biological weapons on a limited scale against Soviet forces in 1939.[10] Between 1939 and 1942, the Japanese also conducted a number of biological attacks against Chinese civilians and soldiers with *Bacillus anthracis* (the bacterium that causes anthrax), *Burkholderia mallei* (the bacterium that causes glanders), *Vibrio cholerae* (the bacterium that causes cholera), *Salmonella* Typhi (the bacterium that causes typhoid), and *Y. pestis.* Although these operations succeeded in causing widespread epidemics, the techniques proved unreliable, caused Japanese casualties as well, and did not provide Japan with a significant advantage over the Chinese opposition forces. These attacks are the only confirmed large-scale use of biological weapons in the twentieth century.

Decades later, Rhodesia and South Africa adopted unsophisticated means of spreading disease among rebel groups and their supporters similar to the methods used by Japan. In the late 1970s, Rhodesian counterinsurgency units used *B. anthracis, V. cholerae,* and various poisons to contaminate clothing, food, drinks, and water supplies used by guerilla groups and their supporters.[11] South Africa's apartheid-era chemical and biological weapons (CBW) program, Project Coast, adopted these techniques in the 1980s. The program supplied members of South African security services with small quantities of poisons, toxins, and pathogens such as *B. anthracis, V. cholerae,* and *Salmonella* Typhimurium (the bacterium that causes salmonellosis) to contaminate food and beverages or in assassination weapons used against members and supporters of the African National Congress.[12]

---

9. This section is drawn from Sheldon Harris, "The Japanese Biological Warfare Programme: An Overview," in *Biological and Toxin Weapons,* ed. Geissler and Moon, 127–52; and Sheldon Harris, *Factories of Death: Japanese Biological Warfare 1932–1945 and the American Cover Up* (London: Routledge, 1994).

10. Although both sides experienced disease outbreaks during the fighting, it is not possible to attribute these outbreaks to Japan's BW activities.

11. Marléne Burger and Chandré Gould, *Secrets and Lies: Wouter Basson and South Africa's Chemical and Biological Warfare Programme* (Cape Town, S.A.: Zebra Press, 2002), 15–16, 221–22; and Chandré Gould, "South Africa's Chemical and Biological Warfare Programme, 1981–1995" (PhD diss., Rhodes University, Grahamstown, S.A., 2005), 35–42.

12. Burger and Gould, *Secrets and Lies,* 18, 31–36, 47, 53–77; and Chandré Gould and Peter Folb, *Project Coast: Apartheid's Chemical and Biological Warfare Programme* (Geneva: United Nations Publications, 2002), 86–99, 103–4, 115–16, 159–67.

Industrial Microbiology and Aerobiology

By the end of World War II, the science and technology applicable to BW had entered a new era and the major powers prepared to introduce a new generation of biological weapons. This third era in biological warfare was characterized by advances in microbiology that enabled the industrial-scale production of microorganisms and the maturation of aerobiology, the scientific study of the dispersion and effects of airborne biological materials, including microorganisms. The ability to mass-produce microorganisms was initially developed for the pharmaceutical, baking, and brewery industries, while aerobiology was developed to study communicable diseases for public health purposes. The large-scale production of pathogens and their dissemination as aerosols formed the basis for virtually all postwar BW programs, such as those pursued by the United States, the United Kingdom, the Soviet Union, and Iraq.[13] During this era, defenders benefited from their improved ability to mass-produce vaccines and antibiotics. This advantage, however, was more than offset by the growing area coverage of aerosolized BW agents and the inability to detect such aerosol clouds, which severely limited the ability of a defender to respond effectively to such an attack.

During World War II, the United States built a large-scale *B. anthracis* production and munition-filling facility in Vigo, Indiana. With its twelve 20,000-gallon fermenters, this plant was the largest BW production facility in the world and dwarfed the production capacities achieved by Japan.[14] The plant never became operational due to difficulties in producing lethal agents safely and because of the ending of the war. The United States built a smaller standby BW production facility at Pine Bluff Arsenal in Arkansas in 1954.

The Soviet Union built BW production facilities on an enormous scale during the postwar era. A BW production facility at Stepnogorsk in Kazakhstan contained ten 20,000-liter fermenters capable of producing one thousand tons of *B. anthracis* per year. Stepnogorsk was one of six such facilities in the Soviet Union that together could be mobilized during wartime to produce thousands of tons of different BW agents a year.[15]

---

13. Notable exceptions include the Rhodesian and South African BW programs described above.

14. While the Vigo facility could produce about one hundred tons of *B. anthracis* a month, Japanese methods were able to produce only eight tons of bacteria a month. John Ellis van Courtland Moon, "U.S. Biological Warfare Planning and Preparedness: The Dilemmas of Policy," in *Biological and Toxin Weapons*, ed. Geissler and Moon, 238–39; and Robert Harris and Jeremy Paxman, *Higher Form of Killing: The Secret History of Chemical and Biological Warfare* (New York: Random House, 2002), 78.

15. Ken Alibek, *Biohazard: The Chilling True Story of the Largest Covert Biological Weapons Program in the World—Told from the Inside by the Man Who Ran It,* with Stephen Handelman (New York: Random House, 1999), 299–301.

This era saw the first large-scale production of viruses as BW agents, although the means of production were relatively crude. Because viruses need to grow inside of cells, fermenters could not be used for production. Instead, both the United States and the Soviet Union employed assembly lines of embryonated chicken eggs as the production vessel of choice. Despite these advances, bacteria and bacterial toxins still dominated the U.S. and Soviet programs throughout this period. Of the eight antipersonnel agents selected by the United States for use as biological weapons, only two were viruses.[16] Similarly, by 1972, only two of nine agents weaponized by the Soviets were viruses.[17] Classical microbiological techniques were capable of modifying BW agents in limited ways. Both the Soviet Union and United States created strains of *Francisella tularensis* (the bacterium that causes tularemia) resistant to a small number of antibiotics by exposing the organism to an antibiotic and then culturing the surviving organisms that exhibited resistance to the drug.[18]

Bacterial, viral, and toxin agents were produced in two versions for use as weapons: as a liquid slurry or as a dry powder. Although the slurry was easier and safer to produce, dry agents were more concentrated, easier to store, and easier to disseminate.[19] Although the United States and Soviet Union produced and stockpiled both forms of BW agents, Iraq's BW program was limited to liquid agents because it was unable to master the production of dry BW agents.

The major innovation of the third-generation BW programs was the application of aerobiology to the problem of dissemination. Aerobiology was the key to the development of an effective means of employing BW agents on a large scale. The most effective means of infecting large populations is via the respiratory tract by dispersing the biological agents as an aerosol or cloud of microscopic droplets in the size range of 1–5 microns.[20] Aerosols composed of particles in this range have several advantages. First, the particles can stay airborne longer, thus increasing the potential area of infection. Second, infection through the respiratory route generally can take place with a smaller dose than other routes of

---

16. The viruses were VEE and yellow fever. Department of the Army, *U.S. Army Activities in the U.S. Biological Warfare Programs* (Washington, DC: Department of the Army, February 24, 1977), 2: C-2, D-2; and Jeffrey Smart, "History of Chemical and Biological Warfare: An American Perspective," in *Medical Aspects of Chemical and Biological Warfare*, ed. Frederick Sidell, Ernest Takafuji, and David Franz (Falls Church, VA: Office of the Surgeon General, U.S. Army, 1997), 50.

17. The viruses were variola and VEE. Testimony by Soviet defector Dr. Kenneth Alibek before the Joint Economic Committee, *Terrorist and Intelligence Operations: Potential Impact on the U.S. Economy,* 105th Cong., 2nd ses., May 20, 1998, http://www.house.gov/jec/hearings/intell/alibek.htm.

18. Wendy Orent, "After Anthrax," *American Prospect* 11, no. 12 (2000); and Richard O. Spertzel, Robert W. Wannemacher, and Carol D. Linden, *Global Proliferation: Dynamics, Acquisition Strategies, and Responses,* vol. 4, *Biological Weapons Proliferation* (Washington, DC: Defense Nuclear Agency, 1994), 21.

19. William C. Patrick III, "Biological Warfare: An Overview," Director's Series on Proliferation 4 (Livermore, CA: Lawrence Livermore National Laboratory, May 1994), 5.

20. Particles smaller than 1 micron will be exhaled instead of being trapped in the lungs. Particles larger than 5 microns will not be able to penetrate past the upper respiratory tract. A micron is one thousandth of a millimeter. A human hair has a diameter of about 50 microns.

entry, and the severity of the resulting disease is typically more severe.[21] For example, the most common form of naturally occurring anthrax is cutaneous anthrax, which is contracted through cuts in the skin and has an untreated case
fatality rate of about 20 percent. In contrast, infection with anthrax through the
respiratory route, called inhalation anthrax, has a 90 percent lethality rate.[22] Another advantage of these types of aerosols is that they are invisible to the human
senses, thus facilitating clandestine attacks. Creating an aerosol containing viable organisms and particles of the correct size is the most difficult step in offensive biological warfare.

There are two principal categories of munitions designed to disseminate
aerosols of biological agents: point sources and line sources. Point source munitions use explosive or gaseous energy to disseminate their payload of biological
agent from a stationary position. The most efficient type of point source munition divides the biological agent payload into a large number of bomblets to
achieve a wider distribution of the agent. Large numbers of bomblets dispersed
from a bomb or missile warhead will saturate the center of the impact area with
BW agent regardless of wind direction and speed. Artillery shells, land and sea
mines, and other devices employed by special operations forces can also be used
as point source biological munitions. Line sources are created by dispersing a biological agent from moving vehicles, ships, aircraft, or cruise missiles in a line per-
pendicular to the direction of the prevailing wind. This type of dissemination is
the most efficient means for delivering BW agents in that it can cover a large area
and is difficult to detect.[23]

The key drawback to dispersing biological weapons as aerosols is their sensitivity to environmental and meteorological conditions that can result in uncertain
area coverage and effects. For example, the integrity of a biological aerosol cloud
and the path it follows after release from a munition are determined by wind
speed, wind direction, terrain, and the degree of atmospheric stability. In addition, biological agents—with the exception of *B. anthracis* and *C. burnetii,* which
can form protective spores—are fragile, and their viability can be sharply reduced
by ultraviolet radiation or unfavorable levels of humidity. The combination of
these factors can significantly influence the performance of a biological weapon.
Thus, an open-air biological weapons attack would require extensive preplan-
ning and access to accurate meteorological information for the target area.

21. Leroy Fothergill, "The Biological Warfare Threat," *Nonmilitary Defense: Chemical and Biological Defenses in Perspective,* Advances in Chemistry Series 26 (Washington, DC: American Chemical
Society, July 1960), 26.

22. Thomas V. Inglesby et al., "Anthrax as a Biological Weapon: Medical and Public Health Management," *Journal of the American Medical Association* 281, no. 18 (1999): 1738.

23. Patrick, "Biological Warfare," 4.

The careful selection of agents, delivery systems, targets, and timing of an attack, however, can compensate for most of these limitations. The timing of an attack can be adjusted to take advantage of the favorable atmospheric conditions typically found after dusk and before dawn and the lack of direct sunlight or ultraviolet radiation at these times. In order to minimize the influence of meteorological conditions, an attacker could employ bombs or missile warheads with dozens or hundreds of submunitions that would saturate the center of the impact area with an aerosol cloud regardless of the wind speed or direction.[24] Terrorists can minimize the impact of unfavorable meteorological conditions by releasing an aerosol indoors.

The United States and the Soviet Union dedicated substantial resources to understanding aerobiology, improving the stability of aerosolized BW agents, improving the dissemination efficiency of munitions, and testing these agents and munitions in both laboratories and in the field. In the United States, the Army conducted this research primarily in a giant, one million–liter explosive aerosol test chamber at its BW research center at Fort Detrick, Maryland. The military also conducted field tests at Dugway Proving Ground in Utah to validate the results of these experiments. In the 1960s under Project 112, an ambitious program to modernize U.S. CBW capabilities, this testing was supplemented with trials conducted at multiple locations in the United States and overseas, principally in the Pacific Ocean.[25] The Soviet Union built explosive aerosol test chambers at several BW facilities and conducted extensive outdoor BW tests, primarily on Vozrozhdeniya Island in the Aral Sea.[26]

Following World War II, biological weapons emerged as a potential rival to nuclear weapons as a weapon of mass destruction. Nuclear weapons, however, quickly eclipsed biological weapons, as their destructive power steadily increased and they were readily embraced by political and military leaders. The assimilation of nuclear weapons into the arsenals of the United Kingdom and France in the 1950s and 1960s led to the decline of postwar BW programs in those countries.[27] A number of developing nations are believed to have launched BW programs between 1945 and 1990, including China, Egypt, Israel, Iran,

---

24. Stockholm International Peace Research Institute (SIPRI), *The Problem of Chemical and Biological Warfare,* vol. 2, *CB Weapons Today* (New York: Humanities Press, 1973), 132–38; Graham S. Pearson, "Prospects for Chemical and Biological Arms Control: The Web of Deterrence," *Washington Quarterly* 16, no. 2 (1993): 147–48; and Patrick, "Biological Warfare," 3.

25. John Ellis Van Courtland Moon, "The U.S. Biological Weapons Program," in *Deadly Cultures,* ed. Wheelis, Rózsa, and Dando, 9–46; and Ed Regis, *The Biology of Doom: The History of America's Secret Germ Warfare Project* (New York: Henry Holt, 1999).

26. Alibek, *Biohazard,* 96–97, 132.

27. See Brian Balmer, *Britain and Biological Warfare: Expert Advice and Science Policy, 1930–1965* (London: Palgrave Macmillan, 2001); and Olivier Lepick, "The French Biological Weapons Program," in *Deadly Cultures,* ed. Wheelis, Rózsa, and Dando, 108–31.

Iraq, Libya, North Korea, Pakistan, Rhodesia, South Africa, Syria, and Taiwan. Some of these programs, such as those of Iraq, Libya, Rhodesia, and South Africa, are known to have been terminated.[28] The status of the other programs is difficult to determine based on publicly available information.

The United States' use of herbicides and tear gas in Vietnam, as well as accidents involving U.S. chemical weapons, subjected chemical and biological weapons to greater scrutiny in the 1960s. In 1969 after a comprehensive review of U.S. CBW policy, the Richard M. Nixon administration decided to unilaterally renounce the use of biological weapons, terminate the offensive BW program, and destroy existing stockpiles of biological agents and munitions.[29] By 1972 international consensus against biological weapons led to the signing of the Biological Weapons Convention, which banned the development, production, acquisition, and possession of biological weapons. The BWC was the first international treaty to outlaw an entire class of weapons. Unlike other WMD nonproliferation treaties, however, the BWC did not contain any verification provisions or an international organization to implement it. The origins and evolution of the BWC are discussed further in chapter 2.

Molecular Biology and Biotechnology

The early 1970s marked not only the negotiation of the BWC but also the birth of genetic engineering and the biotechnology revolution.[30] These scientific

28. On China, Iran, North Korea, and Syria, see Department of State, *Adherence to and Compliance with Arms Control, Nonproliferation, and Disarmament Agreements and Commitments* (Washington, DC: Department of State, 2005), 17–18, 20–21, 26–27, 31. On Egypt, see Arms Control and Disarmament Agency (ACDA), *Adherence to and Compliance with Arms Control Agreements: 1996 Report to the Congress* (Washington, DC: ACDA, 1996). On Israel, see Avner Cohen, "Israel and Chemical/Biological Weapons: History, Deterrence, and Arms Control," *Nonproliferation Review* 8, no. 3 (2001): 27–53. On Iraq, see United Nations Monitoring, Verification and Inspection Commission (UNMOVIC), *Compendium of Iraq's Proscribed Weapons Programmes in the Chemical, Biological and Missile Areas* (New York: United Nations, 2007), 765–1030 [hereafter *Compendium*]. On Libya, see Donald Mahley, "Dismantling Libyan Weapons: Lessons Learned," Chemical and Biological Arms Control Institute's *Arena* 10 (November 2004); and the Commission on the Intelligence Capabilities of the United States Regarding Weapons of Mass Destruction, *Report to the President* (Washington, DC: GPO, 2005), 253–65. On Pakistan, see Defense Intelligence Agency (DIA), *Proliferation of Weapons of Mass Destruction,* DST-2660S-694-92, May 1992, 42, released under the Freedom of Information Act [hereafter FOIA]. On Rhodesia and South Africa, see Burger and Gould, *Secrets and Lies.* On Taiwan, see R. Jeffrey Smith, "China May Have Revived Germ Weapons Program, U.S. Officials Say," *Washington Post,* February 24, 1993, A4.

29. Jonathan B. Tucker, "A Farewell to Germs: The U.S. Renunciation of Biological and Toxin Warfare, 1969–70," *International Security* 27, no. 1 (2002): 107–48.

30. The beginning of the biotechnology revolution can be dated to 1973 when the first recombinant organism was created by splicing a gene that conferred resistance to penicillin into *Escherichia coli.* Stanley N. Cohen, "The Manipulation of Genes," *Scientific American* 233, no. 1 (July 1975): 25–33.

advances have marked the beginning of the fourth era in biological warfare. They have provided states with greater capabilities for agent selection, modification, production, and dissemination. The key difference between third- and fourth-generation biological weapons is not the scale of production or means of dissemination but the type of BW agent employed. Gaining the ability to manipulate the DNA of pathogens created new frontiers for the development of improved and novel biological weapons. With genetic engineering, traditional BW agents can be made more virulent, resistant to antibiotics and vaccines, and better able to avoid detection systems. In addition, harmless microorganisms can be transformed into deadly ones with novel properties. Advances in the life sciences have also increased the range of viral and toxin agents that can be produced and improved the speed and efficiency of BW agent production. Advances in biotechnology also improve the effectiveness of biological weapons by enabling pathogens to better endure the aerosolization process and survive in the atmosphere for longer periods of time. For the first time, scientists also gained the ability to produce bioregulators, chemicals produced by the human body that play a crucial role in regulating key life processes. Manipulation of these biochemicals could cause effects ranging from incapacitation to death. New fields such as synthetic biology, systems biology, and RNA interference, as well as deeper understanding of genomics, neurobiology, and immunology, may create even more opportunities for scientists seeking to design advanced biological weapons.

In 1973—at the dawn of the biotechnology revolution and a year after the signing of the BWC—the Soviet Union created a special organization, Biopreparat, whose purpose was to apply these emerging technologies to creating new and improved biological weapons. The goal of the Soviet program was to develop more lethal and durable strains of BW agents as well as improved means of production and dissemination. To enhance the lethality of BW agents, scientists at the Scientific-Research Institute of Applied Microbiology in Obolensk and the Scientific-Research Institute of Molecular Biology (also called Vector) in Koltsovo engineered pathogens to be resistant to multiple antibiotics, altered antigenic structures to overcome vaccine-induced immunity, inserted genes coding for toxins and bioregulators into microorganisms, and combined genetic material from two different viruses to create "chimera" viruses.[31] Soviet

---

31. Alibek, *Biohazard;* Igor V. Domaradskij and Wendy Orent, *Biowarrior: Inside the Soviet/Russian Biological War Machine* (Amherst, NY: Prometheus Books, 2003); Christopher Davis, "Nuclear Blindness: An Overview of the Biological Weapons Programs of the Former Soviet Union and Iraq," *Emerging Infectious Diseases* 5, no. 4 (1999): 509–11; and Janet R. Gilsdorf and Raymond A. Zilinskas, "New Considerations in Infectious Disease Outbreaks: The Threat of Genetically Modified Microbes," *Clinical Infectious Diseases* 40, no. 8 (2005): 1160–5.

BW scientists also adopted modern cell culture techniques to be able to mass-produce variola virus using bioreactors instead of chicken eggs.[32] The Institute of Ultra-Pure Biological Preparations in Leningrad was dedicated to developing improved methods for stabilizing, drying, milling, and disseminating BW agents, including *Y. pestis* and *F. tularensis*.[33] Biopreparat eventually grew into a massive complex of fifty research and production facilities with over thirty thousand employees.[34] Thankfully, the Soviet Union collapsed before their achievements with genetically modified agents in the lab progressed to production and weaponization.[35]

Aside from the Soviet program, there is no evidence that other states have successfully applied genetic engineering to biological weapons. Iraq launched a genetic engineering program in 1990 with an interest in developing an antibiotic-resistant strain of *B. anthracis,* but the program was cut short by the 1991 Gulf War before it made any progress.[36] After the 2003 invasion of Iraq, a U.S.-led investigation of Iraq's pre-war WMD programs found no evidence that Iraq had conducted BW-related genetic engineering prior to the invasion.[37] A junior scientist in South Africa's Project Coast successfully isolated a toxin-producing gene from *Clostridium perfringens* (the bacterium that causes gas gangrene) and inserted it into *Escherichia coli,* an intestinal bacterium commonly used for genetic engineering experiments. The engineered *E. coli* could produce the toxin more efficiently than the host strain. The scientist, who had previously developed veterinary vaccines, claims that his purpose was to produce a new commercial vaccine for sheep to protect them against endotoxaemia caused by *C. perfringens.*[38]

32. Jonathan B. Tucker, *Scourge: The Once and Future Threat of Smallpox* (New York: Atlantic Monthly Press, 2001), 145–46, 152–55; and Alibek, *Biohazard,* 121–22.

33. James Adams, *The New Spies: Exploring the Frontiers of Espionage* (London: Hutchinson, 1994), 272–73; and Alibek, *Biohazard,* 140.

34. Jonathan B. Tucker, "Biological Weapons in the Former Soviet Union: An Interview with Dr. Kenneth Alibek," *Nonproliferation Review* 6, no. 3 (1999): 4.

35. Joshua Lederberg and George Whitesides, *Report of the Defense Science Board/Threat Reduction Advisory Committee Task Force on Biological Defense* (Washington, DC: Office of the Under Secretary of Defense for Acquisition, Technology and Logistics, 2001), 12, 15, 120, FOIA; and Department of Defense (DOD), *Biotechnology and Genetic Engineering: Implications for the Development of New Warfare Agents* (Washington, DC: GPO, 1996), 2. This assessment, however, is based on defectors whose knowledge at the time was limited by compartmentalization and is now over a decade old. Russia continues to maintain four military BW facilities that are suspected of conducting offensive BW research and are closed to outsiders.

36. UNMOVIC, *Compendium,* 849–50, 855, 918, 942; and UNMOVIC, *Unresolved Disarmament Issues: Iraq's Proscribed Weapons Programmes* (New York: United Nations, 2003), 127–28.

37. Charles Duelfer, *Comprehensive Report of the Special Advisor to the DCI on Iraq's WMD,* vol. 3, *Biological Warfare* (Langley, VA: CIA, 2004), 56–57 [hereafter Duelfer Report].

38. Chandré Gould and Peter Folb, "The Role of Professionals in the South African Chemical and Biological Warfare Programme," *Minerva* 40, no. 1 (2002): 85.

On the positive side, the biotechnology revolution promises to revolution- ize medicine and the fight against infectious diseases. Advanced biotechnolo- gies are being used to develop improved vaccines against traditional BW agents, vaccines that protect against multiple agents, sensors that detect aerosols of BW agents, systems that rapidly diagnose the cause of illnesses, new types of thera- peutic drugs, and new tools for microbial forensics. Progress on applying bio- technology to biodefense, however, has been slow. The ability to detect and identify biological agents in the environment and in clinical samples has ad- vanced the most due to the development of polymerase chain reaction technolo- gies, which makes it possible to analyze even tiny quantities of DNA. Advances in genome sequencing and bioinformatics have enabled the emergence of mo- lecular epidemiology and microbial forensics that seek to attribute the source of natural and man-made disease outbreaks.[39] Exploitation of growing knowledge about the genetic structure and molecular activity of pathogens has been central to the development of new treatments and vaccines.[40] Translating this research into useful products, however, has been stymied as much by political, economic, and regulatory obstacles as by technical hurdles.[41]

Biological Warfare and International Security

There are four major characteristics of biological weapons that are crucial to as- sessing their impact on international security: First, biological warfare strongly favors the attacker. Second, biological weapons have utility as force multipli- ers for conventional military operations. Third, biological weapons are poorly suited to serve as strategic deterrents. Fourth, the constraints on developing and using these weapons may be eroding.

---

39. Roger G. Breeze, Bruce Budowle, and Steven E. Schutzer, eds., *Microbial Forensics* (Burlington, MA: Elsevier Academic Press, 2005).

40. Alexander Kelle, Malcolm Dando, and Kathryn Nixdorff, eds., *The Role of Biotechnology in Countering BTW Agents* (Dordrecht, Netherlands: Kluwer, 2001); Stephen C. Harrison et al., "Discov- ery of Antivirals against Smallpox," *Proceedings of the National Academies of Science* 101, no. 31 (2004): 11178–92; and James C. Burnett, Erik A. Henchal, Alan L. Schmaljohn, and Sina Bavari, "The Evolv- ing Field of Biodefence: Therapeutic Developments and Diagnostics," *Nature Reviews Drug Discovery* 4 (April 2005): 281–97.

41. Institute of Medicine and National Research Council, *Giving Full Measure to Countermeasures: Addressing Problems in the DOD Program to Develop Medical Countermeasures against Biological War- fare Agents* (Washington, DC: National Academies Press, 2004); Jason Matheny, Michael Mair, Andrew Mulcahy, and Bradley T. Smith, "Incentives for Biodefense Countermeasure Development," *Biosecu- rity and Bioterrorism* 5, no. 3 (2007): 228–38; and Scott Gottlieb, *Political Roulette and the Public Health: The Impact of Political Intrusions on Drug Development and the Consequence for America's Biodefense,* AEI Working Paper 113 (Washington, DC: American Enterprise Institute, 2005).

Biological Warfare Favors the Attacker

The offense-defense balance in biological warfare strongly favors the attacker because developing and using biological weapons to cause casualties is significantly easier and cheaper than developing and fielding defenses against them.[42] Four factors give the attacker a significant advantage over the defender in biological warfare: (1) the diversity of threat agents, (2) the potency of biological weapons, (3) the ease of surprise, and (4) the difficulty in defending against such an attack. These four factors may also be dramatically affected by the impact of the biotechnology revolution.

The Diversity of Biological Warfare Agents   Biological warfare agents vary widely in their infectivity (the number of organisms required to cause disease), virulence (the severity of the disease caused), transmissibility (ease of spreading from person to person), and incubation period (the time from exposure to a biological agent to the onset of illness). This diversity provides terrorists and military planners with a great deal of flexibility. Although there are hundreds of infectious diseases and toxins that can cause serious health effects in humans, a limited number of biological agents have the physical and biological characteristics required of a mass casualty–producing biological weapon. The U.S. Department of Defense (DOD) has identified eighteen microorganisms and toxins that have been developed or produced as biological weapons.[43] Most national biological warfare programs have focused on ten to fifteen agents.[44] Even this short list of agents, however, offers a range of potential weapons from the lethal *B. anthracis* to incapacitating agents such as *Coxiella burnetii* (the bacterium that causes Q fever) and Venezuelan equine encephalitis (VEE). Pathogens that cause contagious diseases that have been developed as biological weapons include variola and *Y. pestis.* The major characteristics of these pathogens are summarized in table 1.[45]

This list of agents, however, reflects only known threats. U.S. experts were surprised by some of the agents that Iraq and the former Soviet Union chose to

---

42. This feature of biological warfare has been recognized for more than fifty years. Theodor Rosebury, *Peace or Pestilence: Biological Warfare and How to Avoid It* (New York: Whittlesey, 1946), 135; SIPRI, *The Problem of Chemical and Biological Warfare,* 2:90; and Lederberg and Whitesides, *Biological Defense,* 2.

43. DOD, *Proliferation: Threat and Response* (Washington, DC: GPO, 2001), 94, 113.

44. Spertzel, Wannemacher, and Linden, *Global Proliferation,* 4:11; and David R. Franz, "Medical Countermeasures to Biological Warfare Agents," in *Role of Biotechnology in Countering BTW Agents,* ed. Kelle, Dando, and Nixdorff, 228.

45. For more details about specific biological agents, see Zygmunt Debek, ed., *Medical Aspects of Biological Warfare* (Washington, DC: U.S. Army Surgeon General, 2007); and Donald A. Henderson, Thomas V. Inglesby, and Tara O'Toole, eds., *Bioterrorism: Guidelines for Medical and Public Health Management* (Chicago, IL: American Medical Association, 2002).

TABLE 1. Properties of Biological Warfare Agents

Agent	Disease	Infective Dose (Aerosol)	Incubation Period	Lethality (% if untreated)	Duration of Illness	Person-to-Person Transmission
Bacteria						
Bacillus anthracis	Anthrax	8,000–50,000 spores	1–6 days (up to 60)*	High (>90)	3–5 days	No
Yersinia pestis	Plague	500–15,000 organisms	2–3 days	High (>90)	1–6 days	Moderate
Francisella tularensis	Tularemia	10–50 organisms	3–6 days	Moderate (35)	>2 weeks	No
Brucella spp.	Brucellosis	10–100 organisms	5–60 days	Low (<5)	Weeks–months	No
Burkholderia mallei	Glanders	Unknown, potentially low	10–14 days	Moderate (>50)	7–10 days	Low
Burkholderia pseudomallei	Melioidosis	Unknown, potentially low	1–21 days	Moderate (19–50)	2–3 days	Low
Coxiella burnetii	Q Fever	1–10 organisms	7–41 days	Low (5)	2–14 days	Rare
Viruses						
Variola	Smallpox	Assumed low (10–100 organisms)	7–17 days	Moderate (30)	4 weeks	High
Venezuelan Equine Encephalitis	Viral Encephalitis	10–100 organisms	2–6 days	Low (1)	1–2 weeks	Low
Ebola	Viral Hemorrhagic Fever	Unknown, potentially low	4–21 days	Moderate to High (50–90)	7–16 days	Moderate
Toxins						
Clostridium botulinum	Botulism	.003 μg/kg	12 hours–5 days	High (>90)	24–72 hours	No
Ricin		3–5 μg/kg	18–24 hours	High (>90)	Days	No
Staphylococcus aureus	Staph Enterotoxin B	.003 μg/person	3–12 hours	Low (1)	2 weeks	No

* Laboratory experiments and the 1979 outbreak of inhalation anthrax in Sverdlovsk, USSR, demonstrated that spores of *B. anthracis* in the lungs can remain dormant for several weeks before causing illness. Jeanne Guillemin, *Anthrax: Investigation of a Deadly Outbreak* (Berkeley: University of California Press, 1999), 189, 237.
Source: Jon B. Woods, et al., eds., *USAMRIID's Medical Management of Biological Casualties Handbook*, 6th ed. (Frederick, MD: U.S. Army Medical Research Institute of Infectious Diseases, 2005); and Zygmunt Debek, ed., *Medical Aspects of Biological Warfare* (Washington, DC: U.S. Army Surgeon General, 2007).

produce and weaponize. Because biological terrorism is generally less sophisticated and demanding than the military use of biological weapons, the range of possible agents for terrorists may be larger and more varied.[46] The difficulty in assessing threat agents in a timely manner results in defensive programs lagging behind offensive programs.[47]

The Potency of Biological Weapons   Biological weapons combine a relatively low cost of production with the potential capability of infecting large numbers of people over a wide area. Modern biological weapons are potentially capable of inflicting mass casualties by dispersing pathogens or toxins in an aerosol cloud containing microscopic particles that can be inhaled and retained deep in the lungs of the exposed population. These aerosols are most effective when composed of particles ranging from 1 to 5 microns in size that can stay airborne longer and cause more severe cases of disease. Biological weapons field tests conducted by the United States in the 1950s and 1960s demonstrated that line sources generated by spray tanks mounted on moving vehicles, such as aircraft, helicopters, cruise missiles, and ships, could cover targets eight to thirty kilometers downwind, while point sources, such as bombs, submunitions from cluster bombs or stationary aerosol generators, could cover ten square kilometers.[48] According to former deputy director of Biopreparat, Dr. Ken Alibek (Kanatjan Alibekov), Soviet biological weapons required three to five kilograms of *B. anthracis,* variola, *Y. pestis, F. tularensis,* VEE, or *B. mallei* to cause 50 percent casualties in a one-square-kilometer area.[49]

The capability of biological weapons to cause mass casualties has been illustrated by several studies. In 1970 the World Health Organization (WHO) estimated that the use of *B. anthracis* could cause 48,000 deaths, *Y. pestis* could cause 21,000 deaths, and *F. tularensis* could cause 15,000 deaths in a city the size of Boston.[50] The Office of Technology Assessment (OTA) estimated that a ballistic

---

46. This wider range of agents, however, may not be well suited to large-scale, outdoor aerosolization and would likely be limited to aerosol dissemination inside buildings or the contamination of food and water supplies.

47. Edward Eitzen and Ernest Takafuji, "Historical Overview of Biological Warfare," in *Medical Aspects of Chemical and Biological Warfare,* ed. Frederick R. Sidell, Ernest T. Takafuji, and David R. Franz (Falls Church, VA: U.S. Army Surgeon General, 1997), 443–44.

48. Fothergill, "Biological Warfare Threat," 26; and Spertzel, Wannemacher, and Linden, *Global Proliferation,* 4:17, 28–30.

49. Kenneth Alibek, "Biological Weapons" (Powerpoint presentation to the United States Air Force Counterproliferation Conference, Air War College, Maxwell AFB, Alabama, November 1, 1999), http://www.globalsecurity.org/wmd/library/report/1999/alibek.ppt.

50. These estimates are for attacks using fifty kilograms of high-quality dry BW agent with an inefficient dissemination device. These estimates assume ideal weather conditions and that the victims receive no medical treatment. World Health Organization, *Health Aspects of Chemical and Biological Weapons* (Geneva: WHO, 1970), 96–99.

missile containing thirty kilograms of dry *B. anthracis* could cause 25,000 deaths and that an aircraft disseminating a line source of one hundred kilograms of dry *B. anthracis* could cause 280,000 fatalities.[51] The U.S. Centers for Disease Control and Prevention (CDC) has modeled the effects of a BW attack against a large suburb. This study found that without treatment *B. anthracis* could cause 32,000 fatalities, *F. tularensis* could cause 6,000 fatalities, and *Brucella melitensis* (the bacterium that causes brucellosis) could lead to 600 fatalities.[52]

The creation of an offensive BW capability is also relatively cheap in comparison to other weapons of mass destruction and in comparison to the cost of developing biodefense capabilities. According to OTA, a simple fermentation plant suitable for the production of BW agents could cost ten million dollars. In contrast, chemical plants that can produce nerve agents cost tens of millions of dollars, while facilities to produce highly enriched uranium or plutonium for use in nuclear weapons cost hundreds of millions of dollars.[53] Based on Iraq's own calculations, its pre-1991 Gulf War BW program to research, produce, and weaponize multiple BW agents cost roughly $75 million. In comparison, UNMOVIC has estimated that Iraq's CW and missile programs cost at least a half-billion dollars each.[54] The combination of low production costs and wide area coverage can result in a highly cost-effective weapon. According to a 1969 United Nations study, the cost of causing one civilian casualty per square kilometer was about $2,000 with conventional weapons, $800 with nuclear weapons, $600 with chemical weapons, and only $1 with biological weapons.[55]

In comparison to the relatively low costs of offensive BW programs, developing effective biological defenses is an expensive undertaking. The Department of Defense's program to vaccinate U.S. soldiers against a single threat agent—*B. anthracis*—has cost $525 million since 1998 and only a fraction of the force has been fully vaccinated.[56] In addition, developing a new biodefense vaccine costs

---

51. These estimates are for attacks using high-quality dried agents disseminated by a high-efficiency munition against a city with the population density of Boston. These estimates also assume moderately favorable weather conditions and that the victims receive no medical treatment. Office of Technology Assessment (OTA), *Proliferation of Weapons of Mass Destruction: Assessing the Risks* (Washington, DC: GPO, 1993), 53–54.

52. Arnold F. Kaufmann, Martin I. Meltzer, and George P. Schmid, "The Economic Impact of a Bioterrorist Attack: Are Prevention and Postattack Intervention Programs Justifiable?" *Emerging Infectious Diseases* 3, no. 2 (1997): 83–94.

53. Total program costs for these weapons are also significantly higher. OTA, *Technologies Underlying Weapons of Mass Destruction* (Washington, DC: GPO, 1993), 27, 86, 156–58.

54. UNMOVIC, *Compendium,* 793, 1055–56.

55. United Nations Secretary General, *Chemical and Bacteriological (Biological) Weapons and the Effects of Their Possible Use* (Geneva: United Nations, 1969), 40. The methodology used to determine these figures is not known.

56. Data on procurement costs associated with DOD's Anthrax Vaccine Immunization Program (AVIP) can be found at www.defenselink.mil/comptroller/defbudget. As of December 31, 2006, 5,806,172

$300–400 million and typically takes eight to ten years.[57] In contrast, former U.S. and Soviet BW scientists report that the process of transforming a pathogen into a form suitable for mass-production and use in a munition can take as little as two to three years.[58]

Developing a terrorist capability would be even cheaper. In 1999, the U.S. Defense Threat Reduction Agency built a small facility with commercially available equipment that could be used to produce limited quantities of BW agents for only $1.6 million.[59] The FBI has estimated that the small amount of *B. anthracis* spores sent to media and government officials in fall 2001 cost only $2,500 to produce.[60] In comparison, the cost of responding to the anthrax letter attacks has been estimated at roughly $6 billion.[61]

The Ease of Surprise   Biological weapons have several advantages for conducting surprise attacks. These weapons are relatively easy to develop in secret, are well suited for covert delivery, and do not provide signatures that can be used to easily identify the attacker. As discussed in chapter 4, intelligence on BW threats is hindered by the difficulty in detecting offensive programs and distinguishing between offensive, defensive, and civilian activities.

The small quantity of agent required for an attack, the ability to launch an attack with a spray system from several miles upwind from a target or to clandestinely deliver biological weapons, and the difficulty of detecting biological aerosols makes biological weapons well suited to covert attacks. Field tests conducted by the U.S. Army in the 1950s and 1960s demonstrated the ease of conducting covert attacks with biological weapons against buildings, subway systems, air bases, and cities.[62] The Aum Shinrikyo cult's dissemination of biological agents

---

doses of the vaccine had been administered to 1,492,366 persons. At this time, only 244,781 service members had received the full course of six doses of the vaccine. DOD, *Chemical and Biological Defense Program: Annual Report to Congress* (Washington, DC: DOD, 2007), 96.

57. DOD, *Report on Biological Warfare Defense Vaccine Research and Development Programs* (Fort Belvoir, VA: Defense Technical Information Center, 2001), 2.

58. William Broad and Judith Miller, "Once He Devised Germ Weapons; Now He Defends against Them," *New York Times,* November 3, 1998, D1; and Kenneth Alibek, "Research Considerations for Better Understanding of Biological Threats," in Institute of Medicine, *Biological Threats and Terrorism: Assessing the Science and Response Capabilities* (Washington, DC: National Academies Press, 2002), 64.

59. Judith Miller, Stephen Engelberg, and William Broad, *Germs: Biological Weapons and America's Secret War* (New York: Simon and Schuster, 2001), 297–98.

60. David Rosenbaum and David Johnston, "Single Letter with Anthrax Is Discounted," *New York Times,* November 10, 2001, B1.

61. Leonard A. Cole, "WMD and Lessons from the Anthrax Attacks," in *The McGraw-Hill Homeland Security Handbook,* ed. David G. Kamien (New York: McGraw-Hill, 2006), 170.

62. William C. Patrick III, "Biological Warfare Scenarios," in, - *Firepower in the Lab: Automation in the Fight against Infectious Diseases and Bioterrorism* ed. Scott P. Layne, Tony J. Beugelsdijk, and C. Kumar N. Patel (Washington, DC: Joseph Henry Press, 2001), 215–23.

in Japan on a dozen separate occasions in the early 1990s went undetected at the time, as did the contamination of salad bars in an Oregon town in 1984 by the Rajneeshee cult.[63] The nonspecific nature of the early symptoms of most diseases of concern can mask the beginning of a man-made outbreak and enhance the likelihood that such an attack will catch an adversary unprepared.[64] Due to these characteristics, virtually all BW programs have been closely associated with intelligence agencies and other organizations interested in clandestine means of assassination, counterinsurgency, and sabotage.[65]

While surprise is a well-known force multiplier for conventional forces, biological weapons are especially dependent on this factor for their success. The ability to conceal the identity of an agent, the timing of an attack, the means of delivery, and the planned target is crucial for an effective BW attack. This reliance on surprise has several implications for biological warfare. First, attackers, not defenders, rely on surprise to achieve their objectives.[66] As John Mearsheimer notes, "one important advantage held by the offense is the ability to choose the main point of attack for the initial battles, to move forces there surreptitiously, and to surprise the defender."[67] Aggressors are better prepared not only to employ biological weapons but also to defend against them, because they can anticipate enemy retaliation and prepare accordingly.[68] Second, the need for surprise reduces the utility of these weapons for other strategies such as blackmail or deterrence since they cannot be used to threaten or coerce an opponent. Third, this dependence on surprise exposes biological weapons' Achilles' heel. Accurate intelligence on an adversary's BW capabilities can substantially reduce the

---

63. None of Aum Shinrikyo's BW attacks were successful because the group inadvertently used harmless versions of *B. anthracis* and botulinum toxin. The failed attacks were not revealed until years later during the trial of the cult's leaders. Sheryl Wu Dunn, Judith Miller, and William J. Broad, "How Japan Germ Terror Alerted the World," *New York Times,* May 26, 1998, A1.

The source of the contamination in Oregon was not determined to be the Rajneeshee cult until over a year later. W. Seth Carus, "The Rajneeshees (1984)," in Jonathan B. Tucker, ed., *Toxic Terror: Assessing Terrorist Use of Chemical and Biological Weapons* (Cambridge: MIT Press, 2000), 115–37.

64. Gregory Koblentz, "Biological Terrorism: Understanding the Threat and the Response," in *Countering Terrorism: Dimensions of Preparedness,* ed. Arnold Howitt and Robyn Pangi (Cambridge: MIT Press, 2003), 111.

65. Gregory Koblentz, "Pathogens as Weapons: The International Security Implications of Biological Weapons" (PhD diss., Massachusetts Institute of Technology, 2004), 22–23; and Shlomo Shpiro, "Poisoned Chalice: Intelligence Use of Chemical and Biological Weapons," *International Journal of Intelligence and CounterIntelligence* 22, no. 1 (2009): 1–30.

66. Robert Jervis, "Cooperation under the Security Dilemma," *World Politics* 30, no. 2 (1978): 205–6.

67. John J. Mearsheimer, *Conventional Deterrence* (Ithaca: Cornell University Press, 1983), 26.

68. According to a 1958 U.S. Army Chemical Corps study, "definite advantage will accrue to the nation which initiates BW. Maximum surprise effect will be achieved by that nation. Conversely, if BW is used in retaliation, the impact will fall on troops and civilians who have presumably already taken all possible defensive measure to protect against it." Chemical Corps Board, *Concepts for Employment of Antipersonnel Biological Warfare,* Information Report 1 (Edgewood, MD: Chemical Corps, 1958), 12.

effectiveness of a biological attack by providing the defender with sufficient information to organize public health and medical measures to mitigate the effects of an attack.

The Difficulty of Defense   Biological warfare defenses include measures to prevent, detect, mitigate, or treat the effects of a BW attack. Biological defenses include medical countermeasures, detection and surveillance systems, and physical protection. Defending against biological threats is complicated by the range of available agents, the agent-specific nature of most defenses, the time lag required to develop new vaccines and treatments, and the ease with which an attacker can achieve surprise.

Biological weapons, however, are in some ways more susceptible to countermeasures than high explosives, chemical weapons, or nuclear weapons. They are unique among weapon systems in that vaccines can protect soldiers and civilians before an actual attack. For vaccines to be effective, however, defenders must be able to meet the following conditions: identification of the target population, knowledge of the specific threat agent, availability of the appropriate vaccine, and time for the vaccine to be administered to the target population before an attack.[69] Licensed vaccines are currently available in the U.S. for two of the most dangerous BW agents—*B. anthracis* and variola. In addition, experimental vaccines are available for *F. tularensis, C. burnetii,* and VEE, and toxoids are available for botulinum toxin.[70] Even though immunizing vulnerable populations against the full range of BW threats is not feasible or desirable, the availability of sufficient stockpiles of appropriate vaccines is still valuable as a deterrent to potential attackers, as a defensive measure if warning of an attack is received, as a form of postexposure prophylaxis for anthrax and smallpox, and as a reassuring symbol of preparedness.

Given the limitations of vaccines, defenses against biological weapons rely more on early detection of a biological attack and postexposure prophylaxis or chemotherapy with antimicrobials and antitoxins. The incubation period following infection with a pathogen, typically several days, provides a window of opportunity for the detection and response to a biological attack. Under the right conditions, aerosol detection devices, laboratory or clinical diagnosis, and public health surveillance systems can provide enough warning to launch a medical intervention to mitigate the consequences of a biological attack.[71] Current

69. David R. Franz, "Physical and Medical Countermeasures to Biological Weapons," Director's Series on Proliferation 4 (Livermore, CA: Lawrence Livermore National Laboratory, May 1994), 59–60.
70. DOD, *Chemical and Biological Defense Program: Annual Report to Congress and Performance Plan* (Washington, DC: DOD, 2001), D-11.
71. Koblentz, "Biological Terrorism," 123–43.

detection, diagnostic, and surveillance systems suffer from trade-offs between sensitivity, specificity, timeliness, reliability, and cost that limit their effectiveness. The key to achieving early detection of a BW attack is to integrate the information available from all of these sources into a comprehensive biosurveillance system.

Based on early detection of a biological attack, the administration of antibiotics promptly after exposure (postexposure prophylaxis) or after the onset of symptoms (therapy) can significantly reduce the morbidity and mortality of most bacterial agents. In contrast, there are few effective medical treatments for most toxins and viral agents (see table 2).

Conducting mass immunization or prophylaxis campaigns requires a stockpile of the necessary drugs and a distribution system to provide the drugs to affected individuals within a useful timeframe. Caring for large numbers of BW casualties also requires a robust medical system with surge capacity that can handle an influx of critically ill patients. Isolation, quarantine, and immunization can

TABLE 2. Medical Countermeasures against BW Agents

Agent	Vaccine or Toxoid Available?	Treatment Available?
Bacteria		
Bacillus anthracis	Licensed	Yes
Yersinia pestis	No	Yes
Francisella tularensis	IND	Yes
Brucella spp.	No	Yes
Burkholderia mallei	No	Yes
Burkholderia pseudomallei	No	Yes
Coxiella burnetii	IND	Yes
Viruses		
Variola	Licensed and IND	Licensed vaccine and IND antiviral
Venezuelan Equine Encephalitis	IND	No
Ebola	No	No
Toxins		
Clostridium botulinum	IND	Licensed and IND antitoxins
Ricin	No	No
Staphylococcus aureus	No	No

Licensed: approved for use by the Food and Drug Administration
IND: investigational new drug
Sources: Donald A. Henderson, Thomas V. Inglesby, and Tara O'Toole, eds., *Bioterrorism: Guidelines for Medical and Public Health Management* (Chicago: American Medical Association, 2002); Jon B. Woods, et al., eds., *USAMRIID's Medical Management of Biological Casualties Handbook,* 6th ed. (Frederick, MD: U.S. Army Medical Research Institute of Infectious Diseases, 2005); and Zygmunt Debek, ed., *Medical Aspects of Biological Warfare* (Washington, DC: U.S. Army Surgeon General, 2007).

reduce the impact of transmissible diseases such as smallpox and plague.[72] Since public health infrastructure and medical capacity provides the backbone of a national biodefense program and more specialized defensive countermeasures such as pharmaceutical stockpiles and sensors are quite costly, developing nations will remain even more vulnerable to this form of warfare than developed nations.

Physical defenses prevent exposure to BW agents by filtering the air to remove dangerous particles. Simple masks, such as those used to prevent the inhalation of dust as well as more harmful materials, have been touted as being able to provide relatively inexpensive protection to civilian populations and military forces.[73] To be effective against a surprise attack, the use of these masks would have to be triggered by real-time detection of an attack, a capability that does not yet exist. Alternatively, members of the military, health-care personnel, and other at-risk populations could wear masks when the threat of a BW attack is heightened, such as during a crisis or conflict. The prolonged use of such masks, however, would be difficult for several reasons. Wearers find them increasingly uncomfortable, especially during intense physical activity. Mask integrity and fit erodes with rugged use. These masks also interfere with face-to-face and radio communication. In addition, eating or drinking requires unmasking.[74] Finally, masks do not prevent exposure if not properly fitted or if the concentration of agent is high enough. Given the inability to detect a biological attack in real time, the most feasible physical defenses are buildings and vehicles equipped with High Efficiency Particulate Air (HEPA) filters and positive pressure systems that prevent the infiltration of biological aerosol clouds. Because of their expense, such systems are rare outside of the military. Nonetheless, they hold much promise for defending important buildings against biological attacks since they are not agent specific and can function continuously.[75]

Impact of the Biotechnology Revolution on the Offense-Defense Balance   The revolution in biotechnology, which has been underway since the early 1970s and is

72. Martin I. Meltzer et al., "Modeling Potential Responses to Smallpox as a Bioterrorism Weapon," *Emerging Infectious Diseases* 7, no. 6 (2001): 959–69; and Raymond Gani and Steve Leach, "Epidemiologic Determinants for Modeling Pneumonic Plague Outbreaks," *Emerging Infectious Diseases* 10, no. 4 (2004): 608–14.

73. Karl Lowe, Graham S. Pearson, and Victor Utgoff, "Potential Values of a Simple Biological Warfare Protective Mask," in *Biological Weapons: Limiting the Threat,* ed. Joshua Lederberg (Cambridge: MIT Press, 1999), 263–81; and Stanley L. Weiner, "Strategies for the Prevention of a Successful Biological Warfare Aerosol Attack," *Military Medicine* 161, no. 5 (1996): 251–56.

74. John Martyny, Craig S. Glazer, and Lee S. Newman, "Respiratory Protection," *New England Journal of Medicine* 347 (September 12, 2002): 827.

75. Lester L. Yuan, "Sheltering Effects of Buildings from Biological Weapons," *Science and Global Society* 8, no. 3 (2000): 287–313; and Richard L. Garwin, Ralph E. Gomory, and Matthew S. Meselson, "How to Fight Bioterrorism," *Washington Post,* May 14, 2002, A21.

now a global phenomenon, has profound implications for the offense-defense balance in biological warfare.[76] There have been multiple studies of the impact of advances in the life sciences on biological warfare but no comprehensive net assessment of the impact on the overall offense-defense balance.[77] Favoring the attacker are innovations that widen the range of agents that can be used as weapons, facilitate the safe large-scale production of traditional and novel pathogens, enable the modification of microorganisms to enhance their lethality, and improve the stability and dissemination of biological agents. Favoring the defender are breakthroughs that accelerate the development of improved vaccines and therapeutic agents and the deployment of new detection, diagnostic, and forensic capabilities. The key impediment to developing defenses against improved and advanced BW agents is knowing which of the thousands of potential threat agents the defender may face. Technologies that provide broad-spectrum protection or dramatically reduce the "bug-to-drug cycle"—the time it takes to identify new pathogens and develop vaccines or treatments for them—will provide the greatest benefits to the defender.

At the level of basic research and scientific knowledge, the biotechnology revolution provides far more insights and opportunities for causing harm than for preventing harm. In this realm, the bioweaponeer has more proven tools and techniques at their disposal than does the defender. Knowledge alone, however, is not enough. Whether the biotechnology revolution will strengthen the defender or allow attackers to maintain their edge in this competition will depend on the rate and scale at which this knowledge is applied to developing new weapons and defensive technologies. The United States and its allies have already begun devoting substantial resources to harnessing biotechnology for biodefense. The United States alone has spent over $24 billion on biodefense research and development since 2001.[78]

---

76. On the pace and globalization of the biotechnology revolution, see Institute of Medicine and National Research Council, *Globalization, Biosecurity, and the Future of the Life Sciences* (Washington, DC: National Academies Press, 2006).

77. DOD, *Biotechnology and Genetic Engineering: Implications for the Development of New Warfare Agents* (Washington, DC: GPO, 1996); Steven M. Block, "Living Nightmares: Biological Threats Enabled by Molecular Biology," in *The New Terror: Facing the Threat of Biological and Chemical Weapons*, ed. Sidney D. Drell, Abraham D. Sofaer, and George D. Wilson (Stanford: Hoover Institution Press, 1999), 39–75; Raymond Zilinskas, ed., *Biological Warfare: Modern Offense and Defense* (Boulder, CO: Lynne Reinner, 2000); Lederberg and Whitesides, *Biological Defense;* Kelle, Dando, and Nixdorff, *Role of Biotechnology in Countering BTW Agents;* James B. Petro, Theodore R. Plasse, and Jack A. Mcnulty, "Biotechnology: Impact on Biological Warfare and Biodefense," *Biosecurity and Bioterrorism* 1, no. 3 (2003): 161–68; British Medical Association, *Biotechnology, Weapons, and Humanity II* (London: British Medical Association, 2004); and Mark Wheelis, "Will the 'New Biology' Lead to New Weapons?" *Arms Control Today,* July/August 2004:6–13.

78. Alan Pearson, *Federal Funding for Biological Weapons Prevention and Defense, Fiscal Years 2001 to 2009* (Washington, DC: Center for Arms Control and Non-Proliferation, 2008).

Little is known, however, about the level of effort currently devoted to using biotechnology for malevolent purposes by state and nonstate actors. Russia continues to maintain four military BW facilities that engaged in genetic engineering for military purposes during the Soviet era, are currently closed to outsiders, and are suspected of continuing offensive BW research. The nature of the activities underway inside these facilities is not publicly known although the U.S. Department of State has judged that Russia continues to maintain an offensive BW program in violation of the BWC.[79] In 1999 the Defense Intelligence Agency (DIA) assessed that Iran's BW program would be able to develop enhanced BW agents within three to five years.[80] The report does not indicate, however, if Iran actually has the intent to engage in such activities. The information uncovered about al Qaeda's biological weapons program after the U.S. invasion of Afghanistan indicates that the organization has been interested only in traditional BW agents such as *B. anthracis.*[81] Given the difficulties faced by al Qaeda and other terrorist groups in developing an aerosolized biological weapon based on a naturally occurring pathogen, it is unlikely they will be able to master the art of genetic engineering to develop a more lethal pathogen on their own. Thus, there appears to be a window of opportunity for defenders to exploit the biotechnology revolution to develop new means of detection, protection, and treatment against the traditional BW threat agents that remain the focus of state and nonstate BW programs. Due to the multiuse dilemma, however, even defensive research will generate knowledge that could be used for offensive purposes.

Biological Weapons Are Force Multipliers

The military utility of biological weapons has long been minimized and downplayed based on the United States' experience with these weapons. The United States began developing biological weapons during World War II, but decided to unilaterally abandon these weapons in 1969. The government publicly justified this decision and the 1975 ratification of the Biological Weapons Convention as being due to the unpredictable and uncontrollable consequences of these weapons as well as their lack of military utility.[82] It made these decisions at least

---

79. Department of State, *Adherence to and Compliance with Arms Control, Nonproliferation and Disarmament Agreements and Commitments,* 27–31.

80. DIA, "A Primer on the Future Threat: The Decades Ahead, 1999–2020," July 1999, 89, in Rowan Scarborough, *Rumsfeld's War: The Untold Story of America's Anti-Terrorist Commander* (Washington, DC: Regnery, 2004), 209.

81. The Commission on the Intelligence Capabilities of the United States Regarding Weapons of Mass Destruction, *Report to the President* (Washington, DC: GPO, 2005), 267–78 [hereafter Silberman-Robb Report].

82. "Remarks of the President on Announcing the Chemical and Biological Defense Policies and Programs," Office of the White House Press Secretary, The White House, November 25, 1969, National

in part, however, after concluding that the destructive power of these weapons and their relative accessibility posed a serious proliferation threat.[83] In addition, given its formidable nuclear and conventional forces, the United States did not believe that it needed biological weapons to cause massive civilian casualties or to deter the use of biological weapons by other states. For the United States, the contribution of these weapons to achieving other missions did not justify the price of a heightened risk of proliferation.[84] It is a mistake to extrapolate from this decision that biological weapons are, in the words of Thomas Schelling, "ridiculous weapons that nobody is interested in having even if the other side is foolish enough to procure them."[85] Although biological weapons may have had marginal military utility for the United States in 1969, history has shown that this calculation is not universally applicable. Indeed, shortly after the U.S. decision to abandon these weapons, the Soviet Union decided to dramatically expand its own program and develop a new generation of biological weapons for a range of military missions.[86] As the authoritative Stockholm International Peace Research Institute (SIPRI) study on CBW noted thirty years ago, "because CB weapons have rarely been used in modern warfare, conjecture can scarcely be avoided in discussing their present utility."[87] Despite the lack of operational experience with biological weapons, an examination of evidence from defectors, declassified documents, war games, inspections, government investigations, and open sources makes it possible to assess the utility of biological weapons based

---

Security Council Subject Files. Box 310; folder 5: Chemical, Biological Warfare (Toxins, etc.) vol. 1, Nixon Presidential Materials, National Archives, College Park, Maryland [hereafter Nixon Papers]; Senate Committee on Foreign Relations, *Prohibition of Chemical and Biological Weapons,* 93d Cong., 2d sess., December 10, 1974, 10; Arms Control and Disarmament Agency, *Verification: The Critical Element of Arms Control* (Washington, DC: GPO, 1976), 7, 17–18; *Fiscal Year 1979 Arms Control Impact Statements: Statements Submitted to the Congress by the President Pursuant to Section 36 of the Arms Control and Disarmament Act* (Washington, DC: GPO, 1978), 220.

83. Matthew Meselson, "The Problem of Biological Weapons," n.d., http://www.pugwash.org/reports/cbw/cbw5.htm; Julian P. Perry Robinson, "Some Political Aspects of the Control of Biological Weapons," *Science in Parliament* 53, no. 3 (1996): 6–11; Graham S. Pearson, "Biological Weapons: A Priority Concern," Director's Series on Proliferation 4 (Livermore, CA: Lawrence Livermore National Laboratory, May 1994), 42; and Gradon Carter, "Biological Warfare and Biological Defence in the United Kingdom 1940–1979," *RUSI Journal* 137, no. 6 (1992): 72.

84. For an insider's account of the influence of these considerations in the U.S. decision to renounce biological weapons, see Han Swyter, "Political Considerations and Analysis of Military Requirements for Chemical and Biological Weapons," *Proceedings of the National Academy of Sciences* 65, no. 1 (1970): 261–70.

85. Thomas C. Schelling, *Choice and Consequence* (Cambridge: Harvard University Press, 1984), 253, as cited in Marie Isabelle, Chevrier, "Impediment to Proliferation? Analysing the Biological Weapons Convention," *Contemporary Security Policy* 16, no. 2 (1995): 84.

86. Alibek, *Biohazard;* and Anthony Rimmington, "The Soviet Union's Offensive Program: The Implications for Contemporary Arms Control," in *Biological Warfare and Disarmament: New Problems/New Perspectives,* ed. Susan Wright (Lanham, MD: Rowman and Littlefield, 2002), 103–50.

87. SIPRI, *The Problem of Chemical and Biological Warfare,* 2:116.

on the nature of biological warfare, the specific characteristics of weapons developed and fielded, and the doctrines adopted by different states.

Tactical   At the tactical level of combat the delayed effects of biological agents and the susceptibility of aerosol clouds to vagaries in meteorological and environmental conditions limit their utility to static battles of attrition. The ability of aerosol clouds to penetrate fortifications and buildings could provide an attacker with a means of "softening up" a hardened enemy position before an assault.[88] An attacker can minimize the risk of infecting its own troops by vaccinating them ahead of time, employing biological weapons far from friendly forces, or using only nontransmissible or short-lived agents. States lacking precision-guided munitions and cluster bombs may find the cost-effectiveness of these weapons attractive for attacking large concentrations of soldiers and fortified bunkers.

There is limited evidence of states developing biological weapons for use on the battlefield. Japan reportedly used artillery shells filled with bacterial agents against Soviet forces during the Nomonhan Incident in 1939.[89] Although Iraq experimented with biological warheads for short-range artillery rockets in the late 1980s, none of these weapons were deployed.[90] Ken Alibek has reported that the Soviet military was developing biological weapons for tactical missions during World War II but halted this work after a biological attack against German troops besieging Stalingrad in 1942 caused a massive outbreak of tularemia among Soviet civilians.[91] German and Soviet accounts of the outbreak at the time, and subsequent analyses by independent experts, cast serious doubt on Alibek's claim that the outbreak was intentional.[92]

Operational   Biological weapons may have their greatest military utility at the operational, or theater, level of warfare. The goal of attacks on logistical networks, reinforcements, and command and control facilities is to "to induce operational paralysis, which reduces the enemy's ability to move and coordinate

---

88. U.S. Army, *Employment of Chemical and Biological Agents,* Army Field Manual, no. 3–10 (Washington, DC: Department of the Army, 1966), 47.

89. Although there were outbreaks of plague, cholera, and dysentery subsequent to these attacks, it is not known whether the origins of these outbreaks were natural or man-made. Japan subsequently abandoned the development of bacteria-filled artillery shells. Harris, *Factories of Death,* 60, 76.

90. It is possible that these experiments were in fact intended to develop biological agent-filled submunitions for a cluster bomb. UNMOVIC, *Unresolved Disarmament Issues,* 63–64, 99, 103, 107.

91. Alibek, *Biohazard,* 29–31.

92. Eric Croddy and Sarka Krcalova, "Tularemia, Biological Warfare, and the Battle for Stalingrad (1942–1943)," *Military Medicine* 166, no. 10 (2001): 837–38; and Erhard Geissler, "Alibek, Tularemia, and the Battle of Stalingrad," *CBW Conventions Bulletin* 69/70 (September/December 2005): 10–15.

forces in the theater."[93] Although biological weapons have no direct effect on a defender's tanks and aircraft, they can render these weapons useless by sickening or killing the crews and support personnel. Targets in the enemy's rear area could be selected so that the effects of the biological attack are at their height when friendly forces plan on attacking the objective.

Because biological weapons do not damage or destroy property, they can be used to degrade enemy capabilities while preserving transportation infrastructure. In this way, biological weapons could be used to facilitate the advance of a blitzkrieg-style armored attack. Such weapons could also offer an aggressor the means of seizing valuable natural resources or industrial facilities without risking their destruction. Attackers could reduce the risk of contaminating the desired assets by selecting a biological agent with high decay rate that degrades rapidly on release and minimizing the agent's half-life by launching attacks shortly before sunrise.[94] Power projection forces that rely on a small number of large facilities, such as ports and airfields, are particularly vulnerable to such disruptive attacks.[95] As a result, the employment of biological weapons against theater targets could serve as a potent force multiplier for a conventional military operation.

The use of incapacitating instead of lethal agents for this type of warfare has several advantages. The ability of some biological agents, such as *Brucella* spp., to sicken victims for weeks or months could outweigh the delayed time of onset for such agents. Incapacitating agents would have the additional benefit of burdening the defender with large numbers of wounded soldiers, who typically absorb more resources than fatalities. These types of biological weapons could also be perceived as more useful in areas with heavy concentrations of civilians if the attacker is seeking to minimize collateral damage. In addition, the use of incapacitating agents instead of lethal ones might allow an aggressor to seize its objectives without provoking regime-threatening retaliation from a much stronger opponent.

Incapacitating biological weapons may be particularly useful for states that seek to occupy major cities without engaging in the long, bloody, and destructive battles that have historically characterized urban warfare.[96] John Steinbruner has

---

93. Robert Pape, *Bombing to Win: Air Power and Coercion in War* (Ithaca: Cornell University Press, 1996), 72.

94. On the limited risk of serious contamination with agents besides *B. anthracis,* see Patrick, "Biological Warfare," 6; and Graham S. Pearson, "The Essentials of Biological Threat Assessment," in *Biological Warfare,* ed. Zilinskas, 71.

95. Robert J. Larsen and Robert P. Kadlec, *Biological Warfare: A Post Cold War Threat to America's Strategic Mobility Forces* (Pittsburgh: Ridgway Center for Strategic Studies, 1995), 12–15.

96. On the nature of urban combat, see Michael C. Desch, ed., *Soldiers in Cities: Military Operations on Urban Terrain* (Carlisle Barracks, PA: Strategic Studies Institute, October 2001).

speculated that Soviet military planners "might have calculated that with judicious selection of the agents and timing of their delivery, the urban populations of Western Europe might be sufficiently weakened to allow an occupying army to accomplish an otherwise impossible task."[97] A U.S. Army study of possible Soviet BW operations against the North Atlantic Treaty Organization found that the covert use of an incapacitating agent against West Berlin "represents perhaps the most interesting and potentially profitable employment of biological agents in conjunction with offensive actions in NATO Europe."[98]

Several nations developed biological weapons and doctrine for their use at the operational level of warfare. The United States and the Soviet Union both favored the use of incapacitating agents for this mission. According to Alibek, the Soviet Union selected incapacitating agents such as *B. mallei, Brucella* spp., and VEE for operational missions.[99] The United States also favored incapacitating agents such as *C. burnetii* and VEE. These agents made up the majority of the stockpiled biological agents when the program was terminated in 1969.[100] Iraqi military doctrine also recognized the value of using these types of agents in the enemy's rear area to disrupt their operations.[101] Although Iraq's primary interest was in lethal antipersonnel agents, it began a short-lived program to investigate incapacitating viral agents in 1990.[102] A major Japanese BW campaign in China in 1942 used *B. anthracis, B. mallei,* and other biological agents to attack villages along a strategic railway line southwest of Shanghai in conjunction with a large-scale conventional military operation. The operation was in retribution for the assistance these villagers gave to U.S. pilots following the Doolittle raid on Tokyo in April 1942 and was also intended to prevent future Allied use of airfields in the area.[103]

---

97. John D. Steinbruner, "Biological Weapons: A Plague upon All Houses," *Foreign Policy* 109 (Winter 1997–1998): 90.

98. Don T. Parker et al., *Biological Vulnerability Assessment: NATO Central Front* (Dugway, UT: U.S. Army Dugway Proving Ground, 1976), 2:87.

99. Tucker, "Biological Weapons in the Former Soviet Union," 2.

100. The U.S. stockpile at this time consisted of 10,089 gallons of liquid incapacitating agent and 405 pounds of dry incapacitating agent versus 1,037 pounds of lethal dry agent. DOD, *Environmental Impact Statement for Disposal of Biological Agents and Weapons,* tab A, enclosure 10, September 17, 1970. National Security Council Subject Files. Box 311; folder 2: Chemical, Biological Warfare (Toxins, etc.) vol. 3, Nixon Papers.

101. Timothy McCarthy and Jonathan Tucker, "Saddam's Toxic Arsenal: Chemical and Biological Weapons in the Gulf Wars," in *Planning the Unthinkable: How New Powers Will Use Nuclear, Biological, and Chemical Weapons,* ed. Peter Lavoy, Scott Sagan, and James Wirtz (Ithaca: Cornell University Press, 2000), 62.

102. Iraq conducted research on enterovirus 70, rotavirus, and camelpox. UNMOVIC, *Compendium,* 908, 919.

103. Japan's use of BW was allegedly responsible for causing tens of thousands of casualties among the estimated 250,000 Chinese civilians and Nationalist troops killed during this operation. The Japanese

Strategic   At the strategic level of warfare, the goal of military action is to reduce the willingness or ability of the enemy to continue to prosecute a war. States can achieve this objective through attacks aimed at civilians with the goal of increasing pressure on the government to yield to the attacker or attacks aimed at damaging the enemy's economy enough to prevent effective resistance.[104] Biological warfare can target civilians directly with antipersonnel agents or indirectly with antilivestock and anticrop agents that can ruin an enemy's food supply. The ability of biological warfare agents to be disseminated over large areas and for agents such as variola virus and *Y. pestis* to cause epidemics makes them well suited for strategic attacks. There are also a number of viral and fungal agents that can cause epidemics among livestock and crops, respectively.[105] The delayed effects of biological weapons and uncertainties surrounding the downwind travel of aerosol clouds are less important for strategic attacks, which do not require precision or immediate results. In addition, biological weapons possess a number of properties that evoke disproportionate levels of fear: exposure to these weapons would be invisible and involuntary, while the effects would be delayed, uncontrollable, indiscriminate, poorly understood, and gruesome. As a result, the "dreaded" nature of these weapons could amplify the psychological impact of even a small-scale biological attack.[106] Despite this utility in targeting civilian populations, biological weapons lack several characteristics necessary to serve as strategic deterrents (examined in detail below).

The United States, United Kingdom, Soviet Union, and Iraq developed a range of aircraft and missile-delivered biological weapons and doctrines for their use against urban populations and agricultural targets. The Soviet Union developed an extensive strategic BW capability. According to Ken Alibek, the Soviets sought the most lethal and transmissible agents for use as strategic weapons. The Soviets kept tens of tons of variola, *Y. pestis,* and *B. anthracis* stockpiled for use against targets in the United States and remote parts of Europe. The Soviets developed cluster bombs and spray tanks for medium-range bombers

---

BW campaign also resulted in the sickening of ten thousand Japanese troops who inadvertently entered a contaminated area and contracted cholera. Li Xiaofong, *Blood-Weeping Accusations: Records of Anthrax Victims* (Beijing: CCP Press, 2005); Daniel Barenblatt, *A Plague upon Humanity: The Hidden History of Japan's Biological Warfare Program* (New York: HarperCollins, 2004), 152–63; and Peter Williams and David Wallace, *Unit 731: Japan's Secret Biological Warfare in World War II* (New York: Free Press, 1989), 69–70.

104. Pape, *Bombing to Win,* 42–47.

105. Simon M. Whitby, *Biological Warfare against Crops* (New York: Palgrave Macmillan, 2002); and Terrance M. Wilson et al., "Agroterrorism, Biological Crimes, and Biological Warfare Targeting Animal Agriculture," in *Emerging Diseases of Animals,* ed. Corrie Brown and Carole Bolin (Washington, DC: ASM Press, 2000), 23–57.

106. Jessica Stern, "Dreaded Risks and the Control of Biological Weapons," *International Security* 27, no. 3 (2002/2003): 102–6.

as well as biological submunitions for single- and multiple-warhead intercontinental ballistic missiles. The Soviet Union also developed biological weapons based on antilivestock and antiplant agents.[107] According to Jonathan Tucker of the Center for Nonproliferation Studies, "Soviet military doctrine for strategic biological warfare called for delivering massive quantities of contagious agents against urban targets to cause panic and social disruption, overwhelm the enemy's medical system, and spawn widespread epidemics that would be impossible to control."[108] These objectives are consistent with the Soviet military's nuclear war-fighting strategy, which included impeding the postwar recovery of the United States.[109]

The Anglo-American BW program during World War II was focused on developing strategic biological weapons. Until an antipersonnel weapon based on *B. anthracis* loaded into cluster bombs could be mass-produced in the United States, Great Britain stockpiled five million cattle cakes laced with the organism. The cattle cakes would have been spread across German farms by bombers with the goal of decimating the German cattle industry.[110] During the 1950s, the United States developed antiplant and antipersonnel BW for use in strategic warfare. These agents were loaded into cluster bombs for use by strategic bombers against targets such as industrial facilities and wheat fields in the Soviet Union.[111] Unlike the Soviet Union, the United States did not weaponize any diseases that could be transmitted person to person because of the higher risk during research and development, the increased uncertainty of effects, and the need to protect its own troops.[112]

Iraq also developed and deployed BW for strategic purposes. By the time of the 1991 Gulf War, Iraq had secretly deployed crude biological warheads for its Al Hussein missiles and gravity bombs for delivery by aircraft and was developing spray tanks for use by piloted and unmanned aircraft in strikes against enemy cities.[113] Iraq also produced a large quantity of the anticrop agent *Tilletia*

107. Alibek, *Biohazard,* 5–7; Tom Mangold and Jeff Goldberg, *Plague Wars: The Terrifying Reality of Biological Warfare* (New York: St. Martin's Press, 1999), 84–85; Davis, "Nuclear Blindness," 509–11; Kenneth Alibek, "The Soviet Union's Anti-Agricultural Biological Weapons," *Annals of New York Academy of Sciences* 894 (1999): 18–19; and Rimmington, "The Soviet Union's Offensive Program," 113–15.

108. Tucker, *Scourge,* 143.

109. Stephen M. Meyer, "Soviet Nuclear Operations," in *Managing Nuclear Operations,* ed. Ashton Carter, John Steinbruner, and Charles Zraket (Washington, DC: Brookings, 1987), 531; and Aleksandr' G. Savel'ev and Nikolay N. Detinov, *The Big Five: Arms Control Decision-making in the Soviet Union* (Westport, CT: Praeger, 1995), 1–5.

110. Gradon B. Carter and Graham S. Pearson, "British Biological Warfare and Biological Defence, 1925–1945," in *Biological and Toxin Weapons,* ed. Geissler and Moon, 168–89.

111. Regis, *Biology of Doom,* 138–57; and Whitby, *Biological Warfare against Crops,* 94–117.

112. Spertzel, Wannemacher, and Linden, *Global Proliferation,* 4:12.

113. UNMOVIC, *Compendium,* 945–63.

indica (the fungus that causes wheat cover smut) that may have been intended for use against Iran, whose main crop is wheat.[114] Iraq's experience with strategic BW is discussed in greater depth in the next section.

Biological Weapons Are Poorly Suited for Strategic Deterrence

Biological weapons have been misleadingly labeled the poor man's atomic bomb, which implies that biological and nuclear weapons have similar political effects and implications for international security.[115] This misperception occurs when scholars focus exclusively on the lethality of these weapons and do not pay sufficient attention to the other factors required for weapons to serve as a strategic deterrent.

In a comparative analysis of nuclear, biological, and chemical weapons, Steve Fetter frames the issue as follows: "Do chemical and biological weapons qualify as 'weapons of mass destruction,' and should we think about these weapons in the same way that we have come to think about nuclear weapons? Anthrax weapons (or weapons using similarly lethal pathogens) certainly are able to kill enough people to qualify for this dubious distinction, even if they cannot knock over buildings."[116] According to Susan Martin, the ability of biological weapons to cause mass casualties enables even small states to deter threats to their vital interests and intervention from major powers. Since biological weapons are more easily acquired than nuclear weapons, Martin predicts that the "biological revolution" will have an even more profound impact on international affairs than the nuclear revolution.[117]

Despite their potential lethality, biological weapons do not possess the characteristics necessary to be effective strategic deterrents. Although biological warfare strongly favors the attacker, the uncertain effects of biological weapons, the availability of defenses, and the need for secrecy and surprise greatly reduce the ability of biological weapons to possess the strategic deterrent benefits associated with nuclear weapons. Biological weapons may serve to deter biological attacks or contribute to a state's general deterrence posture, but their effectiveness in these roles will be determined by the offense-defense balance in biological

---

114. Whitby, *Biological Warfare against Crops,* 19–21.

115. Neil C. Livingstone and Joseph D. Douglass Jr., *CBW: The Poor Man's Atomic Bomb* (Cambridge: Institute for Foreign Policy Analysis, 1984); H. Lee Buchanan, "Poor Man's A-Bomb?" *U.S. Naval Institute Proceedings* 123, no. 4 (1997): 83–86; and Al J. Venter, "Biological Warfare: The Poor Man's Atomic Bomb," *Jane's Intelligence Review* 11, no. 3 (1999): 42–47.

116. Steve Fetter, "Ballistic Missiles and Weapons of Mass Destruction: What is the Threat? What Should Be Done?" *International Security* 16, no. 1 (1991): 26.

117. Susan Martin, "The Role of Biological Weapons in International Politics: The Real Military Revolution," *Journal of Strategic Studies* 25, no. 1 (2002): 63–98.

warfare at the time and the relative biological warfare capabilities of the oppos-
ing sides. As a result, these weapons will not eliminate phenomenon such as false
optimism, first-move advantage, arms racing, and perceptions of windows of opportunity and vulnerability that have been identified as key contributors to the
outbreak of wars.[118] Therefore, the spread of BW capabilities is unlikely to exert
a stabilizing influence on international peace and security.

The prerequisite for strategic deterrence is the capability of the target of a
surprise attack to reliably inflict unacceptable damage in retaliation against its
attacker.[119] During the cold war, the possession of such forces by both superpowers gave rise to the situation of mutual deterrence also known as mutual assured destruction (MAD). The nuclear revolution is not only a function of the
destructiveness of nuclear weapons but also of their reliability, the lack of effective
defenses, and the availability of survivable delivery systems.[120] Although biological
weapons have the potential to inflict unacceptable damage against an adversary,
they are unable to offer states an "assured" capability for doing so; this shortfall
significantly undermines their suitability as a strategic deterrent. Biological weapons differ from nuclear weapons in three important ways that raise doubts about
the applicability of strategic deterrence theory to biological warfare.

The first significant difference involves the level of uncertainty associated
with the employment of these weapons. A deep understanding of the fundamental scientific principles underlying nuclear weapons as well as extensive operational and experimental experience with these weapons allowed experts to
document the levels of thermal radiation, nuclear radiation, and blast overpres-
sure that cause specified effects in personnel and matériel.[121] Nuclear weapons
deliver instantaneous and overwhelming destruction; the effects of biological
weapons, on the other hand, are delayed, variable, and difficult to predict. There
are ways to reduce this uncertainty by carefully selecting the agent and delivery
system employed and the conditions under which an attack is conducted. States
that plan on using their biological weapons as a strategic deterrent, however, may
not have the luxury of choosing the time and place for a retaliatory strike.[122] In
addition, the lack of operational experience with these weapons and the inability

---

118. Stephen Van Evera, *Causes of War: Power and the Roots of Conflict* (Ithaca: Cornell University
Press, 2000), 244–45.

119. Bernard Brodie, "Implications for Military Policy," in *The Absolute Weapon: Atomic Power and
World Order,* ed. Bernard Brodie (New York: Harcourt, 1946), 76–77, 89–91.

120. These characteristics are derived from Robert Jervis, *The Meaning of the Nuclear Revolution*
(Ithaca, NY: Cornell University Press, 1989); Shai Feldman, *Israeli Nuclear Deterrence: A Strategy for the
1980s* (New York: Columbia University Press, 1982), 32–33; and Van Evera, *Causes of War,* 240–54.

121. Samuel Gladstone and Dolan J. Philip, eds., *Effects of Nuclear Weapons* (Washington, DC:
GPO, 1977).

122. In contrast, a state contemplating a first strike or surprise attack with biological weapons would
have more flexibility in determining when, where, and how to employ these weapons.

to simulate realistically their effects (short of massive human experimentation) impedes the ability of states to substantially reduce this level of uncertainty.

The second major difference between nuclear and biological weapons concerns the availability of defenses. There are no effective defenses against the effects of a nuclear attack. As discussed earlier, however, there are a number of countermeasures that can be taken before or following a biological attack. Masks and filters can prevent exposure to biological agents. Vaccines can protect those who are exposed. Antibiotics, antitoxins, and antiviral drugs can treat those who are infected. Quarantines can prevent a contagious disease from spreading. Because diseases have an incubation period, defenders have a window of opportunity to detect and treat victims of an attack. There are also vaccines and/or treatments available for the most lethal diseases such as anthrax, plague, smallpox, and tularemia. As a result, the effects of a biological attack are not absolute and incontestable; they can be mitigated and limited by a well-prepared defender. This possibility is likely to reduce the confidence of states in their ability to reliably inflict unacceptable damage against an adversary in a retaliatory strike. The full panoply of defenses need not be deployed constantly at full readiness because the very availability of these defenses may be sufficient to dissuade a state from calculating that it can inflict unacceptable damage. Although civilian populations will remain more vulnerable to biological weapons than will military forces, damage limitation remains a viable option for larger, more advanced states facing less sophisticated adversaries. The December 2002 initiative by the United States to vaccinate nearly one million soldiers, public health officials, and medical workers against smallpox in advance of the looming war with Iraq illustrates how states can adopt precautionary measures to blunt the effectiveness of an anticipated threat.[123]

Third, biological weapons have limited value as strategic deterrents due to the need for states to shroud their weapons programs in strict secrecy. This need for secrecy, which is discussed in greater depth in chapter 3, is driven by normative, legal, and strategic considerations. In the strategic context, the availability of defenses against biological weapons places a premium on the attacker achieving surprise. This causes two problems: First, it is difficult for states to make credible threats based on secret weapons.[124] Second, secrecy is a flimsy means of protecting strategic forces.[125]

---

123. Although fewer than 40,000 of an anticipated 440,000 public health and medical workers were eventually vaccinated, the military successfully vaccinated over 600,000 soldiers and military health personnel. Institute of Medicine, *The Smallpox Vaccination Program: Public Health in an Age of Terrorism* (Washington, DC: National Academies Press, 2005).

124. Avner Cohen and Benjamin Frankel, "Opaque Proliferation," *Journal of Strategic Studies* 13, no. 3 (1990): 31–32; and Feldman, *Israeli Nuclear Deterrence,* 19.

125. Thomas C. Schelling and Morton H. Halperin, *Strategy and Arms Control* (New York: Pergamon, 1985), 37.

The secrecy required to retain the element of surprise in a biological attack reduces a state's ability to issue credible threats to inflict unacceptable damage against an adversary. To make a deterrent threat credible a state would not only have to admit that it was violating international norms and laws but it would also have to reveal details about its offensive BW capabilities such as the types of agents it has developed and their means of delivery.[126] These revelations could reduce the effectiveness of these weapons by compromising the element of surprise and allowing the defender to mobilize appropriate countermeasures. In contrast, the superpowers flaunted their nuclear forces during the cold war for deterrent purposes. They were able to do this because these demonstrations of their nuclear capabilities did not provide the other side with an improved means of defending against them.

Regardless of whether a state develops biological weapons to support a strategy of deterrence by denial or deterrence by punishment, neither strategy will successfully deter a potential adversary if the intention and capabilities to implement the strategy are unknown. The incompatibility between secrecy and deterrence has even been recognized by those who worked on biological weapons. During the cold war, Soviet BW scientist Igor Domaradskij wondered, "if these activities were undertaken for defense purposes, would it not be better, without giving away any secrets, to inform the world community of our successes?"[127]

Secrecy may be an inexpensive and attractive way to gain security for strategic forces, but it is also risky. Forces that depend on secrecy for their protection are vulnerable to intelligence breakthroughs by an adversary. The loss of secrecy could be massive and occur without warning. If a defender were to have inside information about an attacker's capabilities, it would be possible to develop and stockpile new pharmaceuticals, immunize the at-risk population, distribute protective masks and treatments, enhance public health surveillance, and take other precautions that could substantially mitigate the impact of a BW attack. Although such information is difficult to acquire, there have been a number of cases where high-level officials knowledgeable about their nation's BW program have defected.[128]

---

126. It is worth noting that since the BWC entered in force in 1975 no national leader has threatened to use or retaliate with biological weapons.

127. Igor V. Domaradskij and Wendy Orent, "The Memoirs of an Inconvenient Man: Revelations about Biological Weapons Research in the Soviet Union," *Critical Reviews in Microbiology* 27, no. 4 (2001): 246.

128. In 1989 Vladimir Pasechnik, the director of a major Soviet BW research institute, defected to the United Kingdom. In 1992 Ken Alibek (Kanatjan Alibekov), a former deputy director of Biopreparat, the Soviet Union's primary BW research organization, defected to the United States. In 1995 Hussein Kamel,

What little that is known about the perceptions of national security elites regarding the deterrent value of biological weapons supports the view that these weapons have significant shortcomings as deterrents. The difficulty of using biological weapons as retaliatory weapons for deterrent purposes contributed to the decisions by the United States and United Kingdom to renounce biological warfare. According to an influential British arms control study, "it is immediately apparent that CBW agents lack many qualities of an ideal deterrent. The possibilities of effective defence are too great; the adequacy of striking power cannot be made easily manifest. In the case of BW, there is great uncertainty of effect and intolerably slow action."[129] In explaining President Richard Nixon's decision to renounce biological weapons, James Leonard, U.S. ambassador to the United Nations Conference on Disarmament in Geneva, emphasized that these weapons made poor deterrents due to their unpredictability, delayed effects, and the ability of an attacker to protect his forces and blunt the consequences of retaliation.[130] As National Security Adviser Henry Kissinger explained, "We concluded that bacteriological weapons were really primarily useful for first use; that the effect in retaliation would be long delayed, [and] the consequences would be too uncontrollable."[131]

A corollary to the inability of biological weapons to act as a strategic deterrent is that these weapons do not pose a danger of provoking conventional war through the "stability-instability paradox." This concept was developed during the cold war to explain how stability at the nuclear level could encourage conflict at the conventional level.[132] Some scholars believe that non-Western nations may view unconventional weapons as a shield that enables them to safely wield the sword of conventional forces.[133] This logic should not apply to biological weapons, however, because these weapons do not provide the same sort of stable strategic deterrence as nuclear weapons.

---

the head of Iraq's WMD programs, defected to Jordan. Mangold and Goldberg, *Plague Wars,* 91–105, 177–95, 293–94.

129. UK Foreign Office, Arms Control and Disarmament Research Unit, "The Arms Control Implications of Chemical and Biological Weapons: Analysis and Proposals," ACDRU 66(2), 2nd draft, July 4, 1966, 18. FO 371/187448, National Archives, Kew, United Kingdom.

130. "Statement by the United States Representative (Leonard) to the Conference of the Committee on Disarmament: Chemical and Biological Weapons, March 17, 1970," in ACDA, *Documents on Disarmament 1970* (Washington, DC: GPO, 1971), 102–3.

131. "Background Briefing on Chemical and Biological Warfare at the White House with Dr. Henry Kissinger, Assistant to the President for National Security Affairs, and Ron Ziegler, Press Secretary to the President," November 25, 1969, National Security Council Subject Files. Box 310; folder 5, p. 4. Nixon Papers.

132. Glenn Snyder, *Deterrence and Defense* (Princeton: Princeton University Press, 1961), 226; and Jervis, *Meaning of the Nuclear Revolution,* 19–23.

133. Lewis Dunn, Peter Lavoy, and Scott Sagan, "Conclusions: Planning the Unthinkable," in *Planning the Unthinkable,* ed. Lavoy, Sagan, and Wirtz, 234–35.

Iraq's Experience with Biological Weapons as Strategic Deterrent: First Gulf War   The most compelling evidence of the weakness of biological weapons as strategic deterrents was demonstrated by Iraq during its confrontations with the United States in 1991 and in 2003. These cases illustrate the difficulty for states in making biological deterrent threats credible and the likelihood that even inherently credible threats won't have a strong deterrent effect.

Prior to the 1991 Gulf War, Iraq developed a strategic deterrent based on chemical and biological weapons to ensure the survival of the regime.[134] Beginning in December 1990, Iraq began filling bombs and missile warheads with *B. anthracis,* botulinum toxin, and aflatoxin.[135] It hid twenty-five biological and fifty chemical missile warheads near Baghdad and maintained a reserve of seven mobile missiles in western Iraq to deliver these warheads. Iraq also dispersed 157 R-400A biological bombs and 1,000 R-400 chemical bombs to at least four airfields throughout the country.[136]

The purpose of these weapons was to deter attacks that threatened the survival of the Iraqi regime. To achieve this objective, Saddam Hussein predelegated launch authority to airbase and missile commanders in the event that: Baghdad was struck by a nuclear weapon, UN coalition forces marched on the capital, or the commanders lost contact with the national leadership. The warheads and missiles were under the command of the Special Security Organization— the internal security agency composed of the most loyal members of the Baath Party and charged with protecting Saddam Hussein.[137] It is highly likely that if this group lost contact with Baghdad and believed the regime to be in mortal peril they would have ordered the launch of the CBW-armed missiles against Israel and Saudi Arabia. By January 15, the United Nations' deadline for Iraq to withdraw its forces from Kuwait, Iraq had put in place a doctrine and a capability to deter a decapitating strike on the Iraqi leadership.

Iraq's strategy for deterring threats to regime survival failed. From the first night of Operation Desert Storm, the United States made a concerted, albeit unsuccessful, effort to kill Saddam Hussein and the senior Iraqi leadership. The United States devoted 850 air strikes, or about 2 percent of the U.S. air campaign, to attacking leadership targets and command and control facilities. The United States placed a high priority on destroying these targets: over 50 percent of these

134. On Saddam Hussein's preoccupation with his own survival and the centrality of regime survival to Iraqi national security decision making, see Kevin Woods et al., *Iraqi Perspectives Project: A View of Operation Iraqi Freedom from Saddam's Senior Leadership* (Norfolk, VA: Joint Force Command, 2005), 25–28.

135. UNMOVIC, *Compendium,* 958.

136. McCarthy and Tucker, "Saddam's Toxic Arsenal," 72–75; and UNMOVIC, *Unresolved Disarmament Issues,* 45–46.

137. McCarthy and Tucker, "Saddam's Toxic Arsenal," 72–75; and Amatzia Baram, "An Analysis of Iraqi WMD Strategy," *Nonproliferation Review* 8, no. 2 (2001): 34–36.

attacks were conducted with precision munitions, compared to only 8 percent against all other targets. As a result, over half of these leadership targets were damaged or destroyed.[138]

Saddam Hussein's survival was not due to the United States' unwillingness to target him for fear of triggering a chemical and biological retaliatory strike but to an inability to implement a decapitation strategy using airpower. Iraq's strategy failed because it did not communicate to the United States the "red lines" that would trigger a retaliatory strike, the existence of predelegated launch authority for airbase and missile commanders, or the extent of Iraq's deployed strategic chemical and biological weapons capabilities. Indeed, in April 1990 Saddam Hussein admitted to a visiting Congressional delegation that Iraq possessed chemical weapons, but he denied possessing biological weapons.[139] Iraq did not reveal its 1991 deterrent strategy or the existence of its strategic BW arsenal until 1995.

This incident illustrates some of the dangers that scholars have associated with opaque nuclear weapon programs. When opacity delays the deployment of a deterrent force until a crisis, the military is unlikely to have a well-developed doctrine or well-trained troops for handling the weapons. In addition, a national emergency is not conducive to deliberation and debate by elites on the merits and drawbacks of competing policies and doctrines. Although covert weaponization prior to a crisis would allow the political and military leadership to confront and resolve operational dilemmas, secrecy would continue to constrain strategic discourse, awareness of operational issues, and the vetting of trade-offs. As Duke University professor Peter Feaver has observed, "the risks of aberrant behavior are greatest precisely because the opacity has inhibited preparing the national leadership for weighing the trade-offs wisely."[140]

An alternative explanation for the failure of Iraq's CBW deterrent strategy is that it was neutralized by Iraq's fear of nuclear retaliation if it used CBW against the United States. In August 1995, when Iraq admitted to UNSCOM that it had filled bombs and missile warheads with BW agents before the Gulf War, Iraq's foreign minister Tariq Aziz claimed that Iraq did not use these weapons due to the risk of nuclear retaliation by the coalition.[141] This statement, however, should not be taken at face value. Although the United States had repeatedly warned Iraq before Operation Desert Storm that it would suffer severe consequences if

---

138. Pape, *Bombing to Win,* 221–23, 226–40; and Eliot A. Cohen, *Gulf War Air Power Survey,* vol. 2, *Effects and Effectiveness* (Washington, DC: Department of the Air Force, 1993), 274–90.

139. Michael R. Gordon, "C.I.A. Fears Iraq Could Deploy Biological Arms by Early 1991," *New York Times,* September 29, 1990, A4.

140. Peter Feaver, "Proliferation Optimism and Theories of Nuclear Operations," *Security Studies* 2, no. 3/4 (1993): 177.

141. R. Jeffrey Smith, "UN Says Iraqis Prepared Germ Weapons in Gulf War," *Washington Post,* August 26, 1995, A1.

it used CBW against the United States or its allies, the United States followed a strategy of "calculated ambiguity" and did not explicitly threaten nuclear retaliation.[142] In contrast, the George H. W. Bush administration explicitly threatened to expand its war aims to include regime change if Iraq used chemical or biological weapons.

The United States communicated this threat directly to the Iraqi leadership on January 9, 1991, during a meeting between Secretary of State James Baker and Foreign Minister Aziz. At this meeting Secretary Baker delivered a letter from President Bush to Saddam Hussein that warned that if Iraq used chemical or biological weapons, destroyed Kuwait's oil fields, or conducted terrorist attacks against any member of the coalition, "You, the Ba'ath party, and your country will pay a terrible price if you order unconscionable actions of this sort."[143] Baker also told Aziz that if Iraq used chemical or biological weapons, "our objective won't be only the liberation of Kuwait, but also the elimination of the current Iraqi regime, and anyone responsible for using these weapons would be held accountable."[144] Thus, while Iraq could not rule out the possibility of nuclear retaliation, the most direct warnings issued by the United States threatened only the survival of Saddam Hussein's regime.

It is quite likely that Aziz's statement was part of a political strategy to limit the damage caused by Iraq's revelations about the true extent of its WMD programs after the defection of Saddam Hussein's son-in-law Hussein Kamel by portraying Iraq as the victim of Western bullies. Once Iraq admitted that it had produced and deployed biological weapons by January 1991, some justification had to be offered for not using these weapons during the Gulf War. Not surprisingly, there are no public statements by Iraqi officials that they were deterred by threats to overthrow the Baath regime, since this would sound cowardly and acknowledge that the regime felt vulnerable. As one Arab diplomat commented, "the regime had to explain to its military commanders why it was pulling back from the brink, so it looked a lot better to say that it was sparing the Iraqi people from nuclear holocaust than to admit that the leaders were worried about their own skins."[145]

Indeed, during the days following Baker's meeting with Aziz and the beginning of Operation Desert Storm, Iraq moved forward with deploying biological

---

142. See Scott Sagan, "The Commitment Trap: Why the United States Should Not Use Nuclear Threats to Deter Biological and Chemical Weapon Attacks," *International Security* 24, no. 4 (2000): 91–96; and William Arkin, "Calculated Ambiguity: Nuclear Weapons and the Gulf War," *Washington Quarterly* 19, no. 4 (1996): 3–18.

143. George Bush and Brent Scowcroft, *A World Transformed* (New York: Knopf, 1998), 442.

144. James Baker, *The Politics of Diplomacy: Revolution, War, and Peace, 1989–1992* (New York: Putnam, 1995), 359.

145. Quoted in Joseph Fitchett, "Nuclear States See Vindication: Threat of Annihilation Deterred Iraq, They Say," *International Herald Tribune,* September 12, 1995.

weapons and planning how it would use its chemical and biological weapons against the coalition. On January 11, Iraq completed filling 157 R-400A bombs and 25 Al Hussein missile warheads with *B. anthracis,* botulinum toxin, and afla-toxin. By January 13 Iraq had dispersed these weapons to air bases and impro-vised hide sites around Iraq.[146] During the second week of January, most likely just a few days before the United Nations' January 15 deadline for Iraq to with-draw from Kuwait, Saddam Hussein held a high-level meeting to discuss the status of Iraq's chemical and biological weapons and plans on how they could be used. He ordered Iraq's air- and missile-delivered chemical and biological weap-ons to be targeted at major Saudi Arabian and Israeli cities as well as major U.S. troop concentrations in Saudi Arabia. He also issued instructions to predelegate the launch authority for these weapons in the event that air force or missile com-manders could not communicate directly with him.[147]

Because the deployment of Iraq's biological weapons and the meeting to plan their use took place after Baker's meeting with Aziz, it does not appear that U.S. threats to retaliate with nuclear weapons or to seek regime change were the de-ciding factors in shaping Iraq's CBW doctrine. This conclusion is supported by Iraq's violation of the two other "red lines" outlined by Bush and Baker: the destruction of Kuwait's oil fields and committing acts of terrorism against members of the coalition.[148] Iraq's failure to heed U.S. warnings regarding these two issues reduces the likelihood that U.S. threats of retaliation were the pri-mary driver of Iraq's CBW doctrine. The failure of Iraq's chemical and biologi-cal weapons to deter regime-threatening attacks by the United States was more likely due to the shortcomings of Iraq's deterrent strategy than to fear of nu-clear retaliation.

Iraq's Experience with Biological Weapons as Strategic Deterrent: Second Gulf War   The U.S. invasion of Iraq in 2003 provides a different kind of test of the ability of biological weapons to serve as a strategic deterrent. If biological weap-ons really are the poor man's atomic bomb and have the same deterrent effect as nuclear weapons, we should have seen some evidence of this during the run-up to the war.

Although Iraq did not make biological deterrent threats in 2003 during the buildup to Operation Iraqi Freedom, it was believed to have both the motivation

---

146. UNMOVIC, *Compendium,* 788, 961–62.

147. Duelfer Report, vol. 1, *Strategic Intent,* 97–100.

148. See Ali Mohamed Al-Damkhi, "Kuwait's Oil Well Fires, 1991: Environmental Crime and War," *International Journal of Environmental Studies* 64, no. 1 (2007): 31–44; and Andrew W. Terrill, "Saddam's Failed Counterstrike: Terrorism and the Gulf War," *Studies in Conflict and Terrorism* 16, no. 3 (1993): 151–71.

and capability to use these weapons to implement such a strategy. The stated purpose of the invasion was to overthrow Saddam Hussein and his Baath Party. This type of regime-threatening war is exactly the scenario that a strategic deterrent is best suited to preventing. The prospect of being overthrown should have removed any incentive for Hussein to exercise restraint in defending his regime. Iraq's willingness to use unconventional weapons had been demonstrated by its chemical attacks against the Kurds and Iranians in the 1980s and by revelations of Iraq's 1991 plans to use these weapons against Israel and Saudi Arabia if the regime's survival had been threatened by the coalition.

According to U.S. intelligence, Iraq had a large and advanced biological weapons program; possessed a stockpile of BW agents, including *B. anthracis* and perhaps even variola virus; and had the means of delivering these agents by aircraft, missiles, unmanned aerial vehicles, and covert operatives. These assessments were made with a high level of confidence and were taken seriously by the military.[149] U.S. intelligence also assessed that Iraq viewed its biological weapons as a strategic deterrent and would probably use these weapons when Saddam Hussein "perceived that he irretrievably had lost control of the military and security situation."[150] In response to this threat, the military expanded the program of vaccinations it gave to its soldiers to protect them from the agents Iraq was believed to possess. In addition to a mandatory vaccination for anthrax, the military launched a campaign in December 2002 to immunize five hundred thousand soldiers against smallpox. The purpose of the immunization campaign was, in the words of one government official, to "take that card from Saddam's deck."[151] In effect, the United States sought to minimize the casualties that Iraq could inflict using its biological weapons, which would reduce their deterrent value for the Iraqi leadership. The United States' decision to invade Iraq with the goal of overthrowing the regime, despite that regime's presumed possession of CBW and a demonstrated willingness to use them, illustrates biological weapons' weakness as a strategic deterrent.

Constraints on the Use of Biological Weapons May Be Eroding

Despite the major advances in biological warfare since the 1940s and their potential utility in a wide range of operations, there is no evidence that modern

---

149. National Intelligence Council, *Iraq's Continuing Programs for Weapons of Mass Destruction,* National Intelligence Estimate 2002–16HC, October 2002, 5–7.

150. Ibid., 8; and CIA, *Developing Biological Weapons as a Strategic Deterrent,* CIANESAF IA 2001–20072J, August 10, 2001, cited in Senate Select Committee on Intelligence (SSCI), *Report on Whether Public Statements Regarding Iraq By U.S. Government Officials Were Substantiated by Intelligence Information,* (Washington, DC: SSCI, June 5, 2008), 20.

151. John Cohen and Martin Enserink, "Rough-and-Tumble behind Bush's Smallpox Policy," *Science* 298 (December 20, 2002): 2315.

biological weapons based on aerosol dissemination technology have been successfully employed. On the rare occasions when states and terrorists have resorted to the use of biological weapons, they have used less sophisticated means of dissemination. Accounting for the rare use of these weapons in modern times is important to determine the likelihood that the conditions that led to this restraint will continue to remain strong. There are three likely reasons why biological weapons have been rarely used in modern times.

First, there is a strong normative barrier to the use of these weapons. The use of disease as a weapon has long been considered taboo.[152] This taboo can be found in ancient Indian, Greek, Roman, and Muslim traditions, so it is multicultural and has existed since antiquity.[153] This sense of revulsion at using poison or disease as an instrument of war has been codified in national legal prohibitions for centuries and in international law in the twentieth century. The 1925 Geneva Protocol prohibits the use of biological weapons and the 1972 Biological Weapons Convention prohibits the development, production, or acquisition of these weapons. The BWC was a groundbreaking treaty, the first to outlaw an entire class of weapons. The treaty reinforced the long-standing norm against these weapons by declaring the use of biological weapons as being "repugnant to the conscience of mankind."

Second, military organizations have also had practical reasons for not assimilating these weapons into their war plans.[154] Safely storing and handling these weapons presents logistical difficulties, and employing them in combat can pose significant operational problems. Early generations of biological weapons had limited effectiveness and uncertain results due to their reliance on vectors, such as insects or rats, or contamination of food or water to infect the enemy. Modern biological weapons based on aerosol dissemination are susceptible to vagaries in atmospheric conditions. This creates uncertainty for military planners and poses the risk of accidentally infecting friendly troops due to a change in wind direction.

A third reason for the rare use of these weapons is political and strategic. The use of these weapons may have been limited by the fear of retaliation or escalating a conflict. Japan, Rhodesia, and South Africa engaged in biological warfare against opponents that were unable to retaliate in kind. The domestic or international reaction to the use of these illegitimate weapons, rather than the prohibition itself, may have also had a restraining influence.

---

152. For a review of the debate over the sources of this taboo, see Leonard Cole, "The Poison Weapons Taboo: Biology, Culture, and Policy," *Politics and the Life Sciences* 17, no. 2 (1998): 119–32.

153. Adrienne Mayor, *Greek Fire, Poison Arrows, and Scorpion Bombs: Biological and Chemical Warfare in the Ancient World* (Woodstock, NY: Overlook Press, 2003), 24–39.

154. Military organizations are well known for resisting innovation in the absence of operational experience with a new technology. Barry Posen, *The Sources of Military Doctrine: France, Britain, and Germany between the World Wars* (Ithaca, NY: Cornell University Press, 1984), 55.

Unfortunately, there is cause for concern that all three of these constraints on the use of biological weapons have been eroding. The continued proliferation of biological weapons may reflect the diminishing normative power of the BWC. In 1972 the United States believed that four states were pursuing development of biological weapons.[155] The number of states suspected of possessing an offensive BW program had climbed to ten by 1989 and to twelve by 2001.[156] Since then the number of states assessed as having BW programs has dropped to six.[157] Significantly, all of these countries are parties to the BWC.[158] The secretiveness with which these states pursue these weapons is a demonstration of the normative power of the BWC. But the purpose of the treaty was to prevent this activity, not just drive it underground. As Avner Cohen and Benjamin Frankel have observed in the context of covert nuclear proliferation, "beyond a certain point the aggregate weight of an on-going practice overwhelms the rules."[159]

The second constraint, posed by operational and logistical problems, may be less daunting now due to technological advances and organizational innovations. As discussed above, the biotechnology revolution has introduced a range of advanced technologies that may make these weapons easier and safer to produce and store and more effective when employed.[160] Virtually all of these technologies were developed for civilian, not military, purposes. Given the multiuse nature of the technologies that are required to develop and produce biological weapons, and the global growth in civilian applications of biotechnology, states pursuing biological weapons have several incentives to create a separate organization outside of the military establishment to conduct research, development,

155. General Accounting Office, *Arms Control: U.S. and International Efforts to Ban Biological Weapons,* GAO/NSIAD-93–113 (Washington, DC: GAO, 1992), 9–11. These four states were the Soviet Union, Egypt, and Israel and either France or the People's Republic of China. Interdepartmental Political-Military Group, *Annual Review of United States Chemical and Biological Research Programs as of July 1, 1972,* October 26, 1972, p. 19. National Security Council Files, NSC Institutional Files (H-Files). Box H-213: Policy Papers, NSDMs, NSDM-35 [4 of 4], Nixon papers; and Foreign Capabilities Task Force, *Contribution to NSSM-59: Foreign Chemical and Bacteriological (Biological) Warfare Capabilities,* July 25, 1969, p. 36, FOIA.

156. Milton Leitenberg, *Assessing the Biological Weapons and Bioterrorism Threat* (Carlisle Barracks, PA: Strategic Studies Institute, 2005), 10–16.

157. Interview with senior U.S. intelligence official, Washington, DC, May 2008.

158. In 2005 the U.S. Department of State listed six nations that were suspected of not being in compliance with the BWC: China, Cuba, Iran, North Korea, Russia, and Syria. Department of State, *Adherence to and Compliance with Arms Control and Nonproliferation Agreements and Commitments* (Washington, DC: Department of State, 2005).

159. Cohen and Frankel, "Opaque Proliferation," 30.

160. Jonathan B. Tucker, "The Future of Biological Warfare," in *The Proliferation of Advanced Weaponry,* ed. W. Thomas Wander and Eric H. Arnett (Washington, DC: American Association for the Advancement of Science, 1992), 61–71; Block, "Living Nightmares," 39–75; and Robert P. Kadlec and Alan P. Zelicoff, "Implications of the Biotechnology Revolution for Weapons Development and Arms Control," in *Biological Warfare,* ed. Zilinskas, 11–26.

and production. From a scientific and technical perspective, such an organization is better able to recruit and reward scientists and to obtain multiuse knowledge, materials, and equipment from abroad then a military-run agency. By using an ostensibly civilian organization to conduct BW-related activities, a state can also better conceal the existence of a BW program and military interest in biological weapons. Nations as diverse as the Soviet Union, Iraq, and South Africa have adopted this model.

In his pioneering book on innovation in business, *The Innovator's Dilemma,* Harvard Business School professor Clayton Christensen argues that already successful firms fail to invest in and capitalize on new disruptive technologies that represent a break from traditional products.[161] According to Christensen's theory, firms are only able to successfully exploit disruptive technologies when they are being developed by an independent organization spun off from the mainstream company. Biological weapons may represent a type of disruptive technology from the standpoint of militaries wedded to conventional and/or nuclear weapons. Military organizations tend to share the conservatism of the mainstream firms in Christensen's analysis: they are more interested in investing in weapons that are central to their current conception of waging war. Therefore, the creation of autonomous organizations dedicated to the development of biological weapons could serve as a catalyst for states to integrate these weapons into their arsenals and strategic planning. The dangers that such an autonomous organization poses to civilian oversight and management are discussed in greater depth in chapter 3.

Finally, the dominance of the United States and its allies in conventional military technology may provide dissatisfied actors with a strong incentive to employ biological weapons as part of an asymmetric strategy that outweighs the political and strategic hazards of using these weapons. Dissatisfied actors may calculate that they can use their biological weapons as force multipliers to bring about a fait accompli, tailor their use of these weapons to avoid provoking regime-threatening retaliation, or conduct anonymous attacks and avoid retaliation entirely. As with nuclear weapons, the lack of large-scale use of biological weapons since 1945 is a cause for celebration, but it is not grounds for complacency.

In this chapter I discussed the major characteristics of biological weapons and highlighted four findings. First, biological warfare strongly favors the attacker. Second, biological weapons are well-suited to serving as force multipliers, especially at the operational level of warfare. Third, biological weapons are poorly suited to serve as strategic deterrents. Fourth, the constraints on the development

161. Clayton Christensen, *The Innovator's Dilemma* (Boston: Harvard Business School, 1997).

and use of these weapons may be eroding. Thus, biological weapons could provide dissatisfied states with a potent means of engaging in asymmetric warfare and challenging the status quo. Due to the limited value of biological weapons as strategic deterrents, the spread of these weapons will have a destabilizing influence on international security.

The next four chapters describe the implications of these characteristics of biological weapons for verifying international biological arms control agreements, conducting civilian oversight over BW programs, collecting and analyzing intelligence on BW programs, and assessing the threat of biological terrorism. The concluding chapter offers policy prescriptions for reducing the dangers posed by biological weapons.

2

Verification

Preventing the spread of biological weapons is perhaps the most difficult proliferation challenge facing the international community. This does not mean that traditional arms control and nonproliferation tools should be abandoned, but policymakers must recognize that such measures are less effective at halting the spread of biological weapons than other types of weapons. Verification, the ability to confirm whether a nation is complying with its obligations, is the foundation of effective arms control and disarmament. Fortunately, during the cold war, the most threatening military forces—strategic nuclear weapons—required large industrial facilities to develop, produce, and test them. These facilities were either visible to overhead reconnaissance systems or had distinct signatures that could be detected at long range.[1] Even chemical weapons programs require

---

1. On the "reconnaissance revolution," see John Lewis Gaddis, "The Long Peace: Elements of Stability in the Postwar International System," *International Security* 10, no. 4 (1986): 123–25.

industrial-scale production facilities and large stockpiles of munitions in order to pose a significant military threat.[2]

The core problem in verifying compliance with biological arms control and disarmament agreements is that the capabilities for conducting the research, development, production, and testing of biological weapons are virtually identical to those employed by defensive programs and in legitimate civilian enterprises. Biotechnology-related capabilities and activities that cannot be justified as having a civilian purpose—such as working with dangerous pathogens or experimenting with aerosols of biological agents—can be legitimate activities for a biological defense program. There are few aspects of a BW program that are unique to offensive applications and that are readily detectable by outsiders. Advanced biotechnologies may make it unnecessary to maintain large dedicated production plants, stockpiles of bulk agents, or filled munitions that would provide intelligence agencies or inspectors with a smoking gun.

The first part of this chapter provides a primer on the 1972 Biological Weapons Convention and describes the evolution of the treaty to date. The BWC prohibits the development, production, stockpiling, acquisition, and retention of biological weapons. The BWC, however, does not include any mechanism for verifying that states are complying with the treaty. As a result, the international community has been engaged in an ongoing effort since 1975 to strengthen the treaty. International negotiations to create a compliance protocol for the treaty ended in 2001 after the United States rejected the draft protocol. Since 2003 state parties to the treaty have met annually to exchange ideas and proposals on national voluntary mechanisms for strengthening the treaty.

In the second part of this chapter I argue that the multiuse nature of biotechnology, the overlap between offensive and defensive activities, the need for secrecy, and the lack of signatures for offensive BW programs makes it difficult to distinguish between offensive and defensive or civilian activities. When offensive and defensive activities cannot be differentiated, cooperation and arms control become extremely difficult. This is especially true when the military capabilities in question favor the attacker, as was shown to be the case in regard to biological warfare.[3]

In the third part of this chapter I examine the investigation of Iraq's BW program by the United Nations Special Commission from 1991 to 1998. The

---

2. Gordon M. Burck, "Chemical Weapons Production Technology and the Conversion of Civilian Production," *Arms Control* 11, no. 12 (1990): 122–63; and Office of Technology Assessment (OTA), *Technologies Underlying Weapons of Mass Destruction* (Washington, DC: GPO, 1993), 15–55.

3. On the influence of the offense-defense balance on the security dilemma, see Robert Jervis, "Cooperation under the Security Dilemma," *World Politics* 30, no. 2 (1978): 167–214; and Stephen Van Evera, *Causes of War: Power and the Roots of Conflict* (Ithaca: Cornell University Press, 2000), 135–37.

UNSCOM experience represents the most important effort by the international community to verify biological arms control and disarmament. UNSCOM was the most intrusive arms control regime ever devised and had access to an unprecedented range of inspection techniques and technologies. Although UNSCOM was successful in uncovering aspects of Iraq's past BW activities, a comprehensive account of Iraq's biological agent research, production, testing, and weaponization only emerged following the defection of a high-level Iraqi official in August 1995. The UNSCOM experience provides insight into how the multiple uses of biological technologies complicates verification and the extraordinary measures that were required to overcome Iraq's attempts to retain an offensive BW capability based on multiuse technologies.

The chapter concludes with an analysis of the applicability of the UNSCOM experience to strengthening the BWC. While UNSCOM amply demonstrated the utility of a number of technologies and techniques for verifying biological arms control, the conditions required for UNSCOM's success cast serious doubt on the ability of an international organization to achieve similar results in the context of a multilateral BW verification treaty.

The Biological Weapons Convention

The Biological Weapons Convention, formally known as the Convention on the Prohibition of the Development, Production, and Stockpiling of Bacteriological (Biological) and Toxin Weapons and on their Destruction, entered into force on March 26, 1975. As of July 2008, 162 nations had become parties to the treaty and another 13 had signed but not ratified it.

The BWC had its origin in an August 1968 British proposal to separate chemical and biological weapons in international disarmament negotiations and to focus international efforts on banning biological weapons.[4] Until this point, negotiators in Geneva had sought an agreement to prohibit both chemical and biological weapons. International interest in such an agreement had intensified during the mid-1960s in response to the use of tear gas, herbicides, and defoliants in Vietnam by the United States. Negotiations over the British proposal quickly bogged down due to the controversial nature of the U.S. intervention in Vietnam and attempts by Communist nations to use the forum for propaganda purposes.

---

4. For a summary of the negotiations leading to the BWC, see Susan Wright, "Geopolitical Origins," in *Biological Warfare and Disarmament: New Problems/New Perspectives,* ed. Susan Wright, (Lanham, MD: Rowman and Littlefield, 2002), 313–42; and Marie Isabelle Chevrier, "The Politics of Biological Disarmament," in *Deadly Cultures: Biological Weapons since 1945,* ed. Mark Wheelis, Lajos Rózsa, and Malcolm Dando, (Cambridge: Harvard University Press, 2006), 304–28.

The British reasoned that because biological weapons had not been previously used in battle, were not useful for deterrence, and had not yet spread beyond the great powers, it would be easier to negotiate a ban on them then on chemical weapons.[5] The British proposal, however, faced stiff resistance from other states that objected to the exclusion of chemical weapons and the lack of any verification provisions in the draft treaty. Two breakthroughs were required to overcome this logjam and enable the superpowers to reach an agreement on a treaty banning biological weapons.

The first breakthrough came on November 25, 1969, when President Nixon announced that the United States was terminating its offensive BW program. Nixon also announced that the United States would support the British draft convention despite the lack of verification provisions. Although verification had long been a key stumbling block for strategic arms control initiatives during the cold war, the United States was willing to accept this treaty without any verification measures for four reasons. First, the military was convinced that these weapons had little utility and therefore they were not concerned if another country was developing them. Second, the United States had already terminated its offensive BW program—and did not plan on rearming with biological weapons even if others violated the treaty. Third, it was hoped that the norm established by the treaty would deter other nations from developing biological weapons. Finally, the Soviets were opposed to on-site inspections.[6]

The second breakthrough occurred on March 30, 1971, when the Soviet Union, after having long opposed separating chemical and biological weapons in disarmament negotiations, reversed itself and submitted its own draft biological weapons treaty. At the time, the United States concluded that the Soviets were using the treaty to signal its interest in arms control and engage the Nixon administration in strategic nuclear issues.[7] After several months of negotiations, the United States and the Soviet Union jointly introduced a draft convention on biological weapons to the United Nations' Conference of the Committee on Disarmament. The BWC opened for signature on April 10, 1972, and entered into force on March 26, 1975. In recognition of the important roles they played in the negotiation of the BWC, the United States, the United Kingdom, and Russia (originally the Soviet Union) serve as the depositories for the treaty.

---

5. UK Foreign Office, Arms Control and Disarmament Research Unit, "Arms Control Implications of Chemical and Biological Warfare," report written by Hedley Bull, ACDRU (66) 2 (2nd Draft), 4 July 1966, FO 371/187448, National Archives, Kew, United Kingdom.

6. Tom Mangold and Jeff Goldberg, *Plague Wars: The Terrifying Reality of Biological Warfare* (New York: St. Martin's Press, 1999), 55–57, 402 n. 26; and Alan F. Neidle, "The Rise and Fall of Multilateral Arms Control: Choices for the United States," in *Arms Control: The Multilateral Alternative,* ed. Edward C. Luck, (New York: New York University Press, 1983), 13.

7. Ambassador James Leonard, cited in Mangold and Goldberg, *Plague Wars,* 59.

Key Features of the BWC

The BWC was the first international treaty to outlaw an entire class of weapons. In contrast, the recently completed Treaty on the Non-Proliferation of Nuclear Weapons (or Nuclear Non-Proliferation Treaty) allowed the five states that possessed nuclear weapons at the time the treaty was written to keep them. The preamble of the BWC highlights the importance the drafters of the treaty gave to capitalizing on the preexisting stigma against using disease as a weapon and their hope that the treaty would further reinforce this norm. The preamble states that the use of biological weapons is "repugnant to the conscience of mankind" and that the prohibition of these weapons is "for the sake of all mankind."

The heart of the treaty is Article 1, which states:

> Each State Party to this Convention undertakes never in any circumstances to develop, produce, stockpile or otherwise acquire or retain:
> (1) Microbial or other biological agents, or toxins whatever their origin or method of production, of types and in quantities that have no justification for prophylactic, protective or other peaceful purposes;
> (2) Weapons, equipment or means of delivery designed to use such agents or toxins for hostile purposes or in armed conflict.

The language in this article walks a fine line between the aspirations of the drafters to achieve a clear and unequivocal prohibition against biological weapons and the reality of the multiuse nature of biological agents and biological research. As a result, while state parties are obligated "never in any circumstances" to develop, produce, or possess biological weapons, the borders demarcating prohibited and legitimate activities are either vague or undefined. The convention does not prohibit research on biological weapons in recognition of the great difficulty in determining whether such activities are being undertaken for permitted or prohibited purposes.[8] Furthermore, the convention does not define what activities are considered research, and therefore fall outside the scope of the treaty, and what activities constitute development, and therefore subject to the treaty's provisions. In addition, the treaty allows the development, production, and stockpiling of biological agents of appropriate "types and quantities" so long as they have "prophylactic, protective or other peaceful purposes." However, the types, quantities, and purposes that are permitted are not further defined in the treaty.[9] This ambiguous wording and lack of definition was required

---

8. Barend ter Haar, *The Future of Biological Weapons* (New York: Praeger, 1991), 64–65.

9. The United States has interpreted "protective, prophylactic, or other peaceful purposes" to include the prevention, diagnosis, or treatment of disease in humans, plants, and animals; the protection of humans, plants, and animals through vulnerability studies and the development of protective masks,

to allow states to continue conducting medical, scientific, public health, commercial, and defensive work with organisms that could also be used as BW agents. The multiuse dilemma resulted in a treaty that places a heavy burden on interpreting the intent of an activity to determine whether or not it is in compliance with Article I.

Although the BWC was written before the advent of the biotechnology revolution, its drafters were aware of the amazing advances that had already taken place in the life sciences and fully expected further such advances in the future. The inclusion of the phrases "other biological agents" and "whatever their origin or method of production" in Article I was intended to provide as broad as possible coverage of biological threats. The parties to the BWC have reaffirmed at each of the treaty's review conferences that Article I covers all recent developments in science and technology relevant to biological weapons.[10]

The other major obligations for state parties to the BWC are to destroy any BW agents and weapons in their possession (Article II), not to transfer biological weapons or provide assistance to others in producing biological weapons (Article III), to put in place domestic legislation implementing the treaty (Article IV), to reaffirm the Geneva Protocol banning the use of biological weapons (Article VIII), and to provide assistance to states threatened by BW (Article VI). Under Article X, states are encouraged to engage in the fullest possible exchange of biological knowledge and materials and to implement the treaty in a way that does not hamper economic development or international cooperation in the life sciences.

The BWC has two notable differences from the other international WMD nonproliferation treaties: the Nuclear Non-Proliferation Treaty, the Chemical Weapons Convention, and the Comprehensive Test Ban Treaty. First, the BWC does not contain any verification provisions. If a state suspects another state of violating the treaty, it has two options. Under Article V, it can engage in consultations and attempt to resolve compliance concerns in a cooperative manner.[11] Under Article VI, it can lodge a complaint with the United Nations Security

filtration systems, detection, warning and identification devices, and decontamination systems; the development of means for detecting violations of the treaty; biomedical research and biological processing technology for nonweapon purposes; and activities to protect or enhance the use of agriculture and the environment. "Memorandum from Brent Scowcroft, National Security Advisor, to Heads of Executive Departments and Agencies, Subject: U.S. Compliance with the Biological Weapons Convention, December 23, 1975," *CBW Conventions Bulletin* 57 (September 2002): 2.

10. British Medical Association, *Biotechnology, Weapons, and Humanity* (Amsterdam: Harwood Academic, 1999), 37–41.

11. Article V has been invoked only once, in response to allegations by Cuba in 1997 that the United States had spread agricultural pests on the island. Raymond A. Zilinskas, "Cuban Allegations of Biological Warfare by the United States: Assessing the Evidence," *Critical Reviews in Microbiology* 25, no. 3 (1999): 173–227.

Council, which is authorized to initiate an investigation of the allegation. Due to the veto power of the five permanent members of the Security Council, this mechanism has not proven to be of any value. An alternative means of addressing compliance concerns emerged in 1982 when the UN Secretary-General gained the authority to investigate allegations of CBW use brought to its attention by member states.[12] Although this mechanism has never been used to investigate the alleged use of biological weapons, the Secretary-General dispatched several teams to investigate alleged cases of CW use during the Iran-Iraq War, as well as in Mozambique and Azerbaijan in the early 1990s.[13]

The second major difference between the BWC and these other treaties is that the BWC lacks an international organization to support its implementation. When the Nuclear Non-Proliferation Treaty was signed in 1968, the International Atomic Energy Agency (IAEA) was charged with ensuring that non-nuclear states did not divert nuclear material into a weapons program. When the CWC was signed in 1993, the Organization for the Prohibition of Chemical Weapons was created to oversee the destruction of existing chemical weapons and to monitor civilian chemical facilities to ensure that they were not utilized for military purposes. The Comprehensive Test Ban Treaty Organization was created in 1996 to oversee a global verification regime for the test ban treaty including an international monitoring system. Given the absence of an international organization to act as an advocate for the BWC or to serve as a forum for state parties to discuss the treaty's implementation and improvement, the review conferences held every five years have served as the primary venue for discussing measures to strengthen the treaty.

Evolution of the BWC

Since its entry into force in 1975, the BWC has evolved in fits and starts.[14] For the first sixteen years of the treaty, efforts to strengthen the treaty made incremental progress through the adoption of voluntary confidence-building

---

12. Additional General Assembly and Security Council resolutions in 1987 and 1998 empowered the Secretary-General to launch such investigations on its own authority.

13. These episodes demonstrated the ability of international investigations to confirm or disprove allegations of CW use, but only if they were dispatched soon after the attack allegedly took place and the host country provided its full cooperation. Jonathan B. Tucker, "Multilateral Approaches to the Investigation and Attribution of Biological Weapons Use," in *Terrorism, War, or Disease? Unraveling the Use of Biological Weapons,* ed. Anne L. Clunan, Peter R. Lavoy, and Susan B. Martin (Stanford: Stanford University Press, 2008), 269–92.

14. For detailed descriptions of the evolution of the BWC, see Nicholas A. Sims, *The Evolution of Biological Disarmament* (Oxford: Oxford University Press, 2001); and Jez Littlewood, *The Biological Weapons Convention: A Failed Revolution* (London: Ashgate, 2005).

measures (CBMs) intended to improve the transparency of civilian and defensive biological activities. Beginning in 1991, state parties began a process to devise stronger mandatory measures to further improve transparency and provide greater confidence that all state parties were in compliance with the treaty. Negotiations on a compliance protocol for the treaty came to an end in 2001 when the United States announced it would not support the draft protocol (discussed in more detail below). A new process began in 2002 that featured regular exchanges of ideas and proposals on a wide array of voluntary national measures to strengthen the BWC.

At the second review conference in 1986 and at the third review conference in 1991 states adopted a number of voluntary CBMs to increase the transparency of facilities and activities of special relevance to the treaty. In the absence of verification measures built into the BWC, state parties developed these CBMs to enhance their confidence that other parties to the treaty were in compliance. In 1986 the state parties agreed to provide information on maximum containment biological labs on their territory, unusual outbreaks of infectious diseases or illnesses due to toxins, publications on biomedical research, and efforts to promote contact between scientists conducting research related to the BWC. In 1991 the state parties adopted four new CBMs that required states to exchange information on past offensive and/or defensive biological programs, ongoing national biological defense research-and-development programs, human vaccine production facilities, and the implementation of national legislation relevant to the BWC. The lack of widespread and consistent participation in these CBMs and the uneven quality of the submitted information has been a consistent disappointment and a motivating factor in the pursuit of more robust measures to strengthen the treaty.[15]

The third review conference in 1991 also established the Ad Hoc Group of Government Experts to Identify and Examine Potential Verification Measures from a Scientific and Technical Standpoint (or Ad Hoc Group of Verification Experts—VEREX) to evaluate twenty-one possible on-site and off-site measures to strengthen the BWC. The group submitted a consensus report to the state parties in 1993 that found that a combination of both types of measures could increase transparency and enhance confidence in compliance with the treaty.[16] In 1994 a special conference of signatories to the BWC authorized the negotiation of a legally binding protocol to the BWC to enhance compliance.

15. Marie Isabelle Chevrier and Iris Hunger, "Confidence Building Measures for the BTWC: Performance and Potential," *Nonproliferation Review* 7, no. 3 (2000): 24–42.

16. Ad Hoc Group of Governmental Experts to Identify and Examine Potential Verification Measures from a Scientific and Technical Standpoint, *Report*, BWC/CONF.III.VEREX/9 (Geneva: United Nations, 1993).

The newly created Ad Hoc Group began meeting regularly in January 1995, and in July 1997 the chairman of the group introduced a rolling text based on the negotiations to date. In January 1998, after a bruising battle over U.S. Senate ratification of the CWC, the United States announced its support for a protocol to strengthen the BWC based on declarations and on-site inspections administered by an international organization.[17]

By fall 2000, progress on the rolling text had stalled. The chairman of the talks judged that the remaining issues were too interdependent to be resolved individually and would instead require compromises across the entire body of the text. After extensive consultations with the delegations in Geneva, the chairman introduced a composite text of a draft compliance protocol in March 2001. This draft protocol was intended to forge a compromise on contentious issues that were stalling the negotiations, such as the scope of required declarations, the extent and intrusiveness of inspections, the degree of protection afforded to proprietary information, and restrictions on trade in biotechnology.

This text almost immediately encountered opposition. In May a group of developing nations from the Non-Aligned Movement rejected the chairman's text and demanded a return to negotiations.[18] The Non-Aligned Movement's opposition to the protocol revolved around the issue of export controls. The Australia Group, an informal group now consisting of forty-one Western nations (including all OECD members except Mexico, the European Commission, all EU member states, Argentina, Croatia, and Ukraine) that was created with fifteen members in 1985 to strengthen export controls on CW-related materials and equipment, had extended its mandate in 1991 to technology and materials relating to BW.[19] While these nations justified their action under terms of Article III of the BWC to prevent the proliferation of biological weapons, developing nations viewed the arrangement as discriminatory, an impediment to their economic development, and a violation of Article X. The tension between Article III and Article X created by the Australia Group's export controls had been a key issue of contention throughout the protocol negotiations.

In July 2001 the United States announced that it would not accept the draft protocol because it was not intrusive enough to detect clandestine BW activities, but it was invasive enough to compromise proprietary and classified

---

17. The U.S. opposed routine or random visits. White House Press Secretary, "The Biological Weapons Convention," *Fact Sheet,* January 27, 1998.

18. China, Cuba, Islamic Republic of Iran, Indonesia, Libyan Arab Jamahiriya, Pakistan, and Sri Lanka, *Joint Statement on the Process of the BTWC Ad Hoc Group Negotiations,* BWC/AD HOC GROUP/WP.451, May 4, 2001.

19. Robert J. Mathews, "The Development of the Australia Group Export Control Lists of Biological Pathogens, Toxins and Dual-Use Equipment," *CBW Conventions Bulletin* 66 (December 2004): 1–4.

information.[20] Several factors contributed to this decision. The George W. Bush administration that took office in January 2001 was opposed to multilateral treaties, which it viewed as imposing unnecessary limitations on U.S. power and autonomy. Based on this ideology, the Bush administration opposed not only the BWC protocol but also the Kyoto Protocol on greenhouse gases, the Comprehensive Test Ban Treaty, and the Anti-Ballistic Missile Treaty. Aside from these foreign policy considerations, the United States had two substantive concerns about the draft protocol that predated the George W. Bush administration. First, since the late 1990s the United States had dramatically expanded its biodefense program, including classified threat assessment programs, to counter the threat posed by states and terrorists. By 2001 the United States had the largest biodefense program in the world, and it feared that the protocol might compromise intelligence sources and methods associated with the threat assessment programs and reveal vulnerabilities in U.S. defenses against biological weapons.[21] Second, the United States was home to the largest and most dynamic pharmaceutical and biotechnology industries, including ten of the top twenty pharmaceutical companies in the world. U.S. pharmaceutical firms are the biggest spenders on R&D, and they have introduced the most new drugs, including the most popular ones.[22] The United States also leads the world, by a large margin, in the number of biotechnology firms, private biotechnology R&D expenditures, and the number of biotechnology patents filed.[23] These industries, and the government, were wary of declarations and on-site inspections that might compromise proprietary information in these increasingly global and competitive businesses. Industry executives were already wary of BW inspections due to their negative experience with Russian visits to a U.S. pharmaceutical company in the early 1990s as part of the Trilateral Agreement. As part of the Trilateral Agreement signed by the United States, the United Kingdom, and the Russian Federation in September 1992 to address U.S. and British concerns about Russia's compliance with the BWC, the parties agreed to reciprocal visits to nonmilitary biological facilities. In 1993, after Anglo-American visits to Biopreparat facilities in Russia, a Russian delegation visited a pharmaceutical production plant owned by Pfizer and Pfizer's main research center in the United States. After the visit, a Russian newspaper published allegations by an unidentified Russian government official that

---

20. Ambassador Donald Mahley, "Statement by the United States to the Ad Hoc Group of Biological Weapons Convention States Parties," Geneva, Switzerland, July 25, 2001, http://www.state.gov/t/ac/rls/rm/2001/5497.htm.

21. Interview with Ambassador Donald Mahley, Cambridge, Massachusetts, April 3, 2003.

22. European Federation of Pharmaceutical Industries and Associations, *The Pharmaceutical Industry In Figures: 2002* (Brussels: EFPIA, 2002), 6, 13, 21.

23. Brigitte van Beuzekom and Anthony Arundel, *OECD Biotechnology Statistics—2006* (Paris: Organization for Economic Cooperation and Development, 2006), 14, 17, 44.

the United States was violating the BWC and implicated Pfizer in maintaining BW research and production facilities. No official from the Russian government refuted the report.[24]

At the end of the fifth review conference in December 2001, the United States surprised the other state parties by demanding an end to the Ad Hoc Group. Instead of acceding to this demand, the conference was suspended until 2002. On the resumption of the review conference in November 2002, the state parties agreed to hold a series of annual meetings leading up to the next review conference in 2006. These meetings examined new mechanisms to strengthen the treaty, such as national implementing legislation, pathogen security, investigations of BW use and disease outbreaks, disease surveillance, and codes of conduct for scientists.[25] The negotiation of a legally binding compliance protocol was effectively put into abeyance.

At the sixth review conference in 2007, a new agenda was adopted to address the following issues over the next five years: national implementation and regional cooperation on BWC implementation; biosafety and biosecurity; oversight, education, and codes of conduct; assistance with surveillance, detection, diagnosis, and containment of infectious disease; and assistance to states in case of BW use. This meeting also established the Implementation Support Unit (ISU), the treaty's first dedicated organizational capacity, to administer the CBMs, the annual meetings, and the review conferences. While the creation of a dedicated organization to assist with the implementation of the BWC was a long overdue measure, the authority and capability of the ISU are severely limited.[26]

The BWC remains the cornerstone of the BW nonproliferation regime. The treaty has been vital for reinforcing the norm against the use of disease as a weapon. The treaty's CBMs increase transparency of BW-related activities and facilities and help states demonstrate their compliance with the treaty. The perennial shortcoming of the treaty has been its lack of verification provisions. Although efforts to strengthen the treaty through a legally binding compliance protocol have halted, parties to the treaty are continuing to explore other means of reducing the threat posed by biological weapons during the ongoing intersessional meetings.

---

24. Mangold and Goldberg, *Plague Wars,* 203–7; and Will D. Carpenter and Michael Moodie, "Industry and Arms Control," in *Biological Warfare: Modern Offense and Defense,* ed. Raymond Zilinskas (Boulder, CO: Lynne Reinner, 2000), 191.

25. Jonathan B. Tucker, "The BWC New Process: A Preliminary Assessment," *Nonproliferation Review* 11, no. 1 (2004): 4–8.

26. The ISU has a staff of three while the IAEA has 2,200 employees, the Organization for the Prohibition of Chemical Weapons has 500, and the Comprehensive Test Ban Treaty Organization has 260.

Obstacles to Verification of Biological Arms Control

As indicated in the introduction, the difficulty in verifying that a state is complying with its commitment to use biotechnology for peaceful purposes is due to: (1) the multiuse nature of biotechnology, (2) the overlap between offensive and defensive activities, (3) the need for secrecy to protect commercial and national security information, and (4) the lack of signatures of an offensive program. These characteristics make biological arms control and disarmament agreements dramatically harder to verify than similar arrangements regarding nuclear and chemical weapons.

The Multiuse Nature of Biotechnology

Biotechnology is multiuse in the sense that it can be applied to civilian endeavors as well as defensive and offensive military programs. Although chemical weapons technology is commonly characterized by a high degree of multiple uses, there is in fact a range of materials, equipment, production processes, and facilities that have no civilian application.[27] In contrast, many of the raw materials and equipment required for the research, development, production, and weaponization of biological weapons are used in civilian industries.[28] The multiuse nature of biology exacerbates the difficulty in determining the true purpose behind suspicious activities or facilities.

In some cases, the biological agents themselves are multiuse. Botulinum toxin, ten thousand times more lethal than the nerve gas VX, is marketed under the name Botox to treat spastic eye-muscle disorders and migraine headaches and to smooth facial wrinkles.[29] The number of multiuse agents is likely to become more pronounced as the use of toxins in medical research and therapy continues to grow.[30] Even innocuous agents with civilian applications can be used as part of an offensive BW program. The use of nonpathogenic organisms, such as *B. subtilis* and *B. thuringiensis* as simulants for the closely related *B. anthracis,* was integral to the Iraqi BW program.[31]

---

27. Burck, "Chemical Weapons Production Technology," 122–63.

28. OTA, *Technologies Underlying Weapons of Mass Destruction,* 84–87.

29. Jonathan B. Tucker, "Dilemmas of a Dual-Use Technology: Toxins in Medicine and Warfare," *Politics and the Life Sciences* 13, no. 1 (1994): 52–53; and Eric A. Johnson, "Clostridial Toxins as Therapeutic Agents: Benefits of Nature's Most Toxic Proteins," *Annual Review of Microbiology* 53 (1999): 551–75.

30. Alan P. Zelicoff, "The Dual-Use Nature of Biotechnology: Some Examples from Medical Therapeutics," Director's Series on Proliferation 4 (Livermore, CA: Lawrence Livermore National Laboratory, May 1994), 82–83.

31. These simulants were used at every stage of Iraq's BW program: determining the best growth media to use, testing production equipment, scaling up production, developing spray-drying techniques,

Research conducted for scientific or commercial purposes could also potentially be used for military purposes. Many of the BW threat agents are naturally occurring diseases that are endemic in certain parts of the world and periodically cause epidemics for people and animals. Thus, the medical and public health authorities in many countries have legitimate reasons for conducting research on the virulence, pathogenicity, immune-response avoidance, and antibiotic resistance of dangerous pathogens. This research is facilitated by the sequencing of the genomes of more than one hundred microbial pathogens, including *Y. pestis* and *B. anthracis,* with the results posted on the Internet.[32] This information will allow researchers to develop better drugs and improve our understanding of the evolution of microorganisms as well as making it possible modify these pathogens to make them more efficient killers. Likewise, techniques developed for the microencapsulation of pharmaceuticals to improve drug delivery could also be applied to the development of more stable biological weapons.

The field of genetic engineering is rife with examples of multiuse research. Research on gene therapy is aimed at perfecting the art of inserting foreign genetic material into viruses and using them as vectors that can avoid the human immune system.[33] Scientific research may also devise new ways to create dangerous pathogens by accident. In 2001 Australian scientists inserted a gene for the immune regulatory protein interleukin-4 (IL-4) into mousepox, which inadvertently resulted in a virus that could kill all of the mice exposed to it, including those immunized against ordinary mousepox.[34] This experiment demonstrated a possible method for engineering a highly virulent and vaccine-resistant form of variola, the virus that causes smallpox.

The Soviet Union actively sought to apply advances in genetic engineering to the development of new biological weapons.[35] Milton Leitenberg has identified several examples of the same techniques and pathogens being utilized in civilian

---

studying conditions suitable for storing organisms, assessing the viability of these organisms in an aerosol, testing munitions to determine dispersion patterns and dissemination efficiency, and training personnel. United Nations Monitoring, Verification and Inspection Commission (UNMOVIC), *Unresolved Disarmament Issues: Iraq's Proscribed Weapons Programmes* (New York: United Nations, 2003), 131–32.

32. National Research Council, *Seeking Security: Pathogens, Open Access, and Genome Databases* (Washington, DC: National Academies Press, 2004), 3.

33. Steven M. Block, "Living Nightmares: Biological Threats Enabled by Molecular Biology," in *The New Terror: Facing the Threat of Biological and Chemical Weapons,* ed. Sidney D. Drell, Abraham D. Sofaer, and George D. Wilson (Stanford, CA: Hoover Institution Press, 1999), 60–65.

34. Ronald J. Jackson, et al., "Expression of Mouse Interleukin-4 by a Recombinant Ectromelia Virus Suppresses Cytolytic Lymphocyte Responses and Overcomes Genetic Resistance to Mousepox," *Journal of Virology* 75, no. 3 (2001): 1205–10.

35. Interview with Serguei Popov, former Soviet biological weapons scientist, Manassas, Virginia, July 25, 2002; and Ken Alibek, *Biohazard: The Chilling True Story of the Largest Covert Biological Weapons Program in the World—Told from the Inside by the Man Who Ran It,* with Stephen Handelman (New York: Random House, 1999), 231.

biomedical research, in defensive programs within the United States and United Kingdom, and in the former Soviet Union's offensive program. For example, in the 1980s the U.S. Army developed techniques to insert foreign genetic material into vaccinia, the virus used as a vaccine for smallpox, to develop new vaccines. Soviet scientists took advantage of this research and the genetic similarities between vaccinia and variola to develop an improved smallpox weapon.[36]

Biotechnology's multiuse nature is also evident in the equipment used in the production, weaponization, and dissemination of biological agents. The same fermenters, egg incubators, and tissue-cell cultures found in the pharmaceutical, dairy, and brewery industries can also produce biological warfare agents. According to a former UNSCOM inspector, all of the equipment and supplies Iraq used for research and development, testing, pilot plant trials, and production of biological weapons were dual-use.[37] After the 1991 Gulf War, Iraq was able to gain considerable experience in the production of dry bulk bacterial agents under the cover of biopesticide production at Al Hakam. The same equipment and processes could also be applied to the production of *B. anthracis* in dry powder form. The equipment required to dry and mill a pharmaceutical product for aerosol delivery does not differ greatly from equipment needed to produce an easily aerosolized BW agent. The centrifuges used in the Soviet program to purify and concentrate liquid slurries of bacteria were similar to those used to make milk and butter and were produced at a civilian dairy-equipment plant. Even the machines used by Iraq and the Soviet Union to fill munitions with biological agents were commercially available and had civilian uses. Finally, in some cases, civilian equipment can be used to disseminate biological agents. In the 1980s, Iraq modified and successfully tested domestic and imported agricultural sprayers for the dissemination of biological agents.[38]

The multiuse property of biotechnology allows a nation developing biological weapons to hide its activities in civilian institutes that appear to be, or actually are, conducting legitimate pharmaceutical or medical research. Most countries believed to have worked on or be working on biological weapons, including Iran, Iraq, the Soviet Union, and South Africa, have exploited the multiuse nature of biotechnology to conduct the research, development, and production of BW agents in ostensibly civilian facilities.[39] The Soviet Union created Biopreparat

36. Milton Leitenberg, "Distinguishing Offensive from Defensive Biological Weapons Research," *Critical Reviews in Microbiology* 29, no. 3 (2003): 232–34; and Alibek, *Biohazard,* 259–60.

37. Raymond A. Zilinskas, "Verifying Compliance to the Biological and Toxin Weapons Convention," *Critical Reviews in Microbiology* 24, no. 3 (1998): 198.

38. Alibek, *Biohazard,* 98–99; Tim Trevan, *Saddam's Secrets: The Hunt for Iraq's Hidden Weapons* (London: HarperCollins, 1999), 314; and UNMOVIC, *Unresolved Disarmament Issues,* 57–60, 132.

39. Gregory Koblentz, "Countering Dual-Use Facilities: Lessons from Iraq and Sudan," *Jane's Intelligence Review* 11, no. 3 (1999): 48–53.

as a civilian research organization in the 1970s to exploit the emerging field of molecular biology for military applications. According to Ken Alibek (formerly Kantajan Alibekov), deputy director of Biopreparat, "ostensibly operating as a civilian pharmaceutical enterprise, the agency could engage in genetic research without arousing suspicion. It could participate in international conferences, interact with the world scientific community, and obtain disease strains from foreign microbe banks—all activities which would have been impossible for a military laboratory."[40] A similar logic led South Africa to conduct its secret CBW program in front companies that concealed the role of the military, granted scientists free access to the international scientific community, and assisted with the procurement of multiuse equipment and materials from abroad.[41] The remarkable progress of Iraq's BW program before the 1991 Gulf War from research to production in only five years was due in part to its exploitation of civilian vaccine facilities for the production of BW agents.[42]

Overlap between Offensive and Defensive Activities

A second phenomenon that further undermines the ability of states to reliably distinguish between activities prohibited and permitted under the BWC is the substantial overlap between these types of activities. Although biological weapons (munitions designed to disseminate biological agents) and biological defenses (such as syringes filled with vaccine) can be readily distinguished when placed side by side, the research, development, production, and testing activities used to develop these capabilities are similar, if not identical, in many ways. The overlap between offensive and defensive activities provides states with another means of masking an offensive program and complicates efforts to assess compliance with biological arms control and disarmament agreements.

At the research-and-development stage, it is extraordinarily difficult to differentiate between research conducted solely for defensive purposes and research that is undertaken for the development of weapons. The same equipment, materials, technologies, and techniques are used for both types of research. For example, experiments to manipulate an organism's virulence are staples of both defensive and offensive programs and generate similar types of knowledge.

---

40. Alibek, *Biohazard,* 22.

41. Chandré Gould, and Peter Folb, "The South African Chemical and Biological Warfare Program: An Overview," *Nonproliferation Review* 7, no. 3 (Fall/Winter 2000): 14.

42. The fermenters at the civilian facilities were either transferred to the biological weapons production plant at Al Hakam or converted on-site to the production of biological warfare agents. UNMOVIC, *Compendium of Iraq's Proscribed Weapons Programmes in the Chemical, Biological and Missile Areas* (New York: United Nations, 2007), 780–85 [hereafter *Compendium*].

Defensive programs conduct such research to identify ways to decrease an organism's virulence in order to create a better vaccine, while offensive programs explore ways to heighten an organism's virulence. Russian scientists have portrayed research conducted under the former Soviet program on enhancing the virulence of *B. anthracis* and conferring multiple antibiotic resistance to *B. anthracis* as efforts to develop improved defenses against this agent.[43]

The production processes for some vaccines and BW agents are also similar. In 1990–91, when the United States sought to stockpile botulinum antitoxin, it first had to grow large quantities of the toxin, which was then treated with formalin to inactivate it while preserving its immunogenic properties. Killed vaccines go through a similar process that results in the production of large quantities of the pathogen until the organisms are chemically treated and killed.[44]

Both offensive and defensive programs also need to engage in generating and testing aerosols of infectious agents and simulants in both the laboratory and the field. Defensive programs conduct such experiments to develop animal models for studying the pathogenesis of disease, evaluating the effectiveness of vaccines and treatments, and testing detection systems and decontamination procedures. Offensive programs engage in aerosol testing to determine the effectiveness of different strains and preparations of an agent, the optimal environmental parameters for disseminating the agent, and the performance of biological munitions. Both types of programs are also interested in understanding the behavior of aerosols in order to predict the effects of a biological attack. Although the scale of testing and nature of agents employed would differ between these types of programs, such differences would not be readily apparent to outside observers.[45]

Even apparently benign defensive activities such as immunizing soldiers against anticipated biological warfare threats can have an offensive connotation. It would be reasonable to infer that an aggressor contemplating the use of a biological weapon would want to ensure that its own troops are protected in the event of blowback. During the cold war, the United States viewed Soviet chemical and biological defensive preparations as evidence of intent to initiate the use of these weapons.[46] According to press reports, the U.S. government viewed the immunization of Iraqi and North Korean soldiers against smallpox

43. A. V. Stepanov, et al., "Development of Novel Vaccines against Anthrax in Man," *Journal of Biotechnology* 44 (1996): 155–60; and A. P. Pomerantsev, et al., "Expression of Cereolysine AB Genes in *Bacillus Anthracis* Vaccine Strain Ensures Protection against Experimental Hemolytic Anthrax Infection," *Vaccine* 15, no. 17/18 (1997): 1846–50.

44. Tucker, "Dilemmas of a Dual-Use Technology," 56; and Leitenberg, "Distinguishing Offensive from Defensive Biological Weapons Research," 246.

45. Haar, *Future of Biological Weapons,* 66–67.

46. Stockholm International Peace Research Institute (SIPRI), *The Problem of Chemical and Biological Warfare,* vol. 2, *CB Weapons Today* (New York: Humanities Press, 1973), 163–64.

as evidence that these countries possessed variola virus, planned on using it as a weapon, and wanted to protect their own forces. As one anonymous Department of Defense official put it: "The vaccinations are as close to a smoking gun as you can come."[47] This inference, however, is not always warranted. After Operation Iraqi Freedom, it was determined that Iraq did not in fact possess variola virus.[48] Likewise, the vaccination of U.S. soldiers against anthrax and smallpox are not indicators of intent to use these agents as biological weapons.

Perhaps the most vexing challenge to distinguishing between offensive and defensive programs is the need for defensive programs to engage in offensive research to prepare for current threats or to anticipate new ones. This type of research goes beyond that described above in that the goal is to create a limited offensive capability in order to assess vulnerabilities and evaluate the effectiveness of current and planned defenses. As with any other form of warfare, understanding the threats posed by others is a prerequisite for developing an effective defense. In 1969, when the United States terminated its offensive BW program, it was recognized that "maintenance of a defensive RDT&E [research, development, test, and evaluation] program inherently requires some offensive RDT&E effort."[49] Although the new policy limited the United States to conducting only defensive biological research, it was recognized that "this does not preclude research into those offensive aspects of bacteriological/biological agents necessary to determine what defensive measures are required."[50] These types of activities fall into a grey area of the BWC that does not prohibit research on biological and toxin agents. This ambiguity has been exploited by Russian and South African officials who have claimed that their past offensive activities were motivated by external threats and that their sole purpose was to assess these threats and develop countermeasures.[51]

This lack of a clear boundary between offensive and defensive programs has been a source of continuing controversy for the United States' biodefense program. In the 1980s, the U.S. Army increased its spending on defensive biological

---

47. William Broad and Judith Miller, "Government Report Says 3 Nations Hide Stocks of Smallpox," *New York Times,* June 13, 1999, A1.

48. Charles Duelfer, *Comprehensive Report of the Special Advisor to the DCI on Iraq's WMD,* vol. 3, *Biological Warfare* (Langley, VA: CIA, 2004), 3 [hereafter Duelfer Report].

49. Report to the National Security Council, *U.S. Policy on Chemical and Biological Warfare and Agents,* submitted by the Interdepartmental Political-Military Group in response to NSSM 59, November 10, 1969, p. 27, released under the Freedom of Information Act [hereafter FOIA].

50. National Security Council, "United States Policy on Chemical Warfare Program and Bacteriological/Biological Research Program," *National Security Decision Memorandum 35,* November 25, 1969, p. 3, FOIA.

51. "Valentin Yevstigneyev on Issues Relating to Russian Biological Weapons," *Kaderny Control Digest* 11 (Summer 1999); and Marléne Burger and Chandré Gould, *Secrets and Lies: Wouter Basson and South Africa's Chemical and Biological Warfare Programme* (Cape Town, S. A.: Zebra Press, 2002), 183.

research in response to intelligence that Soviet Union had an active BW program, including the application of genetic engineering. The military's research on genetically modified organisms and exotic diseases, as well as construction of a new aerosol test facility were subsequently criticized and restricted due to their perceived association with offensive activities.[52] After September 11, 2001, the United States established a new facility, the National Biodefense Analysis and Countermeasures Center (NBACC), to conduct research on the physical and biological properties of traditional, genetically modified, and emerging BW agents as part of a threat assessment program.[53] Critics have pointed out that the research necessary to characterize biological threats as described by NBACC scientists could cross the line into activities prohibited by the BWC. Without greater transparency into the facility, its activities, and the measures it was taking to ensure that it remained in compliance with the BWC, U.S. biodefense research might be misinterpreted as being for offensive purposes or provide justification for other states to conduct such work in the context of an offensive program.[54]

Secrecy to Protect National Security and Proprietary Information

Facilities engaged in defensive and civilian activities frequently have legitimate needs for a limited degree of secrecy to protect national security and proprietary business information. This secrecy makes it more difficult for outside observers to determine the intent behind a program or capability and can foster suspicion and mistrust. Furthermore, the safeguards for protecting sensitive information demanded by states uninterested in developing biological weapons make it easier for states pursuing these weapons to hide their illicit activities. Even advocates of strengthening the BWC acknowledge that a verification regime that is sensitive to national security and commercial concerns will likely be unable to reliably detect violations of the treaty.[55]

52. Charles Piller and Keith R. Yamamoto, *Gene Wars: Military Control over the New Genetic Technologies* (New York: Morrow, 1988); and Susan Wright and Stuart Ketcham, "The Problem of Interpreting the U.S. Biological Defense Research Program," in *Preventing a Biological Arms Race,* ed. Susan Wright, (Cambridge: MIT Press, 1990), 169–96.

53. James B. Petro and W. Seth Carus, "Biological Threat Characterization Research: A Critical Component of National Biodefense," *Biosecurity and Bioterrorism* 3, no. 4 (2005): 295–308.

54. Milton Leitenberg, James Leonard, and Richard Spertzel, "Biodefense Crossing the Line," *Politics and the Life Sciences* 22, no. 2 (2004): 1–2; and Lois R. Ember, "Testing the Limits," *Chemical and Engineering News* 83 (August 15, 2005): 26–32.

55. Marie Isabelle Chevrier, "Verifying the Unverifiable: Lessons from the Biological Weapons Convention," *Politics and the Life Sciences* 9, no. 1 (1990): 99; Zilinskas, "Verifying Compliance," 211; and Barbara Hatch Rosenberg, "U.S. Policy and the BWC Protocol," *CBW Conventions Bulletin* 52 (June 2001): 2.

States developing defenses against biological weapons may need to keep certain aspects and characteristics of these activities secret to ensure the effectiveness of their preparations. Intelligence on foreign biological threats, specific vulnerabilities, and the range of medical countermeasures available have been cited as "obvious examples where secrecy would be advisable."[56] Making such information publicly available could enable an adversary to identify and exploit weaknesses in defensive preparations and intelligence gathering. Given the diversity of biological warfare agents, an adversary could select an agent for which it knows the target state lacks any or adequate defenses. In addition, the advent of genetic engineering makes it possible to modify pathogens to be resistant to antibiotics, circumvent vaccine-induced immunity, or evade diagnostic and detection systems.[57]

When the United States abandoned its offensive program in 1969, it committed itself to conducting its defensive program as openly as possible. Nonetheless, an interagency group determined that the performance of detection systems, threat assessments, and vulnerability studies may require classification.[58] Although this policy is not believed to have changed, the number and nature of classified biodefense programs has increased since the mid-1990s. These secret biodefense projects have included the construction of a small biological agent production facility, the production of dried *B. anthracis* spores, the testing of copies of a Soviet-designed biological bomblet, and the replication of a genetically engineered strain of *B. anthracis* developed by the Soviet Union that was able to circumvent some vaccines.[59] The United States claimed that the purpose of these research projects was defensive and legal under the BWC, but the combination of capabilities under development and the secrecy of the work raised questions at home and abroad about the commitment of the United States to enforcing the

---

56. Malcolm Dando, *Biological Warfare in the 21st Century: Biotechnology and the Proliferation of Biological Weapons* (London: Brassey's, 1994), 190. In addition, SIPRI has listed methods of dissemination, results of field tests, studies of tactical and strategic implications based on this information, and the nature of countermeasures that an aggressor could bypass as examples of information that should be classified under a defensive program. SIPRI, *The Problem of Chemical and Biological Warfare,* vol. 6, *Technical Aspects of Early Warning and Verification* (New York: Humanities Press, 1975), 25.

57. Department of Defense, *Biotechnology and Genetic Engineering: Implications for the Development of New Warfare Agents* (Washington, DC: DOD, 1996), 4–7; and Block, "Living Nightmares," 39–75.

58. Interdepartmental Political Military Working Group, *Annual Review of United States Chemical Warfare and Biological Research Programs as of 1 November 1970,* December 5, 1970, 23–24, FOIA.

59. Judith Miller, Stephen Engelberg, and William J. Broad, "U.S. Germ Warfare Research Pushes Treaty Limits," *New York Times,* September 4, 2001, A1; Judith Miller, Stephen Engelberg, and William Broad, *Germs: Biological Weapons and America's Secret War* (New York: Simon and Schuster, 2001), 290–98, 308–10; and Scott Shane, "Army Confirms Making Anthrax in Recent Years," *Baltimore Sun,* December 13, 2001.

Crap

BWC.[60] In contrast, some officials involved in biodefense activities believe that there is already an excessive amount of publicly available information on the U.S. biodefense program that exposes current shortfalls and gaps in defensive preparedness.[61] Indeed, the original design of NBACC called for it to be a classified facility requiring a security clearance to enter.[62]

The pharmaceutical and biotechnology industries, which have the greatest concentration of multiuse technological capabilities to research, develop, produce and test biological weapons, rely on secrecy to protect their intellectual property. This secrecy is necessary due to the long, costly, and risky process of developing new drugs, the limited duration of patent protection, and the incentives for rivals to engage in corporate espionage.

The pharmaceutical and biotechnology industries are knowledge intensive and invest heavily in research and development to generate new products.[63] The drug discovery and development process is also a risky one. The pharmaceutical industry estimates that for every 25,000 to 50,000 compounds discovered and investigated by researchers, only one will successfully make it to market and earn a positive return on its R&D costs.[64] The escalating costs of R&D, clinical trials, and regulatory review have boosted the average cost of developing a new drug to between $800 million to $1.2 billion.[65]

Firms seeking to protect their investment in a promising organism or compound must rely on secrecy and security until their discovery has been patented. Since the R&D process for a new drug can take ten to twelve years and drugs are protected by patents for seventeen years, companies typically have only five to seven years to make a profit before a drug is available for generic production.

60. Judith Miller, "When Is a Bomb Not a Bomb? Germ Experts Confront U.S.," *New York Times,* September 5, 2001, A5; Elisa Harris, "Research Not to Be Hidden," *New York Times,* September 6, 2001; Barbara Hatch Rosenberg and Milton Leitenberg, "Who's Afraid of a Germ Warfare Treaty?" *Los Angeles Times,* September 6, 2001; and Mark Wheelis and Malcolm Dando, "Back to Bioweapons," *Bulletin of the Atomic Scientists* 59, no. 1 (2003): 40–46.

61. Robert P. Kadlec and Randall J. Larsen, "Passive Defense," in *Countering the Proliferation and Use of Weapons of Mass Destruction,* ed. Peter L. Hays, Vincent J. Jodoin, and Alan R. Van Tassel, (New York: McGraw-Hill, 1998), 232.

62. Joby Warrick, "The Secretive Fight against Bioterror," *Washington Post,* July 30, 2006, A1.

63. These industries invest a far higher percentage of their revenue in R&D than the chemical industry and even more than other high-technology industries such as aerospace. Office of Technology Policy, *U.S. Corporate R&D Investment, 1994–2000 Final Estimates* (Washington, DC: Department of Commerce, 2002), 7; and Department of Commerce, *A Survey of the Use of Biotechnology in U.S. Industry* (Washington, DC: Department of Commerce, 2003), 73, 76–77.

64. Gillian R. Woollett, "Industry's Role, Concerns, and Interests in the Negotiations of a BWC Compliance Protocol," in Marie I. Chevrier, et al., *Biological Weapons Proliferation: Reasons for Concern, Courses of Action* (Washington, DC: Henry L. Stimson Center, 1998), 41.

65. Joseph A. DiMasi and Henry G. Gabrowski, "The Cost of Biopharmaceutical R&D: Is Biotech Different?" *Managerial and Decision Economics* 28 (2007): 469–79.

Firms can extend the window of profitability by delaying the application for a patent and relying instead on trade secrecy to protect their discovery. Once patent protection does expire, a firm's advantage in competing against generic versions of its product may result from customized production equipment and processes that are also held as trade secrets.[66]

The 1990s saw a boom in the rise of blockbuster drugs, the sales of which are over $1 billion a year.[67] Historically, the first drug to market for a particular disease or condition has been the most profitable.[68] This first-mover advantage places enormous pressure on companies to safeguard their drug-development process and for unscrupulous rivals to seek proprietary information on promising drug candidates. As a result, the pharmaceutical industry has experienced a number of corporate espionage cases in recent years.[69] The industry estimates that corporate espionage in the mid-1990s cost firms over $3 billion in lost sales.[70]

Offensive BW Programs Lack Unique Signatures

The paucity of unique signatures associated with offensive BW programs makes them difficult to detect. Detecting facilities utilized in the production of BW agents is challenging. First, pathogen production facilities can be externally identical to a pharmaceutical facility or double as a pharmaceutical facility during peacetime. High levels of biocontainment are not necessary or sufficient for a plant to produce BW agents. Iraq produced *B. anthracis* and botulinum toxin without these precautions.[71] Meanwhile, modern pharmaceutical facilities have begun incorporating multipurpose containment features in plants to ensure quality control.[72] The physical characteristics of a facility such as heavy security, storage bunkers, and incinerator stacks may look suspicious, but they are not direct evidence of an offensive program. Second, large facilities or stockpiles of agent

---

66. Dane Zabriskie, "Strengthening the Biological Weapons Convention and Implications on the Pharmaceutical Industry and Biotechnology Industry," *Current Opinion in Biotechnology* 9 (1998): 313; and Al Homberg, "Industry Concerns Regarding Disclosure of Proprietary Information," Director's Series on Proliferation 4 (Livermore, CA: Lawrence Livermore National Laboratory, May 1994), 93–97.

67. Robert F. Service, "Surviving the Blockbuster Syndrome," *Science* 303 (March 19, 2004): 1796–99.

68. Homberg, "Industry Concerns," 94.

69. Sharon Mollman Elliott, "The Threat from Within: Trade Secret Theft by Employees," *Nature Biotechnology* 25, no. 3 (2007): 293–95; Douglas Pasternak, "In the DNA Vials, Secrets to Steal," *U.S. News & World Report,* May 21, 2001, 42; and Richard Behar, "Drug Spies," *Fortune,* September 6, 1999, 230–41.

70. Woollett, "Industry's Role, Concerns, and Interests," 41.

71. Raymond A. Zilinskas, "Iraq's Biological Weapons: The Past as Future?" in *Biological Weapons: Limiting the Threat,* ed. Joshua Lederberg (Cambridge: MIT Press, 1999), 138–40.

72. These systems can also be used to prevent the leakage of pathogens into the environment. Haar, *Future of Biological Weapons,* 88; and Peter Hambleton, et al., "A High Containment Polymodal Pilot-Plant Fermenter: Design Concepts," *Journal of Chemical Technology Biotechnology* 50, no. 2 (1991): 167–80.

are not required for a nation to have a significant military capability. Advanced technology such as continuous-flow fermenters and viral reactors reduce the size of a production facility and accelerate the production process, obviating the need to stockpile biological weapons.[73] Third, the production of BW agents does not produce easy-to-detect effluents such as those associated with the production of chemical and nuclear weapons.[74]

The weaponization of biological warfare agents also does not generate readily identifiable signatures. Much of the activity required to design and test a munition can be conducted in specially equipped chambers located in nondescript buildings. Field tests and associated facilities could be camouflaged as CW tests, biopesticide trials, or as vulnerability studies. The munitions themselves may be modified versions of civilian aerosol generators, chemical warheads, conventional bombs, or aircraft fuel tanks.[75] These munitions would be unremarkable and virtually identical to the original items. Only an analysis of their contents would reveal their true identity. In the early 1990s, UNSCOM destroyed what it thought were chemical munitions but were in fact biological munitions; the only feature that differentiated these munitions was black stripes on their exterior.[76] Indeed, a BW program could piggyback on a CW program: the munitions, filling, and testing facilities are all similar.[77] Iraq's weaponization and testing activities were the most difficult aspect of Iraq's BW program for UNSCOM to uncover. The lack of unique signatures associated with BW programs makes these programs notoriously difficult targets for inspectors and spies. The challenges posed by BW programs to intelligence agencies are addressed in chapter 4.

United Nations Special Commission

The investigation of Iraq's BW program by the United Nations Special Commission from 1991 to 1998 was an important test of the international community's ability to verify whether or not a state was complying with its biological arms control obligations. UNSCOM was the most intrusive arms control regime ever devised and had access to an unprecedented range of inspection techniques and technologies. UNSCOM provided a real-world test of many of the inspection

73. Richard O. Spertzel, Robert W. Wannemacher, and Carol D. Linden, *Global Proliferation: Dynamics, Acquisition Strategies, and Responses,* vol. 4, *Biological Weapons Proliferation* (Washington, DC: Defense Nuclear Agency, 1994): 22, 27.

74. OTA, *Technologies Underlying Weapons of Mass Destruction,* 49, 106, 164.

75. Iraq pursued all of these options for developing its biological munitions.

76. Miller, Engelberg, and Broad, *Germs,* 131; and Jean Krasno and James Sutterlin, *The United Nations and Iraq: Defanging the Viper* (Westport, CT: Praeger, 2003), 66.

77. Spertzel, Wannemacher, and Linden, *Global Proliferation,* 4:42.

techniques discussed during VEREX for use in a verification protocol for the BWC. Although UNSCOM was successful in uncovering aspects of Iraq's past biological weapons activities and forcing Iraq to admit that it had had an offensive BW program, a comprehensive account of Iraq's BW research, production, testing, and weaponization only emerged following the defection of a high-level Iraqi official in August 1995. The conditions required for UNSCOM's success cast serious doubt on the ability of an international organization to achieve similar results in the context of a multilateral BW verification regime. This case illustrates the extraordinary measures that were required to overcome a dedicated state's attempts to conceal and retain an offensive BW capability based on multiuse technologies.

The United Nations Security Council created UNSCOM in 1991, in the aftermath of Iraq's defeat in the Gulf War, to oversee the dismantling of Iraq's biological and chemical weapons and ballistic missiles.[78] In April 1991 Iraq declared that it had no biological weapons or programs to develop such weapons. Although early inspections led Iraq to admit that it had conducted biological military research, some inspectors believed that Iraq was hiding a larger offensive BW program. It was only after UNSCOM inspectors had accumulated convincing evidence that Iraq had obtained all of the materials necessary for a BW program and could not credibly account for the peaceful use of such materials that Iraq admitted in July 1995 to the production of BW agents at Al Hakam and other facilities. In the meantime, Iraq had continued to refine its ability to mass-produce BW agents at Al Hakam. In August 1995, after the defection of Hussein Kamel, who had directed Iraq's WMD and missile programs, Iraq admitted to producing even larger quantities of agent, filling them into munitions, testing them, and deploying them on the eve of the 1991 Gulf War. As a result of these disclosures, UNSCOM ordered the destruction of Al Hakam and the disabling of other facilities that had been used to produce BW agents. UNSCOM had still not verified the completeness and accuracy of these Iraqi revelations when it withdrew from Iraq in December 1998. In December 1999 the Security Council disbanded UNSCOM and created a new organization, the United Nations Monitoring, Verification and Inspection Commission, to replace it.

The UNSCOM experience has been used by both proponents and opponents of biological arms control to support their case. One school of thought views UNSCOM's investigation as a failure and attributes the uncovering of Iraq's secret

---

78. The International Atomic Energy Agency, which administers international safeguards on nuclear materials, was given shared responsibility for implementing the Security Council's resolution regarding Iraq's nuclear weapon program.

BW program to the defection of Hussein Kamel.[79] In contrast, another school of thought sees the UNSCOM experience as an unqualified success that demonstrated the possibility of a robust regime to detect a secret BW program.[80] The lessons provided by UNSCOM for BW verification are not that straightforward. Although UNSCOM eventually forced Iraq to admit that it had an extensive offensive program, it was not able to verify the elimination of the program or to confidently assess continued BW-related activities by Iraq. Therefore, it is important to analyze, not only what UNSCOM accomplished, but also how it did so. This is vital for determining the sources of UNSCOM's successes and failures and for understanding how effective a future biological arms control verification regime could be.

UNSCOM's Mandate and Powers

The inspection and monitoring regime imposed by the Security Council on Iraq was the most intrusive ever devised. On April 8, 1991, the Security Council approved Resolution 687, which established the cease-fire terms for the 1991 Gulf War. According to the resolution, Iraq was required, inter alia, to "unconditionally accept the destruction, removal, or rendering harmless, under international supervision" of "all chemical and biological weapons and all stocks of agents and all related subsystems and components and all research, development, support and manufacturing facilities." Iraq was ordered to submit to the Secretary-General, within fifteen days of the adoption of the resolution, a declaration of the locations, amounts, and types of all proscribed items and to agree to inspection by UNSCOM at declared sites and any additional sites designated by UNSCOM. UNSCOM was also authorized to establish a system of ongoing monitoring and verification (OMV) of Iraq's compliance with these demands. UNSCOM thus had four missions: to verify the accuracy and completeness of Iraq's declarations; to conduct inspections to ensure that Iraq did not retain any proscribed items; to construct a system to monitor continued Iraqi compliance with the terms of the resolution; and to oversee the destruction of any prohibited weapons, materials, or facilities.[81]

The Security Council subsequently bolstered UNSCOM's authority and capabilities after evidence emerged of Iraqi noncompliance and obstruction of

---

79. See Robert P. Kadlec, Allan P. Zelicoff, and Ann M. Vrtis, "Biological Weapons Control: Prospects and Implications for the Future," in *Biological Weapons,* ed. Lederberg, 96; Edward J. Lacey, "The UNSCOM Experience," *Arms Control Today* August 1996:11; and Kathleen C. Bailey, *The UN Inspections in Iraq: Lessons for On-Site Verification* (Boulder, CO: Westview Press, 1995), 48.

80. Graham S. Pearson, *The UNSCOM Saga: Chemical and Biological Weapons Non-Proliferation* (New York: St. Martin's Press, 1999), 203–5.

81. United Nations Security Council (UNSC), *Resolution 687 (1991),* S/RES/687, April 8, 1991.

inspections. Resolution 707, passed in August 1991, authorized UNSCOM to conduct aerial reconnaissance and surveillance operations.[82] UNSCOM began flights of U-2 reconnaissance aircraft on loan from the United States in September 1991 and helicopter missions from Baghdad starting in June 1992. Resolution 715, passed in October 1991, extended UNSCOM's right to "anytime, anywhere" inspections indefinitely as part of UNSCOM's ongoing monitoring and verification program, even once Iraq's banned weapons were destroyed, and extended this access to Iraq's dual-use facilities.[83]

As a result of these resolutions, UNSCOM was granted extraordinary powers to implement its mandate. UNSCOM was authorized to conduct an unlimited number of unannounced inspections of any site anywhere in Iraq; ask any questions during interviews; conduct aerial overflights of any location in the country; seize, copy, or photograph any item or record; employ any sensor, take any samples, and use any means of analysis it deemed necessary; install monitoring equipment at designated sites; and search any means of transport. In addition, Iraq was obliged by these resolutions to provide information to UNSCOM on all sites, facilities, materials, equipment, documentation, imports, activities, and intentions relevant to nuclear, biological, chemical, and missile programs and dual-use capabilities.[84]

The next three sections examine how UNSCOM used these authorities to investigate Iraq's BW program. UNSCOM's activities are divided into three phases. The first phase covers UNSCOM's search for an offensive Iraqi program in 1991 following the Gulf War. The second phase involves UNSCOM's collection and analysis of evidence between 1992 and July 1995, which resulted in Iraq's confession of a past offensive program. The third phase began with Hussein Kamel's defection in August 1995. That defection forced Baghdad to provide a comprehensive accounting of its BW research, production, and weaponization activities, which UNSCOM spent the next three years trying to verify. This phase ended with UNSCOM's withdrawal from Iraq in December 1998.

Phase 1: The Search for Iraq's Biological Weapons Program (April 1991–December 1991)

During the first phase of UNSCOM's investigation, the main task of the inspectors was to establish whether or not Iraq had an offensive BW program. On April 18, 1991, Iraq submitted a declaration to UNSCOM stating that "Iraq does

---

82. UNSC, *Resolution 707 (1991)*, S/RES/707, August 15, 1991.

83. UNSC, *Resolution 715 (1991)*, S/RES/715, October 11, 1991.

84. Javrier Perez de Cuellar, Secretary-General of the United Nations, Letter to His Excellency Ahmed Hussein, Minister for Foreign Affairs of the Republic of Iraq, May 6, 1991, http://www.un.org/Depts/unmovic/new/documents/letters.pdf.

not possess any biological weapons or related items as mentioned" in Resolution 687.[85] Between August and December, UNSCOM conducted three inspections to verify Iraq's April 1991 declaration. Inspectors visited eleven facilities that were suspected of being part of Iraq's BW program or had dual-use capabilities. In addition, inspectors visited fifteen airbases and ammunition depots looking for signs of chemical or biological weapons activity.

Based on these inspections, UNSCOM reported to the Security Council in October 1991 that "conclusive evidence that Iraq was engaged in an advanced military biological research programme has been collected. No evidence of actual weaponization has been found."[86] The report singled out Salman Pak as the research center for the program. This conclusion was based on the findings of the first BW inspection team that visited Salman Pak in August 1991.

Salman Pak was the first site inspected by UNSCOM BW inspectors since it had been identified prior to the war as the main Iraqi BW research-and-development center. On their arrival, Iraqi officials told the inspectors that "biological research activities for military purposes" had taken place at Salman Pak between 1986 and August 1990. The program was terminated due to the impending war and Iraq destroyed all of its BW agents at this time. According to the head of the program, Rihab Taha, the effort was small with just ten personnel and the results had been meager. The group had conducted research on and laboratory-scale production of *B. anthracis, C. botulinum, C. perfringens,* and two harmless bacteria used to simulate *B. anthracis.*[87]

During the inspection of Salman Pak, the inspectors found several indications that Iraq was concealing the true extent of its past biological activities. After inspectors found some animal cages, including ones designed for primates, Taha admitted that experiments had been conducted on animals to ascertain the toxicity of agents. Evidence of Iraqi attempts to conceal the true nature of the site included Iraqi demolition of buildings that had survived bombing during the Gulf War, including those that housed fermenters, an aerosol test chamber, and a small incinerator. These sites were also bulldozed with fresh dirt piled on top. The aerosol test chamber had been crushed and dumped two kilometers away from Salman Pak. In addition, large piles of burnt ash outside of buildings and in basements indicated that large amounts of documents had been burned recently.[88]

---

85. Pearson, *UNSCOM Saga,* 127.

86. UNSC, "Note by the Secretary General," S/23165, October 25, 1991, 6.

87. UNSC, S/23165; and Trevan, *Saddam's Secrets,* 28–32.

88. Trevan, *Saddam's Secrets,* 32–34; and Karen Jansen, "Biological Weapons Proliferation," in *Multilateral Verification and the Post-Gulf Environment: Learning from the UNSCOM Experience,* ed. Steven Mataija and J. Marshall Beier (Toronto: York University, 1992), 113.

The inspectors also noted several details that belied Iraq's claim that its program was strictly defensive. First, there was no evidence of Iraqi work on protective equipment or materials despite Iraqi claims that they had developed military vaccines against cholera and typhoid and were working on vaccines against anthrax and botulinum toxin.[89] Second, Salman Pak was part of the Technical Research Center, whose director, Ahmed Murtada, was a brigadier general in the Iraqi military and also director general of the Badr Scientific Establishment, a munitions design-and-production plant. Inspectors saw this affiliation as a connection between biological research and weaponization.[90] Based on this information, chief inspector David Kelly confronted Murtada that given the equipment and research conducted at Salman Pak, the program could not be solely defensive. According to Trevan, "Murtada acquiesced to this statement, implicitly agreeing that there had been an offensive biological weapons program."[91]

When UNSCOM BW inspectors returned to Iraq in September 1991 they visited ten other sites in Iraq capable of conducting BW research or production. Among these sites, the single-cell protein (SCP) plant at Al Hakam was the only one that aroused suspicion among inspectors about its intended purpose and past activities.

Al Hakam had several distinctive features that appeared inappropriate given its stated civilian purpose. Its remote location in the desert made no sense from a civilian perspective since the facility required a skilled workforce as well as large volumes of high-quality water. In addition, the layout of the complex was too large and spread out for a civilian site but appropriate for preventing an accident at one building from affecting the entire facility. The facility also had physical security measures, fortified bunkers, dummy bunkers, and air defenses that were hardly standard features for a civilian SCP production facility. Inspectors found evidence that the site had been sanitized recently, including evidence that an airlock at the laboratory building had been removed.[92] Inspectors also discovered organizational and personnel linkages between Al Hakam and Salman Pak. In addition, Al Hakam had been quickly and secretly built by an Iraqi military construction company, and its establishment had not been publicized despite its status as the nation's premier SCP production facility. Although the Iraqis had answers for all of the inspectors' questions, the answers were unsatisfactory and

---

89. Jonathan B. Tucker, "Lessons of Iraq's Biological Warfare Programme," *Arms Control* 14, no. 3 (1993): 254.

90. Trevan, *Saddam's Secrets,* 147; and Bailey, *UN Inspections in Iraq,* 39.

91. Higher-ranking Iraqi officials subsequently disavowed Murtada's statement and denied that the research at Salman Pak had an offensive orientation. Trevan, *Saddam's Secrets,* 34.

92. Trevan, *Saddam's Secrets,* 116–17; Bailey, *UN Inspections in Iraq,* 43; and Jansen, "Biological Weapons Proliferation," 113–14.

the team was unable to determine the scope and commercial viability of the SCP program. Furthermore, the Iraqis could not produce any documentation supporting their claims about the purpose and history of the facility.[93]

Al Hakam possessed an impressive fermentation capability that could support large-scale BW agent production, although at the time of the inspection none of the fermenters were functioning. The facility also housed a large building that had been intended to hold a 5,000-liter fermenter produced by the Swiss firm Chemap. After the inspection, UNSCOM learned that Chemap was shown a site at Latifiyah, thirty kilometers away, as the intended destination of the fermenter and that, in contrast to other projects in Iraq, the firm was not supposed to establish on-site support for the equipment. In addition to the secrecy surrounding this procurement, the inspectors also found it suspicious that the 5,000-liter fermenter that Iraq had ordered was not large enough to satisfy the nation's SCP needs.[94]

Although the inspectors were able to collect evidence that Al Hakam was not the simple civilian site portrayed by the Iraqis, the inspectors did not find any evidence of BW agents or weapons. All of the samples taken from the fermenters tested negative for the presence of BW agents.[95] In addition, a crucial indicator of BW production was missing: the air-handling and containment equipment necessary to work with dangerous pathogens. Also, the fermenters were not designed for use with dangerous pathogens and would require special seals, filters, and other modifications for large-scale production of BW agents. As a result of the lack of appropriate biosafety measures, most of the inspectors believed that large-scale production of pathogens at the site would be too dangerous. Only the chief inspector David Kelly was convinced that the site was a BW production facility.[96] Other inspectors assessed the site as "embryonic" and not yet operational. In the view of team member Karen Jansen, the fermentation capability at Al Hakam was "junk" and the facility "wasn't far enough along to have produced SCP or anything else."[97]

In addition to Salman Pak and Al Hakam, UN inspectors visited nine civilian sites that could be used for BW research or production. These sites included a pharmaceutical plant at Samarra, a foot-and-mouth disease vaccine plant at

---

93. Trevan, *Saddam's Secrets*, 148; Bailey, *UN Inspections in Iraq*, 43; Jansen, "Biological Weapons Proliferation," 113–14; and Tucker, "Lessons of Iraq's Biological Warfare Programme," 256.

94. Bailey, *UN Inspections in Iraq*, 43, 48; Pearson, *UNSCOM Saga*, 147; and Jansen, "Biological Weapons Proliferation," 114.

95. Bailey, *UN Inspections in Iraq*, 43, 50.

96. Tucker, "Lessons of Iraq's Biological Warfare Programme," 257; Trevan, *Saddam's Secrets*, 117; Bailey, *UN Inspections in Iraq*, 43; Milton Leitenberg, *The Problem of Biological Weapons* (Stockholm: Swedish National Defence College, 2004), 198; and General Accounting Office, *Arms Control: U.S. and International Efforts to Ban Biological Weapons*, GAO/NSIAD-93-113 (Washington, DC: GAO, 1992), 56.

97. Jansen, "Biological Weapons Proliferation," 114.

Al Daura, the Al Kindi Company for Serum and Vaccine Production in Abu Ghraib, the Serum and Vaccine Institute at Amiriyah, a SCP plant at Taji, an agricultural research facility at Al Fudaliyah, a blood bank at Medical City in Baghdad, a slaughterhouse in Baghdad, and a bakery in An Najaf. The range of sites visited indicates the range of civilian facilities that can be used to develop biological weapons. Based on physical inspection, interviews, and access to documents, the inspectors concluded that these nine facilities were legitimate civilian enterprises and were not involved in the development of biological weapons. The blood bank, slaughterhouse, bakery, and the Samarra pharmaceutical facility were immediately cleared of suspicion. The other sites, however, exhibited varying levels of capabilities for conducting research on or production of biological weapons.[98]

Vaccine-production plants are commonly viewed as the most suitable civilian facilities for use in producing BW agents due to the availability of the necessary equipment and skilled personnel needed to grow large volumes of microorganisms. The foot-and-mouth disease vaccine plant at Al Daura, the Al Kindi Company for Serum and Vaccine Production in Abu Ghraib, and the Serum and Vaccine Institute at Amiriyah were all judged as being used for their declared purposes. Since each of these facilities was also assessed as being capable of producing BW agents, inspectors recommended that all of these facilities be monitored in the future.[99]

The inspectors also visited two abandoned sites. The Agricultural and Water Resources Center at Al Fudaliyah contained two fermenters designed for the production of foodstuffs that could also be used to produce pathogens. The site at Taji had been used to produce SCP before being abandoned, and its fermenter was transferred to Al Hakam. Both sites were assessed by inspectors as not being useful for producing BW agents.[100] According to biological inspector Karen Jansen, all of these facilities "were obviously legitimate.... The Iraqis were able to answer any questions to the complete satisfaction of the inspectors and provide documents to validate any uncertainties."[101]

Evaluation of Phase 1

An assessment of UNSCOM's first year of conducting biological inspections in Iraq by the British government concluded that the inspectors were able to

---

98. Bailey, *UN Inspections in Iraq,* 41.

99. Gordon Vachon, "Chemical and Biological Weapons: Working Group Summary," in *Multilateral Verification,* ed. Mataija and Beier, 128; Jansen, "Biological Weapons Proliferation," 113; and Trevan, *Saddam's Secrets,* 118.

100. Bailey, *UN Inspections in Iraq,* 42–43.

101. Jansen, "Biological Weapons Proliferation," 113.

TABLE 3. Assessment of UNSCOM's Performance

Facility	Declared Purpose	UNSCOM Assessment	Actual Purpose
Salman Pak	Military biological defense research	BW research	BW research
Al Hakam	Single-cell protein plant	Suspected future BW production plant	BW production plant
Al Daura	Veterinary vaccine plant	True	BW production and research
Al Kindi	Veterinary vaccine plant	True	Transferred production equipment to Al Hakam
Amiriyah	Vaccine production and research	True	As stated
Al Fudaliyah	Abandoned research center	True	BW production
Taji	Abandoned single-cell protein pilot plant	True	Abandoned BW production plant
Baghdad slaughterhouse	Slaughterhouse	True	As stated
Najaf	Bakery	True	As stated
Medical City	Blood bank	True	As stated
Samarra	Pharmaceutical plant	True	As stated

produce "reasonably definitive" assessments of the eleven sites they visited, that they identified indicators differentiating between BW research and legitimate civilian activity, and that the level of openness and cooperation exhibited at legitimate sites differed from that experienced at suspected weapons facilities.[102] In addition, aside from Salman Pak, the inspectors were able to determine with confidence what the current activities of the facilities were and they were "reasonably assured" that past activities did not differ from the peaceful civilian work declared by Iraq.[103] As we now know based on Iraq's revelations of its past offensive BW program, this confidence was misplaced and this early assessment of UNSCOM's performance was overly optimistic. Of the eleven sites visited by UNSCOM BW inspectors in 1991, six were later found to be part of Iraq's BW program. A summary of UNSCOM's performance in identifying Iraqi BW sites in 1991 is provided in table 3.

UNSCOM's only unqualified success during this first phase was confirming U.S. and British intelligence reports that Salman Pak was Iraq's BW research center. Iraq later revealed to UNSCOM that Salman Pak had been engaged in applied research, laboratory-scale production, and animal testing of *B. anthracis,*

---

102. United Kingdom, *UN Special Commission BW Inspections in Iraq: Lessons for the Ad Hoc Experts Group on Verification,* BWC/CONF.III/VEREX.WP5, 1992, 5.

103. Ibid., 8.

botulinum toxin, *C. perfringens,* and mycotoxins between 1987 and 1991. This success should be tempered, however, by the fact that most of the inspectors interviewed by Kathleen Bailey agreed that if Iraq had chosen to stonewall the inspectors on the first team, the physical inspection of Salman Pak would not have enabled the inspectors to uncover the information provided by Iraq on the nature and extent of their biological program. Inspectors were unable to locate documents, equipment, matériel, or other information that the Iraqis did not disclose. Due to damage caused by the air campaign, Iraq's concealment activities, and Iraq's lack of cooperation, it was not possible for the inspectors to develop a complete picture of what Iraq had been doing at Salman Pak.[104] Nonetheless, the inspectors correctly determined that despite Iraqi denial and deception efforts, Salman Pak reflected an intent and capability by Iraq to develop biological weapons.

The inspectors were also right to be suspicious about Al Hakam, but they failed to discover that the facility was a BW production plant and had been used to produce BW agents for almost two years prior to the inspection. This failure was due to several factors. First, UNSCOM believed that Iraq's BW program was still engaged in research, so Al Hakam was viewed as possibly having a future role in the BW program as a production facility.[105] Second, the poor state of the fermentation equipment and the lack of adequate containment systems to work with dangerous pathogens was viewed by inspectors with experience in Western biodefense and microbiological laboratories as being unsuited to producing pathogenic BW agents. Since sampling of the fermenters did not reveal the presence of BW agents, the inspectors did not have any hard evidence that Al Hakam had been part of an Iraqi BW program. According to Jansen, "whatever the true intent of this site [Al Hakam], there is no way to conclusively determine what it was by an on-site inspection."[106]

The inspectors also failed to detect pre–Gulf War BW research and production activity at the foot-and-mouth disease vaccine plant at Al Daura, the SCP plant at Taji, and the water and agricultural research facility at Al Fudaliyah. Iraq later revealed that before the war Al Daura had produced 5,000 liters of botulinum toxin, Taji had produced 8,000 liters of botulinum toxin, and Al Fudaliyah had produced 1,800 liters of aflatoxin. This failure has three important implications for verification. First, it demonstrates the utility of civilian dual-use

104. Bailey, *UN Inspections in Iraq,* 41, 53; Jansen, "Biological Weapons Proliferation," 113; and David L Huxsoll, "The Nature and Scope of the BW Threat," *Director's Series on Proliferation* 4 (Livermore, CA: Lawrence Livermore National Laboratory, May 1994), 27.

105. Paul Lewis, "UN Weapons Inspectors Renew Hunt in Iraq," *New York Times,* November 17, 1991, A12.

106. Jansen, "Biological Weapons Proliferation," 114.

facilities in BW research and production. None of these sites had to be significantly modified to switch from producing vaccines, SCP, or sugar, respectively, to
BW agents.[107] Second, it illustrates the need for a verification regime to monitor
a large number and variety of facilities to prevent their diversion to a BW program. Third, the ability of Iraq to conceal its past BW production at these dual-
use sites, particularly at Al Daura, highlights the difficulties in detecting when a
legitimate civilian site is also used for BW activities.

Intelligence played a minimal role in this stage of UNSCOM's investigation of Iraq's BW program. Salman Pak was the only Iraqi BW facility visited
by UNSCOM that had previously been identified by intelligence agencies. The
other five sites visited by UNSCOM that had been part of the Iraqi BW program
had been declared by Iraq as possessing dual-use capabilities. The three sites targeted for inspection based on intelligence were the slaughterhouse, blood bank,
and bakery; all three were determined to be legitimate enterprises with no connection to BW. Even accurate intelligence is of limited value if it is out of date. In
November 1991, based on intelligence provided by the United States, UNSCOM
inspectors used metal detectors in an unsuccessful search for buried biological
munitions at an airbase known as Airfield 37.[108] The CIA had first received information about buried biological munitions at Airfield 37 in June 1991.[109] Unbeknownst to the CIA, Iraq dug up those munitions, moved them, and destroyed
them by the end of the summer.[110]

By the end of the second inspection, UNSCOM had visited all of Iraq's
major BW research and production sites, although this would not be known for
several years. At that point, UNSCOM believed Iraq had a minor offensive R&D program before the Gulf War that did not involve large-scale production. UNSCOM had used Iraq's declarations and intelligence to pinpoint
sites for inspections, but it was unable to prove the suspicions of inspectors and
lacked additional intelligence on which to base new inspections.[111] By early 1992
one senior inspector concluded, "one thing is for sure, without any tangible evidence that contradicts what we have been told, we are unlikely to uncover anything more."[112]

107. UNMOVIC, *Compendium of Iraq's Proscribed Weapons Programmes in the Chemical, Biological and Missile Areas* (New York: United Nations, 2007), 827–32, 915–23, 937–40 [hereafter *Compendium*].

108. Rod Barton, *The Weapons Detective: The Inside Story of Australia's Top Weapons Inspector* (Melbourne: Black Inc. Agenda, 2006), 81–92; and Trevan, *Saddam's Secrets,* 171–72.

109. Central Intelligence Agency (CIA), *Intelligence Related to Possible Sources of Biological Agent Exposure during the Persian Gulf War* (Langley, VA: CIA, August 2000), http://www.gulflink.osd.mil/
library/43917.htm.

110. Duelfer Report, 3:50–51.

111. The United States did have additional intelligence on Iraq's BW program but, for unknown reasons, did not share it with UNSCOM for several years. See chapter 4.

112. Jansen, "Biological Weapons Proliferation," 115.

Phase 2: Putting the Pieces Together (January 1992–July 1995)

UNSCOM's investigation of Iraq's BW program was largely dormant through-out 1992 and 1993.[113] The lack of priority accorded to Iraq's BW program was in part due to the lack of new information to act on and the lack of an adequate full-time staff to generate new information.[114] As UNSCOM prepared to establish a monitoring system for Iraq's chemical, biological, and missile-related facili-ties in 1994, the organization increased the size of its BW unit and the pace of its BW inspections.[115] By mid-1995 UNSCOM had accumulated enough evidence to confront Iraq about its past BW activities and to discredit Iraqi cover stories and denials. UNSCOM scored an important victory on July 1, 1995, when Iraq finally admitted to having had an offensive BW program and that Al Hakam had produced BW agents.

Iraq's acceptance of Resolution 715 in November 1993 and the implemen-tation of UNSCOM's plan for the ongoing monitoring and verification system beginning in 1994 generated new information and opportunities for the inspec-tors. In addition, crucial information was obtained from outside of Iraq that pro-vided UNSCOM with new avenues of investigation. The key to the unraveling of Iraq's deception was an innocuous material called "complex growth media" that is used to culture and grow bacteria. Iraq's inability to provide a credible ac-count of its importation and utilization of this growth media played a crucial role in the nation's disclosure in July 1995 that it had an offensive BW program and had produced a large quantity of BW agents.

The success of the OMV system was predicated on the ability of UNSCOM to gain a complete understanding of Iraq's dual-use capabilities. The system was designed to monitor declared dual-use sites, equipment, and materials that were being used for legitimate civilian purposes and to detect diversions of these sites and items for proscribed purposes. The OMV system was not designed to de-tect undeclared or proscribed sites or items, which was a function of UNSCOM's disarmament mission.[116] UNSCOM BW inspectors followed a two-pronged approach to address this issue: establishing an inventory of Iraq's BW-capable

113. By the end of 1993, there had been only three biological inspections, compared to twelve chemi-cal inspections and nineteen missile inspections. UNSC, *Seventh Report of the Executive Chairman of the Special Commission Established by the Secretary-General pursuant to paragraph 9 (b) (i) of Security Council Resolution 687 (1991) on the Activities of the Special Commission*, S/1994/750 (New York: United Nations, June 24, 1994), 30–31.

114. In October 1992, UNSCOM had only one biologist on staff.

115. By the end of 1994, UNSCOM's BW unit had five members. Barton, *Weapons Detective,* 121; and Graham S. Pearson, *The Search for Iraq's Weapons of Mass Destruction* (London: Palgrave Macmillan, 2005), 43.

116. Stephen Black, "Investigating Iraq's Biological Weapons Program," in *Biological Weapons*, ed. Lederberg, 164.

dual-use equipment and conducting interviews with Iraqis who had been part of the defensive program or associated with it. Despite Iraq's refusal to provide UNSCOM with the names of its foreign suppliers and attempts to hide such information, UNSCOM was able to obtain the names of Iraq's foreign suppliers of cell cultures, fermenters, aerosol generators, milling machines, inhalation chambers, and growth media. In addition, UNSCOM learned that most of these shipments had gone through the Technical and Scientific Materials Import Division (TSMID), which on paper was part of the Ministry of Trade but actually reported to the Military Industrialization Commission and was the sole ordering arm for the Technical Research Center, the organization responsible for Salman Pak and Al Hakam.[117] Through interviews, the inspectors also learned of connections between Al Hakam and Salman Pak and linked both of these facilities to the CW program based at Muthanna. In addition, inspectors discovered that several Iraqis who had worked on the military research program at Salman Pak were now managing civilian facilities such as the vaccine plants at Al Daura, Al Kindi, and Amiriyah. All of these sites had been on UNSCOM's initial list of suspected BW sites, although no evidence had yet been found to link them to BW activities. The behavior of Iraqi scientists during interviews with UNSCOM inspectors was also revealing. The Iraqis interviewed were evasive, appeared to have been thoroughly coached beforehand, and exhibited collective amnesia, which implied that Iraq was still hiding something.[118]

At the end of 1994, UNSCOM reported to the Security Council that its greatest verification challenge was accounting for Iraq's past biological program. According to UNSCOM, "Iraq's account is minimal and has no inherent logic.... While Iraq maintains that the programme was in the early research stages and would be defensively oriented, the indications all point to an offensive program."[119] UNSCOM's assurance that Iraq was concealing an offensive program was strengthened by an interview in February 1995 with General Wafiq al-Samarra'i, the former head of Iraq's military intelligence. Samarra'i, who had recently

---

117. Trevan, *Saddam's Secrets*, 169, 271–72; and John Barry, "Unearthing the Truth," *Newsweek*, March 2, 1998, 40.

118. UNSC, *Addendum to the Eighth Report of the Executive Chairman of the Special Commission Established by the Secretary-General Pursuant to Paragraph 9 (b) (i) of Resolution 687 (1991)*, S/1994/1422/Add. 1 (New York: United Nations, December 15, 1994), 11; Rod Barton, "Unraveling Iraq's Biological Weapons Program: A Personal Account," (lecture and slide presentation at the Harvard Sussex Program CBW Colloquia, Belfer Center for Science and International Affairs, Harvard University, Cambridge, Massachusetts, January 29, 2001); Black, "UNSCOM and the Iraqi Biological Weapons Program," 292; Rod Barton, "The Application of the UNSCOM Experience to International Biological Arms Control," *Critical Reviews in Microbiology* 24, no. 3 (1998), 222; and Trevan, *Saddam's Secrets*, 284.

119. UNSC, *Eighth Report of the Executive Chairman of the Special Commission Established by the Secretary-General Pursuant to Paragraph 9 (b) (i) of Resolution 687 (1991)*, S/1994/1422 (New York: United Nations, December 15, 1994), 6–7.

defected to Turkey, was the first Iraqi defector interviewed by UNSCOM with credible knowledge of Iraq's BW program. He told the inspectors that the BW program had been underway at Salman Pak since at least 1982 under the supervision of the intelligence service. He also reported that in 1991 Iraq had two hundred biological bombs that weighed either 500 kilograms or 500 pounds and that weapons-related documents had been hidden at the Samarra Drug Company.[120]

By April 1995 UNSCOM had developed a strong case that Iraq was continuing to conceal an offensive program, based on information about its importation of growth media and other dual-use equipment and the nature of the Al Hakam facility.[121] Iraq's inability to credibly refute this assessment over the next three months, and its increasingly tenuous economic situation, led it to disclose its offensive program in July 1995.

The major breakthrough that allowed UNSCOM to expose Iraq's past BW program centered around Iraq's importation of massive quantities of growth media from European companies. Through discussions with European suppliers and information provided by Israel, UNSCOM was able to document TSMID's importation of roughly forty tons of growth media between 1987 and 1990.[122] This quantity of growth media was sufficient to support a modest-sized pharmaceutical plant, but Iraq did not have such a facility. By Iraq's own calculations, its hospitals consumed only two hundred kilograms of growth media a year.[123] Given the connection between TSMID and the Iraqi BW program, UNSCOM believed that Iraq imported the growth media for the purpose of producing biological weapons. UNSCOM was eventually able to locate twenty-three tons of growth media, but this left seventeen tons unaccounted for. Throughout early 1995 UNSCOM sought a credible explanation from Iraq regarding the fate of the growth media. In response, Iraq presented a number of increasingly improbable explanations as to why it had imported such large quantities of the material and what happened to the missing growth media. By April 1995 all of these

---

120. In August 1995 Iraq admitted to having had 166 bombs (which weighed 400 kilograms each) and 25 missile warheads filled with biological agent in 1991, very close to the figure Samarra'i gave of 200. Trevan, *Saddam's Secrets,* 298–300, 331; and Charles Duelfer, "The Inevitable Failure of Inspections in Iraq," *Arms Control Today* September 2002:11.

121. UNSC, *Report of the Secretary-General on the Activities of the Special Commission Established by the Secretary-General Pursuant to Paragraph 9 (b) (i) of Resolution 687 (1991),* S/1995/284 (New York: United Nations, April 10, 1995), 16.

122. Rolf Ekeus, *Iraq's Biological Weapons Program: UNSCOM's Experience* (New York: United Nations, November 20, 1996), 3; Barton, "Unraveling Iraq's Biological Weapons Program"; Trevan, *Saddam's Secrets,* 725, 287; Barry, "Unearthing the Truth," 40; James Bone, "Chemical Agents," *Times of London,* December 13, 1997; and William Broad and Judith Miller, "Iraq's Deadliest Arms: Puzzles Breed Fear," *New York Times,* February 26, 1998, A1.

123. Barton, "Application of the UNSCOM Experience," 223; and Trevan, *Saddam's Secrets,* 288.

claims had been investigated and had been rebutted, were deemed implausible, or remained unsupported by any evidence.[124]

At the same time that inspectors were knocking holes in Iraq's account of its purchase and utilization of growth media, they were also uncovering new information about Al Hakam's true purpose and past history. As noted earlier, since the original inspection in October 1991, some UNSCOM inspectors had remained suspicious about Iraqi claims that Al Hakam was a civilian SCP-production plant.[125] Although the secrecy, security, and physical characteristics of the facility undermined the Iraqi claim that it was a civilian SCP-production plant, the lack of containment to prevent the escape of dangerous pathogens led some inspectors to conclude that the site was not involved in Iraq's BW program.[126]

In early 1995 UNSCOM uncovered evidence that Iraq had planned on installing advanced air-filtration systems in two buildings at Al Hakam. After reviewing the architectural drawings of Al Hakam, inspecting the facility, and interviewing the engineers who designed the facility, UNSCOM inspectors learned that Iraq had planned to install high-efficiency particulate air, or HEPA, filters on two buildings at Al Hakam, which they referred to as Project 324. Inspectors also had intelligence provided by the United States and Israel about Iraq's purchase of HEPA filters for two buildings at an unidentified facility code-named Project 324.[127] The use of such sophisticated equipment was inconsistent with the declared purpose of these buildings but would be required for work with BW agents.[128]

Although not reported publicly at the time, UNSCOM had also discovered an anomaly in the ongoing activities at Al Hakam. In addition to the production of SCP, Iraq also claimed that the facility was engaged in the production of the biopesticide *Bacillus thuringiensis,* commonly known as Bt, which is a spore-forming bacteria closely related to *B. anthracis.* UNSCOM's analysis of samples taken from the spray driers at Al Hakam in December 1994 found that Bt was being produced in dry powder form with particles less than 10 microns in

124. Trevan, *Saddam's Secrets,* 288–89, 295, 303–10; Barton, "Unraveling Iraq's Biological Weapons Program"; and Black, "UNSCOM and the Iraqi Biological Weapons Program," 292.

125. Aside from David Kelly, this assessment was shared by Richard Spertzel, former deputy commander of the U.S. Army Medical Research Institute of Infectious Diseases, and William Patrick, who had previously worked in the U.S. offensive BW program. Miller, Engelberg, and Broad, *Germs,* 144–45; and Barton, *Weapons Detective,* 125.

126. In addition to Karen Jansen, this judgment was shared by Volker Beck, the chief inspector of the fourth BW inspection team, by David Franz, former commander of USAMRIID, and by two microbiologists on staff at UNSCOM, Rod Barton and Raymond Zilinskas. Barton, *Weapons Detective,* 118, 125; Leitenberg, *Problem of Biological Weapons,* 198; and Trevan, *Saddam's Secrets,* 261.

127. Trevan, *Saddam's Secrets,* 274, 291–92; Barton, *Weapons Detective,* 126, 137; and Miller, Engelberg, and Broad, *Germs,* 148–49.

128. UNSC, S/1995/284, 19.

size. This size was inconsistent with biopesticide applications but was ideal for the dissemination of a biological weapon. In addition, UNSCOM discovered that the Bt from Al Hakam lacked the characteristic protein-crystal inclusions needed for insecticidal activity.[129] UNSCOM concluded that the dry powder Bt was being used to practice production of dry *B. anthracis*.[130] Dry powders of BW agents are more potent, more stable, easier to disseminate, and survive longer in aerosol form in arid environments such as the Middle East than the liquid slurries that Iraq produced before the 1991 Gulf War.

Finally, thanks to foreign suppliers and intelligence agencies, UNSCOM was able to document attempted and successful efforts by TSMID to procure a range of dual-use equipment and materials needed to produce, process, and weaponize BW agents. For example, TSMID's purchase of four filling machines, a spray drier, an inhalation chamber, and a sophisticated laboratory were linked by UNSCOM to Al Hakam. In addition, TSMID attempted to order three large fermenters and disguise the fact that Al Hakam was the equipment's ultimate destination. UNSCOM also learned that TSMID had attempted to obtain a highly virulent strain of *B. anthracis* from the United Kingdom that would be well suited for use as a biological warfare agent.[131] Based on these findings, UNSCOM reported to the Security Council that Iraq had obtained or sought all of the dual-use equipment required for a BW program, and Iraq's failure to account for the legitimate use of these materials lead to the conclusion that they had been acquired for use in a BW program.[132]

UNSCOM's BW inspectors are convinced that Iraq's failure to account for the growth media was crucial to Iraq's decision to admit that it had had an offensive program.[133] The detailed documentation available to UNSCOM regarding Iraqi imports of the material, the sheer quantity of missing growth media, and the direct correlation between growth media and BW agent production meant that Iraq could not dismiss the issue. Although Iraq tried to stonewall UNSCOM, its support within the Security Council was slipping. The thoroughness of the April 1995 report, combined with Iraq's clumsy and implausible denials, undercut the support they had been receiving from their French and Russian allies

---

129. UNMOVIC has reported, however, that one of the samples of Bt did have the requisite toxin gene and that the gene may have been missing from the other samples due to instability in the strain of Bt being used by Iraq. UNMOVIC, *Compendium,* 1029.

130. Trevan, *Saddam's Secrets,* 314–15; and Richard O. Spertzel, "Sampling and Analysis as a Monitoring Tool: Lessons from the UNSCOM Experience," in *The Utility of Sampling and Analysis for Compliance Monitoring of the Biological Weapons Convention,* ed. Jonathan B. Tucker, (Livermore, CA: Lawrence Livermore National Laboratory and Monterey Institute for International Studies, 1997), 22–23.

131. Trevan, *Saddam's Secrets,* 314–16; and Pearson, *UNSCOM Saga,* 140–41.

132. UNSC, S/1995/284, 16.

133. Margaret Sloane, "UNSCOM's Inspections for Biological Weapons in Iraq, 1991–1998" (master's thesis, Fletcher School, Tufts University, 2002), 18–21.

on the Security Council. In order to recover their credibility, Russia and France began pressuring Iraq to come clean so that sanctions might be lifted.[134] Iraq was increasingly susceptible to such pressure due to the damage that four years of sanctions had inflicted on its economy. During this period, Iraq's gross domestic product per capita fell dramatically, inflation increased precipitously, the government's ability to provide social services suffered, and the value of the dinar tumbled to new lows.[135] The regime in Baghdad now saw an opportunity to get out from under the sanction regime that was threatening to destabilize the domestic political situation.

In late May 1995, Deputy Prime Minister Tariq Aziz offered UNSCOM chairman Rolf Ekeus a deal. If Iraq saw significant progress on closing the chemical and missile investigations in UNSCOM's next report to the Security Council, then Iraq would address the sole significant outstanding issue for UNSCOM: the BW program. In its June report, UNSCOM stated that it had sufficient confidence in its knowledge of Iraqi chemical and missile capabilities, that Iraq no longer retained significant proscribed chemical or missile capabilities, and that the chemical and missile OMV systems were operational. The report also noted lack of progress on resolving the concerns in the biological field that had been raised in the April 1995 report.[136]

The combination of Ekeus's positive report, Iraq's continued inability to adequately explain the fate of the missing growth media, the prospect that more incriminating evidence could be revealed, the regime's fear that economic problems might cause political instability, and pressure from a unified Security Council forced Iraq to provide a new accounting of its past BW activities. On July 1, 1995, Iraq admitted to UNSCOM that it had had an offensive BW program that had begun in April 1986 at Salman Pak. Iraq also acknowledged that beginning in 1989, Al Hakam had produced 600 liters of *B. anthracis* and 9,000 liters of botulinum toxin. The program was said to have been terminated in October 1990, and all bulk agent was reportedly destroyed at that time. Iraq denied that the CW facility at Muthanna was part of the BW program, that BW agents had been produced at any site besides Al Hakam, that biological agents had been filled into munitions and tested, and that the BW program had any connection with the military.[137] The briefing appeared to be a rather clumsy attempt to disclose enough information to account for what Iraq believed UNSCOM already knew while minimizing disclosures about other aspects of

134. Trevan, *Saddam's Secrets,* 324–25.

135. Duelfer Report, vol. 1, *Regime Finance and Procurement,* 9, 15, 21, 207–15.

136. Rolf Ekeus, "UN Biological Inspections in Iraq," in *The New Terror,* ed. Drell, Sofaer, and Wilson, 245–46.

137. Ekeus, *Iraq's Biological Weapons Program,* 4; and Trevan, *Saddam's Secrets,* 325–27.

the offensive program. UNSCOM strongly suspected that Iraq's new account of agent production was "manipulated to provide what Iraq hoped would pass as a credible accounting of the missing media."[138] In addition, UNSCOM experts calculated that the Iraqi report of its biological agent production was contradictory, inaccurate, and still did not account for at least five tons of missing growth media.[139] UNSCOM also remained skeptical of Iraq's claim that it terminated the BW program in fall 1990, since it had already admitted to expanding its production of chemical weapons at that time. Instead of resolving UNSCOM's suspicions about its BW program, the limited disclosure was seen as another example of Iraq's strategy of "cheat and retreat."

Evaluation of Phase 2

Iraq's disclosure of an offensive biological weapons program in July 1995, after four years of denial, was a great victory for UNSCOM. Ekeus attributes this success to the "crushing" evidence accumulated by UNSCOM, the analytical efforts of the BW inspectors who pieced together the information into a coherent and persuasive case, and the political pressure exerted by UNSCOM and a unified Security Council. The most compelling evidence was the growth media that had been imported in massive quantities, Iraq's increasingly convoluted attempts to account for the missing media, the direct link between the missing media and production of BW agents, and the ability of even nontechnical diplomats to understand this issue and grasp its significance for BW verification.[140] The range of evidence gathered by UNSCOM that indicated Iraq was hiding a BW program was the result of dogged detective work by the BW inspectors, the cooperation of companies in foreign countries, and the assistance of national intelligence services. In the case of the growth media, information on Iraq's foreign procurement provided by Israel and by foreign suppliers gave inspectors several leads to investigate on the ground in Iraq. The inspectors were able to either link these imports directly to Iraq's BW program or force Iraq to invent increasingly complicated and less plausible cover stories.

Although UNSCOM deserves recognition and praise for its success in forcing Iraq to concede that it had an offensive BW program and had produced BW agents at Al Hakam, UNSCOM's experience up to this point offers several cautionary tales about BW verification. First, on-site inspections of Al Hakam were not sufficient to determine the facility's role in the Iraqi BW program.

---

138. UNSC, S/1995/864, 21; and Barton, "Application of the UNSCOM Experience," 225.

139. United Nations, "Press Briefing by Executive Chairman of Special Commission on Monitoring Iraqi Disarmament," August 11, 1995; and Trevan, *Saddam's Secrets,* 328.

140. Ekeus, "UN Biological Inspections in Iraq," 245; and Ekeus, *Iraq's Biological Weapons Program,* 9.

Inspectors who visited the site had diverging views on the nature of the facility. After UNSCOM's first inspection of Al Hakam, the inspection team submitted one report, which stated that "there is absolutely no evidence of participation in a biological weapons program" and another report, which assessed that the plant was "highly suspicious."[141] The running debate within UNSCOM about the potential role of Al Hakam in Iraq's BW program illustrates the ambiguity that surrounds multiuse biological capabilities, the potential for experts to have different interpretations of the same evidence, and the importance of inspectors' judgments in assessing the intent behind a facility.[142] Second, UNSCOM found no direct evidence of Iraq's production of BW agents despite extensive sampling at Al Hakam and Salman Pak.[143] Iraq tried to persuade members of the Security Council that these negative results demonstrated Iraqi compliance with Resolution 687 and that the biological file should be closed.

A third consideration is that Iraq continued to maintain a BW capability at Al Hakam through the mid-1990s. At a minimum, Iraq was able to use this ostensible SCP and biopesticide facility to maintain the equipment and skilled team necessary to produce BW agents. A more alarming interpretation is that Iraq was able to use its research on the biopesticide Bt to upgrade its capability to produce biological weapons from a liquid slurry to a dry powder with the proper size particles for effective dissemination.[144] According to UNMOVIC, Iraq did not intend to produce dry Bt in such a small particle size and did not know the particle size of the final product.[145] This explanation is undercut, however, by evidence that Iraqi scientists were aware that the dry Bt product was unsuitable for agricultural use since it had a tendency to aerosolize easily, a favorable property for a biological weapon.[146] Nonetheless, the process used to produce dry Bt was not suitable for safely producing dry *B. anthracis* spores, since the spray drier lacked biosafety containment features and the Iraqis mixed the bentonite manually with the Bt.[147]

---

141. UNMOVIC, *Compendium,* 1134–35.

142. A senior State Department arms control official who participated in inspections of suspected BW sites in the former Soviet Union compared offensive BW activities to pornography: "you know it when you see it." Interview with Ambassador Donald Mahley, Cambridge, Massachusetts, April 3, 2003.

143. Spertzel, "Sampling and Analysis as a Monitoring Tool," 22–23; Raymond A. Zilinskas, "Detecting and Deterring Biological Weapons: Lessons from United Nations Special Commission (UNSCOM) Operations in Iraq," in *Arms Control in a Multi-Polar World,* ed. James Brown, (Amsterdam: VU University Press, 1996); and Alan J. Mohr, "Biological Sampling and Analysis Procedures for the United Nations Special Commission (UNSCOM) in Iraq," *Politics and the Life Sciences* 14, no. 2 (1995): 240–43.

144. Kadlec, Zelicoff, and Vrtis, "Biological Weapons Control," 105.

145. The particle size of the dry Bt product was dictated by the particle size of bentonite used in the drying process, and only one grade of bentonite was available within Iraq. UNMOVIC, *Compendium,* 1004–7, 1028–30.

146. Duelfer Report, 3:14–15.

147. Communication with Rod Barton, March 27, 2008; and Communication with Kay Mereish, March 24, 2008.

Fourth, while UNSCOM believed that Iraq had weaponized biological agents due to its self-professed production of bulk agent, it did not have any direct evidence of weaponization.[148] UNSCOM did not know how many munitions there were, what kind they were, where they were stored or deployed, or what happened to them after the Gulf War.[149] This aspect of the Iraqi BW program was only revealed in the aftermath of Hussein Kamel's defection to Jordan in August 1995.

Phase 3: Defection and Disclosure (August 1995–December 1998)

After the July disclosure of its past BW activities, Iraq sought to place UNSCOM on the defensive and revitalize its efforts to have the sanctions lifted. The defection of a senior Iraqi official to Jordan in August 1995, however, dramatically changed the balance of power between Iraq and the inspectors. The defection forced Iraq to reveal an even larger and more advanced BW program than it had acknowledged only a month earlier.

In early August, Iraq submitted a new Full, Final, and Complete Disclosure (FFCD) to UNSCOM that codified the information it had provided in July. During a meeting with Ekeus in Baghdad, Aziz made it clear that Iraq's cooperation with UNSCOM was nearing an end. He issued an ultimatum that the biological investigation must be closed by the end of August or else all cooperation with UNSCOM would cease.[150] Iraq apparently calculated that its limited disclosure in July would allow it to offer a credible explanation of the missing growth media, thereby removing UNSCOM's most potent example of Iraqi noncompliance with Resolution 687, and that its ultimatum would place pressure on UNSCOM to close the BW investigation. The resolution of the biological file would allow Iraq to regain the support of France and Russia on the Security Council in lifting the UN sanctions.

Iraq's plans for UNSCOM to close the biological file and to have sanctions lifted were dashed by the defection of Hussein Kamel to Jordan on August 7, 1995.[151] Prior to his defection, Kamel had spent over ten years developing and

148. UNSCOM had two potential leads. First, UNSCOM knew that the four filling machines imported by TSMID in 1989 had been well used before the 1991 Gulf War, based on the type and amount of spare parts the foreign supplier had also provided. Communication with Rod Barton, March 17, 2008. Second, UNSCOM had received information from Israel that TSMID had also imported components necessary to build an agricultural spray device that was suspected of being designed for aeoroslizing BW agents. Barton, *Weapons Detective,* 151–52, 159.

149. Zilinskas, "Detecting and Deterring Biological Weapons," 195.

150. Trevan, *Saddam's Secrets,* 329.

151. The motivation for Kamel's defection is not known for certain. Rolf Ekeus, UNSCOM's first executive chairman, has alleged that his defection was directly triggered by UNSCOM's successes in

concealing Iraq's conventional and unconventional weapons programs and protecting the senior leadership from internal and external threats. Kamel, a cousin of Saddam Hussein and a member of his clan, parlayed his ambition, management skills, and relationship with Hussein into a bureaucratic empire that eventually controlled Iraq's WMD programs, civilian and military industries, and the regime's internal security. By 1988 Hussein Kamel was described as being the second most powerful person in Iraq. At this time, Kamel oversaw the Amn al-Khass, or Special Security Organization, which was responsible for presidential security and supervising the rest of Iraq's internal security and intelligence agencies, and the Ministry of Industry and Military Industrialization, which was responsible for civilian and military industries, including WMD and missile programs. Kamel served as the minister of defense in 1991, and after the Persian Gulf War he returned to his prior role as head of the renamed Military Industrialization Commission.[152]

Baghdad immediately began taking action to limit the damage that could be inflicted by Kamel's revelations regarding Iraq's proscribed weapons. Ekeus was invited back to Baghdad and given a new account of Iraq's proscribed weapons programs. Iraq informed UNSCOM that Kamel had been responsible for hiding elements of Iraq's WMD programs without the knowledge of senior Iraqi officials. Iraqi officials now acknowledged that their BW program had included greater production, more agents, and more facilities than previously admitted and had also included the testing and deployment of biological munitions. According to this new account, Iraq's pursuit of biological weapons began in 1974, not 1985. The early program, based at Salman Pak, was managed by an intelligence agency and was terminated in 1979. A new BW program began in 1985 at the CW facility at Muthanna. In addition to Salman Pak and Al Hakam, Iraq reported that facilities involved in BW research, production, and weaponization included Muthanna, the SCP plant at Taji, the agricultural and water resources research center at Al Fudaliyah, and the foot-and-mouth disease vaccine facility at Al Daura. Iraq also admitted that it had produced 19,000 liters of botulinum toxin, 8,500 liters of *B. anthracis,* 2,200 liters of aflatoxin, and 340 liters of

---

uncovering Iraq's past BW program. Barton, *Weapons Detective,* 167. A more likely cause of Kamel's defection was an internal family feud between Kamel and Saddam Hussein's eldest son, Uday. According to King Hussein of Jordan, "as far as we know, this was a family crisis, in the personal context, for a fairly long period." Amatzia Baram, *Building toward Crisis: Saddam Husayn's Strategy for Survival* (Washington, DC: Washington Institute for Near East Policy, 1998), 8–13. See also, Duelfer Report, vol. 1, *Regime Strategic Intent,* 45–46.

152. Scott Ritter, *Endgame: Solving the Iraq Problem Once and For All* (New York: Simon and Schuster, 1999), 76–93; Kenneth Timmerman, *The Death Lobby: How the West Armed Iraq* (Boston, MA: Houghton Mifflin, 1991), 36, 257–58, 288; Duelfer Report, vol. 1, *Regime Strategic Intent,* 45–47; and "Iraq's Military Industrial Capability: Evolution of the Military Industrialization Commission," 5–7, in Duelfer Report, vol. 4, *Addendums.*

C. perfringens. Iraq also disclosed that it had conducted research on trichothecene mycotoxins, ricin, *T. indica* (wheat cover smut), hemorrhagic conjunctivitis virus, rotavirus, and camelpox. Finally, Iraq revealed that it had tested bombs, artillery rockets, artillery shells, and spray tanks with BW agents and filled 18,000 liters of *B. anthracis,* botulinum toxin, and aflatoxin into 166 bombs and twenty-five Al Hussein missile warheads. Iraq claimed that after the 1991 Gulf War these munitions were filled with deactivation chemicals and then destroyed and buried. The remaining bulk agent was similarly neutralized and then dumped out of Al Hakam's waste system.[153] Table 4 provides a summary of Iraq's changing claims regarding its BW program.

Before departing Baghdad, Ekeus was directed to a farm said to have been owned by Hussein Kamel. In a locked chicken house on the farm were 150 boxes of hardware, documents, and other records from the proscribed weapons programs. Iraq admitted that, contrary to their initial claim that all relevant documents had been destroyed during the summer of 1991, orders had been issued at the time to sites working on proscribed weapons to collect and package important documents relating to the technology of weapons production and transfer them to the Special Security Organization.[154] Kamel, as head of the organization, had been responsible for preserving these documents and hiding them from the UN inspectors.

Among this collection containing more than a million pages of documents, one box with some two hundred documents was related to Iraq's BW program. Most of the documents were previously published papers on biological weapons from universities and think tanks or scientific articles that dealt with various aspects of bacterial agents that did not add to UNSCOM's understanding of the BW program. The cache did include several annual reports of the BW program and a red book that described the testing of biological weapons, including photographs. The documents still left important gaps in UNSCOM's knowledge of Iraqi work on viruses, weaponization, the "know how" of producing and processing biological warfare agents, procurement networks, sources of supply, and the roles of the Military Industrialization Commission and Ministry of Defense in the BW program.[155]

Following this visit to Baghdad, Ekeus and other officials from UNSCOM and IAEA traveled to Amman to meet with Kamel.[156] He was able to confirm

---

153. UNSC, S/1995/864, 22–27.

154. Ibid., 11.

155. Krasno and Sutterlin, *The United Nations and Iraq,* 61; Mangold and Goldberg, *Plague Wars,* 293; William J. Broad and Judith Miller, "Germs, Atoms and Poison Gas: The Iraqi Shell Game," *New York Times,* December 20, 1998, WK5; UNSC, S/1995/864, 11; and UNSC, S/1999/94, 98, 104.

156. Unless otherwise noted, this section is drawn from United Nations Special Commission, "Note for the File," August 22, 1995, http://www.un.org/Depts/unmovic/documents/hk.pdf.

TABLE 4. Evolution of Iraqi Disclosures Regarding Its BW Program

	April 1991	August 1991	July 1, 1995	August 17, 1995
History of BW Program	No BW program	Defensive only; from 1986 to August 1990	Offensive; from April 1986 to October 1990	Offensive; from 1974 to May–June 1991
Facilities	None	Salman Pak	Salman Pak, Al Hakam	Salman Pak, Al Hakam, Muthanna, Taji, Al Daura, Al Fudaliyah
Agents	None	B. anthracis, C. botulinum, C. perfringens	B. anthracis, C. botulinum, C. perfringens	B. anthracis, C. botulinum, C. perfringens, aflatoxin, mycotoxins, ricin, wheat smut, hemorrhagic conjunctivitis virus, rotavirus, and camelpox
Production	None	None	9,000 liters of botulinum toxin and 600 liters of B. anthracis	19,000 liters of botulinum toxin, 8,500 liters of B. anthracis, 2,200 liters of aflatoxin, and 340 liters of C. perfringens
Weaponization	None	None	None	LD-250 and R-400 bombs, 122 mm artillery rockets, 155 mm artillery shells, aerosol generators, and spray tanks tested; R-400 bombs and Al Hussein warheads filled and deployed

the command structure for Iraq's WMD programs and their overall aims, as well as providing interesting information on how Iraq concealed proscribed items from UNSCOM. Kamel identified the key managers of the BW program as Amer al-Saadi, General Amer Rashid, and Murtada, the former head of Muthanna and TSMID.[157] Kamel also identified Nasser Hindawi as a key scientist who had been part of the program from the beginning and who had been Rihab Taha's boss. Kamel also provided an overview of the project's history, facilities, and agents that matched the information that Iraq had just provided. Regarding weaponization, Kamel confirmed that aerial bombs and twenty-five missile warheads were filled with biological agents at Muthanna in December 1990. Kamel also reported that Iraq had destroyed its biological agents and weapons, but he was unclear as to when this occurred. Overall, Kamel gave UNSCOM high marks for their efforts to uncover Iraq's prohibited weapons. He told the inspectors, "You have [an] important role in Iraq with this. You should not underestimate yourself. You are very effective in Iraq."

The value of the information provided by Kamel has generally been rated as less than impressive by UNSCOM officials.[158] At a minimum, the information that Kamel provided could be used to confirm the most recent disclosures by Baghdad. Far more important than what Kamel revealed, however, was Baghdad's response to his defection. Given Kamel's key role in the development and concealment of Iraq's proscribed weapons for so many years, Baghdad was forced to make sweeping new disclosures regarding all of its proscribed weapons programs and provide a huge cache of documents and other materials to the UN inspectors.

As a result of these revelations, in May and June 1996 UNSCOM demolished the Al Hakam facility, disabled the air-handling system at the Al Daura site, and destroyed the remaining growth media and the equipment at Al Daura and Al Fudaliyah that had been used for BW-agent production.

Following Kamel's defection and Iraq's new disclosures, UNSCOM renewed its effort to verify Iraq's declarations about its past BW activities. Between August 1995 and February 1997, UNSCOM launched twenty-five inspections to

---

157. Al-Saadi and Rashid had been Kamel's deputies at the Ministry of Industry and Military Industrialization. Timmerman, *Death Lobby,* 36, 79.

158. Stephen Black, "Verification under Duress: The Case of UNSCOM," in *Verification Yearbook 2000,* ed. Trevor Findlay, (London: VERTIC, 2000), 121; Rolf Ekeus, "Yes, Let's Go into Iraq," *Washington Post,* September 15, 2002, B1; and Zilinskas, "Detecting and Deterring Biological Weapons," 195. At the time of the defection it was not clear if Kamel was being completely truthful or if he was withholding information to improve his bargaining position. Based on a document written shortly after Kamel's defection by Hossam Amin, then head of the National Monitoring Directorate that served as the official Iraqi liaison with UNSCOM and the IAEA, it appears that Kamel provided the UN with everything he knew about Iraq's proscribed weapons programs. Barton Gellman, "Iraq's Arsenal Was Only on Paper," *Washington Post,* January 7, 2004, A1.

verify Iraq's newest BW declaration. Initially, Iraqi officials were cooperative and the inspectors were able to conduct a large number of interviews, including with previously inaccessible senior officials. But Iraq soon began stonewalling the inspectors again, and subsequent interviews and inspections were not very fruitful. As a result, UN inspector Rod Barton recalls that "the inspections had gone nowhere and none of the issues we had singled out back then were any closer to resolution."[159]

The sampling of former BW facilities produced useful information for the first time. The sampling of Salman Pak and Al Hakam in 1991, 1992, and 1994 had not revealed any incriminating information. By 1996 UNSCOM had access to new techniques based on polymerase chain reaction technology that made it possible to detect the traces of BW agents on pieces of equipment that had earlier tested negative. Direct evidence of Iraqi production of BW agents was found by UNSCOM in May 1996 when fifteen samples taken from dismantled equipment from Al Hakam, the Al Daura vaccine plant, and Al Fudaliyah tested positive for the presence of BW agents. UNSCOM found evidence of *B. anthracis* spores of the same strain as that used in Iraq's BW program on two fermenters and a mobile storage tank at the foot-and-mouth disease vaccine plant at Al Daura.[160] This finding contradicted Iraq's claim that it had produced *B. anthracis* only at Al Hakam and raised the question of how much additional *B. anthracis* Iraq had produced beyond what it declared already and what else they were hiding from UNSCOM.[161]

In 1997 and 1998, sampling and analysis of excavated munitions that had been unilaterally destroyed by Iraq in 1991 provided UNSCOM with conclusive evidence that Iraq had filled bombs and missile warheads with BW agents. In February 1997 UNSCOM recovered three intact bombs from their destruction site at Al Aziziyah and found them partially filled with a liquid that tested positive for the presence of botulinum toxin or *C. botulinum*. In 1998 UNSCOM found traces of *B. anthracis* on at least seven different Al Hussein missile warheads recovered from the disposal site at Al Nibai, two more than Iraq claimed to have been filled with this agent. In response to this finding, Iraq changed its accounting of its BW missile warheads and reported that it had in fact filled sixteen warheads with *B. anthracis* and five with botulinum toxin instead of the other way around. Iraq claimed, however, that this change did not affect its declaration

159. Barton, *Weapons Detective,* 162–63. 181.

160. Ekeus, *Iraq's Biological Weapons Program,* 5; Stephen Morse, "Detecting Biological Warfare Agents," in *Biological Warfare,* ed. Zilinskas, 98; Spertzel, "Sampling and Analysis as a Monitoring Tool," 22–23; and UNSC, S/1999/94, 128, 157.

161. The interpretation of the analytical data underlying this assessment was later disputed within UNMVOIC. Compare UNMOVIC, *Unresolved Disarmament Issues,* 95–97 with UNMOVIC, *Compendium,* 928–32.

about the total quantity of BW agents produced and weaponized.[162] The ease with which Iraq adjusted these numbers to accommodate new information presented by UNSCOM did not inspire confidence in their accuracy.

Since its first revelations of an offensive BW program in July 1995, Iraq had submitted three Full, Final, and Complete Disclosures of its proscribed biological program to UNSCOM. Given the lies, half-truths, and omissions contained in these declarations, one inspector dubbed these documents "full, final and complete fairy tales."[163] Due to the slow and frustrating pace of verifying these declarations, UNSCOM commissioned four independent reviews of Iraq's BW declarations.

All four reviews found the declarations deficient in completeness and accuracy. In March 1997 an international panel of experts reviewed Iraq's June 1996 FFCD and recommended its rejection because of the inadequacy of the material presented throughout the document.[164] An international panel of BW experts reviewed Iraq's September 1997 FFCD in October 1997 and unanimously concluded that it "was incomplete and contained significant inaccuracies. It is in no way a full account of the scale and scope of the BW programme."[165] In March 1998 UNSCOM convened a technical evaluation meeting between Iraqi officials and a new panel of international experts with the goal of conclusively resolving all outstanding issues in the BW field. The panel found that the most recent FFCD was deficient in all areas and contained "major mistakes, inconsistencies, and gaps in information."[166] As a result, the experts found that the meeting yielded, "no additional confidence in the veracity and expanse of the FFCD."[167]

In July 1998 another team of international experts conducted another review of the September 1997 FFCD and found that Iraq's accounting of growth media, bulk agent production and disposal, and munitions was "inadequate." The group recommended that no further verification or assessment of the Iraqi biological declaration should be conducted until Iraq provided new information.

---

162. UNSC, S/1999/94, 118; Pearson, *UNSCOM Saga,* 164; and CIA, *Intelligence Related to Possible Sources of Biological Agent Exposure during the Persian Gulf War.*

163. Trevan, *Saddam's Secrets,* 11.

164. UNSC, *Report of the Secretary-General on the Activities of the Special Commission Established by the Secretary-General Pursuant to Paragraph 9 (b) (i) of Resolution 687 (1991),* S/1997/301 (New York: United Nations, April 11, 1997), 17.

165. UNSC, *Report of the Secretary-General on the Activities of the Special Commission Established by the Secretary-General Pursuant to Paragraph 9 (b) (i) of Resolution 687 (1991),* S/1997/774 (New York: United Nations, October 6, 1997), 37.

166. UNSC, *Letter dated 8 April 1998 from the Executive Chairman of the Special Commission Established by the Secretary-General Pursuant to Paragraph 9 (b) (i) of Resolution 687 (1991) Addressed to the President of the Security Council,* S/1998/308 (New York: United Nations, April 8, 1998), 4.

167. Ibid., 11.

The team concluded that "any other approach would be a waste of time."[168] This meeting proved to be Iraq's last opportunity to account for its past activities and to present evidence to UNSCOM that it had eliminated its BW program.

On December 16, 1998, UNSCOM withdrew its inspectors due to a lack of cooperation from Iraq. That same day, U.S. and British forces began a three-day aerial assault on Iraqi leadership, military, and WMD-related sites as part of Operation Desert Fox. UNSCOM did not return to Iraq. On December 17, 1999, UNSCOM was disbanded by the Security Council and replaced by the newly created United Nations Monitoring, Verification, and Inspection Commission.[169]

Evaluation of Phase 3

The last phase of UNSCOM's investigation of Iraq's BW program began with a bang and ended with a whimper. Kamel's defection and Baghdad's subsequent revelations in August 1995 unveiled an extensive BW program. For a brief period, Iraq cooperated with UNSCOM in verifying this new account of its offensive program, but then it returned to obstruction and obfuscation. In its final report to the Security Council, UNSCOM reported that the thirty-five BW-related inspections it had undertaken since July 1995 to verify Iraq's declarations of its past BW activities "has been negated by Iraq's intransigence and failure to provide cooperation concerning its biological weapons since January 1996."[170] UNSCOM's inspections continued to find inconsistencies, contradictions, omissions, and outright lies in Iraqi declarations about past activities. UNSCOM and four groups of international BW experts identified serious problems with almost every aspect of Iraq's BW declarations, including history, organization, facilities, procurement, R&D, production, weaponization, and concealment efforts. As a result of these problems, UNSCOM judged its attempts to verify Iraq's FFCDs as "generally without success."[171] Furthermore, during this phase, UNSCOM was unable to develop another lead as important and compelling as the missing growth media.

The only breakthrough achieved by UNSCOM was in the field of biological sampling and analysis, but this was too little, too late. Thanks to advances in technology and improved sampling methodologies, UNSCOM was able, for the first time, to detect traces of BW agents on production equipment and munitions.[172]

168. UNSC, *Letter Dated 5 August 1998 from the Executive Chairman of the Special Commission Established by the Secretary-General Pursuant to Paragraph 9 (b) (i) of Security Council Resolution 687 (1991) Addressed to the President of the Security Council,* S/1998/719 (New York: United Nations, August 5, 1998), 9.

169. UNSC, *Resolution 1284 (1999),* S/RES/1284, December 17, 1999.

170. UNSC, S/1999/94, 105.

171. Ibid.

172. Kay Mereish, "Technical Advances and Field Experiences for Use in Biological Verification,"

Sampling proved useful for verifying some Iraqi claims and provided some indications that the current Iraqi accounts of production and weaponization were still not accurate.[173] The sampling did not provide UNSCOM with the kind of smoking gun evidence that would have been most useful prior to July 1995, since Iraq had already admitted by this time to having produced and weaponized BW agents. It should also be noted that the sampling of Iraq's BW munitions was made possible only because Iraq showed UNSCOM the site where it had destroyed and buried these weapons in 1991.[174] This incident illustrated once again UNSCOM's dependence on Iraqi disclosures and cooperation to collect evidence of past BW activities.

The most dramatic revelation in August 1995, that Iraq had tested a range of biological munitions and deployed close to two hundred biological bombs and missile warheads on the eve of the Gulf War, was probably only obtainable from a knowledgeable defector or a direct Iraqi admission. Until Kamel's defection, Iraq steadfastly denied that it had weaponized any of the bulk BW agents it had admitted to producing. Aside from the information provided by General Samarra'i and information on Iraqi imports of filling machines and aerosol-generator components, UNSCOM lacked any useful information on the nature or extent of Iraq's weaponization of BW agents before Kamel's defection.[175] Since Iraq's biological munitions were produced indigenously, based on conventional munitions, or were modified versions of innocuous items such as auxiliary fuel tanks, UNSCOM would not have been able to follow the paper trail generated by import and export activities that had been so useful in the cases of the growth media and dual-use equipment. Without information from external sources such as national intelligence agencies or records of foreign procurement, Iraq's munition-related activities and capabilities would likely have continued to elude UNSCOM.

Net Assessment of UNSCOM's Verification of Iraq's BW Program

A net assessment of UNSCOM's investigation of Iraq's BW program does not yield a simple and clear-cut conclusion. UNSCOM's success was neither swift nor complete, but it was significant. Between 1991 and 1994, UNSCOM visited

(paper presented to the NGO Committee on Disarmament, Peace and Security, UN Headquarters, New York City, New York, April 19, 2007), http://disarm.igc.org/unmovic19april.pdf.

173. As noted earlier, however, the interpretation of some of the analysis of these samples was a source of disagreement within UNSCOM and UNMOVIC.

174. A November 1996 UNSCOM mission to collect samples of BW agents disseminated during outdoor testing of biological munitions was unsuccessful due to Iraqi unwillingness to identify the specific locations where the testing took place. Pearson, *UNSCOM Saga,* 158.

175. Communication with Richard Spertzel, former head of UNSCOM biological inspectors, March 27, 2004.

several dual-capable sites in Iraq, including Al Hakam, Al Daura, Taji, and Al Fudaliyah and failed to find any incriminating evidence that directly linked them with BW activities. As a result, until 1995, Iraq was able to retain the facilities, equipment, growth media, and personnel at Al Hakam to restart production of BW agents. In part this delay in uncovering Iraq's past BW program was due to the lack of any new information on Iraq's BW program and the low priority assigned to BW compared to CW and ballistic missiles.

UNSCOM's investigation, supported by information from foreign suppliers and national intelligence agencies, eventually led to the collection of a large amount of compelling yet circumstantial evidence that indicated that Iraq was hiding an offensive BW program. UNSCOM was also able to refute Iraq's claims to the contrary or demonstrate the implausibility of Iraq's alternative explanations. Although UNSCOM's detective work forced Iraq to admit to an offensive program and the production of BW agents at Al Hakam, it took the defection of Hussein Kamel for Iraq to reveal a more complete history of the program, the scope of research and production activities, and the extent of weaponization. This disclosure allowed UNSCOM to destroy the production equipment, facilities, and growth media that Iraq had used in its offensive program. UNSCOM, however, was unable to satisfactorily verify Iraq's newest account of the program.

UNSCOM and the Future of BW Verification

Verification is the holy grail of the BW arms control regime. Although UNSCOM was the most intrusive arms control regime ever devised, it enjoyed mixed success at best in verifying Iraq's compliance. UNSCOM was able, after many years of effort, to uncover Iraq's production of BW agents prior to 1991, but it is unlikely that UNSCOM would have been able to discover the scope of Iraqi research and production or the extent to which these agents had been weaponized without Iraqi disclosures prompted by Hussein Kamel's defection. UNSCOM field-tested many of the methods under consideration for use in verifying biological arms control and pioneered some new ones as well. These methods, however, were insufficient to dispel Iraqi deception or confirm Iraqi honesty. As a result, UNSCOM could not technically and analytically verify Iraqi compliance with Resolution 687. It is not possible to judge the effectiveness of UNSCOM's monitoring of civilian biological facilities since there is no evidence that Iraq conducted illicit research, development, production, or weaponization in such facilities after 1995. To the extent that this compliance was motivated by fear of detection, it represents a successful experiment in deterring the misuse of biotechnology through a verification regime.

UNSCOM's accomplishments were due in large part to the range of inspection techniques and technologies it was able to employ. UNSCOM's investigative arsenal included intrusive anyplace and anytime inspections, information on imports and exports, document collection and analysis, interviews, unrestricted right to aerial photography, unlimited authority to conduct biological sampling and analysis, intelligence provided by governments and defectors, and the capability to analyze the information from all of these sources. The foundation for many of these techniques was laid in the early 1990s as a result of the work of VEREX. This group was charged with developing verification measures to strengthen compliance with the BWC. UNSCOM's investigation of Iraq's BW program provided the first opportunity to field-test many of these methods, and their collective contribution to UNSCOM's success has been cited as evidence of the feasibility of an international verification regime to strengthen the BWC.[176]

While the UNSCOM experience highlighted the value of individual verification measures and the synergy between such measures in uncovering an illicit BW program, the conditions that made this accomplishment possible are not readily generalizable to the verification of the BWC by an international organization. UNSCOM had several advantages that a multilateral verification regime for the BWC would not have.

First, the Security Council authorized a robust carrot-and-stick strategy to promote Iraqi compliance with its obligations and cooperation with UNSCOM. The Security Council imposed the most comprehensive economic sanctions ever on Iraq for its invasion of Kuwait. These sanctions cost Iraq roughly $20 billion a year in lost oil-export revenue and could only be lifted once UNSCOM and the IAEA certified that Iraq had been disarmed of nuclear, biological, and chemical weapons.[177] Because Iraq's disarmament obligations were part of the cease-fire resolution for the Gulf War, military action in response to Iraqi violations was authorized under Chapter VII of the UN Charter. Given Iraq's decisive defeat at the hands of the coalition in 1991 and the continued presence of significant U.S. military forces in the region, the threat of renewed military operations was ever present. The benefits of cooperation and the costs of noncompliance faced by Iraq were far greater than those available for enforcing any other arms control agreement.

Second, the United Nations Security Council required Iraq to make exhaustive declarations regarding virtually every aspect of its biological activities and heavily restricted Iraqi capabilities in this field. Iraq had to declare to UNSCOM all microorganisms, toxins, and related equipment and facilities that could be

---

176. Pearson, *UNSCOM Saga*, 203–5; and Black, "Verification under Duress," 127.

177. Meghan L. O'Sullivan, *Shrewd Sanctions: Statecraft and State Sponsors of Terrorism* (Washington, DC: Brookings, 2003), 168.

used for biological warfare and all research on pathogenic microorganisms and toxins. Iraq was also required to disclose all labs that worked with these agents, had biosafety containment features, had a fermentation capacity in excess of forty liters, or produced vaccines. Iraq's biological research was restricted to unclassified civilian activities on indigenous diseases or diseases that posed an imminent threat of emerging in the country. The Iraqi military was prohibited from conducting or sponsoring any work whatsoever with microorganisms or toxins. Iraq was also barred from breeding vectors or importing pathogenic microorganisms, toxins, or vaccines without UNSCOM's permission. Finally, Iraq was allowed to possess only one biosafety level-4 lab and two biosafety level-3 labs for working with dangerous pathogens.[178] These limitations on Iraqi biological research and facilities greatly aided UNSCOM monitoring by reducing Iraq's ability to exploit the multiuse nature of biology to conduct offensive work under the guise of defensive or public health research. Despite this advantage, UNSCOM had to monitor eighty-two dual-use facilities including vaccine and pharmaceutical plants, breweries, distilleries, dairies, university labs, and public health and diagnostic laboratories. UNSCOM also tagged 1,334 pieces of dual-use biological equipment, more than in the missile and chemical fields combined.[179] The number and diversity of the facilities and pieces of equipment that needed to be monitored illustrates the ease with which civilian dual-use sites could be converted to hostile purposes.

Third, UNSCOM was given a single clear mandate and extraordinary powers to fulfill this mandate. UNSCOM's focus on disarming Iraq provided the organization with clarity of purpose usually lacking in international organizations that have multiple competing agendas and constituencies. As described earlier, UNSCOM was given a broad set of rights within Iraq and employed a range of highly intrusive inspection techniques and technologies. The extent of UNSCOM's rights demonstrates "how complex and multifarious" an inspection regime must be to detect and deter a state suspected of developing biological weapons.[180] Even with the restrictions placed on Iraq's dual-use biological activities noted above, UNSCOM needed every single one of these rights and techniques to uncover Iraq's proscribed programs, verify their destruction, and monitor facilities for signs of proscribed activities. Indeed, UNSCOM had to

178. UNSC, *Plan for Future Ongoing Monitoring and Verification of Iraq's Compliance with Relevant Parts of Section C of Security Council Resolution 687 (1991)*, S/22871/Rev. 1 (New York: United Nations, October 2, 1991), 9–11, 26–28.

179. UNSC, S/1995/864, 20; UNSC, S/1999/94, 223, 247, 256; and Barton, "Application of the UNSCOM Experience," 228–29.

180. Ekeus, "UN Biological Inspections in Iraq," 252–53.

constantly develop new techniques and employ new technologies in response to Iraqi intransigence.[181]

The conditions required for UNSCOM's success cast serious doubt on the ability of an international organization to achieve similar results in the context of a multilateral biological verification treaty. The severity of the restrictions placed on Iraq's multiuse biological activities, the range of techniques employed by UNSCOM, and the authority that UNSCOM had to employ them were not only unprecedented but also unpalatable for a voluntary arms control regime. The scope and level of detail of the required declarations, intrusiveness of inspections, range of facilities placed under monitoring, and extent of restrictions on dual-use activities imposed on Iraq went far beyond what states negotiating the BWC compliance protocol were willing to contemplate. An international verification regime would have to take into account the risks to proprietary and national security information, financial costs, and the legal rights of member states to a much greater degree than UNSCOM did with Iraq. The UNSCOM experience highlighted both the obstacles and opportunities in designing an international BW verification regime.

---

181. Some UNSCOM innovations included the use of U-2 reconnaissance aircraft, chemical and biological sampling, ground-penetrating radar, and equipment to intercept radio communications. Black, "UNSCOM and the Iraqi Biological Weapons Program," 304–5.

3

OVERSIGHT

On January 29, 1997, the South African police's narcotics bureau made a routine drug bust. In a sting operation, they caught a Pretoria cardiologist handing over 1,040 capsules of the drug Ecstasy to a business acquaintance in return for 60,000 rand in cash. The target of the sting, however, was no ordinary cardiologist. He was Dr. Wouter Basson, the former head of South Africa's apartheid-era chemical and biological weapons program, code-named Project Coast. The arrest triggered a series of events that led to the exposure of the sordid history and nefarious activities of the top-secret program. Trafficking in illegal street drugs was only the tip of the iceberg. In hearings before South Africa's Truth and Reconciliation Commission (TRC) and during Basson's two-and-a-half-year criminal trial, startling details emerged about the program. Evidence presented to the TRC and in court revealed massive corruption, blatant deception of the highest levels of the South African government, violations of international law, and other illegal and unethical behavior. South Africa's CBW program, established in 1981, was officially defensive and managed by the Surgeon General, but in reality it was offensive and intimately tied to the military's highly secretive Special Forces Command. The ability of Basson and Project Coast to engage in these activities and hide them from senior officials for as long as they did was due in no small part to the extensive secrecy and compartmentalization that characterized the program.

In this chapter I examine the adverse effects that secrecy can have on the management and oversight of BW programs. The range of pathologies that secrecy can introduce into the decision making and supervision affecting BW programs is illustrated by the Soviet, Russian, and South African programs. In each case, BW organizations turned the secrecy adopted to foil external enemies against civilian leaders perceived as threats to the organization or its managers. Before examining each of these cases, it is worth investigating the incentives that states have for wrapping their BW programs in secrecy, how these states achieve such high levels of secrecy, and the corrosive effects that this secrecy has on oversight.

Motivations for Secrecy

States pursuing biological weapons have normative, legal, and strategic reasons to subject these programs to stringent secrecy. The use of pathogens and poisons in war has long been stigmatized and the subject of international opprobrium.[1] The general revulsion against biological warfare has motivated states to conceal their research into these weapons. In Secretary of War Henry Stimson's April 1942 request to President Franklin D. Roosevelt to launch a BW program, he wrote that biological warfare was a "dirty business" and that "the matter must be handled with great discretion and for the most part with great secrecy."[2] As a British study of CBW policy noted, "in order to avoid provoking the critics of CBW in peacetime, while forearming itself against charges of shortsightedness in case war should find the country unable to retaliate against CBW, a responsible government can hardly be blamed for procuring the weapons but keeping them dark."[3]

Secrecy became even more important for states developing biological weapons after the Biological Weapons Convention was established in 1972. Prior to

---

1. Leonard A. Cole, "The Poison Weapons Taboo: Biology, Culture, and Policy," *Politics and the Life Sciences* 17, no. 2, (1998): 119–32; and John Ellis van Courtland Moon, "Controlling Chemical and Biological Weapons through World War II," in *Encyclopedia of Arms Control and Disarmament*, vol. 2, ed. Richard Burns (New York: Scribner's Sons, 1993), 657–74.

2. Barton J. Bernstein, "America's Biological Warfare Program in the Second World War," *Journal of Strategic Studies* 11, no. 3 (1988): 294.

3. United Kingdom Foreign Office, Arms Control and Disarmament Research Unit, "The Arms Control Implications of Chemical and Biological Weapons: Analysis and Proposals," ACDRU 66(2), 2d draft, July 4, 1966, p. 25, FO 371/187448, National Archives, Kew, United Kingdom.

the advent of the BWC, the only controlling international legal authority for biological weapons was the 1925 Geneva Protocol. The protocol, however, outlaws only the *use* of chemical and biological weapons. Even this prohibition is not absolute, in that many states reserved the right to retaliate in kind if an opponent violated the treaty first. By prohibiting the development, production, stockpiling, or acquisition of biological weapons, the BWC outlawed an entire class of weapons and reinforced the long-standing norm against use of these weapons. Although the treaty lacks verification or enforcement measures, its widespread adoption (175 parties and signatories as of July 2008) raises the political costs for a state if it is discovered to have a BW program. Since the treaty's entry into force, no government has openly proclaimed their development or production of biological weapons.

Finally, there is a strategic motivation for wrapping BW programs in secrecy. Biological weapons, like certain other military capabilities, favors the attacker and relies on surprise for effectiveness. The premium for secrecy arises from the availability of countermeasures against specific biological agents and the potential for an adversary to create new countermeasures.

Regimes of Secrecy

Although all military programs are subject to some level of secrecy to prevent adversaries from learning about capabilities and vulnerabilities, the secrecy surrounding BW programs has been unusually high. One of the primary means of achieving this secrecy has been through compartmentalization. Limiting access to sensitive information through classification or the principle of "need to know" reduces the risk that such information will fall into the wrong hands (either intentionally or inadvertently). The Soviet Union and South Africa established elaborate secrecy regimes to prevent outsiders from learning about their BW programs. These regimes were abused by program managers to shield their activities, not just from foreigners, but from their own political leaders.

Those who have studied the Soviet BW program cannot help but be impressed by its devotion to secrecy. According to a trio of *New York Times* reporters, "the program had been a deliberate maze of false fronts, secret projects, and parallel organizations that often conducted both military and peaceful research. The structure was designed to enhance secrecy."[4] The ability of Biopreparat to stay so secret for as long as it did was in part because the organization was subject

---

4. Judith Miller, Stephen Engelberg, and William Broad, *Germs: Biological Weapons and America's Secret War* (New York: Simon and Schuster, 2001), 222.

to strict need-to-know compartmentalization and was monitored by Soviet intelligence officers. The BW program was conducted under the highest security classification in the Soviet system, even higher than the nuclear weapons program.[5] These elaborate security measures stemmed in part from the close association of the BW program with the Soviet internal security services.[6] According to one former high-level participant, the Soviet BW program had been "plunged into the deepest possible obscurity since its inception."[7]

Like a *matryoshka,* a Russian nesting doll, the Soviet BW program relied on multiple levels of secrecy that controlled access to increasingly sensitive information. At the first level, the "open legend" was that there was no BW program and that the agency's research on genetic engineering and biotechnology was completely civilian. To provide some legitimacy to this legend, at the same time that the Soviets created Biopreparat they also issued a public decree on enhancing the development of molecular biology and genetics. The decree created the Interdepartmental Science and Technology Council for Molecular Biology and Genetics at the USSR Academy of Sciences to oversee its implementation. Yuri Ovchinnikov, a molecular biologist and vice president of the Soviet Academy of Sciences, headed this council. Ovchinnikov also served on the secret Interagency Science and Technology Council for Molecular Biology and Genetics that served as the nerve center for the Soviet effort to apply these emerging technologies to biological weapons. At the second level, there was a "closed legend" that explained that Soviet research was strictly defensive and the purpose was to produce vaccines and antibiotics. This closed legend was also false, but it was supported by the existence of a biological defense program called Problem No. 5. Soviet civilian microbiological institutes had been engaged in Problem No. 5 since at least the 1950s, but by the 1970s this project was being used as a smokescreen for offensive research.[8] At the third level, the offensive nature of the research was acknowledged. However, this research on dangerous

5. Tom Mangold and Jeff Goldberg, *Plague Wars: The Terrifying Reality of Biological Warfare* (New York: St. Martin's Press, 1999), 65, 182.

6. From its beginning in the 1920s, the Soviet BW program was under the supervision of the internal security agencies. Even after the BW program was transferred from the KGB to the Ministry of Defense, the KGB continued to play a key role in providing security for the program and conducting oversight over some of its activities. Valentin Bojtzov and Erhard Geissler, "Military Biology in the USSR, 1920–1945," in *Biological and Toxin Weapons: Research, Development and Use from the Middle Ages to 1945,* ed. Erhard Geissler and John Ellis van Courtland Moon (Oxford: Oxford University Press, 1999), 153–67; Ken Alibek, *Biohazard: The Chilling True Story of the Largest Covert Biological Weapons Program in the World— Told from the Inside by the Man Who Ran It,* with Stephen Handelman (New York: Random House, 1999), 33–35, 92–93; and Anthony Rimmington, "The Soviet Union's Offensive Program," in *Biological Warfare and Disarmament,* ed. Susan Wright (Lanham, MD: Rowman and Littlefield, 2002), 113–15, 122–23.

7. Igor V. Domaradskij and Wendy Orent, *Biowarrior: Inside the Soviet/Russian Biological War Machine* (Amherst, NY: Prometheus Books, 2003), 135.

8. Domaradskij and Orent, *Biowarrior,* 111, 151.

pathogens was justified as an investigation of the potential threat posed by the U.S. BW program.[9] Only the managers and senior scientists at civilian institutes would have access to this information.[10] At the fourth level, the purpose of specific projects, such as the creation of genetically modified biological weapons and the interconnections between projects was revealed.[11] Each project had its own code name, and access to information was based on a need-to-know basis. As a result, scientists and managers in one ministry were usually not aware of related activities in other ministries. At the fifth and highest level of security, available only to the most senior members of the directorates and ministries involved in the BW program, was a full description of the entire BW program as laid out in the Five-Year Plan. The information contained in the document was classified as Special Importance, which was even more restricted than Top Secret. Only ten to twelve people in the entire Soviet government were authorized to see this document. For example, within Biopreparat, only Yuriy Kalinin, the director, and Kanatjan Alibekov (Ken Alibek), the first deputy, had access to it.[12]

South Africa's CBW program, code-named Project Coast, was shrouded in secrecy from its inception. The program was established in 1981 by the South African Defense Force (SADF) as part of South Africa's response to the perceived "total onslaught" by communists and black Africans against the white-ruled nation. At the time, South Africa was not only a party to both the 1925 Geneva Protocol and the 1972 Biological Weapons Convention but it was also subject to a United Nations arms embargo and strong international criticism for its apartheid policy. As a result of these considerations, Project Coast was cloaked in secrecy and structured in a highly compartmentalized fashion in order to minimize the risk that SADF could be linked to the development of chemical and biological weapons.[13]

South Africa established two front companies to conceal the military's involvement in CBW research, development, and production: Delta G Scientific, for research and production of chemical agents and weapons, and Roodeplaat Research Laboratory (RRL), for research on toxins and biological agents.[14]

---

9. Interview with Serguei Popov, Manassas, Virginia, July 25, 2002.

10. Domaradskij and Orent, "The Memoirs of an Inconvenient Man," *Critical Reviews in Microbiology* 27, no. 4 (2001): 251; and Jonathan B. Tucker, *Scourge: The Once and Future Threat of Smallpox* (New York: Atlantic Monthly Press, 2001), 151.

11. Interview with Serguei Popov, Manassas, Virginia, July 25, 2002.

12. Interview with Ken Alibek, Manassas, Virginia, November 16, 2004.

13. The secrecy, compartmentalization, and autonomy that characterized Project Coast was similar to that enjoyed by South Africa's covert special operation forces. The links between Project Coast and these units reinforced the need for secrecy and plausible deniability.

14. Project Coast established a range of other front companies to provide ancillary services to the program such as administrative support, security, testing, physiological research, and research on protective clothing materials.

RRL's cover story was that it was a contract research facility in the fields of biology, medicine, pharmacology, and veterinary medicine. Scientists at RRL conducted some peaceful research in these areas to sustain this cover.[15] In addition to disguising the CBW program, the use of front companies also provided the scientists with free access to the international scientific community, facilitated the recruitment of top-level scientists whom they could offer higher salaries, and assisted with the procurement of dual-use material from abroad.

Since Project Coast was as highly classified as the nuclear weapons program and covert units of Special Forces, the program was heavily compartmentalized at all levels. The principle of "need-to-know" was strictly applied at even the highest levels of South Africa's political-military leadership. The Defense Command Council, the structure that connected the minister of defense and the chief of SADF, did not meet as a whole to discuss these programs. Instead, the Reduced Defense Command Council, composed only of officials with the requisite need to know, met after a meeting of the whole council. The next layer of oversight was the Coordinating Management Committee (CMC), composed of high-ranking military officers, which was supposed to supervise the budget and direction of Project Coast. But the CMC met to discuss budgetary issues and reported to the minister of defense only once a year.[16] Responsibility for day-to-day management of Project Coast was officially lodged with Surgeon General Daniel P. Knobel as the program manager, but in reality it was exercised by Wouter Basson as the project officer. According to Knobel, Basson reported to the CMC on the progress of Project Coast toward objectives established by the CMC only in broad terms. This was said to be because the members of the CMC did not have the scientific knowledge or background to address the technical details of the project.[17]

Civilian employees at RRL and Delta G were reportedly ignorant of the sponsor and purpose of their research and believed that they worked at a legitimate private research institute. Scientists worked under strict secrecy regulations and were not supposed to talk among themselves about their project. In addition, scientists were not allowed to know how the results of their research were to be used. The microbiologist in charge of culturing organisms at RRL never knew what happened to the pathogens he turned over to the head of his

15. About 15% of RRL's projects were commercial with the results published in professional journals. Chandré Gould and Peter Folb, *Project Coast: Apartheid's Chemical and Biological Warfare Programme* (Geneva: United Nations, 2002), 72.

16. The lack of minutes of CMC meetings after 1988 raises doubts about whether the group met after this date. E-mail communication with Chandré Gould, November 30, 2004.

17. Marléne Burger and Chandré Gould, *Secrets and Lies: Wouter Basson and South Africa's Chemical and Biological Warfare Programme* (Cape Town, S. A.: Zebra Press, 2002), 13, 20; and Gould and Folb, *Project Coast,* 169–73.

department, who secretly served as RRL's liaison with various clandestine military and paramilitary units.[18]

Corrosive Effects of Secrecy

The intense secrecy that shrouds BW programs obstructs civilian oversight and distorts decision making by military and political leaders.[19] The strict compartmentalization that is a central feature of secrecy restricts the information available to senior officials about the nature and conduct of these programs and limits the range and knowledge of participants involved in such oversight. This compartmentalization exacerbates the existing information asymmetries between political leaders and the military officers or scientists who run BW programs. According to principal-agent theory, large information asymmetries enable subordinates such as military officials or program managers to take actions for the benefit of themselves or their organization that are against the interests of their superiors. Secrecy also makes it more difficult for overseers to detect such behavior or hold responsible officials accountable.[20]

These problems are particularly acute for organizations that already operate under a high degree of secrecy and compartmentalization for security reasons. National security organizations have a noted tendency to use secrecy to increase their autonomy.[21] In addition, the overlap between offensive, defensive, and civilian biological activities facilitates the establishment of BW programs in ostensibly civilian institutions or outside the traditional military chain of command in order to shield the true nature of the program.[22] Such arrangements involve an implicit trade-off in favor of maintaining secrecy at the expense of exercising effective oversight.

The stigma surrounding biological weapons can also discourage policymakers from exercising proper oversight. In announcing the results of a review of U.S. CBW programs in 1969, President Nixon stated, "This has been the first

18. Gould and Folb, *Project Coast,* 7, 58, 72; Burger and Gould, *Secrets and Lies,* 25, 29; and Mangold and Goldberg, *Plague Wars,* 239.

19. The literature on opaque nuclear proliferation has observed similar effects among states with covert nuclear weapons programs. Avner Cohen and Benjamin Frankel, "Opaque Proliferation," *Journal of Strategic Studies* 13, no. 3 (1990): 22, 34; and Peter Feaver, "Proliferation Optimism and Theories of Nuclear Operations," *Security Studies* 2, no. 3/4 (1993): 175–78.

20. Peter D. Feaver, *Armed Servants: Agency, Oversight, and Civil-Military Relations* (Cambridge: Harvard University Press, 2003), 68–71.

21. Barry Posen, *The Sources of Military Doctrine: France, Britain, and Germany between the World Wars* (Ithaca: Cornell University Press, 1984), 45.

22. Gregory Koblentz, "Countering Dual-Use Facilities: Lessons from Iraq and Sudan," *Jane's Intelligence Review* 11, no. 3 (1999): 48–53.

thorough review ever undertaken of this subject at the Presidential level....I recall during the eight years that I sat on the National Security Council in the Eisenhower Administration that these subjects, insofar as an appraisal of what the United States had, what our capability was, what other nations had, were really considered taboo."[23]

As a result of these factors, programs escape review, decisions by national leaders are made with incomplete or inaccurate information, and the exercise of appropriate civilian oversight is hindered. Secrecy also allows BW organizations to achieve a high degree of autonomy and self-sufficiency that increases the risk that subordinates will avoid accountability by concealing damaging information, obstructing the implementation of policies they disagree with, and engaging in illegal or unethical behavior. Such behavior can hinder, or even prevent, governments from complying with international arms control obligations, which increases the risks of proliferation. Secrecy allowed BW program managers and scientists in the Soviet Union, Russia, and South Africa to engage in corruption, insubordination, and proliferation.

Soviet Union

By the 1980s the Soviet BW program was the largest and most advanced in the world with 65,000 personnel at over sixty research, development, production, and testing facilities sponsored by the Ministries of Defense, Agriculture, Health, and Medical and Microbiological Industries as well as the Soviet Academy of Sciences and the KGB.[24] One of the major components of the program was the quasi-civilian agency, Biopreparat, that was tasked with conducting research and development on new agents; improving methods of agent production, storage, and dissemination; and maintaining mobilization facilities for the mass production of BW agents. Although Biopreparat's management drew heavily from the military and its only customer was the Ministry of Defense, it enjoyed "virtually autonomous authority" as the principal organization for Soviet antipersonnel BW research and development.[25]

---

23. "Remarks of the President on Announcing the Chemical and Biological Defense Policies and Programs," Office of the White House Press Secretary, The White House, November 25, 1969, National Security Council Subject Files. Box 310; folder 5: Chemical, Biological Warfare (Toxins, etc.) vol. 1, p. 1, Nixon Presidential Materials, National Archives, College Park, Maryland.

24. Alibek, *Biohazard,* 310–13; and Amy Smithson, *Toxic Archipelago: Preventing Proliferation from the Former Soviet Chemical and Biological Weapons Complexes* (Washington, DC: Henry L. Stimson Center, 1999), 9.

25. Alibek, *Biohazard,* 298.

In the late 1980s, President Mikhail Gorbachev and Foreign Minister Eduard Shevardnadze attempted to rein in the Soviet BW program and make it more transparent. This effort was part of their broader initiative to ease tensions with the West and reduce the burden of defense spending on the Soviet economy.[26] They experienced serious problems in obtaining accurate information from the military regarding BW activities, making informed decisions about the future of the program, ensuring the implementation of new policies, and earning the trust of their U.S. and British counterparts. These problems were due in large part to the program's extreme level of compartmentalization and the autonomy that it enjoyed within the Soviet system.

This compartmentalization severely restricted the range of political actors who were knowledgeable about the Soviet BW program. Only members of the senior leadership who were directly responsible for agencies involved in the program and provided funding were fully briefed on the program. In the late 1980s, this small coterie reportedly included President Gorbachev, KGB chairman Vladimir Kryuchkov, Defense Minister Dmitry Yazov, and Lev Zaikov, the Politburo member responsible for military industries.[27] This compartmentalization also excluded regional Communist Party leaders whose jurisdictions included BW facilities. At the time of the 1979 anthrax outbreak in Sverdlovsk, the regional Communist Party leader, Boris Yeltsin, was unaware of the existence of the military BW facility responsible for the outbreak.[28] This compartmentalization not only prevented significant penetration of the program by foreign intelligence agencies but also shielded the program from internal scrutiny. At first, information about the BW program was withheld from other agencies within the Soviet government, but eventually BW officials began misleading even their civilian leaders in the Kremlin to protect their program. These lies and distortions made it difficult for Gorbachev and Shevardnadze to engage in arms control with the United States and United Kingdom and to be seen as reliable negotiating partners.

---

26. On the struggle of Gorbachev and Shevardnadze to impose greater civilian control over the military and the defense industrial complex, see Carolyn M. Ekedahl and Melvin A. Goodman, *The Wars of Eduard Shevardnadze* (University Park: Pennsylvania State University Press, 1997); and William C. Green and Theodore Karasik, eds., *Gorbachev and His Generals: The Reform of Soviet Military Doctrine* (Boulder, CO: Westview Press, 1990).

27. Alibek, *Biohazard,* 149–50; and Mangold and Goldberg, *Plague Wars,* 183. The ministers of health and agriculture may also have been included in this select group since these ministries were also part of the Soviet BW program.

28. When he became president Yeltsin publicly acknowledged, for the first time, the responsibility of a military facility for the outbreak. R. Jeffrey Smith, "Yeltsin Blames '79 Anthrax on Germ Warfare Efforts," *Washington Post,* June 16, 1992, A1.

Compartmentalization Undermined Diplomacy

In January 1987 the Soviet Union created an interagency commission to co-ordinate its responses to external requests for information relating to its BW program. Throughout the 1980s, the United States sought additional information from Moscow regarding the 1979 anthrax outbreak in Sverdlovsk and facilities suspected of being part of the Soviet BW program.[29] In addition, the commission was charged with preparing a declaration on BW-related facilities that was required by a new confidence-building measure adopted at the second review conference of the BWC in 1986. The commission was chaired by the Ministry of Foreign Affairs, and its members included the deputy ministers of the Ministries of Defense, Health, and Agriculture, as well as representatives of the military's 15th Main Directorate, Military-Industrial Commission, Soviet Academy of Sciences, and Biopreparat. Through 1990 the responses drafted by the commission denied that the Soviet Union was engaged in offensive biological warfare or that the 1979 Sverdlovsk anthrax outbreak was caused by anything other than tainted meat.[30] Ministry of Foreign Affairs officials, including the deputy foreign minister who chaired the commission, were never told about the existence of the Soviet BW program.[31] According to Alibek, even Politburo member and foreign minister Eduard Shevardnadze was not privy to this information.[32] A former Soviet disarmament diplomat, however, believes that Shevardnadze's status as a Politburo member gave him access to all of the relevant information on the BW program.[33]

Western governments believed that Shevardnadze must be knowledgeable about the Soviet BW program by dint of his status as a member of the Politburo, an assumption that cast a shadow over their dealings with the Soviet foreign ministry. The British government received reports from two separate sources that Shevardnadze had chaired high-level meetings in 1988 and 1990 that had approved Biopreparat's plans and budget. These revelations created serious

---

29. Between 1984 and 1989, Washington submitted six demarches to Moscow regarding suspected Soviet violations of the BWC. Senate Committee on Governmental Affairs and Permanent Subcommittee on Investigations, *Global Spread of Chemical and Biological Weapons,* 101st Cong., 1st sess., May 17, 1988, 184.

30. Interview with former Soviet Ministry of Foreign Affairs official, 2000 (where date and location are not included with interview information it is to protect the confidentiality of the source); and Alibek, *Biohazard,* 146–48, 151.

31. The diplomats, however, were not completely naive. A former Soviet diplomat in the disarmament department admitted that although he did not "officially" know about the nature of the Soviet BW program, he was aware of it through unofficial channels. Interview with former Soviet Ministry of Foreign Affairs official. See also ibid., 151.

32. Alibek, *Biohazard,* 146.

33. Interview with former Soviet Ministry of Foreign Affairs official.

doubts among senior arms control officials in the George H. W. Bush administration about Shevardnadze's trustworthiness. A former State Department official said, "Frankly, the US did not know what Gorbachev and Shevardnadze were hearing behind the scenes in their own government. Initially, in 1990, it seemed that Gorbachev and Shevardnadze were lying to us. We believed they knew about the BW program. But we were just guessing."[34] Information gathered later, however, strongly suggested that Shevardnadze's meetings with military officials regarding the BW program were attempts by Shevardnadze to discover what the military was doing and how it was spending its money. Based on long-standing Ministry of Defense policy to keep the foreign ministry out of the loop on biological weapons, Shevardnadze was not in a position to approve the program or have any influence over it.[35]

Although this conclusion assuaged worries in Washington about Shevardnadze's sincerity and honesty, it raised the equally troubling implication that the Soviet political leadership did not have complete control over the military and the BW program. The Soviet response to the defection of Vladimir Pasechnik, a high-ranking BW scientist, to the United Kingdom in October 1989 and subsequent Anglo-American pressure on the Kremlin to address BWC compliance issues illustrates that Western concerns about the Kremlin's control over the BW program were well founded.

The Military Misleads the Kremlin

The defection of Pasechnik was a major blow to the secrecy of the Soviet BW project, especially the portion managed by Biopreparat. Pasechnik had been in charge of three research institutes and two manufacturing plants under Biopreparat, and he served on Biopreparat's board of directors, which afforded him an overview of the highly compartmentalized and classified program.[36] As a result of his revelations, British and U.S. intelligence agencies doubled their estimates of the number of Soviet BW facilities.[37] More important, the West had obtained for the first time direct evidence of massive and long-standing Soviet violations of the BWC, including the application of genetic engineering to biological weapons. The quantity and quality of Pasechnik's information allowed

---

34. Cited in Mangold and Goldberg, *Plague Wars,* 108.

35. Ibid., 111–13.

36. James Adams, *The New Spies: Exploring the Frontiers of Espionage* (London: Hutchinson, 1994), 272–73; and Simon Cooper, "Life in the Pursuit of Death," *Seed* 4 (January/February 2003): 104.

37. Bill Gertz, "Defecting Russian Scientist Revealed Biological Arms Efforts," *Washington Times,* July 4, 1992, A4; and R. Jeffrey Smith, "Russia Fails to Detail Germ Arms," *Washington Post,* August 31, 1992, A1.

Washington and London to place Soviet compliance with the BWC higher on the diplomatic agenda and provided them with more ammunition to use in their diplomacy.

The defection of Pasechnik also marked the beginning of the Soviet military's efforts to deceive the civilian leadership in the Kremlin. In an attempt to limit the internal political fallout from the defection, the military sent a memo to Gorbachev minimizing the seriousness of the incident and the security risk posed by the defection. On April 30, 1990, the United States and the United Kingdom presented a joint demarche based on information supplied by Pasechnik regarding Soviet violations of the BWC to Anatoly Chernyaev, Gorbachev's senior foreign policy adviser. On May 2, 1990, U.S. Secretary of State James Baker followed up with a memo to Shevardnadze laying out in more detail the information that the United States had on Soviet violations of the BWC. After reading the document, Shevardnadze appeared shocked. He said he "didn't think they could be doing that" and promised to respond to Baker as soon as possible. As a result of these demarches, Gen. Yuriy Kalinin, the head of Biopreparat, was asked to prepare a response for the Kremlin. Based on what it was believed Pasechnik would be able to tell the British, Kalinin and his staff decided that the best strategy was to continue denying any wrongdoing. The one-page memo Kalinin sent to Gorbachev stated that the Soviet Union was not in violation of the BWC and had only a defensive program that worked on vaccines and tested defensive equipment.[38] The lie that had served the military so well for use against the Americans now also served a new role: deceiving the leadership in the Kremlin.

Perhaps sensing that the Pasechnik defection would give the West the leverage they needed to force Gorbachev and Shevardnadze to put pressure on the biological weapons program, Kalinin and his allies in the military also sought to further insulate the program from civilian oversight. On May 5, 1990, Gorbachev issued a secret decree halting the research, development, and testing activities of Biopreparat, effectively ending its role in offensive biological warfare. The formulation of the decree, however, had been manipulated by Kalinin to preserve as much of the program as possible. The final decree included a loophole inserted by Kalinin that allowed the continued funding of the full range of Biopreparat's activities. The final paragraph instructed Biopreparat "to organize the necessary work to keep all of its facilities prepared for further manufacture and development." These production facilities would be retained as mobilization plants in the event that a "special period" was declared prior to a war. Although the directors of Biopreparat's institutes knew of the decree's

---

38. Mangold and Goldberg, *Plague Wars,* 106–8, 415 n. 10.

existence, Kalinin withheld its text from them. As a result, the directors were unable to implement the decree without guidance from headquarters, which Kalinin was unwilling to provide.[39] Alibek, who by this time had grown disillusioned with the Soviet BW program, claims that he was able to use the decree to close the Soviet's largest explosive aerosol test chamber, located at Stepnogorsk, and to convert some buildings at Vector to civilian use. He also learned, however, that Vector continued to build a new viral-agent production plant and that Biopreparat continued to develop railcars for use as mobile BW agent production plants.[40] In effect, the decree allowed Gorbachev to believe that he had terminated the offensive program while imposing only limited constraint's on Biopreparat's activities. More important, the decree further complicated oversight of the program by civilians in the Kremlin.[41]

In response to continued Anglo-American diplomatic pressure to resolve concerns regarding Soviet compliance with the BWC, the Soviets agreed in August 1990 to allow an Anglo-American team to visit four Biopreparat sites.[42] Behind the scenes, Biopreparat was busily preparing for the inspections by hiding or sanitizing as much evidence as possible of its role in the development of biological weapons. Following the Anglo-American visit in January 1991, Biopreparat reported to the Kremlin that although the visitors had seen enough to be suspicious, they had found no evidence of an offensive program and couldn't prove anything. In fact, the Anglo-American team had seen enough to conclude that the Soviet Union had a massive offensive program run by Biopreparat and the Ministry of Defense. The team had uncovered evidence of research on variola (the virus that causes smallpox), genetic engineering of dangerous pathogens, explosive aerosol testing for munition development, and a large-scale capability to produce pathogens far in excess of legitimate civilian or defensive needs.[43]

Gorbachev's Reliability as Arms Control Partner

Concerns similar to those that dogged Shevardnadze were raised in Washington and London regarding the reliability of Gorbachev as an arms control partner. Within the British government, Prime Minister Margaret Thatcher believed that Gorbachev's desire to end the BW program was sincere and that he was being

---

39. Alibek, *Biohazard*, 187–91; and Mangold and Goldberg, *Plague Wars*, 417 n. 20.

40. Alibek also claims that under this decree, the production lines at Omutninsk, Berdsk, Stepnogorsk, Kurgan, and Penza were destroyed. Alibek, *Biohazard*, 190–91, 263.

41. Mangold and Goldberg, *Plague Wars*, 109–10, 417 n. 20; Alibek, *Biohazard*, 190–91.

42. The sites selected were the Institute of Ultra-Pure Biological Preparations in Leningrad, the Scientific-Research Institute of Applied Microbiology in Obolensk, the Scientific-Research Institute of Molecular Biology (Vector) in Koltsovo, and the Institute of Immunology in Lyubuchany near Moscow.

43. Alibek, *Biohazard*, 204; and Mangold and Goldberg, *Plague Wars*, 113–14, 138–40.

deceived by his generals. Sir Percy Cradock, then chairman of Britain's Joint Intelligence Committee, thought that was as likely as Thatcher being deceived by her generals.[44] He believed that the program was so large that Gorbachev would have to have known about it and known that it was not defensive.[45]

Shortly after the failed Kremlin coup in August 1991, British Prime Minister John Major reportedly confronted Gorbachev on the Soviet BW program. Instead of denying the existence of an offensive program as he had done before, Gorbachev blamed the coup plotters, including Minister of Defense Dmitry Yazov, for misleading him about the true nature of the program. Gorbachev also promised to get to the bottom of it and establish mutual confidence with the West. On November 18, 1991, the Kremlin informed the British ambassador to Moscow that an order had been issued to terminate the Soviet BW program. But by this time officials in Washington and London believed that Gorbachev was too weak to take effective action anyway.[46]

It remains unclear how much Gorbachev knew about the offensive program and how hard he tried to halt and roll back the program. Alibek claims that Gorbachev belonged to the small circle of senior officials who were fully informed about the Soviet offensive program and that he has seen Gorbachev's signature on key documents authorizing offensive activities.[47] On the other hand, Gorbachev also authorized measures in the 1980s to eliminate some aspects of the biological weapons program such as a BW agent production plant at Sverdlovsk and a large stockpile of *B. anthracis* that had been produced at Sverdlovsk.[48] Whether the intent of these measures was to roll back the offensive program or simply to hide it better from inspectors is unknown. When asked in a 1995 interview if he had been deceived by his generals on the issue of chemical and biological weapons, Gorbachev replied that these men had been "in no great hurry to introduce conversion [to civilian production], rather they preferred to preserve their military industrial complex." However, he added, that ultimately they had followed his lead on arms control.[49] This response implies that Gorbachev was aware of the military's resistance to his efforts to reduce and open up the offensive program, but he had limited power to compel their compliance.

44. Mark Urban, *UK Eyes Alpha: Inside British Intelligence* (London: Faber and Faber, 1996), 132–33.

45. Mangold and Goldberg, *Plague Wars,* 108.

46. Adams, *New Spies,* 277; and Mangold and Goldberg, *Plague Wars,* 141–42.

47. Alibek, *Biohazard,* 117, 145, 150.

48. Alibek, *Biohazard,* 263; and Paul Quinn-Judge, "The Breeding of Death," *Time,* February 16, 1998. The stockpile of *B. anthracis* spores, estimated at between one hundred and two hundred tons, was transferred to Vozrozhdeniya Island in 1988 for sterilization and burial. Judith Miller, "At Bleak Asian Site, Killer Germs Survive," *New York Times,* June 2, 1999, A1; Miller, Engelberg, and Broad, *Germs,* 178, 352n; and Jonathan B. Tucker, "Biological Weapons in the Former Soviet Union: An Interview with Dr. Kenneth Alibek," *Nonproliferation Review* 6, no. 3 (1999): 6.

49. Urban, *UK Eyes Alpha,* 134.

The misleading reports sent to Gorbachev regarding Pasechnik's defection and the results of the Anglo-American visit to Biopreparat sites, as well as the subterfuge to resist Gorbachev's May 5, 1990, decree, indicate that the military and Biopreparat perceived Gorbachev's desire to halt, if not roll back, the offensive program as genuine. It appears that Gorbachev played a two-level game. He persisted in denying the existence of an offensive program to the West to avoid embarrassment and a confrontation with the military while he and Shevardnadze engaged in a bureaucratic struggle to rein in the offensive program.

According to Jack Matlock, U.S. ambassador to Moscow from 1987 to 1991, "from their behavior, I think the people at the top [in the Kremlin] probably did not know everything. There is plenty of evidence that shows these people were not able to get the information they wanted, because the system was so secret and the political authorities had so little control over the military and KGB. And they had no reliable way to check up on the information they did get."[50] Biopreparat and the Soviet military took advantage of the intense secrecy surrounding the BW program, and the autonomy it offered, to shield it not only from foreigners but also from perceived domestic interlopers.

Russia

After the collapse of the Soviet Union, Russian president Boris Yeltsin encountered the same problems as Gorbachev and Shevardnadze in their bid to dismantle the BW program. Although Yeltsin declared his resolve to bring Russia into compliance with the BWC and cooperate with the West, he faced great difficulties implementing these pledges.

Soon after entering office, Yeltsin took the diplomatic offensive by publicly acknowledging past violations of the BWC, promising to halt such activities, and vowing "rigorous implementation" of the BWC.[51] Privately, however, Yeltsin also told U.S. and British officials that his office was having trouble penetrating the secrecy that surrounded the program and that he was still being deceived by the military. Yeltsin called the generals in charge of the BW program "fanatics" and "misguided geniuses."[52]

During his first meeting with President George H. W. Bush in February 1992, Yeltsin told him, "We are still deceiving you, Mr. Bush. We promised to eliminate bacteriological weapons. But some of our experts did everything possible

---

50. Quoted in ibid., 109.
51. Mangold and Goldberg, *Plague Wars,* 158–59.
52. Quoted in Ibid. See also James A. Baker III, *The Politics of Diplomacy: Revolution, War, and Peace, 1989–1992* (New York: Putnam, 1995), 621.

to prevent me from learning the truth. It was not easy but I outfoxed them."[53] Yeltsin explained the program was so compartmentalized that there were few knowledgeable officials, even fewer who were forthcoming, and that the military continued to hide certain facilities. These impediments forced Yeltsin to repeatedly extend the amount of time he told Western leaders was necessary to dismantle the former Soviet program.[54]

The Military Misleads the Kremlin

Furthermore, the British learned in early 1992 from sources in Moscow that the military and Biopreparat remained committed to continuing the BW program and were lying to Yeltsin in order to justify the program. In December 1991 the Soviet Union had dispatched a team to visit former offensive and current defensive BW sites in the United States as part of a reciprocal confidence-building exercise. By the time the team returned to Moscow, the Soviet Union had been replaced by Russia and fourteen other independent states. In order to ensure the continuation of their program, Biopreparat and military officials reported to the Kremlin that their visit had uncovered evidence that the United States continued to maintain a BW program, including mothballed production and testing facilities. Therefore, the 15th Main Directorate, the organization within the Ministry of Defense responsible for the BW program, recommended that Russia's offensive program should continue.

In fact, there was no such evidence and the outcome of the visit had been preordained. Both General Valentin Yevstigneev, head of the 15th Main Directorate, and Yuriy Kalinin, head of Biopreparat, told members of the team before their departure to find evidence of a U.S. BW program—or else.[55] The mothballed facilities were in fact the abandoned remnants of the United States' former offensive program.[56] The testing facility highlighted in the report to the Kremlin was a one-million liter spherical aerosol test chamber, called the Eight Ball, that had not been used since 1969 and whose surrounding wooden structure had burned down long ago. The decrepit nature of the former offensive sites, the limited size of the defensive facilities, and the openness of the U.S. scientists convinced one of the team members, Ken Alibek, that the United States no longer had an offensive program. As a result, he defected to the United

---

53. M. Zahkarov, "A Visit with the President," *Izvestiya*, April 22, 1992, in JPRS-TND-92-104 (Washington, DC: Joint Publications Research Service, May 4, 1992).

54. Mangold and Goldberg, *Plague Wars*, 158–60.

55. Ibid., 157, 160–61; and Alibek, *Biohazard*, 227, 242–43.

56. David C. Kelly, "The Trilateral Agreement: Lessons for Biological Weapons Verification," in *Verification Yearbook 2002*, ed. Trevor Findlay and Oliver Meier (London: VERTIC, 2002), 96.

States later that year and revealed the full extent of the former Soviet BW program and the struggle for its survival in Russia.[57]

Throughout 1992 the military succeeded in undermining Yeltsin's major efforts to increase civilian control over the former BW program, to make it more transparent, and to cooperate with Anglo-American efforts to verify Russian compliance with the BWC. On February 28, Yeltsin announced the creation of the Committee on the Convention Problems of Chemical and Biological Weapons to implement Russia's commitments not to develop, produce, or stockpile these weapons. While on paper this was a promising development, reliable sources in the Russian foreign ministry warned the British that the military still controlled decision making on BW issues and was seeking to hijack the committee.[58] Indeed, the membership of the committee left much to be desired and caused a great deal of concern in Washington and London. Retired army general Anatoly Kuntsevich, who served as a presidential adviser on chemical and biological disarmament, was appointed chairman of the committee. One of his deputies was General Yevstigneev. These generals were old-guard conservatives who had been at the forefront of Soviet efforts to secretly develop new chemical and biological weapons in contravention of international treaties.[59]

On April 11 Yeltsin took his most significant step to date in bringing Russia into compliance with the BWC. The Kremlin issued Edict 390, "On Ensuring the Implementation of International Obligations Regarding Biological Weapons," which prohibited all biological warfare activities on Russian territory that violated the BWC. The decree also placed the Committee on Convention Problems of Chemical and Biological Weapons under the office of the president to oversee the fulfillment of the requirements of the decree and international treaty obligations. Although this decree codified the BWC's prohibition against development, production, and stockpiling of biological weapons, it did not regulate research or defensive activities. The British Joint Intelligence Committee

---

57. Mangold and Goldberg, *Plague Wars,* 149–51, 193–94.

58. Ibid., 160–61.

59. Kuntsevich had been an architect of the Soviet CW program that continued developing new agents even after Gorbachev announced the termination of all offensive CW research in 1987. He was awarded a Lenin Prize in 1991 for supervising the development of a new binary chemical nerve agent designed to circumvent the forthcoming Chemical Weapons Convention. Adams, *New Spies,* 280; and Mangold and Goldberg, *Plague Wars,* 162. In April 1994 Kuntsevich was fired from his post as chairman of the committee due to "numerous and gross violations" of his duties, including allegations that he sold CW precursors to Syria. In November 1995 he was sanctioned by the United States for engaging in CW proliferation activities. R. Jeffrey Smith, "U.S. Officials Allege That Russians Are Working on Biological Arms," *Washington Post,* April 8, 1994, A28; Sergei Shargorodsky, "Former Chemical Weapons Chief Investigated for Chemical Smuggling," *Associated Press,* October 23, 1995; and Department of State, "Imposition of Chemical and Biological Weapons Proliferation Sanctions on a Foreign Person," *Federal Register* 60, no. 234 (1995): 62526–27.

later concluded that the Russian military was circumventing the decree by classifying all of its ongoing offensive scientific research as "defensive." The generals reportedly argued to the Kremlin that the defensive research was necessary in case Russia was ever attacked from the west by NATO or from the east by China.[60] As Alibek observed after his defection, "after Yeltsin signed a decree in April 1992 to stop all offensive biological work, suddenly all [of the] offensive biological facilities overnight became defensive facilities. And, you know, dozens of thousands of people who were involved in offensive programs became expert in defensive issues."[61]

Russia as Unreliable Biological Arms Control Partner

In late April 1992, Russia shared with the United States and United Kingdom its draft declaration on past and present BW activities as required by a BWC confidence-building measure. In a presentation to U.S. and British officials, Deputy Foreign Minister Grigoriy Berdennikov tried to put a positive spin on the document: the declaration admitted that the Soviet Union had violated the BWC and pledged that all such work had been halted. Berdennikov also told the officials that producing the document had been difficult due to the resistance of the military, which did not want to disclose any previous offensive activity, and the inability of the Ministry of Foreign Affairs and Yeltsin's civilian advisers to acquire accurate information.[62]

The Russian declaration acknowledged that an offensive BW program had been maintained from 1946 to March 1992.[63] The declaration claimed that munition development never proceeded past the prototype stage and that no biological weapons were produced or stockpiled. While the declaration listed the known Soviet military BW sites, it listed only the four Biopreparat facilities at Leningrad, Obolensk, Koltsovo, and Lyubychany previously visited by the United States and United Kingdom. A dozen other Biopreparat facilities involved in BW activities were not listed. Furthermore, the activities of the Biopreparat facilities were marginalized and downplayed. Although the declaration listed a number of bacterial agents that the Soviet Union worked on, there was no mention of work with viral agents such as variola, Marburg, and Ebola. The declaration also contained no information about Soviet research on

60. Mangold and Goldberg, *Plague Wars,* 196–97.

61. Potomac Institute for Policy Studies, *Conference on Countering Biological Terrorism: Strategic Firepower in the Hands of Many?* (Arlington, VA: Potomac Institute for Policy Studies, 1997), 67.

62. Mangold and Goldberg, *Plague Wars,* 165.

63. Although the Soviet BW program began in 1928, the confidence-building measure only required states to declare their offensive activities since 1946.

124   *Living Weapons*

anticrop or antianimal biological agents. The declaration did not mention the BW programs and facilities associated with the Academy of Sciences, Ministry of Health, Ministry of Agriculture, or KGB. The declaration also failed to address several outstanding issues such as evidence of Soviet genetic engineering for offensive purposes, the 1979 anthrax outbreak at Sverdlovsk, the defection and revelations of Vladimir Pasechnik, and the findings of the January 1991 Anglo-American visit.[64] Kuntsevich refused to answer subsequent U.S. questions about specific omissions from the declaration and maintained that the declaration met all legal requirements.[65]

Clearly, Yeltsin and the Ministry of Foreign Affairs lost this round to the military and Kuntsevich's committee. Equally disturbing was that many of the details, denials, and shortcomings in the declaration appeared to match those found in a report on the former Soviet BW program submitted by Kuntsevich to Yeltsin in March.[66] As in the Soviet era, the military was telling the same lies to both the United States and the civilian leadership in the Kremlin.

Kuntsevich's report to Yeltsin in March and the Russian declaration in April demonstrated that the Russian military was willing to concede only what it believed that the White House, 10 Downing Street, and the Kremlin already knew about the BW program. Given these signs of military insubordination and cover-up, U.S. secretary of state Lawrence Eagleburger and British foreign secretary Douglas Hurd raised their concerns directly with Russian foreign minister Andrei Kozyrev. In an August 24, 1992, letter, they wrote that "we are very concerned that some aspects of the offensive biological warfare program, which President Yeltsin acknowledged as having existed and which he then banned in April, *are in fact being continued covertly and without his knowledge.*"[67]

Corruption and Proliferation

Biopreparat's ability to maintain its autonomy and elude civilian control led to reports of corruption and possibly proliferation. Although Biopreparat had been transferred to federal civilian control under the Russian Ministry of Health, "it

64. Russian Federation, "Declaration of Past Activity in Regard to Offensive and Defensive Programs of Biological Research and Development," United Nations Form F, DDA/4–92/BWIII, 1992.

65. For example, Kuntsevich claimed that all ongoing Russian research on *Y. pestis* was defensive, while the United States had intelligence from a recent defector that Pasechnik's old institute was still trying to develop a means to mass-produce an antibiotic-resistant strain of the pathogen. Mangold and Goldberg, *Plague Wars,* 163–64, 430 n. 38.

66. Adams, *New Spies,* 278; and R. Jeffrey Smith, "Russia Fails to Detail Germ Arms," *Washington Post,* August 31, 1992, A1.

67. Letter from U.S. secretary of state Lawrence Eagleburger and British foreign minister Douglas Hurd to Russian foreign minister Andrei Kozyrev, August 24, 1992 (emphasis added).

would appear that these changes were cosmetic in nature and that, despite its official incorporation within this ministry, Biopreparat continued to operate autonomously with little or no government control."[68] In 1995 Yuri F. Doshchitsyn, head of medical industry within the Russian Ministry of Health and Medical Industry (also known as Minzdravmedprom) and the official with direct responsibility for Biopreparat, reported that his agency had "been unable to sort out its relation with Biopreparat. The reason for this is that Biopreparat has recently succeeded in securing budget finance outside of Minzdravmedprom and, having acquired economic independence, it's attempting to take factories of the same profile with it."[69] The bulk of this outside finance likely came from the Ministry of Defense, with commercial sales and black market activities playing a smaller role. Amy Smithson reports that stories of corruption within the chemical and biological weapons communities circulated in Russia throughout the 1990s.[70] Anthony Rimmington has identified around thirty private companies that were created on the basis of organizations and facilities that contributed to the Soviet BW program.[71] The firm Bioeffect, created by a former BW scientist, has advertised for sale recombinant strains of *F. tularensis* with altered virulence genes and offered to cooperate in research on the virulence factors of different pathogens and the development of novel microorganisms.[72]

The most alarming example of how autonomy can contribute to proliferation is a deal struck in July 1995 between Iraq's Military Industrialization Corporation and Biopreparat for a 50,000-liter fermentation capability. Iraq and Russia claimed that the fermenters were for a single-cell protein factory. This was the same story used by Iraq to hide its BW production facility at Al Hakam from UNSCOM. Indeed, the key Iraqi negotiators were affiliated with Al Hakam and had previously worked on Iraq's BW program. In addition, Iraq was negotiating for five 10,000-liter fermenters, not one 50,000-liter fermenter as might be expected for a legitimate single-cell protein factory. One of the Russians reportedly involved in the negotiations was Vilen Matveyev, formerly with the 15th Main Directorate and later a senior deputy at Biopreparat, who specialized in

68. Anthony Rimmington, "Fragmentation and Proliferation? The Fate of the Soviet Union's Offensive Biological Weapons Programme," *Contemporary Security Policy* 20, no. 1 (1999): 91.

69. Quoted in Rimmington, "Fragmentation and Proliferation?" 91.

70. Smithson, *Toxic Archipelago,* 14.

71. For example, the firm Binom has advertised its role in the design and construction of several major BW factories. Rimmington, "The Soviet Union's Offensive Program," 119.

72. Testimony of Dr. Kenneth Alibek before the Joint Economic Committee, *Terrorist and Intelligence Operations: Potential Impact on the U.S. Economy,* 105th Cong., 2nd sess., May 20, 1998; and Wendy Orent, *Plague: The Mysterious Past and Terrifying Future of the World's Most Dangerous Disease* (New York: Free Press, 2004), 229.

the development of weapons-manufacturing equipment.[73] Russia has assured UNSCOM that no contract was concluded, and no attempt was made to export the equipment in 1995 or after.[74] According to the Iraq Survey Group, the deal fell through when the Russian company was unable to obtain an export control license.[75] UNMOVIC, however, suggests that the deal was never consummated because it was preempted by Iraq's admission that Al Hakam had been part of the BW program and the subsequent closure and destruction of the facility.[76] The episode serves to illustrate the dangers that highly autonomous BW organizations or entrepreneurial scientists can pose if they choose to place their own material interests above the political interests of their superiors.

Assessment

While Yeltsin appears to have genuinely desired to comply with the BWC, his ability to implement this pledge and establish the level of transparency necessary to demonstrate compliance was limited. Yeltsin made limited progress after the initial breakthroughs in 1992 such as the decree banning work on biological weapons, the submission of the confidence-building declaration to the UN, and the signing of the so-called Trilateral Agreement in September 1992. Russia, however, refused to clarify omissions and falsehoods in its UN declaration, address issues raised by Anglo-American visits to former BW sites as part of the trilateral process, or grant the promised access to military sites. In addition, the continued presence of Kuntsevich, Yevstigneev, and Kalinin in senior positions reinforced concerns in the West about the dangers of Kremlin complicity in the offensive program or lack of control over the military. According to a Western intelligence official, "Yeltsin is certainly telling us what he believes. But that is not what is actually happening. If the military are really able to defy

73. Judith Miller, "Official Confirms 1995 Russian-Iraq Deal," *New York Times*, February 18, 1998, A8; R. Jeffrey Smith, "Russians Admit Firms Met Iraqis," *Washington Post*, February 18, 1998, A16; R. Jeffrey Smith, "Did Russia Sell Iraq Germ Warfare Equipment?" *Washington Post*, February 12, 1998, A1; Ritter, *Endgame*, 220; Alibek, *Biohazard*, 275; and Statement of Richard O. Spertzel before the House Armed Services Committee, *State of the Iraqi Weapons of Mass Destruction Program*, 107th Cong., 2nd sess., September 10, 2002.

74. United Nations Security Council, *Report of the Executive Chairman on the Activities of the Special Commission Established by the Secretary General pursuant to paragraph 9 (b) (i) of Resolution 687 (1991)*, S/1998/332 (New York: United Nations, April 16, 1998), 17.

75. Charles Duelfer, *Comprehensive Report of the Special Advisor to the DCI on Iraq's WMD*, vol. 3, *Biological Warfare* (Langley, VA: CIA, 2004), 13–14 [hereafter Duelfer Report].

76. United Nations Monitoring, Verification and Inspection Commission, *Compendium of Iraq's Proscribed Weapons Programmes in the Chemical, Biological and Missile Areas* (New York: UNMOVIC, 2007), 1025.

him in this way, it tells us a lot about the power structure in Russia."[77] As one senior U.S. official observed, "it's really a debate about whether Russian bio-warfare research is a national policy or run by entrenched interests that are out of control. Did Yeltsin mean what he said? Probably yes. Did he have the ability to tear it down? Probably no."[78]

Problems with Russian compliance with the BWC persisted beyond Yeltsin's tenure as president. In January 2000, on the eve of Vladimir Putin's ascension to Russia's presidency, the Department of Defense reported that "we have little information on the extent of control and oversight by the Government of Russia over the military and civilian-military biological warfare programs formerly controlled or overseen by the Soviet Union. We are concerned, however, that the same generals who led the former Soviet offensive BW program are still in charge at military institutes that are said to be part of the greatly reduced defensive program."[79] Although Putin's government has publicly reaffirmed its commitment to the BWC on several occasions, the United States has been unable to certify that Russia is fully implementing the treaty.[80]

South Africa

Similar problems of control and oversight beset the South African CBW program, Project Coast, which operated from 1981 to 1995. Secrecy, compartmentalization, and organizational autonomy impeded effective oversight, undermined civilian control, and distorted decision making. An investigation by the TRC found that the military committee charged with oversight of the project was "grossly negligent in approving programmes and allocating large sums of money for activities of which they had no understanding, and which they made no effort to understand."[81] This mismanagement resulted in scientific and financial fraud by a "nepotistic, self-serving and self-enriching group of people, misled by those who had a technical grasp of what was happening."[82] Furthermore, the program managers misled President F. W. de Klerk and later President Nelson

---

77. Quoted in James Adams, "Russia's Secret Weapons for Germ Warfare," *Sunday Times* (London), March 27, 1994.

78. Quoted in Wendy Orent, "Escape from Moscow," *The Sciences* 38, no. 3 (1998): 30.

79. Department of Defense, *Report to Congress on Biological Weapons Programs in Russia* (Washington: DOD, January 11, 2000), 2.

80. Department of State, *Adherence to and Compliance with Arms Control, Nonproliferation, and Disarmament Agreements and Commitments* (Washington, DC: Department of State, 2005), 27–31.

81. Truth and Reconciliation Commission (TRC), *Truth and Reconciliation Commission of South Africa Report*, vol. 2 (Basingstoke, UK: Macmillan Reference, 1999), 522.

82. Ibid., 520.

Mandela about the offensive orientation of the program and its role in assassination operations. The oversight mechanism put in place to monitor Project Coast was undermined by the secrecy, compartmentalization, and divided chain of command that characterized the program. As a result, the program's documents and pathogens were not properly destroyed or accounted for when the program was terminated, and they continued to present a proliferation risk many years later. In addition, Dr. Wouter Basson, head of Project Coast from 1981 to 1993, is suspected of aiding Libya's CBW program in the early 1990s. In 1997 Basson was arrested for drug trafficking, and in 1999 he went on trial with sixty-seven charges of possession of illegal drugs, murder, attempted murder, conspiracy to murder, and fraud. All of these charges stemmed from his actions as the head of South Africa's CBW program. Although Project Coast scientists testified to the production of assassination weapons under orders from Basson, and members of Special Forces units testified to using such devices to carry out murders, Basson denied that he was involved in any way with these operations. On April 11, 2002, the judge acquitted him of all charges.[83]

Chandré Gould and Peter Folb, who worked on the TRC investigation of Project Coast, believe that the ability of Project Coast to evade SADF's normal financial and security controls was not due solely to Basson's efforts. They believe that there was a decision made by the senior SADF leadership that the project should operate with the minimal amount of control in order to ensure plausible deniability.[84] According to Surgeon General Knobel, Basson was given carte blanche to obtain the desired results. As Burger and Gould paraphrase Knobel, "the end totally justified the means, and if that meant that Basson had to lie, steal or bribe people, no one in SADF would blink an eye. Who he dealt with and how he achieved the desired results were 'details' that members of the CMC [Coordinating Management Committee] specifically did *not* want to know."[85]

The lack of controls allowed Project Coast to develop sufficient autonomy to resist later efforts to exercise more stringent oversight over the program's finances and activities. In addition, the highest levels of the South African, U.S., and British governments as well as the United Nations were consistently misled about the nature of Project Coast by Knobel and Basson. The lack of adequate oversight also made it difficult for Pretoria to shut down the program in a complete and verifiable manner. This allowed Basson and other Project Coast scientists to

83. For a thorough description of the shortcomings of the judge's rulings in this case, see Center for Conflict Resolution, "Report on the Judgment in the State vs. Wouter Basson, delivered on 11 April 2002," *Trial Report no. 63,* n.d., http://ccrweb.ccr.uct.ac.za/archive/cbw/63.html. In September 2005 the South African Constitutional Court ruled that Basson could be tried on six of the dismissed murder charges, but the South African government decided not to prosecute.

84. Gould and Folb, *Project Coast,* 186.

85. Burger and Gould, *Secrets and Lies,* 20 (emphasis in original).

divert project materials for their own purposes, which increased the risk of the proliferation of chemical and biological weapons to states and terrorists.

Autonomy

The structure of Project Coast and autonomy enjoyed by Basson were driven primarily by the SADF's need for plausible deniability as the SADF could not afford to be linked to his activities. To compensate for the risks involved, Basson was provided with a generous level of funding and minimal oversight. The only restrictions placed on his activities, aside from the injunction for secrecy and deniability, were that he operate within the approved annual budget, did not transport hazardous materials on commercial aircraft, and did not enrich himself at the project's expense.[86] The responsibility, freedom, and financial rewards granted to Basson due to the perceived need for secrecy led him to realize that no one else in SADF knew anything about chemical and biological weapons and that "in the land of the blind, the one-eyed man is king."[87]

Basson was able to leverage his supposed expertise in CBW and his superiors' desire for secrecy to serve as their sole source of information on the project. Due to the strict compartmentalization of Project Coast, Basson served as the only direct link between CMC and the project's front companies.[88] Basson also controlled the three working groups established by the CMC to guide its decision making and exercise oversight over the project.[89] This arrangement allowed him to prepare all of the documentation for the committee and therefore monopolize the information flowing to it.

The high degree of compartmentalization of Project Coast allowed Basson to circumvent the usual organizational and procedural checks and balances of secret military programs. All secret SADF projects were assigned a security officer, who would report to the chief of staff for intelligence, to handle the physical security of facilities, proper classification and handling of documents, screening of personnel, advice on how to route finances to prevent them from being linked back to the SADF, and other counterintelligence activities. To fulfill his duties, the security officer would have to know as much as possible about the project to

---

86. Burger and Gould, *Secrets and Lies*, 17, 20.

87. Ibid., 17, 179.

88. Knobel was the only member of the CMC to ever set foot on the premises of Delta G or RRL. He visited Delta G once and RRL twice, always outside of normal working hours. Burger and Gould, *Secrets and Lies*, 20.

89. On paper, the technical working group was composed of Basson, the directors of RRL and Delta G, and some of the scientists in these front companies. In fact, Basson was the only constant member of the group and many scientists claimed that they had never heard of the technical working group. Ibid., 518; and Gould and Folb, *Project Coast*, 170–71.

anticipate or detect breaches in the project's secrecy. Johan Theron, the security officer for Project Coast, testified at Basson's trial that he had been denied access to all transactions conducted by Basson and that he reported directly to Basson, not to the chief of staff for intelligence. As a result, the security officer had no ability to act as a check on Basson.[90]

As Burger and Gould observe, "even the highest echelon of the SADF was entirely dependent on Basson for every detail of the CBW programme it had created."[91] D. John Tuter, who managed one of Project Coast's front companies, testified at Basson's trial that "Wouter Basson *was* Project Coast—end of story."[92] As a result, Basson could control the entire program and manipulate his overseers as desired. Basson oversaw personnel decisions, the program's research agenda, budgetary matters, overt and black market procurement, and was responsible for keeping senior political and military leaders informed about the status of his program. The investigation by the TRC as well as Basson's two-and-a-half-year criminal trial revealed how he was able to exploit the desire for secrecy and the autonomy of his program to abuse all of these responsibilities.

Fraud and Corruption

Basson used his position as the sole source of his superiors' information about Project Coast to exaggerate the program's achievements and to enrich himself and his cronies. In the words of Princeton Lyman, U.S. ambassador to South Africa in the mid-1990s, "Basson proved to be a combination of Dr. Strangelove and Walter Mitty."[93] According to Knobel, Project Coast's achievements, which were stored for posterity on sixteen CD-ROMs, were a "national asset." Even the judge at Basson's trial believed that the project had been a huge success.[94] The TRC assessment of this aspect of Project Coast is worth quoting at length:

> One of the curious aspects of the CBW programme was the high level of respect it enjoyed with the military and the government of the day. The facts, as they emerged in the Commission's hearings, show that this respect was misplaced. The scientific research undertaken by the project was pedestrian, misdirected, ineffectual and unproductive. It was also exorbitantly expensive, costing the nation tens if not hundreds of millions of rands.[95]

---

90. Gould and Folb, *Project Coast,* 174, 185–86.
91. Burger and Gould, *Secrets and Lies,* 20–21.
92. Ibid. (emphasis in original).
93. Princeton N. Lyman, *Partner to History: The U.S. Role in South Africa's Transition to Democracy* (Washington, DC: United States Institute of Peace Press, 2002), 190.
94. Burger and Gould, *Secrets and Lies,* 23.
95. TRC, *Truth and Reconciliation Commission of South Africa Report,* vol. 2, 511.

After Basson's arrest for drug dealing in 1997, the CD-ROMs that were supposed to contain highly classified information on South Africa's scientific achievements in the CBW field were reviewed and found to contain only previously published literature on these weapons.[96] Instead of a national asset, Project Coast was unmasked as a national embarrassment.

Basson also exploited his superiors' desire for secrecy and the technique of compartmentalization to enrich himself and his colleagues. The extent of corruption within Project Coast illustrates the dangers posed by an autonomous organization whose leadership is not held accountable for its actions. State prosecutors accused Basson of structuring Project Coast's financial arrangements so that select insiders benefited from the program's implementation and privatization. Basson arranged the replacement of the civilian scientists in charge of Delta G and RRL with two personal friends who also served with him in the Special Forces and Seventh Medical Battalion. This management shake-up was timed to occur just before the commercialization phase of Project Coast and resulted in Basson and his friends becoming millionaires after the "sale" of these companies to their management.[97]

Prosecutors also accused Basson of misappropriating funds designated for the procurement of CBW-related materials from abroad to support a luxurious lifestyle in South Africa and abroad for himself and select colleagues, most of whom also worked for Project Coast. Basson claims he used the funds to purchase a range of drugs and materials. However, only he knew what substances the program was procuring, how much they cost, and whether and how they were being used. Surgeon General Knobel justified this practice by claiming that the overriding priority was to prevent foreign suppliers, or anyone else, from knowing of the military's connection to Basson's activities. These purchases were never physically verified, and scientists at Delta G and RRL testified that they did not obtain black market goods from Basson and were able to procure required items through normal commercial channels.[98]

As a result of the covert nature of Project Coast, the stated need to acquire equipment and material on the black market or to smuggle it into the country due to the international embargo, and the limited oversight exercised by CMC, Basson was able to divert virtually all of the money allocated for overseas procurement from Project Coast and launder it through a network of shell companies

---

96. Ibid., 144; and Burger and Gould, *Secrets and Lies,* 26, 204–5.

97. Wynand Swanepoel, managing director of RRL, received a payment of 4 million rand ($1.5 million) when RRL was privatized in 1991, and Dr. Philip Mijburgh, managing director of Delta G, made a profit of 15 million rand ($5.4 million) from the privatization of Delta G. Burger and Gould, *Secrets and Lies,* 39–41; and Gould and Folb, *Project Coast,* 67, 100, 143–44, 148–52.

98. Gould and Folb, *Project Coast,* 177–84, 200.

and offshore accounts he had established in the Cayman Islands. A forensic auditor found that over a seven-year period, 86 million rand ($31 million) of Project Coast funds flowed through a labyrinth of offshore accounts that Basson had access to but which were never reported to Knobel or CMC. Government investigators found that Basson and his colleagues used this money to buy real estate in Europe and South Africa and to enjoy extravagant vacations in the United States and Europe.[99]

When financial irregularities came to the attention of military auditors in 1992, Knobel rejected their request to conduct an independent investigation based on Basson's advice that such an audit could represent a security risk.[100] As Knobel testified, "his word was enough. After all, the man was a brigadier, a senior military officer. If you can't trust him, who can you trust?"[101] Once again, Basson used the need for secrecy as a means to shield his project's autonomy and hide his wrongdoing.

The Misleading of Senior Civilian Officials

When F. W. de Klerk replaced P. W. Botha as president of South Africa in 1989 it was the beginning of the end of Project Coast. De Klerk ushered in a new era in South Africa's domestic politics and international relations by beginning a dialogue with opposition groups, including the African National Congress, which eventually led to the end of apartheid and genuine democratic elections in South Africa. Project Coast, however, refused to fade away.

During this time, the senior civilian leadership was briefed by Knobel and Basson that Project Coast was developing defenses against chemical and biological weapons and that its only offensive activities were the development of incapacitating and irritant chemical agents for use in crowd control. Basson reported that "our biological capacity is focused on staying up to date with the changing threat. To do this we are constantly producing new organisms in order to develop a preventative strategy as well as a strategy for treatment."[102] Accordingly, de Klerk approved the continuation of Project Coast as it was described in the briefing.[103]

---

99. Burger and Gould, *Secrets and Lies,* 91–96, 121–40, 199; and Gould and Folb, *Project Coast,* 183, 204–5.

100. Gould and Folb, *Project Coast,* 175, 178–81.

101. Burger and Gould, *Secrets and Lies,* 108.

102. Wouter B. Basson, "Projek Coast: Voorligtig aan Statspresident" [Project Coast: briefing of the state president], GG/UG/302/6/C123/BK, March 26, 1990. Available from the Chemical and Biological Warfare Project for the Centre for Conflict Resolution collection at the South African History Archive, University of Witwatersrand, Johannesburg, South Africa [hereafter SAHA].

103. Wouter Basson and Gen. D. P. Knobel, "Voorligting aan die Minister van Verdediging oor die verloop en huidige status van Projeke Coast en Jota te George op 7 Jan 1993" [Presentation to the minister

Unbeknownst to de Klerk, the ostensibly defensive biological research program at RRL conducted almost exclusively offensive research.[104] According to a 1989 document authored by Basson, the purpose of Project Coast was to develop both offensive and defensive capabilities and to support the employment of these capabilities by the security forces. According to this report, "current biological warfare research focuses on offensive, epidemic agents. The researchers are also working on the development of new agents."[105] In addition, the biological program included research on weaponization "to create a bridge between the agent on the one side and the ammunition on the other. Researchers are trying to develop the best possible distribution techniques for the agent."[106] A senior scientist at RRL claims that Basson insisted that "the Holy Grail of all research was the perfect murder weapon: a tasteless, colorless, odorless toxin that could not be traced *post mortem*."[107]

President de Klerk first learned of Project Coast's nefarious activities in 1992 when Gen. Pierre Steyn provided him with a secret report on criminal activities conducted by the SADF. Steyn reported that the Seventh Medical Battalion under Basson's command was engaged in drug trafficking and assassinations of opponents of the apartheid regime. On March 31, 1993, de Klerk ordered the BW portion of Project Coast closed down, and Basson was dismissed from the military. He was immediately rehired for one year to tie up loose ends.[108] President de Klerk, however, continued to receive misleading reports about the apartheid-era CBW program. A March 1994 document prepared for de Klerk repeated the claim that South Africa's biological research was defensive only and that "officially no biological agents were used offensively."[109]

President de Klerk's successor, Nelson Mandela, was also deceived about Project Coast's past activities. In August 1994 Mandela received his first full briefing on South Africa's CBW programs from Surgeon General Knobel. Knobel claimed that South Africa's biological program had been engaged in only defensive research. He briefed Mandela that "as an offensive option for SADF, BW were considered too dangerous because of the difficulty in controlling the spread of the organisms, and in any case would be ethically and morally unacceptable. For

of defense about the course and current status of projects Coast and Jota at George on January 7, 1993], GG/UG/302/6/J1282/5, January 8, 1993, SAHA.

104. Burger and Gould, *Secrets and Lies,* 26.

105. Wouter B. Basson, "Projek Coast: Moontlikhede vir privatisering" [Project Coast: possibilities for privatization], SADF Document GG/UG/302/6/COAST/BFW, November 28, 1989, 2–4, SAHA.

106. Ibid.

107. Burger and Gould, *Secrets and Lies,* 29.

108. Gould and Folb, *Project Coast,* 116–17, 209; and Mangold and Goldberg, *Plague Wars,* 267.

109. "Further Background Information with Regards to the Biological Warfare Project for the State President," March 1994, SAHA. The author of the document is unknown. The document was found in 1997 in a trunk belonging to Basson that contained other Project Coast documents.

these reasons it was decided that the SADF would only undertake extensive research into the BW threat possibilities and concentrate on countermeasures in case of the possible manipulation of local organisms by hostile parties."[110]

South Africa as Unreliable Arms Control Partner

Neither the de Klerk nor Mandela governments took further action to examine the history and conduct of the CBW program. Project Coast's past offensive activities, both research and employment, were effectively sanitized from South African government documents and briefings for South African and foreign officials. In December 1993 South Africa submitted a declaration to the United Nations on its past and current offensive and defensive biological activities as required by a BWC confidence-building measure. The declaration stated that South Africa had not conducted offensive biological research and that defensive biological research had been conducted only in 1990 and 1992. The declaration failed to mention the activities of RRL from the mid-1980s through 1991 and did not discuss South Africa's research, development, production, and deployment of biological agents and devices for offensive purposes.[111]

South Africa's refusal to fully declare its past BW activities led to an April 1994 meeting between the U.S. and British ambassadors and President de Klerk. South African officials resisted the Anglo-American demand to fully declare their past offensive activities, which they contended were unauthorized and against official policy. De Klerk, however, also sought more information from the ambassadors about the project's past activities in order to investigate the matter more fully.[112] At this meeting, Basson provided the ambassadors with a misleading overview of Project Coast. Basson stated that the goal of Project Coast was to develop self-sufficiency in chemical and biological defense through the establishment of defensive research and production facilities. This emphasis on defense is misleading since South Africa's chemical and biological defensive work did not begin until 1988, seven years after Project Coast began. The briefing also claimed that no biological weapons or delivery systems were developed by Project Coast.[113] Although RRL did not produce sophisticated biological weapons capable of aerosol dissemination and causing massive casualties, they did

110. D. P. Knobel, "Briefing to President Mandela on the Defensive Chemical and Biological Warfare Programme of the SADF and the RSA's Position with Regard to the CWC and BWC," CG/UG/302/J1282/5, August 18, 1994, 3, http://cryptome.org/mandela-cbw.htm.

111. South Africa, *Confidence Building Measure F: Declaration of Past Activities,* December 15, 1993, cited in Gould and Folb, *Project Coast,* 100–101, 213–14.

112. Gould and Folb, *Project Coast,* 210–11; and Lyman, *Partner to History,* 192.

113. "The South African CBW Programme," n.d., cited in Gould and Folb, *Project Coast,* 212.

produce biological agents and munitions for use in assassination and clandestine attacks. The United States and United Kingdom presented another demarche to Mandela's government in January 1995 requesting that his government submit a credible CBM declaration.[114] Despite this Anglo-American pressure, South Africa has refused to amend its initial declaration that it did not conduct offensive activities and continues to maintain the fiction that it had engaged only in defensive biological research.[115]

Proliferation

The secrecy and autonomy with which Project Coast had been run for over ten years not only made it very difficult for the senior political leadership to gain a complete understanding of the program and to make it transparent to outsiders, but it also compromised their efforts to properly dismantle the program. In January 1993 the minister of defense ordered Basson to destroy the chemical and biological materials produced and purchased by Project Coast and to destroy the project's files after key data were transferred to CD-ROMs. Basson later reported to the CMC that he had accomplished both tasks although he did not submit any documents or witnesses to certify the destruction of either the materials or the files.[116] Nevertheless, South African officials accepted Basson's claims and reassured the United States and United Kingdom that the offensive program had been terminated and all materials of proliferation importance had been destroyed or were "under strict centralized control."[117]

Basson's January 29, 1997, arrest demonstrated that he had not followed these orders and had lied to his superiors. After his arrest, authorities seized two trunks linked to him that contained over three thousand capsules of MDMA (methylenedioxymethamphetamine, also known as Ecstasy), 96.9 grams of methaqualone (also known as Mandrax), and 14 grams of cocaine. All of these drugs had been produced or acquired by Delta G before the termination of Project Coast as part of a research program on using street drugs as incapacitating chemical weapons for crowd control.[118] In addition, numerous classified technical documents from

114. Gould and Folb, *Project Coast,* 213.

115. South Africa has not updated its CBM declaration since 1994. Nicolas Isla, *Transparency in Past Offensive Biological Weapon Programmes: An Analysis of Confidence Building Measure Form F, 1992–2003* (Hamburg: Hamburg Center for Biological Arms Control, 2006), 18–19.

116. Burger and Gould, *Secrets and Lies,* 26–27; and Gould and Folb, *Project Coast,* 214–16, 222.

117. Knobel, "Briefing to President Mandela on the Defensive Chemical and Biological Warfare Programme," 13.

118. The actual fate of the 1,000 kilograms of methaqualone (Mandrax), 912 kilograms of MDMA (Ecstasy), 37 kilograms of cocaine, and 980 kilograms of the chemical incapacitating agent BZ that Basson claimed to have disposed of in January 1993 is unknown. Gould and Folb, *Project Coast,* 216–18.

Project Coast that were supposed to have been destroyed in 1993 were found in the trunks. Scientists from RRL reported that they had also retained copies of their research reports.[119] It later emerged that Basson and his staff had also failed to destroy the stocks of biological cultures as directed when the program was closed down. Daan Goosen, the former director of RRL, claims that he retained a personal collection of 150 strains collected by or developed by the project, including *B. anthracis,* and six genetically modified strains, such as an *E. coli* strain that produces the toxin of *C. perfringens.*[120] Other scientists were also reported to have retained copies of strains to continue working on vaccines and therapeutic treatments with commercial prospects.[121]

Perhaps even more dangerous than documents or strains of microorganisms was the potential for scientists to "freelance" with their knowledge to other nations and nongovernment organizations. Basson made several trips to Libya between 1993 and 1995 that were believed to be linked to Libya's pursuit of foreign expertise for its CBW program.[122] The Mandela government decided to rehire Basson in October 1995 as a means of keeping a closer eye on him. Goosen and other scientists previously involved with Project Coast have reported being approached by representatives of foreign countries and extremist groups seeking materials or expertise relating to chemical and biological weapons.[123] Basson's involvement with Libya and drug trafficking illustrates the risk that former weapons scientists could sell their know-how or access to highly valuable materials on the black market.

Secrecy, Oversight, and International Security

BW programs operate under extreme secrecy and compartmentalization for legal, normative, and strategic reasons. As a result, these programs are able to attain a high degree of autonomy that obstructs civilian oversight and distorts decision making. The security implications are subtle but disturbing.

---

119. Ibid., 222.

120. Goosen attempted unsuccessfully to sell this collection to the U.S. government in 2002. Joby Warrick and John Mintz, "Lethal Legacy: Bioweapons for Sale," *Washington Post,* April 20, 2003, A1. Goosen may be exaggerating the size of his collection to increase its value. For example, there is evidence of only one genetically modified organism, not six, being created under the auspices of Project Coast. E-mail communication with Chandré Gould, November 30, 2004.

121. Joby Warrick, "Biotoxins Fall into Private Hands," *Washington Post,* April 21, 2003, A1.

122. Mangold and Goldberg, *Plague Wars,* 269; James Adams, "Gadaffi Lures South Africa's Top Germ Warfare Scientists," *Sunday Times,* February 26, 1995; and Paul Taylor, "Toxic S. African Arms Raise Concern," *Washington Post,* February 28, 1995, A14.

123. Robert Block, "Bitter Researchers Are Big Question in Germ Warfare," *Wall Street Journal,* May 20, 2002, A1; Warrick and Mintz, "Lethal Legacy," A1; and Gould and Folb, *Project Coast,* 207–8.

Biological weapons program are able to escape review by senior officials, leading to a dissonance between military means and political ends in a state's grand strategy.[124] As a result, reviews are typically triggered by external pressure that raises the cost of this dissonance. The continuation of the Soviet BW program in violation of the BWC undermined Moscow's strategy under Gorbachev and Yeltsin of reconciliation and cooperation with Western powers. The efforts by Gorbachev and Yeltsin to rein in the offensive program were triggered by, and sustained by, diplomatic pressure from the United States and United Kingdom. The public pressure exerted by the United States at the third review conference of the BWC in 1991 led the Soviet delegation to worry that the United States would insist that the Soviet Union be singled out and named for noncompliance in the meeting's final declaration. This approach appeared to promote a more cooperative attitude from Moscow and Soviet agreement to a new CBM on declaration of past offensive BW programs.[125] The United States later used this CBM as a means of testing Russian willingness to comply with the BWC. Similarly, the United States made the most progress resolving concerns with Russian compliance with the BWC when it made these concerns public in 1992.

Likewise, South Africa's CBW program was shut down due to a series of investigations into illegal activities committed by Basson, the program's manager. A fuller and more accurate accounting of the program's activities emerged only as a result of the public hearings held by the TRC and pressure from the United States and United Kingdom. In these cases, it was not only external pressure but also the information provided by outsiders that enabled political leaders to regain leverage over these secret programs.

Another example of the role of external pressure in triggering a long-overdue review of CBW policies can be found in the United States' unilateral abandonment of its BW program in 1969. Mounting scientific and congressional opposition to the use of riot control agents and herbicides in Vietnam and the testing of chemical weapons in the United States led to the first National Security Council review of the United States' CBW program in over fifteen years. The review resulted in the termination of the offensive BW program and the United States' renunciation of the use of biological weapons.

Even if senior officials attempt to closely monitor a BW program, such oversight may be compromised by uncooperative program managers who can exploit the compartmentalization of knowledge to mislead senior officials. The motive for such manipulation may be merely bureaucratic maneuvering to maintain

124. On the dangers of a lack of political-military integration in grand strategy, see Posen, *Sources of Military Doctrine,* 24–29.
125. Michael Moodie, "The Soviet Union, Russia, and the Biological and Toxin Weapons Convention," *Nonproliferation Review* 8, no. 1 (2001): 65–67.

or increase budget, prestige, or autonomy, or it could be an attempt to avoid accountability for unethical or illegal activities. The leaders of the Soviet BW program repeatedly lied to the civilian leadership in the Kremlin in order to justify the program's continuation. Basson also misled his superiors in order to conceal his involvement in assassination operations and to cover up his alleged fraud, embezzlement, and drug trafficking. As a result, government leaders may not know the full extent and nature of past and current activities. However, since these leaders have an incentive to distance themselves from such activities, it may be difficult to determine to what extent they are truly ignorant or are turning a blind eye. The false information provided by program managers may also be propagated internationally through incomplete and inaccurate declarations to the United Nations and negotiating partners.

We now know that Iraqi BW scientists hid vital information regarding their unilateral destruction of BW agents in 1991 from their own leaders and UN inspectors, which greatly complicated efforts by the UN to verify Iraqi disarmament. In July 1991 Hussein Kamel issued emergency orders to immediately dispose of all bulk BW agents. Faced with a broken semitrailer, which prevented the transportation of a cache of *B. anthracis* spores back to the main BW facility at Al Hakam for disposal, Iraqi scientists deactivated and dumped the agent within sight of one of Saddam Hussein's presidential palaces. Once they realized their mistake, they were too scared to tell the regime leadership, even after UN weapons inspectors had identified gaps and flaws in Iraq's account of its 1991 unilateral BW destruction activities.[126] According to the Iraq Survey Group, a US-led fact-finding mission that searched Iraq for weapons of mass destruction after the 2003 invasion, "this deception, in effect, prevented any possibility of the UN accepting the Iraqi account of its BW program. Whether those involved understood the significance and disastrous consequences of their actions is unclear."[127]

Organizations that enjoy a high degree of autonomy also allow managers to hinder the implementation of unwelcome policies and resist efforts to comply with international obligations. Kalinin's manipulation of Gorbachev's May 1990 decree and the military's domination of CBW policymaking under Yeltsin allowed the continuation of illegal activities, the maintenance of offensive capabilities, and a failure to fully divulge the program's past activities. This resistance, coupled with the withholding of information from senior political leaders, can make it more difficult to negotiate arms control measures in good faith, especially if the other party has access to information that the leadership does not.

126. Duelfer Report, 3:52, 56, 62; and Rod Barton, *The Weapons Detective: The Inside Story of Australia's Top Weapons Inspector* (Melbourne: Black Inc. Agenda, 2006), 239.
    127. Duelfer Report, 3:62.

The United States and United Kingdom faced these problems when working with the Soviet, Russian, and South African governments to bring them into compliance with the BWC and the requirements of the treaty's confidence-building measures.

The lack of adequate oversight increases the risk that such programs, or the remnants of these programs, could become the source of expertise, materials, or weapons for terrorists or other states. In both Russia and South Africa, former BW scientists have offered such resources on the international market or been approached to supply these resources to states or terrorists. Future nonproliferation successes should be accompanied by efforts to employ former weapon scientists in peaceful research and to secure sensitive materials to prevent further proliferation.

These problems affect not only authoritarian states prone to poor civil-military relations but also strong liberal democracies. The 1969 U.S. decision to renounce biological weapons and destroy it BW stockpile is the exception that proves the rule. This decision was made by President Nixon after extensive interagency deliberations. When the civilian leadership at the DOD was not satisfied with the advice they were getting from the uniformed military, they turned to civilian experts within the DOD and obtained independent analyses from science advisers in the Office of Science and Technology in the White House and outside scientists who were members of the President's Science Advisory Committee. To ensure that the destruction of biological agents was conducted in a safe manner, the DOD was required to have destruction plans approved by multiple federal and state environmental agencies.[128] The decision and its implementation demonstrate the value of pluralistic decision-making structures and processes not constrained by compartmentalization. The exception to this emerged in the most secretive, and least accountable, agency of the government: the Central Intelligence Agency. In 1975 a congressional investigation exposed a secret stockpile of toxins at the CIA that should have been destroyed when the United States decided to terminate its offensive BW program.[129] The toxins were the result of cooperation between the CIA and the U.S. Army to develop biological agents and weapons for clandestine operations. An internal CIA review of the program found that it was "characterized by a compartmentation [sic] that was extreme even by CIA standards."[130] In contrast to the review of the DOD's

---

128. Jonathan B. Tucker, "A Farewell to Germs: The U.S. Renunciation of Biological and Toxin Warfare, 1969–70," *International Security* 27, no. 1 (2002): 107–48.

129. Senate Select Committee to Study Governmental Operations with Respect to Intelligence Activities, *Intelligence Activities,* vol. 1, *Unauthorized Storage of Toxic Agents,* 94th Cong., 1st sess., September 16, 17, and 18, 1976.

130. *Summary Report on CIA Investigation of MKNAOMI,* n.d. (declassified September 15, 1975), p. 4 in Senate Committee on Human Resources, Subcommittee on Health and Scientific Research, *Biological*

plans to destroy its stocks of agents and munitions by appropriate federal, state, and local agencies, the destruction of the CIA's holdings of biological and toxin agents stored at Fort Detrick was not subject to any external oversight. As a result, CIA scientists were able to decide on their own to retain a small stockpile of toxins despite the presidential decision to destroy all such agents. To prevent a repeat of this embarrassing incident, the National Security Council required all government agencies to certify in writing that they were in compliance with the BWC.[131] This episode highlights the corrosive effects of secrecy on civilian oversight and management of BW programs even within liberal democracies.

The adverse effects of secrecy on oversight emerged again in 2001 when it was reported that the CIA and DOD were conducting classified biodefense projects that entailed the small-scale production of *B. anthracis* spores in dry powder form, the construction of a pilot plant capable of producing a stimulant for *B. anthracis* spores, the design and testing of a bomblet to disseminate biological agents, and the creation of a genetically modified strain of *B. anthracis* that could overcome the protection offered by some vaccines. Some of these projects had not been subject to an official arms control compliance review, and none of them were included in annual confidence-building declarations of biodefense activities to the United Nations.[132] The United States claimed that the purpose of these research projects was defensive and legal under the BWC, but the combination of capabilities under development and the secrecy of the work have raised questions at home and abroad about the commitment of the United States to enforcing the BWC.[133]

Testing Involving Human Subjects by the Department of Defense, 95th Cong., 1st Sess., March 8 and May 23, 1977, 247.

131. "Memorandum from Brent Scowcroft, National Security Advisor, to Heads of Executive Departments and Agencies, Subject: U.S. Compliance with the Biological Weapons Convention, December 23, 1975," *CBW Conventions Bulletin* 57 (September 2002): 2.

132. Milton Leitenberg, *Assessing the Biological Weapons and Bioterrorist Threat* (Carlisle Barracks, PA: Strategic Studies Institute, 2005), 54–55, 59–70, 84.

133. Judith Miller, "When Is a Bomb Not a Bomb? Germ Experts Confront U.S.," *New York Times,* September 5, 2001, A5; Elisa Harris, "Research Not to Be Hidden," *New York Times,* September 6, 2001; and Malcolm R. Dando and Mark Wheelis "Back to Bioweapons?" *Bulletin of the Atomic Scientists* 59, no. 1 (2003): 41–45.

4

INTELLIGENCE

In October 2002, the U.S. intelligence community published a National Intelligence Estimate (NIE) on Iraq's weapons of mass destruction programs. One of the key judgments of this highly influential report was that "all key aspects—R&D, production, and weaponization—of Iraq's offensive BW program are active and that most elements are larger and more advanced than they were before the Gulf war."[1] This program was believed to include multiple mobile BW agent production units; a stockpile of lethal and incapacitating BW agents, including *B. anthracis* and possibly variola virus and genetically engineered agents; and related munitions and delivery systems. The intelligence community declared that it had a high degree of confidence in this assessment.[2] This report became the basis for Secretary of State Colin Powell's February 2003 presentation to the United Nations Security Council to rally international support for the invasion of Iraq and the overthrow of Saddam Hussein.

---

1. National Intelligence Council (NIC), *Iraq's Continuing Programs for Weapons of Mass Destruction: Key Judgments,* NIE 2002–16HC, October 2002, 6, http://www.dni.gov/nic/special_keyjudgements.html.
   2. Ibid., 9.

The Iraq Survey Group, a U.S.-led 1,200 member multinational task force that was responsible for investigating Iraq's WMD programs following the war, failed to uncover any evidence to support any of the NIE's assessment on Iraq's BW program.[3] The bipartisan Silberman-Robb Commission investigation of 2004–5 concluded that the U.S. intelligence community "seriously misjudged" the status of Iraq's biological weapons program.[4] An investigation by the Senate Select Committee on Intelligence found that the United States' prewar assessment of Iraq's BW program either overstated, or was not supported, by the underlying intelligence.[5] How did the United States get so much so wrong about Iraq's BW program?

This episode illustrates another key security implication of biological weapons: states tend to have flawed assessments of the biological warfare intentions and capabilities of their adversaries. As discussed in chapter 3, states developing biological weapons have strong incentives to keep their plans and capabilities secret. As a result, these states engage in extensive deception-and-denial operations to conceal the existence and capabilities of offensive programs.[6] Properly assessing the information that is collected is complicated by the same factors discussed in chapter 2 that hinder verification—the multiuse nature of biotechnology; the overlap between offensive, defensive, and civilian activities; and the lack of easily detectable signatures for offensive programs.

As a result, biological weapons are a notoriously difficult target for intelligence agencies. According to the CIA's top nonproliferation analyst in 1999, "biological weapons (BW) pose, arguably, the most daunting challenge for intelligence collectors and analysts."[7] According to the Silberman-Robb Commission, biological weapons are "the mass casualty threat the Intelligence Community is least prepared to face."[8] The commission found that the intelligence community's analyses of national and nonstate BW programs often rely on assumptions of potential agents and delivery systems unsupported by data. This is in large part

3. Charles Duelfer, *Comprehensive Report of the Special Advisor to the DCI on Iraq's WMD,* vol. 3, *Biological Warfare* (Langley, VA: CIA, 2004) [hereafter Duelfer Report].

4. The Commission on the Intelligence Capabilities of the United States Regarding Weapons of Mass Destruction, *Report to the President* (Washington, DC: GPO, 2005), 80 [hereafter Silberman-Robb Report].

5. Senate Select Committee on Intelligence (SSCI), *Report on the U.S. Intelligence Community's Prewar Intelligence Assessments on Iraq* (Washington, DC: GPO, 2004), 14 [hereafter SSCI Report].

6. Denial refers to attempts to prevent an adversary from obtaining accurate information. Deception refers to efforts to cause an adversary to believe false information. For example, camouflage is a form of denial whereas decoys are a means of deception.

7. Statement by John A. Lauder, Special Assistant to the Director of Central Intelligence for Nonproliferation, to the House Permanent Select Committee on Intelligence, "Worldwide Biological Warfare Threat," March 3, 1999, http://www.cia.gov/cia/public_affairs/speeches/archives/1999/lauder_speech_030399.html.

8. Silberman-Robb Report, 503.

because traditional collection methods such as imagery and signal intelligence are poorly suited to collecting useful information on biological threats and the community is not properly configured to monitor the large volume of BW-relevant information available from open sources.[9] Assessing the biological threat posed by terrorists is even more difficult given the intensely secretive nature of such organizations and the smaller scale of their operations.

Biological threat assessments must take into account not only multiuse capabilities that are challenging to monitor but also intentions that are even more difficult to discern. Due to the multiuse nature of biotechnology, properly gauging intent is crucial to determining the purpose and significance of an observed capability or activity. Assessing intentions, however, has traditionally been the most difficult challenge for intelligence agencies. Intentions are not physical objects that can be easily observed but beliefs and plans that may be subject to rapid change and be known to only a handful of people. In addition, indicators of intent are frequently ambiguous, fragmentary, and contradictory. This leads to two pitfalls for intelligence analysts.

The first pitfall is that the nature of BW-related intelligence, which revolves around questions of intent and judgments about the purpose of multiuse capabilities, is susceptible to distortion due to cognitive biases, bureaucratic politics, and political pressure. As Lawrence Freedman has observed, "the more estimators have to guess, speculate, infer, induce, and conjecture in order to reach a conclusion, the greater the possibility of open disagreement."[10]

The second pitfall is that the most valuable source of intelligence on biological threats can also be the most misleading. The defection of well-placed individuals with inside knowledge of their nation's BW activities was crucial to gaining a fuller understanding of the Soviet program and Iraq's program immediately after the 1991 Gulf War. Human sources can also be highly unreliable and difficult to corroborate. The case of Curveball, the Iraqi chemical engineer whose reporting formed the basis for the NIE's claim that Iraq had mobile BW production facilities, demonstrates the danger of relying on such sources.

In this chapter I evaluate the U.S. intelligence community's assessments of the Soviet BW program during the cold war and Iraq's BW program from the 1980s through Operation Iraqi Freedom in March 2003. These are the only modern cases where sufficient material is available to compare intelligence assessments with the "ground truth" as revealed by defectors, inspectors, scholars, and investigative journalists. The evaluations in this chapter are as comprehensive as possible given the restrictions on the release of intelligence documents and the lack

---

9. Ibid., 504, 507.

10. Lawrence Freedman, *U.S. Intelligence and the Soviet Threat* (Princeton: Princeton University Press, 1986), 188.

of access to definitive accounts of Moscow's and Baghdad's BW capabilities and intentions.

During the cold war, the United States and its allies lacked a clear understanding of the size, scope, and sophistication of the Soviet BW program. Although the United States gradually obtained more intelligence on Soviet BW activities from human sources, overhead imagery, communication intercepts, and scientific publications, it continued to underestimate the Soviet BW program. This miscalculation was only revealed in 1989 by the defection of Vladimir Pasechnik, a high-ranking member of Biopreparat and the director of a key BW research institute. Based on his information, British and U.S. intelligence agencies doubled their estimates of the number of Soviet BW facilities.[11] When the full extent of the Soviet BW program was finally revealed by additional defectors, the skeptics in the intelligence community had to acknowledge that even the most alarmist analysts had underestimated the threat.

U.S. intelligence on Iraq's BW program prior to the 1991 Gulf War had significant gaps, but it was far superior to the deeply flawed intelligence on Iraq's BW program in 2002. Although the United States correctly assessed in 1991 that Iraq had begun production of two BW agents and had probably filled these agents into munitions, the intelligence community failed to identify virtually all of Iraq's BW facilities, including the main production plant at Al Hakam. As a result, Iraq's BW production infrastructure emerged virtually unscathed from the 1991 Gulf War. Prior to Operation Iraqi Freedom in March 2003, the U.S. intelligence community fundamentally misread Iraq's intentions and grossly exaggerated Iraq's BW capabilities. The intelligence community believed that Iraq had an active BW program that was even larger and more advanced than it was in 1991, as well as stocks of biological weapons and mobile production facilities. The Iraq Survey Group, which was responsible for investigating Iraq's WMD programs following the war, has shown that every aspect of the U.S. biological threat assessment prior to the war was deeply flawed.

Accurate and timely intelligence has long been regarded as a crucial element in defending against biological weapons. In 1969 President Nixon stated that the unilateral renunciation of biological weapons by the United States would not "leave us vulnerable to surprise by an enemy who does not observe these rational restraints. Our intelligence community will continue to watch carefully the nature and extent of the biological programs of others."[12] The sobering conclusion

---

11. Bill Gertz, "Defecting Russian Scientist Revealed Biological Arms Efforts," *Washington Times,* July 4, 1992, A4; and R. Jeffrey Smith, "Russia Fails to Detail Germ Arms," *Washington Post,* August 31, 1992, A1.

12. "Statement by the President," Office of the White House Press Secretary, November 25, 1969, 2, National Security Council Subject Files. Box 310; folder 5: Chemical, Biological Warfare (Toxins, etc.)

of this chapter is that intelligence on biological threats will most likely not be sufficient to prevent surprises.

U.S. Assessment of the Soviet BW Program

U.S. intelligence on the Soviet BW program is divided into two periods, from 1945 to 1970 and from 1971 to 1990. During the first period, the United States struggled to piece together a coherent picture of the Soviet program from human sources, scientific publications, and overhead reconnaissance systems. The lack of hard evidence, however, frustrated analysts and contributed to misinterpretations of Soviet activities in this field. During the second period, more compelling information from satellites and human sources became available regarding suspect BW sites, but the purpose and activities of most of these sites remained ambiguous. The scope, scale, and sophistication of the BW program were not revealed until the defection of key Soviet scientists beginning in 1989.

The Soviet Union was particularly adept at exploiting secrecy and the overlap between offensive, defensive, and civilian biological activities to conceal its BW program. The Soviet Union's totalitarian government, intrusive security services, and the vastness of its territory facilitated the creation of a highly secret BW program. The Soviet BW program was closely associated with the internal security services from its inception.[13] Even within the obsessively secretive Soviet Union, the BW program was "one of the best-guarded secrets."[14] The variety and extent of diseases in the Soviet Union caused by pathogens that were also viewed as candidate BW agents also made it difficult to interpret the purpose of Soviet activities in this field. Since these diseases were legitimate public health, veterinary, or agricultural problems, extensive research on these diseases for peaceful purposes was justifiable. The Soviets were also known to have a robust biological defense program, which was seen as an extension of the overall Soviet investment in civil defense. In addition, the Soviet emphasis on live vaccines and aerogenic immunization (delivering vaccines through an aerosol instead of direct injection) provided additional cover for research, production, and testing activities with direct applicability to developing biological weapons.[15]

vol. 1, Nixon Presidential Materials, National Archives, College Park, Maryland [hereafter Nixon Papers].

13. See chapter 3.

14. Russian deputy foreign minister Grigory Berdennikov quoted in John Barry, "Planning a Plague," *Newsweek,* February 1, 1993, 40.

15. Defense Intelligence Agency (DIA), *Chemical and Biological Warfare Capabilities—USSR,* DST-1600S-034–76-SUP-1, March 1976, 247–248, Chemical and Biological Warfare Collection, box 13, National Security Archives [hereafter NSA].

The Soviet Union also possessed a vast biological research-and-industrial complex with over 100,000 workers, 200 factories, and 150 research centers.[16] The Soviets used this civilian industry to conceal offensive facilities and activities as part of a denial-and-deception campaign. In effect, the U.S. intelligence community had to contend with lots of "noise" as well as an adversary that was skilled in masking "signals" that could reveal information about its development of biological weapons.

U.S. Intelligence on the Soviet BW Program, 1945–1970

The U.S. assessment of Soviet BW activities during this period oscillated considerably due to the paucity of hard evidence and the multiple plausible interpretations of the available information. From the end of World War II through the late 1950s, the United States remained suspicious that the Soviet Union had an offensive BW program, but it lacked the evidence to demonstrate this. Instead, analysts had to rely on reports of Soviet human sources obtained by German intelligence during World War II and highly ambiguous indirect indicators of current Soviet interest in BW. By the late 1950s, overhead imagery provided by U-2 reconnaissance aircraft as well as Soviet scientific publications provided enough valuable, yet still ambiguous, information for the intelligence community to reach a firmer conclusion about the existence of a Soviet offensive BW research-and-development program. The United States, however, was unable to successfully gauge the size, scope, and maturity of the BW program. In addition, the intelligence community failed to detect the existence of the Soviet Union's extensive antiagriculture program. A flawed reassessment of Soviet BW intelligence in the mid-1960s led the CIA to judge that the Soviet program was still in the research stage and relatively primitive. Although compelling new information emerged in the late 1960s that indicated that the Soviet BW program was much more advanced than believed, a high-level review of intelligence on Soviet BW raised new doubts about the status of the Soviet program.

The United States knew virtually nothing about Soviet BW intentions or capabilities until the end of World War II.[17] For the next decade or so, the most important sources of information on the Soviet BW program were German personnel knowledgeable about Soviet BW activities who were debriefed after the war. The most valuable information was obtained from Heinrich Kliewe,

---

16. The Soviet Union was the world's largest producer of single-cell protein and microbial pesticides. Anthony Rimmington, *Ex-USSR Biotechnology Industry* (York: Technology Detail, 1994), 5.

17. Central Intelligence Agency (CIA), *The Soviet BW Program: Scientific Intelligence Research Aid,* OSI-RA/61-3, Office of Scientific Intelligence, April 24, 1961, 1, Freedom of Information Act [hereafter FOIA].

a leading bacteriologist who was part of the German biological research program during World War II, and Walter Hirsch, former chief of German chemical weapons research and development and head of the German BW planning committee.[18] According to two Soviet sources debriefed by German intelligence in 1942, the Soviet Union had an active BW research-and-development program at multiple locations that included testing of munitions filled with BW agents.[19] At that time, the United States had no way of confirming the validity of the information provided by these sources. Nevertheless, fifteen years later the CIA still considered the information provided by Hirsch as "one of the pillars upon which the still incompletely known historical developments of Soviet BW activities has been partially reconstructed."[20]

As a result of the paucity of useful information, intelligence assessments of Soviet BW activities through the 1950s were based primarily on extrapolations from the Hirsch report, assumptions derived from the U.S. experience with biological warfare, the study of Communist propaganda regarding alleged U.S. use of biological weapons during the Korean War for clues to Soviet sophistication and knowledge about BW agents and delivery systems, and speculation about Soviet motivations and capabilities.[21]

In 1958 the CIA reported that it had "confirmed" the existence of an active Soviet BW research-and-development program based on an analysis of Soviet scientific publications and imagery of a suspect test site on Vozrozhdeniya Island in the Aral Sea.[22] The breakthrough in BW intelligence came in August 1957 when a U-2 reconnaissance aircraft photographed Vozrozhdeniya Island.[23] Vozrozhdeniya Island had been identified by Hirsch and Kliewe in the 1940s as a BW testing site. However, no description of the installation or confirmation of

---

18. Erhard Geissler, "Biological Warfare Activities in Germany, 1923–1945," in *Biological and Toxin Weapons: Research, Development and Use from the Middle Ages to 1945,* ed. Erhard Geissler and John Ellis van Courtland Moon (Oxford: Oxford University Press, 1999), 97.

19. Walter Hirsch, *Soviet BW and CW Preparations and Capabilities* (Washington, DC: U.S. Army Chemical Intelligence Branch, May 1951), 101–13. The information provided by Kliewe is summarized in Office of Naval Intelligence, *Naval Aspects of Biological Warfare,* August 1947, 46–51, General Records of the Department of the Navy, RG 80, National Archives II, National Archives and Records Administration, College Park, Maryland [hereafter NARA].

20. CIA, *Soviet BW Program,* 1.

21. Wilton E. Lexow and Julian Hoptman, "The Enigma of Soviet BW," *Studies in Intelligence* 9 (Spring 1965): 15–16.

22. CIA, *Main Trends in Soviet Capabilities and Policies, 1958–1963,* NIE 11–4-58, December 23, 1958, 35, FOIA. In contrast, between 1948 and 1952 U.S. intelligence had only "strongly suggested" a R&D program, and by 1956 the CIA was estimating that the Soviets "almost certainly" had an active program. CIA, *Soviet BW Program,* 7.

23. Photographs of Vozrozhdeniya Island were taken during U-2 Mission 4035 on August 5, 1957. Some of these photographs can be found at http://www.globalsecurity.org/wmd/world/russia/vozrozh denly.htm.

its existence was possible until the U-2 overflight. These pictures led the CIA to conclude that the island was probably a BW test site with the potential for self-sufficient research, development, and testing as well as the production of enough biological agents for experiments or clandestine weapons. Since the CIA had not been able to identify any other BW facilities in the Soviet Union, it was possible that Soviet BW development took place solely on the island with the exception of any large-scale agent and munitions production.[24]

Soviet scientific publications that began emerging in 1956 provided indirect evidence that the Soviet Union was conducting an active research program on both the offensive and defensive aspects of BW.[25] These publications provided a wealth of data on Soviet applied research for public health and defensive purposes, some of which could have offensive implications. Such multiuse research included studies of aerobiology and aerosolized agents; immunity against respiratory infection; immunogenic properties of airborne organisms; and development of new vaccines, treatments, detection devices, and disinfection techniques.[26]

In 1964 this conventional wisdom on the Soviet BW program was challenged by two CIA analysts. Wilton Lexow and Julian Hoptman stated that "there is no firm evidence of the existence of an offensive Soviet BW program."[27] As a result of this reassessment, the 1964 National Intelligence Estimate (NIE) on the Soviet BW program concluded that "we believe that a BW research program exists in the USSR, but we know of no facility devoted exclusively to offensive BW research and we have no evidence of field testing."[28]

The centerpiece of this reappraisal was a reinterpretation of the evidence linking Vozrozhdeniya Island to the Soviet BW program. The NIE acknowledged that the intelligence community had accumulated indications of possible BW activity at a few locations, with Vozrozhdeniya Island as the most suspicious, but noted that there was "no strong evidence, however, that this activity is connected with BW research."[29] Lexow and Hoptman believed that there were several features of the island's installations that did not fit the profile for a BW research-and-testing facility. First, the five test sites on the southern part of the island, each of which comprised a tower and one or two small buildings, were too small, had poorly defined configurations, and were unlike those

---

24. CIA, *Soviet BW Program,* iii, 68, 77, 83–84.

25. For an overview of the intelligence community's efforts to analyze Soviet scientific publications during this time, see J. J. Bagnall, "The Exploitation of Russian Scientific Literature for Intelligence Purposes," *Studies in Intelligence* (Summer 1958): 45–49, FOIA.

26. CIA, *Soviet BW Program,* iii, 3, 8, 54.

27. Lexow and Hoptman, "Enigma of Soviet BW," 15.

28. CIA, *Soviet Capabilities and Intentions with Respect to Biological Warfare,* NIE 11–6-64, August 26, 1964, 1, Declassified Document Reference Service.

29. CIA, *Soviet Capabilities and Intentions,* 2.

used for Soviet CW or U.S. CBW testing. Second, the island appeared to lack the necessary air support for BW testing activities such as a sophisticated landing strip, decontamination capabilities, or night-landing facilities. Third, the buildings and inhabitants of nearby Konstantin Island lay in the path of prevailing winds and this would preclude conducting tests with live BW agents on Vozrozhdeniya.[30]

The initial CIA assessment that Vozrozhdeniya Island was a BW test facility, based on German human intelligence and U-2 photographs, was accurate. Vozrozhdeniya Island was used to test biological weapons in 1936–37 and then abandoned until the early 1950s, when a new laboratory was built on the island to conduct experiments and a military unit was garrisoned there to support the test program. Until 1991 the island was the site of tests conducted to study the aerobiology of a variety of dangerous pathogens, the dissemination pattern of munitions, and the effectiveness of defensive equipment and materials.[31]

The reassessment of Vozrozhdeniya Island's role as a BW test site in the mid-1960s represents an example of the analytical bias known as mirror-imaging. Mirror-imaging is "assuming that other states or individuals will act just the way we do."[32] The reasons provided by the analysts for their reassessment—the small and oddly configured test grids, the lack of sophisticated air-support capabilities, and the proximity of an inhabited compound to the test girds—reflect an expectation that the Soviet Union would construct and operate a BW test site the same way the United States would.[33] In fact, the island was equipped with an airport in the northern part of the island that provided regular plane and helicopter transportation to the mainland. It may not have been as well equipped as a U.S. counterpart, but this may have simply reflected the more primitive nature of Soviet air-support operations. In addition, the presence of the compound on nearby Konstantin Island in the path of the prevailing winds from the test site did not deter the Soviets from conducting tests with live agents.[34]

---

30. Lexow and Hoptman, "Enigma of Soviet BW," 18–19.

31. Gulbarshyn Bozheyeva, Yerlan Kunakbayev, and Dastan Yeleukenov, *Former Soviet Biological Weapons Facilities in Kazakhstan: Past Present and Future,* Occasional Paper 1 (Monterey, CA: Center for Nonproliferation Studies, 1999), 5–7.

32. Mark M. Lowenthal, *Intelligence: From Secrets to Policy* (Washington, DC: CQ Press, 2003), 8.

33. During the 1950s, the CIA photointerpreters who analyzed foreign nuclear, biological, and chemical weapon research and production facilities were given tours of such facilities in the United States to familiarize them with their salient characteristics. Dino A. Brugioni, "Photo Interpretation in the 1950s," in *Early Cold War Overflights, 1950–1956 Symposium Proceedings,* vol. 1, *Memoirs,* ed. R. Cargill Hall and Clayton D. Laurie (Washington, DC: National Reconnaissance Office, 2003), 315.

34. This proved to be a mistake, however, and the island had to be evacuated and abandoned in 1960 after it was contaminated due to a wind shift during a BW test. Bozheyeva, Kunakbayev, and Yeleukenov, *Former Soviet Biological Weapons Facilities in Kazakhstan,* 6.

Lexow and Hoptman also took issue with what they deemed an "unrewarding" twenty-year search for indirect indicators of a Soviet BW program in Soviet scientific and military publications.[35] They argued that the intelligence community lacked sufficient evidence to conclude that Soviet research on dangerous pathogens was part of an offensive program or to estimate the types and quantities of BW agents that might be part of such a program. The potential BW agents that the Soviets were known to have conducted research on were either endemic to the Soviet Union and thus legitimate subjects for medical, public health, or veterinary research or were known to be under investigation by the U.S. BW program. In addition, the Soviets were known to have a biological defense program administered by the Ministry of Defense to protect military forces and civilian populations against biological weapons. Only Soviet studies on botulinum toxin, *Y. pestis,* and *B. anthracis* were believed to have offensive applications.[36]

The intelligence community also lacked any evidence of Soviet development, production, or stockpiling of biological munitions and delivery systems or doctrine or training for the employment of biological weapons. The Soviets were judged as being highly unlikely to consider biological weapons as useful weapons during limited or general warfare due to the delayed effects of these weapons and the greater predictability and destructiveness of nuclear weapons.[37] As a result of this reassessment of Soviet BW intelligence, the 1964 NIE "depart[s] radically from the old assumption and look[s] at Soviet military doctrine realistically in terms of limited BW activity and the unsure potential of BW weapons."[38] The Soviet offensive program was judged to be at the research stage and the Soviet military only capable of conducting clandestine attacks with biological weapons.[39]

This view of the Soviet BW program became the new conventional wisdom. Although it was briefly challenged in 1969 as a result of new information from a defector, after a review led by the National Security Council (NSC) it emerged even more deeply entrenched than before.

In February 1969, the intelligence community issued a new NIE on the Soviet BW program that reported that the Soviet Union was conducting research and development on the possible military application of biological agents.[40] Although virtually all of the available evidence regarding Soviet BW-related activities could be attributed to legitimate work in public health and defensive aspects of biological warfare, new information regarding Soviet BW doctrine indicated

35. Lexow and Hoptman, "Enigma of Soviet BW," 15–16.

36. CIA, *Soviet Capabilities and Intentions,* 2–4.

37. Ibid., 1, 3, 5.

38. Lexow and Hoptman, "Enigma of Soviet BW," 20.

39. CIA, *Soviet Capabilities and Intentions,* 2–4.

40. CIA, *Soviet Chemical and Biological Warfare Capabilities,* NIE 11–11–69, February 13, 1969, 10, FOIA.

a more mature offensive program than previously suspected. The United States had obtained information from a high-level Czechoslovakian defector on the existence of Warsaw Pact contingency plans to deliver biological weapons from the Soviet Union to front commanders in Eastern Europe in the event of a decision to use these weapons to stop or slow an invasion.[41] Additionally, Warsaw Pact military organizational plans depicted components responsible for employing biological weapons.[42] This type of contingency would presumably require the Soviets to have standardized BW agents and munitions and either stockpiles of such weapons or the ability to produce them rapidly. While the intelligence community judged that the Soviet Union had the technical ability to develop, produce, and stockpile militarily significant quantities of BW agents, analysts had no information on such activities and could not estimate the types and quantities of agents that might be available to the Soviets for offensive use. Although the Soviets were still considered unlikely to employ biological weapons in an initial strategic attack, their subsequent use during a general war was now deemed to be possible.[43]

A review of U.S. CBW policy by the National Security Council in 1969 under the auspices of National Security Study Memorandum 59 included an evaluation of U.S. intelligence on Soviet CBW capabilities and intentions. By the end of this review, the U.S. assessment of the Soviet BW program had softened significantly. Although the report of the Czechoslovakian defector Sejna on Soviet planning for the use of biological weapons was included in both draft and final papers, it was consistently followed by a disclaimer that the United States had no direct evidence of Soviet production, weaponization, stockpiling, or testing of biological weapons.[44]

According to one account based on interviews with participants in the review process, the State Department's Bureau of Intelligence and Research objected to analyses by the CIA and Defense Intelligence Agency that included quantitative estimates of Soviet CW and BW stockpiles. When the intelligence agencies

---

41. Jan Sejna had been chief of staff of the Czechoslovakian Ministry of Defense as well as secretary of the Military Committee of the Central Committee, the state's highest military policy-making body, before his defection in February 1968. Jan Sejna, *We Will Bury You* (London: Sidgwick and Jackson, 1982), 32–34, 109. On Sejna's revelations about Soviet CBW policy, see Joseph D. Douglass Jr., "The Expanding Threat of Chemical-Biological Warfare: A Case of U.S. Tunnel Vision," *Strategic Review* (Fall 1986): 42–43.

42. Foreign Capabilities Task Force, "The Nature of the Threat to the U.S. and its Allies," September 29, 1969, 3, FOIA.

43. CIA, *Soviet Chemical and Biological Warfare Capabilities,* 9–10.

44. See Foreign Capabilities Task Force, "Nature of the Threat," August 29, 1969, 6, FOIA; Foreign Capabilities Task Force, "Nature of the Threat," September 12, 1969, 6, FOIA; and Foreign Capabilities Task Force, "Nature of the Threat," September 29, 1969, 3, FOIA; Interdepartmental Political-Military Group, *U.S. Policy on Chemical and Biological Warfare and Agents,* Report to the National Security Council submitted in response to National Security Study Memorandum 59, October 15, 1969, 8, FOIA.

were unable to provide evidence supporting these "elaborate, precise estimates" to National Security Council staffers, the U.S. intelligence estimates of Soviet BW activity had to be severely downgraded.[45] After the completion of National Security Study Memorandum 59, the head of the interagency review committee wrote to a colleague in the Bureau of Intelligence and Research to report that during the course of the review it had become clear that some of the intelligence on Soviet CBW capabilities was out of date. As a result, the National Security Study Memorandum reflected new views on Soviet capabilities that had not been incorporated officially into the national intelligence estimates.[46] It was later reported that, as a result of this intelligence review, "there are now growing indications that more and more U.S. officials do not believe the Soviet Union to possess, or have possessed, an offensive BW capability of much, or even any, military significance."[47] By 1970 the lack of hard evidence led the U.S. government to conclude that "useful intelligence on actual production, weaponization and stockpiling remains nonexistent, and information on the Soviet biological warfare program remains incomplete in almost all important details."[48]

During this period, the U.S. intelligence community had an extremely limited ability to detect, identify, and monitor Soviet BW facilities. Although the United States identified dozens of facilities in the Soviet Union in the 1950s that could possibly be engaged in BW research, it was unable to conclusively link any of them to a BW program.[49] The intelligence community was unable to confirm the identity, location, and activities of the three Soviet military BW research centers in Kirov, Zagorsk, and Sverdlovsk that were active during this period. The CIA successfully identified the Scientific Research Institute of Epidemiology and Hygiene of the Armed Forces in Kirov as the center of antipersonnel BW research in the Soviet Union, but soon lost track of it. The institute was best known for its development of live dry vaccines against *B. anthracis, Y. pestis, F. tularensis,* and *Brucella* spp. The CIA believed that these diseases were the most likely Soviet antipersonnel agents, since there were close parallels between the research

45. Forrest Russell Frank, "U.S. Arms Control Policymaking: The 1972 Bacteriological Treaty Case" (PhD diss., Stanford University, 1974), 180.

46. Department of State, Memorandum from Ronald I. Spiers, PM, to Mr. Cline, INR, Subject: "Chemical and Biological Warfare," December 5, 1969, FOIA.

47. Stockholm International Peace Research Institute, *The Problem of Chemical and Biological Warfare,* vol. 2, *CB Weapons Today* (New York: Humanities Press, 1973), 174.

48. Interdepartmental Political-Military Working Group, *Annual Review of United States Chemical Warfare and Biological Research Programs as of 1 November 1970,* 19, FOIA.

49. Department of the Army, *Preliminary Report on Soviet Activities and Capabilities in Biological Warfare Research and Development* (Washington, DC: Intelligence Division, General Staff of the United States Army, October 12, 1950), U.S. Army Military History Institute [hereafter MHI]; and Department of the Army, *Soviet Biological Warfare Capabilities* (Washington, DC: Office of the Assistant Chief of Staff, G-2, September 9, 1955), MHI.

and production of live vaccines and BW agents. Soviet scientific publications were crucial to the identification of the institute, but tracking the institute's activities became extremely difficult after 1948 when it stopped publishing in scientific journals. As a result, by 1961 it was unknown if the institute still existed and, if active, if it was still located in Kirov.[50] It is now known that this facility, renamed the Scientific Research Institute of Microbiology, became the hub of the Soviet Union's expanded BW program after World War II and the most important BW institute in the Soviet military.

In the late 1950s, the United States received intelligence from human sources on suspected Soviet BW sites at Zagorsk and Sverdlovsk.[51] Neither of these facilities, however, is mentioned in any of the intelligence reports on the Soviet BW program that have been declassified so far.[52] It is possible that the information provided by these sources was not sufficiently detailed and credible enough to be included in the intelligence reports or that their importance was recognized only in hindsight when additional information came to light that implicated these sites in BW activities. According to Gary Crocker, who was responsible for CBW at the Bureau of Intelligence and Research beginning in the mid-1970s, Sverdlovsk and Zagorsk were considered probable BW sites by analysts, but managers were more skeptical and so these assessments weren't included in higher-level intelligence reports.[53] The facility at Sverdlovsk was established in the late 1940s and specialized in bacterial BW agents such as *B. anthracis* and *C. botulinum*.[54] The facility at Zagorsk, which was established in 1954 as the Scientific Research Institute of Sanitation, became the Soviet military's primary research center on viral and rickettsial agents.[55]

In addition, the United States failed to detect the existence of "mobilization" BW production plants at Omutninsk and Berdsk, which were built or expanded in the 1960s.[56] During peacetime, these plants produced civilian products, but they were designed to produce BW agents on a large scale during wartime.

---

50. CIA, *Soviet BW Program,* 60–64, 87–98.

51. Mangold and Goldberg, *Plague Wars,* 50–51; and interview with Gary Crocker, Washington, DC, November 12, 2004.

52. This includes a comprehensive 1961 review of the Soviet BW program by the CIA's Office of Scientific Intelligence and the 1964 and 1969 NIEs on the Soviet BW program.

53. Interviews with Gary Crocker, Washington, DC, November 12, 2004, and January 21, 2005.

54. Anthony Rimmington, "From Offence to Defence? Russia's Reform of its Biological Weapons Complex and the Implications for Western Security," *Journal of Slavic Military Studies* 16, no. 1 (2003): 12–15.

55. R. N. Lukina, E. P. Lukin, and V. K. Bulavko, eds., *Dostoiny Izvestnosti: 50 let Virusologicheskomu Tsentru Ministerstva Oborony* [Worthy of fame: 50 years of the Ministry of Defense's Virology Center] (Sergiev Posad, Russia: Ves' Sergiev Posad, 2004).

56. Ken Alibek, *Biohazard: The Chilling True Story of the Largest Covert Biological Weapons Program in the World—Told from the Inside by the Man Who Ran It,* with Stephen Handelman (New York: Random House, 1999), 51–52, 59–61.

The intelligence community did not fare well in its assessment of the BW agents being developed by the Soviet Union. Although the intelligence community consistently reported that they had no evidence of the type and quantities of BW agents being developed by the Soviet Union, it did generate lists of the most likely threat agents. These agents were generally the same as those developed by the United States and its allies during World War II. In addition, Soviet defectors interrogated by Germany during World War II indicated that the Soviets were primarily interested in *B. anthracis, F. tularensis, Y. pestis,* and *V. cholerae.*[57] Soviet scientific publications did not provide enough evidence to determine which biological agents were under investigation for offensive purposes, but there were indications of at least sixteen agents being studied. The most commonly discussed agents were *B. anthracis, F. tularensis, Y, pestis,* and *Brucella* spp. (there are several species of bacteria in the *Brucella* genus that cause brucellosis).[58]

Based on the 1992 Russian confidence-building declaration to the United Nations, the intelligence community accurately identified six agents and missed two with two false positives.[59] Based on Ken Alibek's account of the agents weaponized by the Soviet Union prior to 1972, the intelligence community accurately identified five BW agents and missed four, with three false positives.[60] The United States' assessment of Soviet BW threat agents is evaluated in table 5.

The United States was only partially successful in its effort to detect Soviet preparations for antiagricultural biological warfare. It correctly identified Soviet interest in certain animal pathogens for BW purposes but failed to detect its interest in anticrop BW or the establishment of a dedicated antiagricultural BW program. As early as 1954, the intelligence community had judged that the Soviet Union was capable of developing anticrop and antilivestock biological weapons.[61] The Soviets were believed to have only a marginal interest in anticrop biological warfare, and there was no evidence of Soviet interest in developing plant pathogens.[62] In contrast, the intelligence community believed that the Soviets were investigating the use of rinderpest and foot-and-mouth disease, both highly contagious viruses lethal to livestock, for use in antilivestock

57. Hirsch, *Soviet BW and CW Preparations and Capabilities,* 101–13.

58. CIA, *Soviet BW Program,* iii, 3, 8, 54.

59. Russian Federation, "Declaration of Past Activity in Regard to Offensive and Defensive Programs of Biological Research and Development," United Nations Form F, DDA/4–92/BWIII, 1992, 52.

60. Testimony of Dr. Kenneth Alibek before the Joint Economic Committee, *Terrorist and Intelligence Operations: Potential Impact on the U.S. Economy,* 105th Cong., 2nd sess., May 20, 1998.

61. Scientific Estimates Committee, *Estimate of Soviet Biological Warfare Capabilities through 1960,* SEC 2–54, April 20, 1954, 14–33, FOIA.

62. CIA, *Soviet BW Program,* iii, 3, 8, 54; CIA, *Soviet Capabilities and Intentions,* 2–4.

TABLE 5. Evaluation of U.S. Assessment of Soviet Biological Threat Agents, 1945–1970

Pathogen	1964 NIE	1992 Russian Declaration	Alibek	Evaluation
Y. pestis	X	X	X	Accurate
B. anthracis	X	X	X	Accurate
F. tularensis	X	X	X	Accurate
Brucella spp.	X	X	X	Accurate
C. burnetii	X	X	X	Accurate
Botulinum toxin	X	X		Accurate/false positive
Yellow fever	X			False positive
Tick-borne encephalitis	X			False positive
R. prowazekii		X	X	False negative
VEE		X	X	False negative
Variola			X	False negative
B. mallei			X	False negative

biological warfare.[63] This assessment was based on reports of suspected antilivestock BW research conducted during World War II, the presence of animal pens on Vozrozhdeniya Island suitable for large domestic animals, and the known vulnerability of North American livestock to these diseases.[64] The United States, however, lacked information on the locations where antilivestock BW research was conducted or the status of the program.

In 1958 the Soviet Union established an ambitious program, code-named Ecology, to develop and produce plant and animal pathogens for military purposes. The program reportedly developed foot-and-mouth disease and rinderpest for use against cattle, African swine fever for use against pigs, and *Chlamydia psittaci* (the bacterium that causes psittacosis) for use against poultry. Anticrop agents targeted wheat, rye, corn, and rice. The Ministry of Agriculture established six research institutes under this program, split between the anticrop and antilivestock missions.[65] None of these sites were detected by U.S. intelligence. The cause

63. CIA, *Soviet Gross Capabilities for Attack on the U.S. and Key Overseas Installations and Forces through Mid-1959,* NIE 11–56, March 6, 1956, 5, FOIA; and CIA, *Soviet Science and Technology,* NIE 11–6-59, July 21, 1959, 31, FOIA.

64. CIA, *Soviet BW Program,* 104–7.

65. Anthony Rimmington, "The Soviet Union's Offensive Program: The Implications for Contemporary Arms Control," in *Biological Warfare and Disarmament,* ed. Susan Wright (Lanham, MD: Rowman and Littlefield, 2002), 113–15; Alibek, *Biohazard,* 37–38, 301; Kenneth Alibek, "The Soviet Union's Anti-Agricultural Biological Weapons," *Annals of New York Academy of Sciences* 894 (1999): 18–19; and Igor V. Domaradskij and Wendy Orent, "Achievements of the Soviet Biological Weapons Programme and Implications for the Future," *Scientific and Technical Review* 25, no. 1 (2006): 157.

of this failure to detect such a large undertaking is unclear. To the extent that the program was engaged primarily in research during this period and focused on plant and animal pathogens that were legitimate threats to Soviet agriculture, Soviet scientific publications and overhead imagery would not have made it possible to differentiate between hostile and peaceful research. It appears that without human intelligence to guide analysts, the available sources of information were not sufficient to enable the detection of this program and its related facilities.

Overall, the elements of the Soviet BW program correctly identified by the intelligence community can be attributed primarily to human sources, including information provided by Hirsch and Kliewe in the 1940s. Although the history of the Soviet BW program before and during World War II remains murky, the information provided by Hirsch and Kliewe has generally been accepted as accurate.[66] The collection and analysis of Soviet scientific publications supplemented this information, particularly regarding potential BW agents and the activities of the Scientific Research Institute of Epidemiology and Hygiene at Kirov. These publications, however, failed to reveal the Soviet offensive antiagriculture program, the full extent of Soviet research on antipersonnel BW agents, or any information on the military's other BW research centers at Sverdlovsk and Zagorsk. Overhead imagery was useful in confirming the existence of a previously reported test site in the Aral Sea, but it did not lead to the discovery of any new BW facilities. Despite the conventional wisdom that imagery intelligence provides hard intelligence, the imagery obtained of the installations on Vozrozhdeniya Island was ambiguous enough to allow analysts to wrongly dismiss the site as a BW-testing facility.

This reassessment of the role of Vozrozhdeniya Island drove a more fundamental shift in the intelligence community's view of the Soviet BW program. Based on this new perspective, the absence of firm evidence for an offensive military program was interpreted as evidence that such a program did not exist. Lexow and Hoptman believed that if the Soviet Union had a BW program, even a highly secretive one, the United States would have already detected it as it had done with the Soviet nuclear and chemical weapons programs.[67] This perception gained ground during the 1969 intelligence review, which again emphasized how little hard evidence the intelligence community had on Soviet BW capabilities and intentions. The information provided by defecting Czechoslovakian general Jan Sejna on the Soviet Union's preparedness to use biological weapons was apparently not sufficient to alter this view of the Soviet program.

---

66. Valentin Bojtzov and Erhard Geissler, "Military Biology in the USSR, 1920–1945," in *Biological and Toxin Weapons:* ed. Geissler and Moon, 153–67; and Rimmington, "The Soviet Union's Offensive Program," 121–27.

67. Lexow and Hoptman, "Enigma of Soviet BW," 20.

The paucity of direct and unambiguous intelligence on Soviet BW activities continued to be a problem that plagued the intelligence community until the defection
of a senior Soviet BW scientist in 1989.

U.S. Intelligence on the Soviet BW Program, 1971–1990

During the 1970s and 1980s, the United States received new evidence of continued Soviet interest in biological weapons, including the expansion of suspicious sites, construction of new facilities, a suspicious outbreak of anthrax near
a suspected BW facility, and reports of research on genetic engineering applicable to biological weapons. This evidence began emerging at a politically in-
opportune time. During the early 1970s, the United States was in the process of
closing down its offensive program, negotiating the BWC to outlaw biological
weapons, and pursuing a policy of détente with the Soviet Union. Additional evidence of Soviet BW capabilities and intentions emerged in the late 1970s with
the defection of a senior Soviet official and the anthrax outbreak in Sverdlovsk.[68]
This new evidence coincided with the end of détente, and the Reagan administration began publicizing this intelligence as part of a wider effort to discredit
the Soviet Union as a reliable arms control partner and to reinforce its image as
"the evil empire."

On the macro level, U.S. intelligence was able to outline the basic contours of
the Soviet offensive program including the major sponsors of research. Although
many of the Soviet Union's BW research and production sites were identified
at one time or another by U.S. intelligence agencies, there does not appear to be
have been a consistent assessment of the role of these facilities over time or an
appreciation of the range of other facilities involved in the BW program. During the 1980s, the intelligence community identified seven BW facilities controlled by the Soviet Ministry of Defense and the Ministry of Medical and
Microbiological Industry.[69] Based on the information provided by Pasechnik,

68. In 1978 Arkady Shevchenko, a senior Soviet diplomat and adviser to Prime Minister Andrei
Gromyko, defected to the United States. Shevchenko reported that the Soviet Union had a large CBW
program and had signed the BWC because of its lack of any verification measures. The military planned
on maintaining its BW stockpiles and continuing its development of these weapons. Although Shevchenko
is not believed to have offered any hard evidence of these claims, his seniority and access to the inner circle of Soviet decision making lent weight to his assertions. Arkady N. Shevchenko, *Breaking with Moscow*
(New York: Knopf, 1985), 173–74.

69. See Department of Defense (DOD), *Soviet Military Power 1984* (Washington, DC: GPO, 1984),
73; Douglas J. Feith, Deputy Assistant Secretary of Defense for Negotiations Policy, "Testimony before
the House Permanent Select Committee on Intelligence Subcommittee on Oversight and Evaluation, August 8, 1986"; and DIA, *Biological Warfare Capabilities—Warsaw Pact,* DST-1610S-123–90, March 1990, 12
http://www.gwu.edu/~nsarchiv/NSAEBB/NSAEBB61/Sverd29.pdf.

the U.S. and British intelligence agencies doubled their estimate of the number of Soviet BW sites.[70]

At the micro level, U.S. intelligence was more fragmentary, more ambiguous, and less detailed. According to Christopher Davis, who worked on BW issues for the British Defense Intelligence Staff and debriefed Pasechnik, "we knew quite a lot of the bones, it you like, a little bit of the flesh here and there, but we really didn't have the kind of detail, the kind of bottom line on the weapons."[71] The intelligence community lacked reliable information on the type of research being conducted inside these facilities, the agents being produced, or the types of weapons that would disperse them. This lack of fidelity had a negative impact on the overall assessment of Soviet BW capabilities and intentions at the macro level. As one former CIA official remarked, "you must understand, there was still a dearth of intelligence on the Soviet BW program [in 1988]. Even some senior CIA analysts still did not believe that the Soviets had a BW program. So some people in authority did not believe they had this capability. The believers didn't know for sure."[72]

The gaps and shortfalls in U.S. knowledge of the Soviet BW program were revealed in 1989 when Vladimir Pasechnik defected to the United Kingdom.[73] Pasechnik offered firsthand evidence of Soviet research, development, and production of biological weapons in violation of the BWC. More details became available when Kantajan Alibekov (who later changed his name to Ken Alibek), deputy director of Biopreparat, defected to the United States in 1992. These defectors revealed that the Soviet BW program was a massive enterprise employing over sixty thousand workers at over fifty facilities spread across four major ministries. The intelligence provided by Pasechnik and Alibek highlights the invaluable contribution that defectors can provide to biological threat assessments. When the full extent of the Soviet BW program was finally revealed by Pasechnik and Alibek, even the skeptics in the intelligence community had to acknowledge that the most alarmist analysts had, in fact, been underestimating the threat.

The intelligence community's overall assessment that the Soviet Union had an offensive BW program that included the development and production of BW agents, the testing and evaluation of dissemination and delivery systems, and the development of new and improved biological weapons was correct.[74] As early

70. Gertz, "Defecting Russian Scientist Revealed Biological Arms Efforts"; and Smith, "Russia Fails to Detail Germ Arms."

71. Christopher Davis, "Plague War: Interview with Christopher Davis," *Frontline,* PBS, July 1998, http://www.pbs.org/wgbh/pages/frontline/shows/plague/interviews/davis.html.

72. Former senior CIA official cited in Mangold and Goldberg, *Plague Wars,* 85.

73. See chapter 3 for details on Pasechnik's position within the Soviet BW program.

74. DIA, *Soviet Biological Warfare Threat,* DST-1610F-057–86 (Washington, DC: DIA, 1986).

as 1980, the Defense Intelligence Agency concluded that the Soviet Union possessed an illegal stockpile of BW agents and was probably involved in the development or production of biological weapons. The agency, however, lacked any sources that could describe Soviet biological munitions, the agents contained in such munitions, or the facilities where these were produced.[75] The intelligence community successfully identified most of the major participants in the Soviet BW such as the Ministries of Agriculture, Defense, Health, and Medical and Microbiological Industry, as well as the Soviet Academy of Sciences.[76] The intelligence community also identified most of the BW research, testing, and production facilities associated with the Ministry of Defense and the Ministry of Medical and Microbiological Industry, with a few important exceptions. The assessment of which institutes of the Ministry of Agriculture, Ministry of Health, and Soviet Academy of Sciences were engaged in BW research was more uneven. The community was slow to identify the Soviet BW genetic engineering program and did not fully understand the objectives of the program. The assessments of Soviet BW agent selection were poor, and there is no evidence that the United States understood the scope or scale of Soviet BW production, stockpiling, and weaponization.

The United States was able to identify four of the five military BW sites active during this time. Although the United States had been suspicious of military facilities at Sverdlovsk and Zagorsk since the 1950s, this suspicion was only confirmed following the construction of production and storage units at these sites in the late 1960s.[77] These new units included capabilities to prepare nutrient media, produce and process BW agents on a large scale, treat the resulting waste, and berm storage areas to hold munitions.[78] This new construction was first detected by photoreconnaissance satellites in 1971.[79] Satellite imagery

---

75. DIA, *USSR: Biological Warfare,* March 25, 1980, 1, http://www.gwu.edu/~nsarchiv/NSAEBB/NSAEBB61/Sverd9.pdf.

76. Unless otherwise noted, this section is based on DIA, *Biological Warfare Capabilities—Warsaw Pact.* This report is particularly significant because it was prepared using information available as of January 1989. Thus, it provides the best available snapshot of U.S. intelligence on the Soviet BW program before the defection of Vladimir Pasechnik in November 1989.

77. It is not known exactly when these units were built, but they were probably the result of a top-secret August 1967 decree issued by the Central Committee of the Communist Party and the USSR Council of Ministers that called for a buildup of Soviet CBW capabilities to offset perceived U.S. leads in these weapons. Raymond L. Garthoff, "Polyakov's Run," *Bulletin of the Atomic Scientists* 56, no. 5 (2000): 37–40. It is possible that the decision to implement this decree was not made until 1969. This timing also fits a report that in 1969 the Soviets increased the budget of the BW program to 3% of the total military budget. Confidential interview cited by Mangold and Goldberg, *Plague Wars,* 52.

78. Russian Federation, "Declaration of Past Activity," 52–53.

79. Memorandum from W. E. Colby, Director, Central Intelligence, to Dr. Albert C. Hall, Assistant Secretary of Defense (Intelligence), Subject: "Soviet BW Activity," TCS-2497-75, February 4, 1975." Box 75 [3 of 4]; folder 14, p. 1, Record Group 273: Records of the National Security Council, 1947–1969, NARA.

of Soviet military installations at Sverdlovsk and Zagorsk revealed very tall incinerator stacks and large cold-storage bunkers that could be used for stockpiling biological weapons.[80] As a result, the United States concluded that "there is good evidence that facilities necessary for BW research and production are present at both sites (i.e., research type buildings, animal holding facilities, buildings sufficiently large to house production and storage, revetted structure for munition storage)."[81]

Although satellite imagery played a key role in identifying suspect BW sites in the 1970s, this photographic evidence was not judged by all members of the intelligence community to provide a high level of confidence as to the purposes of these sites. The initial reaction of CIA analysts to the photos was that they were "inconclusive."[82] The analysts charged with conducting foreign biological threat assessments for the military said that "though there is some indication in newly acquired intelligence of the manufacture and stockpiling of biological weapons by the USSR, it is not 'hard' intelligence and not sufficient to warrant full confidence in the existence of such weapons."[83] In addition, DIA analysts considered the intelligence supporting the Soviet Union's continued development of biological agents and weapons after World War II as "largely hearsay."[84]

Policymakers were divided about how to respond to this new intelligence in the era of détente. Some government officials regarded the evidence as sufficiently ambiguous to warrant only further surveillance.[85] Although some Pentagon analysts thought that there was enough evidence to seek an explanation from the Soviet Union, and the Arms Control and Disarmament Agency urged a comprehensive National Security Council study, neither was done because the evidence was "dismissed as too flimsy."[86] This refusal to act on the available intelligence may have been motivated by a desire not to cause a crisis with Moscow during the early stages of détente and so soon after the signing of the BWC. The differences of opinion among the intelligence agencies prevented the formation

80. William Beecher, "Soviets Feared Violating Germ Weapons Ban," *Boston Globe,* September 28, 1975, 1.

81. Interdepartmental Political-Military Group, *Annual Review of United States Chemical and Biological Research Programs as of July 1, 1972,* October 26, 1972, 19, NSC, H-Files, Policy Papers, NSDMs, NSDM-35 [4 of 4]; box H-213, Nixon Papers.

82. Memorandum from Colby to Hall, Subject: "Soviet BW Activity," 2.

83. Don T. Parker, Dale O. Galloway, and J. Clifton Spendlove, *Defense against Biological Attack: A General Assessment,* Dugway Proving Ground, May 1975, 15, NSA.

84. DIA, *Chemical and Biological Warfare Capabilities—USSR,* DST-1600S-034–76-SUP-1, March 1976, 5–7, NSA.

85. Beecher, "Soviets Feared Violating Germ Weapons Ban."

86. William Beecher, "Logging Arms Tests Crucial," *Boston Globe,* October 15, 1976.

of a unified intelligence community position on the purpose of these facilities.[87] This lack of consensus allowed policymakers to emphasize the assessment that best supported their own policy preferences.

The role of the Sverdlovsk facility in the BW program was confirmed by an outbreak of anthrax in the city in 1979. The intelligence community was already suspicious of the Sverdlovsk facility's involvement in BW because of satellite photos of the installation's ventilation system, smokestacks, refrigeration facilities, animal pens, revetments, and physical security measures.[88] Beginning in late summer 1979, the intelligence community began receiving reports from eyewitnesses and émigrés of an accident having occurred at a BW facility in Sverdlovsk resulting in dozens of cases of inhalation anthrax.[89] By mid-January 1980, the intelligence community had collected enough circumstantial but compelling information to conclude that the anthrax outbreak was most likely caused by an accidental release of *B. anthracis* spores from a military facility.[90] The most detailed and convincing evidence that the outbreak involved inhalation anthrax, and not the naturally occurring gastrointestinal form of anthrax, came from a surgeon in Sverdlovsk who was involved in the response to the outbreak.[91] After the outbreak, intelligence officials also observed evidence of quarantine and decontamination efforts in the city inconsistent with the later Soviet claim that the outbreak was caused by tainted meat.[92] Analysts estimated that up to ten kilograms of *B. anthracis* spores escaped the facility, which indicated that the facility was engaged not just in research but also in production and storage of BW agents.[93] After the collapse of the Soviet Union, Russian president Boris Yeltsin acknowledged that the 1979 anthrax outbreak in Sverdlovsk had been caused by an accident at a military BW facility.[94]

The military microbiological institute at Kirov, the Soviet's oldest military BW facility, managed to elude U.S. intelligence throughout the 1970s and 1980s.[95] This failure is particularly striking in that the Soviets had even declared to the United Nations in 1987 the existence of a high-containment laboratory at

---

87. House Permanent Select Committee On Intelligence (HPSCI), *Soviet Biological Warfare Activities* (Washington, DC: GPO, 1980), 3.

88. Leslie H. Gelb, "Keeping an Eye on Russia," *New York Times Magazine,* November 29, 1981, 33.

89. DIA, *USSR: Biological Warfare,* 2.

90. CIA, *Soviet Biological Warfare Agent: Probable Cause of the Anthrax Epidemic in Sverdlovsk,* January 16, 1980, http://www.gwu.edu/~nsarchiv/NSAEBB/NSAEBB61/Sverd4.pdf.

91. DIA, *USSR: Biological Warfare,* 3–4.

92. Elisa Harris, "Sverdlovsk and Yellow Rain: Two Cases of Soviet Noncompliance?" *International Security* 11, no. 4 (1987): 49.

93. DIA, *USSR: Biological Warfare,* 4; and DIA, *Soviet Biological Warfare Threat,* 4.

94. R. Jeffrey Smith, "Yeltsin Blames '79 Anthrax on Germ Warfare Efforts," *Washington Post,* June 16, 1992, A1.

95. The facility is not listed in the 1986 or 1990 DIA reports on the Soviet BW program.

the Ministry of Defense's Scientific Research Institute of Microbiology in Kirov.[96] The cause of the failure to identify Kirov is unknown. If the 1992 Russian BWC declaration is accurate, the Soviet Union did not build production and storage capabilities at Kirov similar to those that U.S. intelligence detected at Sverdlovsk and Zagorsk. The lack of production and storage facilities at Kirov is not consistent, however, with reports by Alibek and Pasechnik that Kirov produced and stockpiled twenty tons of *Y. pestis.*[97]

The intelligence community properly identified two other military BW sites, but details on how these assessments were made is lacking. Vozrozhdeniya Island was reassessed as a BW test site by the mid-1980s.[98] When and why this occurred is unknown. The newest military BW institute, the Kirov-200 BW facility in Levintsy near Strizhi was built in the late 1980s.[99] Although this facility was not listed in the 1990 DIA report, a former U.S. State Department intelligence official claims that the United States identified this facility before the fall of the Soviet Union.[100]

The intelligence community correctly identified the Ministry of Medical and Microbiological Industry as playing a key role in the Soviet BW program. Although analysts were aware of the existence of Biopreparat, they did not grasp the central role of this organization in the Soviet Union's BW program. Biopreparat, created in 1974, played two important roles: conducting R&D on new and improved biological weapons and maintaining a network of BW mobilization plants for the production of BW agents in the event of war. The intelligence community did a much better job of identifying these BW facilities than understanding the activities taking place inside them.

U.S. intelligence did a very good job of identifying the locations of Biopreparat's research and production facilities. Biopreparat's primary R&D centers—the Institute of Ultra-Pure Biological Preparations in Leningrad, the Institute of Molecular Biology at Koltsovo (near Novosibirsk), the Institute of Applied Microbiology at Obolensk, and the Special Design Bureau of Biologically Active Substances at Berdsk—had been identified by the mid-1980s.[101] There were, however, some mistakes. The 1990 DIA report failed to list the

96. Union of Soviet Socialist Republics, *Information presented by the USSR in Compliance with the Agreements Reached at the Second Review Conference of the Convention on the Prohibition of Development, Production and Stockpiling of Bacteriological (Biological) and Toxin Weapons,* United Nations Department of Disarmament Affairs, October 13, 1987, 15.

97. Alibek, *Biohazard,* 166, 297; and Mangold and Goldberg, *Plague Wars,* 94.

98. DIA, *Soviet Biological Warfare Threat,* 1.

99. Alibek, *Biohazard,* 298; and Rimmington, "The Soviet Union's Offensive Program," 127.

100. Interview with Gary Crocker, Washington, DC, January 21, 2005.

101. William Kucewicz, "The Science of Snake Venom," *Wall Street Journal,* April 25, 1984; William Kucewicz, "A Non-Stop Russian Response to WWI," *Wall Street Journal,* May 10, 1984; and Gary Thatcher, "Disease as an Agent of War," *Christian Science Monitor,* December 15, 1988, B1.

Institute of Immunology at Lyubuchany near Moscow, which conducted research on biological agents to suppress the human immune system, and wrongly listed the Institute of Biological Testing of Chemical Compounds as part of the BW program.[102]

The United States successfully used imagery and signal intelligence to correctly identify the network of six production plants that made up the Soviet BW mobilization capacity. The CIA first identified Omutninsk as a suspect BW production plant in 1971, based on the analysis of satellite photos.[103] The Omutninsk Chemical Factory began producing biopesticides in the 1960s and was subsequently expanded by the military to serve as a BW mobilization plant.[104] By 1976 the CIA had evidence implicating ostensibly civilian facilities at Omutninsk, Pokrov, and Berdsk with the BW program, with another suspected production site under construction at Aksu (also known as Stepnogorsk).[105] By the late 1980s, two other Biopreparat mobilization-production facilities, at Penza and Kurgan, were mentioned in U.S. press reports as suspect BW production plants.[106] Each of these plants produced legitimate civilian products during peacetime, such as antibiotics, vaccines, diagnostic kits, or biopesticides. In the event of an imminent war, production could be switched over to BW agents. Each of these sites also had the capability to fill and store biological munitions in reinforced bunkers.[107]

The most suspicious indicators of BW activity at the suspect sites were bunkers designed to store explosives. The presence of these bunkers at military biological facilities suggested that the plants were involved not just in research but also in production and/or storage of biological weapons. The presence of identical configurations at civilian microbiological sites, such as Omutninsk, Pokrov,

102. DIA, *Biological Warfare Capabilities—Warsaw Pact*, 12.

103. The CIA was less certain about the involvement of this site in the Soviet BW program compared to Sverdlovsk and Zagorsk. Memorandum from Colby to Hall, "Soviet BW Activity," 2. In contrast, the State Department's Bureau of Intelligence and Research believed that the evidence was equally strong for all three facilities. According to Gary Crocker, a Bureau of Intelligence and Research CBW analyst who wrote a comprehensive assessment of the Soviet BW program in 1975, Omutninsk featured the same munition storage bunkers observed at Sverdlovsk and Zagorsk and was also implicated in military activities based on intercepts collected by the National Security Agency. Interview with Gary Crocker, Washington, DC, November 12, 2004.

104. Alibek, *Biohazard*, 51–52. This expansion probably occurred around the same time that Sverdlovsk and Zagorsk were upgraded.

105. Beecher, "Soviets Feared Violating Germ Weapons Ban"; and William Beecher, "Logging Arms Tests Crucial," *Boston Globe*, October 15, 1976.

106. Jack Anderson and Dale Van Atta, "Poison and Plague: Russia's Secret Terror Weapons," *Readers Digest*, September 1984, 56; Jack Anderson and Dale Van Atta, "Sanitation Institute a Soviet Front," *Washington Post*, August 3, 1989, cited in Milton Leitenberg, "The Biological Weapons Program of the Former Soviet Union," *Biologicals* 21, (1993): 188; and Thatcher, "Disease as an Agent of War."

107. Alibek, *Biohazard*, 298–301.

and Berdsk also suggested a military purpose for these sites.[108] In addition, analysts used communication intercepts to determine if a civilian facility was engaged in suspicious behavior such as employing encrypted communications or communicating frequently with known military sites.[109] The fact that none of these plants were listed in the 1990 DIA report as major facilities in the Soviet BW program raises questions about the intelligence community's confidence in the earlier assessment that these were indeed BW sites. This uncertainty may have been due to the "signal" of BW capabilities being masked by the "noise" of these facilities' legitimate civilian activities and the success of Soviet denial-and-deception operations.

Despite the success of intelligence agencies in identifying Soviet BW research and production facilities, insight into the activities within these facilities was harder to come by. The intelligence community took ten years to collect sufficient information to warn senior policymakers about the Soviet program launched in 1974 to apply genetic engineering and other advanced biotechnologies to the creation of new and improved biological weapons. This program, code-named Ferment (Enzyme), entailed the creation of a new organization, Biopreparat, to oversee the research, development, and testing of new and improved biological weapons at a number of newly created institutes.[110] This delay looks less dramatic when one considers that the Biopreparat R&D centers did not begin working with dangerous pathogens until 1982–83 due to safety concerns.[111] Nonetheless, it remains disturbing that the true intention behind the Soviet Union's massive investment in advanced biotechnologies went undiscovered for so long.

The intelligence community's assessment of Soviet interest in biotechnology and genetic engineering for military purposes grew from vague concern to alarm by the mid-1980s. Although the CIA had picked up reports of military-funded genetic engineering research in closed microbiological institutes in the late 1970s, analysts assessed that it was "improbable that this work is directed toward or is capable of achieving significant biological warfare applications."[112] This judgment was based in part on the skepticism of Western biologists that genetically engineered biological weapons were either feasible or necessary given the variety

108. DIA, *USSR: Biological Warfare,* Intelligence Appraisal, March 25, 1980, 2, http://www.gwu.edu/~nsarchiv/NSAEBB/NSAEBB61/Sverd9.pdf; HPSCI, *Soviet Biological Warfare Activities,* 3; and interview with Gary Crocker, Washington, DC, November 12, 2004.

109. Interviews with Gary Crocker, Washington, DC, November 12, 2004 and January 21, 2005; and interview with former National Security Agency CBW analyst, 2008.

110. Rimmington, "The Soviet Union's Offensive Program," 110–11; and Alibek, *Biohazard,* 41–42.

111. Russian Federation, "Declaration of Past Activity," 55.

112. National Foreign Assessment Center, *Soviet Recombinant DNA Research: Status and Trends,* September 1978, FOIA.

of naturally occurring lethal diseases already in existence. During the early 1980s, the United States continued to observe Soviet genetic engineering research that could have military implications, but it did not possess evidence that such research was related to biological weapons.[113]

By 1984 the intelligence community had reassessed existing intelligence or collected new intelligence of unknown origin that indicated a concerted Soviet effort to develop new and improved biological weapons using genetic engineering. The intelligence agencies now believed that in the early 1970s the Soviet Union had launched a multifaceted research-and-development program with a budget of $2 billion to field a new generation of improved chemical and biological weapons. The Soviet military was believed to be using biotechnology to develop new and more effective biological weapons by enhancing the virulence of pathogens, making them antibiotic resistant, enabling them to overcome vaccine immunity, and modifying them to complicate detection. In addition, the Soviets were suspected of modifying agent properties, such as stability, persistence, dissemination characteristics, and rapidity of effect, to tailor them for specific operational requirements.[114] This assessment of the Soviet BW program has largely been borne out by the accounts of former Soviet BW scientists.[115]

The intelligence community, however, lacked a solid understanding of the purpose of some of the Soviet research on novel biological agents. The intelligence community believed that the Soviets were interested in developing genetically modified organisms that could produce large quantities of bioregulators and toxins in civilian fermentation plants for use as weapons.[116] It now appears that the Soviets were primarily interested in inserting genes that coded for toxins and bioregulators into microorganisms to enhance their virulence, not for the production and harvesting of the compounds themselves. Under Project Factor, Soviet scientists sought to transform normally harmless microorganisms into dangerous microbes or make pathogens even more deadly.[117]

The intelligence community was less successful at understanding the scope of BW activities and identities of research institutes affiliated with other parts of

113. DOD, *Soviet Military Power* (Washington, DC: GPO, 1981), 79; and Director of Central Intelligence (DCI), *Soviet Genetic-Engineering Capabilities,* December 1983, 8–9, 13–14, FOIA.

114. DCI, *New Directions in Soviet BCW Agent Development and Their Implications,* Special National Intelligence Estimate (SNIE) 11/17–84/CX, January 24, 1984, 1–2, FOIA; DCI, *Soviet Offensive Chemical Warfare Threat to NATO,* SNIE 11/17-2-84/L, November 20, 1984, 13, FOIA; DCI, *Soviet Chemical and Biological Warfare Program,* NIE 11–17–86/5, August 1986, 1, 4, FOIA; and DIA, *Soviet Biological Warfare Threat.*

115. See Alibek, *Biohazard;* and Domaradskij and Orent, *Biowarrior.*

116. DCI, *New Directions in Soviet BCW Agent Development and Their Implications,* 1–2; and DCI, *Soviet Offensive Chemical Warfare Threat to NATO,* 13.

117. See Alibek, *Biohazard,* 154–55; Domaradskij and Orent, *Biowarrior,* 181, 206; and interview with Serguei Popov, former Biopreparat scientist, Manassas, Virginia, July 25, 2002.

the Soviet BW program, such as the Ministry of Agriculture, Ministry of Health, and Academy of Sciences. In part this was due to the greater emphasis of these organizations on basic and applied research that had offensive, defensive, and civilian applications and the lack of associated production facilities. Although the DIA identified the Ministry of Agriculture as a participant in the BW program, the intelligence community was only able to identify one of the ministry's seven facilities engaged in antiagricultural biological warfare. Notably, this was the production site at Pokrov, not one of the ministry's six anticrop and antianimal research institutes. The Pokrov Factory of Biopreparations produced diagnostics and vaccines for animal diseases during peacetime and served as a mobilization-production plant for antianimal and antipersonnel viral pathogens during wartime.[118]

The intelligence community had limited insight into the BW activities of the Ministry of Health. The DIA accurately judged the role of the Soviet antiplague system in conducting basic research on dangerous pathogens and identifying promising strains of biological agents for the military. The agency also correctly identified two of the three institutes involved in the BW program.[119] This record is not surprising given the amount of information that was openly available about these institutes and that their role in combating disease outbreaks led them to engage in a large amount of multiuse research. The ministry's 3rd Directorate completely escaped the DIA's attention. This directorate was composed of at least three research institutes that developed psychotropic and neurotropic agents for the KGB under Project Flute to induce altered mood and behavior or to cause sudden death in its victims.[120] Since only laboratory-scale production was probably required to fulfill the operational needs of the KGB, this program did not require the large-scale production facilities of the military BW program. The affiliation of this program with the KGB probably also engendered very high levels of secrecy.

The DIA correctly identified the role played by the Gamaleya Institute of Epidemiology and Microbiology and the Ivanovsky Institute of Virology within the Soviet system of scientific academies in coordinating and conducting basic research in support of the Soviet Union's biodefense program.[121] The agency's record on identifying other institutes within this system conducting BW-related

118. Alibek, *Biohazard,* 301.

119. The DIA believed that the antiplague institutes in Rostov-on-Don, Saratov, and Alma Ata were part of the Soviet BW program. DIA, *Biological Warfare Capabilities—Warsaw Pact,* 12, 21. According to Russian sources, the institutes at Rostov-on-Don, Saratov, and Volgograd were engaged in offensive BW research. Raymond A. Zilinskas, "The Anti-Plague System and the Soviet Biological Warfare Program," *Critical Reviews in Microbiology* 32 (2006): 47–64.

120. Alibek, *Biohazard,* 171–72, 302.

121. DIA, *Biological Warfare Capabilities—Warsaw Pact,* 12, 20.

research was mixed. The DIA believed that eight institutes affiliated with the Soviet Academy of Sciences conducted basic and applied research for scientific, civilian, and defensive purposes that was also used to support the offensive program.[122] Only four of these institutes were actually involved in the BW program.[123] In addition, four other institutes that did conduct fundamental research for the BW program were not listed.[124]

During this period, intelligence agencies had a poor grasp of the agents selected by the Soviets for weaponization (see table 6). The DIA believed that the Soviets had selected *B. anthracis, F. tularensis, Y. pestis,* botulinum toxin, enterotoxin, *V. cholerae,* and mycotoxins as antipersonnel BW agents.[125] Only the first four agents have been confirmed by Russian sources.[126] In addition, by the late 1980s the Soviets had standardized variola, *Brucella* spp., *C. burnetii,* VEE, and *B. mallei* as BW agents.[127]

The most startling intelligence shortcoming regarding Soviet BW agent selection was the failure to detect the Soviet development of variola (smallpox) virus as a weapon over the course of forty years. The Soviet Union stockpiled twenty tons of the virus and planned on using it against the continental United States as a strategic weapon in the event of war.[128] Meanwhile, the United States had stopped immunizing its civilian population against this disease in 1972. The intelligence community also failed to appreciate the emphasis the Soviets placed on *Y. pestis* as a strategic biological weapon. *Y. pestis* was the number one bacterial

---

122. Ibid.

123. These institutes were the Gamaleya Institute of Epidemiology and Microbiology, the Ivanovsky Institute of Virology, the Institute of Molecular Biology, and the Shemyakin Institute of Bioorganic Chemistry.

124. These institutes were the Scientific Research Institute of Poliomyelitis and Viral Encephalitis, the Institute of Proteins, the Institute of Biochemistry and Physiology of Microorganisms, and the Pacific Ocean Institute of Bioorganic Chemistry. These lists were derived from Alibek, *Biohazard,* 303; Domaradskij and Orent, *Biowarrior,* 303; and Zilinskas, "The Anti-Plague System and the Soviet Biological Warfare Program," 47–64.

125. DIA, *Soviet Biological Warfare Threat,* 2.

126. It has been reported that the Soviet BW mobilization plant at Stepnogorsk conducted research on or produced staphylococcal enterotoxin. Bozheyeva, Kunakbayev, and Yeleukenov, *Former Soviet Biological Weapons Facilities in Kazakhstan,* 9; and Anthony Rimmington, "Conversion of BW Facilities in Kazakstan," in *Conversion of Former BTW Facilities,* ed. E. Geissler et al. (Dordrecht, Netherlands: Kluwer, 1998), 167. These reports are not consistent, however, with accounts of Stepnogorsk's activities given by Ken Alibek, who directed the facility from 1983 to 1987. Alibek, *Biohazard,* 87–106; e-mail communication with Ken Alibek, October 5, 2005; and Sonia Ben Ouagrham and Kathleen M. Vogel, *Conversion at Stepnogorsk: What the Future Holds for Former Bioweapons Facilities,* Occasional Paper 28 (Ithaca: Cornell University Peace Studies Program, February 2003).

127. Kenneth Alibek, "Biological Weapons," (Powerpoint presentation at the United States Air Force Counterproliferation Conference, Air War College, Maxwell AFB, Alabama, November 1, 1999); and Alibek, *Biohazard,* 198, 202.

128. Tucker, "Biological Weapons in the Former Soviet Union," 2; Tucker, *Scourge,* 141–42; and Alibek, *Biohazard,* 112.

TABLE 6. Evaluation of U.S. Assessment of Soviet Biological Threat Agents, 1971–1990

Pathogen	1986 DIA	1992 Russian BWC Declaration	Alibek	Evaluation
Y. pestis	X	X	X	Accurate
B. anthracis	X	X	X	Accurate
F. tularensis	X	X	X	Accurate
Botulinum toxin	X	X		Accurate
Enterotoxin	X			Uncertain
Mycotoxin	X			False positive
Brucella spp.		X	X	False negative
C. burnetii		X	X	False negative
VEE		X	X	False negative
Variola			X	False negative
B. mallei			X	False negative

agent for the Soviets because of its virulence and transmissibility.[129] The source of these failures can be attributed at least in part to mirror-imaging. During its offensive BW program, the United States conducted very little work with pathogens that cause contagious diseases due to the increased risks to its own researchers, the additional level of unpredictability introduced by transmissible diseases, and the possibility of a boomerang effect that would endanger its own troops. In addition, the United States had failed to produce *Y. pestis* in large quantities that also retained its infectivity. The failure of the intelligence community and policymakers to appreciate the extent of Soviet work on producing and weaponizing biological agents, such as variola and *Y. pestis,* for use as strategic weapons reflects a Western bias toward equating strategic weapons with nuclear weapons.

As in the 1960s, U.S. intelligence analysts again fell prey to mirror-imaging, which led them to dramatically underestimate the size and scope of the Soviet BW program. The existence of the facilities subordinate to Biopreparat had been discovered in the 1970s and 1980s, but not their relationship with the organization or their role in the Soviet BW program. According to Gary Crocker, a long-time CBW expert with the State Department, analysts expected the Soviet BW program to be mainly a military effort, based in large part on how the United States structured its own offensive program. Analysts were surprised to find a large research infrastructure in the ostensibly civilian Biopreparat directly supporting the military BW program.[130] One factor that contributed to this focus on

---

129. Interview with former British intelligence official, 2004; and Orent, *Plague,* 215–16, 221.

130. Gary Crocker, "Plague Wars: Interview with Gary Crocker," *Frontline,* PBS, July 1998, http://www.pbs.org/wgbh/pages/frontline/shows/plague/interviews/crocker.html.

the military component of the Soviet BW program was the military background of most of the intelligence community's CBW analysts.[131]

The intelligence community's lack of investment in collection and analysis of BW intelligence also contributed to these gaps and shortfalls in assessing the Soviet Union's BW capabilities and intentions. Although the collection and analysis of intelligence on CBW had been assigned a relatively low priority through the 1970s, by 1981 it had been raised to the top tier of targets for the intelligence community.[132] Nonetheless, the level of resources devoted to CBW intelligence lagged far behind that devoted to nuclear weapons issues. Gary Crocker estimates that in the 1970s, the intelligence community fielded at most fifty CBW analysts, compared to thousands of analysts devoted to nuclear weapons issues.[133] In 1985 a group of outside experts warned that "the Department of Defense does not have an adequate grasp of the biological warfare threat and has not been giving it sufficient attention. Both intelligence and research in this area, although improved after a virtual halt during the 1970s, are strikingly deficient."[134] The United States ultimately required the defection of well-placed scientists to pierce the veil of secrecy surrounding the Soviet program and develop a comprehensive understanding of the size, scope, and sophistication of the Soviet BW program.

U.S. Assessment of Iraq's BW Program

U.S. intelligence on Iraq's BW program from the 1980s through 2003 can be evaluated by comparing declassified intelligence reports on Iraq's BW program with the information obtained by UN weapons inspectors and by the United States after Operation Iraqi Freedom in 2003. Prior to the 1991 Gulf War, the United States detected the emergence of Iraq's offensive BW program in a timely fashion and accurately identified Iraq's main BW research center and two of its three weaponized BW agents. The United States failed, however, to identify Iraq's BW agent production plants that emerged from the war unscathed. The poor performance of the intelligence community in identifying these production facilities was due to U.S. reliance on communication intercepts to track Iraqi imports of dual-use equipment and matériel along with

---

131. Interview with Gary Crocker, Washington, DC, January 21, 2005.

132. The turning point was the 1973 Yom Kippur War, which revealed how well prepared Soviet-equipped Egyptian forces were to operate on a chemical battlefield. Jack Anderson, "Upgrading Germ Warfare Intelligence," *Washington Post,* November 30, 1984.

133. Interview with Gary Crocker, Washington, DC, January 21, 2005.

134. *Report of the Chemical Warfare Review Commission* (Washington, DC: GPO, 1985), 67, 71.

good operational security by the Iraqis, which included an elaborate denial-and-deception effort.

Prior to the March 2003 invasion of Iraq, the U.S. intelligence community believed with a high degree of confidence that Iraq had a large and active BW program with large-scale and redundant biological production capabilities, including mobile production facilities and stockpiles of BW agents and munitions. In contrast to 1991 when the United States accurately assessed Iraq's intentions and made several correct judgments regarding Iraq's capabilities, every single intelligence assessment of Iraq's BW intentions and capabilities in 2002 were wrong. Iraq possessed, at most, only a small-scale CBW effort geared toward assassination. Iraq's success at shielding its BW program from intelligence agencies before the 1991 Gulf War and from UN inspectors in the early 1990s facilitated the emergence of a strong mindset that Iraq continued to develop BW. This mindset contributed to three analytical problems. First, analysts were seduced by human sources that provided information that confirmed what the analysts already believed. Second, this mindset led to the interpretation of ambiguous information about dual-use sites as threatening. Third, analysts used Iraq's past success with denial-and-deception measures to both justify their inability to verify reporting from human sources and to explain the presence of conflicting information. In addition, political and bureaucratic pressure suppressed dissenting views before and after the war about the reliability of the evidence underlying the assessment of Iraq's BW program.

U.S. Intelligence on Iraq's Pre-1991 BW Program

The United States began tracking Iraq's interest in biological weapons in the late 1980s. Understanding Iraq's BW intentions and capabilities became a high-priority issue after Iraq's invasion of Kuwait in August 1990 and the deployment of U.S. forces to Saudi Arabia to defend that nation against further Iraqi aggression. During Operation Desert Shield, intelligence agencies worked furiously to update their assessment of the Iraqi BW threat. The 1991 Gulf War marked the first time that the United States had confronted a nation armed with biological weapons. As a result, military leaders were desperate to know what agents Iraq was likely to have and how they could be delivered. The military also needed to pinpoint the location of Iraqi BW research, production, and storage sites for targeting during the air campaign. The United States sought not only to prevent Iraq from using these weapons during the war but also to eliminate Iraq's capability to produce these weapons after the war.

At the dawn of the Gulf War, the U.S. intelligence community assessed that Iraq had the most advanced BW program in the Arab world. Iraq was believed to have produced large quantities of *B. anthracis* and botulinum toxin and to have filled these agents into artillery rockets, aerial bombs, and missile war-heads.[135] This intelligence was crucial for instilling a sense of urgency in Wash-ington regarding the threat posed by Iraqi biological weapons and the need to take defensive precautions prior to the 1991 war. Based on this intelligence, the United States began vaccinating its forces against anthrax and botulinum toxin and distributed packages of antibiotics to soldiers.[136] By the end of the Gulf War, the United States had identified and targeted five suspected BW production sites and twenty-one bunkers suitable for the storage of BW agents. After the war, the DIA assessed that bombing had destroyed or severely damaged the thirteen buildings associated with the five suspected BW sites and destroyed nineteen of the twenty-one bunkers.[137] As a result of these attacks, Iraq's BW program was believed to have been eliminated. This would turn out to be an optimistic assessment.

After an initial lag in detecting the establishment of Iraq's BW program, the United States developed very good intelligence on the status and progress of the Iraqi program and the primary BW agents Iraq was developing. It took two years for the intelligence community to detect the establishment of Iraq's BW program. Iraq initiated its BW program at its CW facility at Muthanna in 1985 and then transferred the program to the Technical Research Center at Salman Pak in 1987. The United States first began receiving reports of Iraqi inter-est in biological weapons in 1987.[138] By 1988 the United States and Israel had identified Salman Pak as Iraq's BW research center and *B. anthracis* and botu-linum toxin as Iraq's primary BW agents.[139] The speed with which these as-pects of Iraq's BW was identified is impressive since Iraq was engaged at this time in relatively early stage BW activities such as applied research, laboratory-scale production of *B. anthracis* and botulinum toxin, and testing these agents on

135. CIA, *Intelligence Related to Possible Sources of Biological Agent Exposure during the Persian Gulf War* (Langley, VA: CIA, August 2000), http://www.gulflink.osd.mil/library/43917.htm.; CIA, *Iraq Inter-agency Biological Warfare Working Group,* n.d., http://www.gulflink.osd.mil [hereafter Gulflink website]; and CIA, *Prewar Status of Iraq's Weapons of Mass Destruction,* March 20, 1991, 27, http://www.gwu.edu/~nsarchiv/NSAEBB/NSAEBB80/wmd04.pdf.

136. Albert J. Mauroni, *Chemical-Biological Defense: U.S. Military Policies and Decisions in the Gulf War* (Westport, CT: Praeger, 1998), 75, 87.

137. DIA, *Iraq's Chemical and Biological Warfare Capabilities: Surviving Assets and Lack of Use during the War,* DIM 88–91, March 1991, 2, FOIA.

138. CIA, *Iraqi Development of Biological Agent for Military Purposes,* October 1987, Gulflink website; and CIA, *BW Capabilities in Iraq,* December 1987, Gulflink website.

139. Stephen Engelberg, "Iraq Said to Study Biological Arms," *New York Times,* January 18, 1989, A7; W. Seth Carus, *"The Poor Man's Atomic Bomb?" Biological Weapons in the Middle East,* Policy Paper 23 (Washington, DC: Washington Institute for Near East Policy, 1991), 7–8; and Milton Leitenberg, *Bio-logical Weapons Arms Control* (College Park: Center for International and Security Studies at Maryland, 1996), 23; and CIA, *Chemical and Biological Weapons: The Poor Man's Atomic Bomb,* December 1988, FOIA.

animals.[140] Intelligence from human sources (HUMINT) reportedly played a role in the association of Salman Pak with Iraq's BW program and Iraqi interest in *B. anthracis* as a biological weapon.[141]

By 1990 the CIA had concluded that Iraq had been producing large quantities of *B. anthracis* and botulinum toxin for at least two years and had produced 15 kilograms of botulinum toxin and 1,000 kilograms of *B. anthracis*.[142] Iraq had, in fact, commenced pilot-scale production of botulinum toxin in 1988 and large-scale production of both agents in 1989.[143] Although the intelligence community accurately estimated the amount of botulinum toxin produced by Iraq, it significantly overestimated *B. anthracis* production. Iraq admitted to producing roughly 19,000 liters of botulinum toxin and 8,500 liters of *B. anthracis* before the 1991 Gulf War. Based on a conservative estimate that Iraq could produce one gram of dry agent for every liter of culture, these amounts are the equivalent of 19 kilograms of botulinum toxin and 8.5 kilograms of *B. anthracis* spores.

Iraq's production and weaponization of aflatoxin, a toxin produced by strains of the fungus *Aspergillus,* completely surprised the intelligence community. Iraqi production of this agent was difficult to detect because it did not rely on an imported strain of the fungi or imported production equipment. In addition, no other nation is known to have developed this toxin for use as a weapon. Aflatoxin has a relatively low toxicity compared to other toxins, and the primary health effects associated with it are long term. Given these limitations, Iraq's choice to weaponize this agent remains a puzzle.[144]

The intelligence community's assessment of biological agents under research and development in the Iraqi program was much less accurate than its assessment of agents in production. Before the war, the DIA believed that Iraq was investigating *V. cholerae, C. perfringens, Y. pestis,* and staphylococcus enterotoxin.[145] Of these agents, Iraq has admitted to working only on *C. perfringens.* Iraq also conducted research on ricin, wheat smut, trichothecene mycotoxins, and three viral agents: camelpox, hemorrhagic conjunctivitis, and rotavirus.[146]

140. United Nations Monitoring, Verification and Inspection Commission (UNMOVIC), *Compendium of Iraq's Proscribed Weapons Programmes in the Chemical, Biological and Missile Areas* (New York: United Nations, 2007), 779–80 [hereafter *Compendium*].

141. Rod Barton, *The Weapons Detective: The Inside Story of Australia's Top Weapons Inspector* (Melbourne: Black Inc. Agenda, 2006), 53; and Sharon Begley, "The Germ Warfare Alert," *Newsweek,* January 7, 1991, 25.

142. CIA, *Beating Plowshares into Swords: Iraq's Defense Industrialization Program,* NESA 90–10009, July 1990, 3, FOIA; and CIA, *Iraq Interagency Biological Warfare Working Group,* n.d., Gulflink website.

143. UNMOVIC, *Compendium,* 780–82.

144. UNMOVIC, *Compendium,* 853, 938–39.

145. Armed Forces Medical Intelligence Center (AFMIC), *Iraq Biological Warfare Threat,* October 22, 1990, Gulflink website; and DIA, *Iraqi BW Capabilities,* 1991, Gulflink website.

146. UNMOVIC, *Compendium,* 836, 849, 919.

The United States' assessment of Iraq's weaponization of biological agents was accurate despite a lack of hard evidence on which to base this assessment. The United States had no evidence that biological agents had been filled into munitions or that such munitions had been tested by Iraq.[147] Despite this lack of information, the intelligence community's assessment that Iraq had filled bombs and missile warheads with *B. anthracis* and botulinum toxin was a reasonable inference given the estimate of Iraq's sizable agent stockpile and the impending war. The failure to detect aflatoxin production also meant that analysts did not know that Iraq had weaponized this agent as well. Due to the poor military utility of aflatoxin as a BW agent, the military significance of the failure to detect Iraq's weaponization of this agent was minimal.

Although the speed with which Iraq's production of BW agents was detected is impressive, the United States badly miscalculated which sites were involved in the production and storage of these agents (see table 7). Salman Pak was identified as the primary BW research-and-development center in Iraq as well as a production and storage site. A plant located in a military complex at Taji was believed to be the site for pilot-scale production of *B. anthracis*. The Al Kindi veterinary vaccine plant in Abu Ghraib was identified as the location of botulinum toxin production. Another site in Abu Ghraib, advertised as an infant-formula plant, was suspected of being a backup BW production facility. A possible production site was identified at Latifiyah based on the tracking of fermentation equipment sought by Iraq.[148]

The only active BW site struck by the United States during the 1991 Gulf War was Salman Pak. The other targeted sites had either never been involved in the BW program or had not been involved for several years. Furthermore, the United States failed to identify and strike the three sites used by Iraq to produce BW agents immediately prior to the war: Al Hakam, the foot-and-mouth disease vaccine plant at Al Daura, and the agricultural research station at Al Fudaliyah. The poor performance of the intelligence community in identifying the proper targets was due to U.S. reliance on monitoring Iraqi imports of multiuse equipment and materials and good operational security by the Iraqis, which included an elaborate denial-and-deception effort.

The mistaken attacks on the Al Kindi veterinary vaccine plant in Abu Ghraib and on the facilities at Taji and Latifiyah were directly connected to

---

147. Between 1988 and 1991 Iraq tested a range of biological munitions, including aerial bombs, artillery rockets, a helicopter-mounted aerosol generator, and aircraft-mounted spray tanks. CIA, *Intelligence Related to Possible Sources of Biological Agent Exposure.*

148. CIA, *Iraq Interagency Biological Warfare Working Group;* AFMIC, *Iraq Biological Warfare Threat;* DIA, *Iraqi BW Capabilities;* DIA, *Iraqi Chemical Warheads,* 1991, Gulflink website; and DIA, *Iraqi BW,* February 15, 1991, Gulflink website.

TABLE 7. Evaluation of U.S. Assessment of Iraqi BW Facilities, 1991

Facility	Assessment	Purpose	Evaluation
Salman Pak	BW research	BW research	Accurate
Al Hakam	None	BW production	False negative
Al Daura	None	BW production	False negative
Al Fudaliyah	None	BW production	False negative
Al Kindi	BW production	Veterinary vaccine plant	False positive
Infant formula plant	Backup BW production	Infant formula plant	False positive
Taji	BW production	Abandoned BW production	False positive
Latifiyah	BW production	Decoy site	False positive

the intelligence community's failure to detect Iraq's main BW agent production plant at Al Hakam. Al Hakam was constructed in great secrecy in 1988. Iraq's initial plan was to equip the plant with three 5,000-liter fermenters purchased abroad. In order to conceal the true destination of the equipment, Iraq falsified the end-use certificates for the fermenters and claimed that they would be used for peaceful purposes at a facility in Latifiyah. To prevent foreigners from gaining access to Al Hakam, Iraq modified an existing facility at Latifiyah for a tour by representatives of the European supplier. When the firm postponed delivery of the fermenters, Iraq sought out domestic sources of fermentation equipment. As a result, the fermenters at the Al Kindi veterinary vaccine plant at Abu Ghraib were transferred to Al Hakam in late 1988.[149] At the same time, the fermenter at Taji, which had been engaged in the production of botulinum toxin—and not *B. anthracis* as believed by the intelligence community—was also transferred to Al Hakam. To conceal the transfer of these fermenters to Al Hakam, Iraq continued to list Taji and Al Kindi as the end users for the equipment's imported spare parts. These orders were apparently intercepted by the United States or its allies. Thus, the intelligence community believed that these sites were still active and engaged in BW production. As a result of these transfers, Al Hakam began large-scale production of botulinum toxin in 1989 and *B. anthracis* in June 1990.[150] Iraq's denial-and-deception operation successfully concealed the location of its primary BW-agent production facility. As a result, the coalition bombed sites at Latifiyah, Taji, and Al Kindi instead of Al Hakam.

---

149. Tim Trevan, *Saddam's Secrets: The Hunt for Iraq's Hidden Weapons* (London: HarperCollins, 1999), 316–17; Graham S. Pearson, *The UNSCOM Saga: Chemical and Biological Weapons Non-Proliferation* (New York: St. Martin's Press, 1999), 141; and UNMOVIC, *Compendium,* 805, 884–89.

150. Trevan, *Saddam's Secrets,* 316; and UNMOVIC, *Compendium,* 782–83.

The bombing of the infant-formula plant at Abu Ghraib provided Iraq with a rare propaganda victory during the war.[151] Both UNMOVIC and the ISG concluded that the suspected backup BW production site in Abu Ghraib was in fact an infant-formula plant as Iraq claimed.[152] The misjudgment of this plant stemmed from analysts falling victim to mirror-imaging and applying a Western mindset to Iraq's industrial development. Analysts believed the plant was suspicious because it was not a commercially viable project, it had not actually produced any infant formula since its construction in the early 1980s by a foreign firm, and Iraq continued to maintain the plant in perfect working condition. Based on this background information, the presence of dual-use equipment at the site, and security features that were inconsistent with a civilian facility, the plant was listed as a backup BW production site.[153] Analysts apparently discounted a report that after the completion of the plant by a foreign contractor, the foreign workers were replaced with Iraqis who were unable to produce infant formula that met the required hygienic standards.[154] Flush with oil money, Iraq had commissioned several such turnkey projects with foreign companies in the late 1970s with the goal of building up its industrial infrastructure and becoming a leading regional exporter, only to run into problems when attempting to operate the facilities on its own.[155] What appeared suspicious to outside analysts was in fact a result of overly ambitious industrial planning by Iraqi bureaucrats.

The intelligence community's assessment of the role of the refrigerated twelve-frame bunkers in Iraq's BW program was also incorrect.[156] Three of these bunkers underwent secondary explosions when bombed during the Gulf War indicating the storage of conventional explosives. UNSCOM found no evidence that Iraq used these bunkers to store biological agents or munitions.[157] Instead of using bunkers, Iraq adopted unorthodox storage techniques to protect these weapons from coalition air strikes. Iraq buried its biological bombs at a military airbase and a military test range and stored its biological missile warheads in pits along the banks of the Tigris Canal and in an abandoned railroad tunnel. In contrast to the key role that bunkers played in identifying suspected Soviet BW

151. For additional details about this incident, see Gregory Koblentz, "Countering Dual-Use Facilities: Lessons from Iraq and Sudan," *Jane's Intelligence Review* 11, no. 3 (1999): 48–53.

152. UNMOVIC, *Compendium,* 807–10; and Duelfer Report, 3: 11.

153. DIA, "Position Paper, Subject: Biological Warfare (BW) Association of Abu Ghurayb 'Infant Formula' Plant," March 22, 1991, Gulflink website.

154. DIA, *Iraqi Biological Warfare,* n.d., Gulflink website.

155. UNMOVIC, *Compendium,* 833, 908, 925–26.

156. Intelligence analysts made a similar mistake in focusing on S-shaped bunkers as a signature for Iraqi CW storage sites. Persian Gulf War Illnesses Task Force, *Lessons Learned: Intelligence Support on Chemical and Biological Warfare during the Gulf War and on Veterans' Illnesses Issues* (Langley, VA: CIA, December 1997), Gulflink website.

157. CIA, *Intelligence Related to Possible Sources of Biological Agent Exposure.*

facilities, Iraq's twelve-frame bunkers were a red herring. This incident highlights the danger of standard analytical procedures that apply lessons learned about one state's standard operating procedures to the identification of other states' BW activities.

The intelligence community successfully warned policymakers and the military that Iraq had a stockpile of biological munitions filled with *B. anthracis* and botulinum toxin. Based on this intelligence, the military was able to provide medical countermeasures against Iraq's two primary BW agents to U.S. troops deployed to Saudi Arabia in 1990–91. The intelligence agencies, however, failed to identify the locations of Iraq's BW agent production plants, which escaped the 1991 Persian Gulf War unscathed. This combined intelligence success and intelligence failure was due to the United States' reliance on signal intelligence to monitor Iraqi procurement of critical materials and equipment from foreign suppliers for insight into Iraq's BW program.

Iraq's large-scale efforts to develop ballistic missiles and nuclear, biological, and chemical weapons depended heavily on foreign suppliers for materials and equipment.[158] Iraq used the Technical and Scientific Materials Import Division as a front company for obtaining dual-use items for the BW program. TSMID was ostensibly part of the Ministry of Trade, but in fact it reported to the Military Industrialization Commission and was the sole ordering agency for the BW program.[159] By tracking TSMID's activities, the United States and its allies were able to chart Iraq's interest in and procurement of all of the components necessary for a BW program: strains of dangerous pathogens, growth media, fermenters, spray dryers, and filling machines.[160] While this method was effective in determining Iraq's interest in specific BW agents and how much progress the program was making, it failed to provide an accurate picture of which facilities were involved and the extent of Iraq's preparedness to use these weapons. The limited utility of this approach was due in part to Iraq's extensive use of denial-and-deception measures to shield the locations of its BW agent production sites.

U.S. Intelligence on Iraq's BW Program, 1991–2003

In October 2002 the intelligence community issued a National Intelligence Estimate on Iraq's WMD programs. The NIE stated, with a high degree of confidence,

---

158. CIA, *Iraq: Foreign Dependency in Developing Weapons of Mass Destruction,* January 1991, Gulflink website.

159. Rod Barton, "The Application of the UNSCOM Experience to International Biological Arms Control," *Critical Reviews in Microbiology* 24, no. 3 (1998): 222.

160. CIA, *Iraq's Biological Warfare Program,* August 1990, Gulflink website; and AFMIC, *Iraq Biological Warfare Threat.*

that Iraq possessed an active BW program that was larger and more advanced than its program before the 1991 Gulf War. Iraq was now believed to possess a large-scale and redundant BW production capability, including the ability to produce dry agents, as well as stockpiles of BW agents and munitions.[161] The key assessments of Iraq's BW capabilities and intentions were based almost entirely on reports that Iraq had a fleet of mobile BW production units.[162] These unconfirmed reports were relayed to the United States by a foreign intelligence service from a single source, code-named Curveball, to whom U.S. officials did not have direct access. According to the Silberman-Robb Commission, "that Iraq was cooking up biological agents in mobile facilities designed to elude the prying eyes of international inspectors and Western intelligence services was, along with the aluminum tubes, the most important and alarming assessment in the October 2002 NIE."[163]

Not one of these assessments has been proven correct. The United States fundamentally overestimated Iraqi BW capabilities and exaggerated Iraqi intentions. The Iraq Survey Group, a 1,200-member task force that searched Iraq for evidence of WMD from July 2003 to December 2004, found no evidence that Iraq conducted BW research or production for military purposes after 1996. Indeed, the ISG found that from the mid-1990s "there appears to be a complete absence of discussion or even interest in BW at the Presidential level."[164] The ISG also concluded that Iraq had destroyed its pre-1991 stocks of biological agents and weapons in 1991, although the ISG acknowledged that it could not verify the complete destruction of these materials. In addition, the ISG failed to find any evidence that Iraq possessed mobile BW production facilities. Instead of a large military program, Iraq may have had a covert research effort run by intelligence agencies geared toward the production of limited quantities of toxins for use in assassination operations. The ISG judged that these small-scale laboratory-level activities were not part of a military program and that the purpose of the labs was not to retain the technical expertise required to restart a large-scale CBW program.[165]

The intelligence community's failure to accurately estimate any aspect of Iraq's BW intentions and capabilities was part of a broader breakdown in understanding Baghdad's political intentions and assessing Iraq's military capabilities. This intelligence failure stemmed from faults at every stage of the intelligence

---

161. DCI, *Iraq's Weapons of Mass Destruction Programs,* October 2002, 13–17; and NIC, *Iraq's Continuing Programs for Weapons of Mass Destruction,* 6–9.

162. SSCI Report, 148–50; and Silberman-Robb Report, 48, 87, 558–59.

163. Silberman-Robb Report, 80.

164. Duelfer Report, 3:1.

165. Duelfer Report, 3:1–3, 16–18, 69–70, 73–78.

cycle and represents a microcosm of the intelligence community's failure to accurately assess Iraq's WMD capabilities and intentions. An examination of the intelligence community's record with regard to Iraq's BW program provides insight into the systemic and deep-seated problems that led to this catastrophic failure.

The most important source of information on Iraq's BW program was an Iraqi chemical engineer who left Iraq in 1999 to seek political asylum in Germany. Beginning in January 2000, the German Federal Intelligence Service (Bundesnachrichtendienst, or BND) began debriefing the engineer, code-named Curveball, who claimed to have been involved in a program to design and build mobile BW agent production facilities before fleeing Iraq in 1999. According to the engineer, the mobile BW program began in May 1995 with the goal of producing seven mobile production units: six truck mounted and one rail mounted. The mobile units were designed by the Chemical and Engineering Development Center (CEDC) under the cover of a seed purification project for the Mesopotamia State Company for Seeds. Each truck-mounted production unit was composed of two or three trailers that contained all of the equipment necessary for the production, processing, and storage of BW agents. The trailers would be linked together and connected to water and electrical utilities at six "docking stations" located throughout Iraq. These mobile units were capable of producing several hundred tons of five different biological agents in liquid slurry form per year. Even more worrisome was that the mobile facilities had the capability to process the BW agents into dry powder form, an important technological achievement for Iraq. The first mobile unit began producing a BW agent in 1997, and three of the units were fully functional by 1999.[166]

These reports had an immediate impact on the U.S. intelligence community's assessment of the BW threat posed by Iraq. According to a December 2000 NIE on worldwide BW programs, "new intelligence acquired in 2000...causes [the IC] to adjust our assessment upward of the BW threat posed by Iraq.... The new information suggests that Baghdad has expanded its offensive BW program by establishing a large scale, redundant, and concealed BW agent production capability."[167] The U.S. repeatedly requested the right to interview Curveball in order to learn more details and validate his reporting, but the BND refused

166. NIC, *Iraq's Continuing Programs for Weapons of Mass Destruction,* 5, 7; CIA and DIA, *Iraqi Mobile Biological Warfare Agent Production Plants,* May 28, 2003, 1–2; Lord Butler, *Review of Intelligence on Weapons of Mass Destruction: Report of a Committee of Privy Counselors* (London: The Stationery Office, 2004), 127–28 [hereafter Butler Report]; Silberman-Robb Report, 83, 90; SSCI Report, 149–50; Duelfer Report, 3:74–77; and Bob Drogin, *Curveball: Spies, Lies, and the Con Man Who Caused a War* (New York: Random House, 2007), 58.
167. NIC, *Worldwide Biological Warfare Programs: Trends and Prospects, Update,* NIE 2000–12HCX, December 2000, 22, cited in Silberman-Robb Report, 83.

to provide access to him.[168] Instead, the BND provided reports on these debriefings to the DIA, which in turn disseminated them throughout the intelligence community. By 2002 the DIA had disseminated ninety-five reports based on Curveball's debriefings.[169] The lack of direct access to Curveball had two important consequences for U.S. assessment of Iraq's BW program. First, it hampered the ability of intelligence agencies to vet Curveball's reporting. Second, it forced U.S. analysts to rely on thirdhand reports of what Curveball told his German debriefers.

Both the Senate inquiry and the Silberman-Robb Commission harshly criticized the DIA for failing to take effective measures to vet Curveball, such as checking his bona fides, testing his reliability and motivations for cooperating, and ensuring that he was not under the influence of a foreign actor.[170] Without German cooperation this would have been a difficult task, but the DIA exacerbated the problem by not following its usual procedure of assigning the source a grade indicating his reliability. Instead, a DIA official in Germany watered down the original German warning that the reliability of the source "cannot be verified," to the milder "could not be determined."[171] Despite the lack of any basis for assessing the reliability of Curveball, the DIA marked all of the reports from this source as having "Major Significance," the highest ranking for intelligence reports.[172]

Despite the lack of direct access to Curveball, intelligence agencies did try, and often succeeded, in verifying information provided by him. The British Secret Intelligence Service (SIS) verified that Curveball had worked where he claimed and that his position would have given him access to the information he claimed to have.[173] Curveball demonstrated, in the words of a December 2003 DIA assessment, "knowledge of and access to personalities, organizations, procurement, and technology relating to Iraq's BW program."[174] Analysts used overhead imagery to confirm the existence and identity of the locations described by Curveball as being involved in the mobile BW program such as agricultural sites where the mobile units were hidden and the Baghdad office building housing

168. The BND claimed that the source did not speak English, disliked Americans, and would refuse to speak with them, Silberman-Robb Report, 90–91, 217 n. 274. Instead, BND's decision appears to have been driven by the agency's acrimonious relationship with the CIA and embarrassment over information from Curveball that Iraq was using German-made equipment in its BW program. Drogin, *Curveball,* 6, 14–18, 28–36, 64, 74–77.

169. SSCI Report, 149; and Silberman-Robb Report, 84, 215 n. 235.

170. Silberman-Robb Report, 88–89; and SSCI Report, 191.

171. Drogin, *Curveball,* 64, 67–68.

172. Drogin, *Curveball,* 73.

173. Butler Report, 101.

174. SSCI Report, 156–57.

CEDC.[175] A CIA attempt to determine if Curveball had been exposed to, or vaccinated against, BW agents to test his claim that he had been present during BW-agent production runs, including one in 1998 that led to an accidental release of an unidentified organism that killed twelve technicians, was inconclusive.[176]

Curveball's deception was so effective because his reports contained enough accurate and verifiable information to make his entire account seem credible. Curveball had worked, albeit briefly, at the CEDC in the mid-1990s and was involved with, or at least very familiar with, a seed-purification project underway there at the time. This experience most likely supplied the inspiration for his information about Iraq's mobile BW production systems. Between 1994 and 1997, the CEDC designed, manufactured, and installed ten agricultural seed-sorting and fungicide-treatment systems for the Mesopotamia State Company for Seeds. Almost all of the sites that Curveball named as hide sites for the mobile BW production units were linked to this enterprise.[177] The CEDC also had long-standing links to Al Hakam, Iraq's main BW agent production facility prior to the 1991 Gulf War. Shortly after the war, the CEDC was responsible for establishing a single-cell protein line at Al Hakam, which Iraq used as one of its cover stories to retain its BW production capability at the site.[178] The CEDC had also been responsible for the attempted 1995 procurement from Russia of a 50,000-liter fermentation capacity for Al Hakam, ostensibly to produce SCP.[179] Most of the individuals Curveball identified as being part of the mobile BW production program were part of the CEDC and were also involved in the seed purification project as well as the installation of the SCP line at Al Hakam.[180]

Only after the war did the intelligence community learn key facts about Curveball that would have been helpful in validating his reporting. Curveball had graduated last in his class instead of first as he had claimed. He had been a low-level trainee at CEDC and not a project head or site manager. He had been fired from his job in 1995 at the time when he said he was beginning to work on the mobile BW production units. In addition, he had been traveling outside of the country during the period he claimed to have been involved in the project. Curveball had also run afoul of the law in Iraq, which provided an ulterior motive

175. SSCI Report, 149–50; and Silberman-Robb Report, 92, 98.

176. SSCI Report, 155–56.

177. Of the six locations Curveball identified as housing mobile units, three were operated by the company and involved in the seed purification project, one was a railroad station where the company had hidden seed purification equipment during Operation Desert Fox in 1998, one was a pesticide storage facility, and one was an unrelated warehouse for a construction company. Duelfer Report, 3:75–77.

178. Duelfer Report, 3:74–77.

179. R. Jeffrey Smith, "Russians Admit Firms Met Iraqis," *Washington Post,* February 18, 1998, A16; and Scott Ritter, *Endgame: Solving the Iraq Problem Once and For All* (New York: Simon and Schuster, 1999), 220.

180. Duelfer Report, 3:75.

for his willingness to cooperate with the BND in return for resettlement in Germany.[181] The CIA also learned that Curveball's brother was an official in the Iraqi National Congress, the Iraqi opposition group headed by Ahmed Chalabi.[182] In May 2004 the CIA issued a fabrication notice for Curveball and began recalling all of his reports.[183]

The lack of direct access to Curveball meant that American BW analysts had only thirdhand reports of his debriefings and had to rely on the BND to debrief him properly. The BND's handling of Curveball, however, was problematic. A U.S. intelligence official who had access to the original German summaries found that Curveball's handlers failed to practice proper interrogation tradecraft by asking leading questions and signaling what issues were important to them. Due to the technical nature of the source's information, the BND assigned a BW analyst, supported by a multidisciplinary technical team, to lead the questioning of Curveball instead of an experienced interrogator.[184] The German BW analyst may have been guilty of "compensating for errors" in technically implausible reports, which allowed him to interpret otherwise sketchy information in support of his own conclusions.[185] A senior BND official has admitted that "we filled in [the] gaps" in Curveball's accounts of the mobile BW production facilities.[186] The SIS has accused the BND of omitting significant technical details from its reports, which led SIS to believe that the mobile facilities could produce BW agent as a dry powder.[187]

The process by which Curveball's debriefings were shared with the United States introduced additional problems. The debriefings were conducted by the BND in a mix of Arabic, English, and German, which were then summarized into one- to five-page memos written in German. These summaries were sent

---

181. Drogin, *Curveball,* 231–32, 239–41; and Silberman-Robb Report, 106, 108.

182. The CIA found no evidence that Curveball was influenced or controlled by the Iraqi National Congress. The Senate Select Committee on Intelligence does not believe that the CIA has enough information to make this determination, so it considers Curveball's relationship with the Iraqi National Congress an open question. SSCI, *Report on the Use by the Intelligence Community of Information Provided by the Iraqi National Congress* (Washington, DC: GPO, 2006), 105–9, 121–22 [hereafter SSCI, INC Report]. For a dissenting view that Curveball was most likely not a source controlled by the Iraqi National Congress, see ibid., 150–55.

183. Drogin, *Curveball,* 271.

184. Drogin, *Curveball,* 26, 68–69.

185. A CIA CW analyst committed this type of error by interpreting a report that Iraq had built a castor oil production plant that could produce sarin nerve gas (castor oil can be used to produce ricin, not sarin) as evidence that Iraq had built a facility that could produce both ricin and sarin. Silberman-Robb Report, 128–29.

186. Drogin, *Curveball,* 51.

187. Butler Report, 100–102. In October 2004 the SIS designated Curveball a fabricator and recalled his entire line of reporting. Intelligence and Security Committee, *Annual Report 2004–2005* (London: HMSO, 2005), 23.

to the DIA, which translated them into English, reorganized them into a standard DIA format, and further summarized them into one- or two-page reports before disseminating them to the rest of the intelligence community.[188] This convoluted reporting chain led a former CIA official to express concern that Curveball's information "was analyzed and translated and reanalyzed and retranslated, and comments got added, it could have gotten sexed up by accident."[189]

The unprofessional handling of Curveball's debriefing and the convoluted reporting process may explain the recurring reports that Curveball did not actually say what was attributed to him. According to five senior BND officials, Curveball never claimed to have produced biological weapons or witnessed anyone else doing so. He told the Germans that his job was to design and test laboratory equipment for the trucks that he could describe in detail, but he could not identify what bacteria the trucks would produce. According to a BND official, "his information to us was very vague. He could not say if these things functioned, if they worked."[190] According to the DIA case officer who had primary responsibility for collecting and reporting Curveball's debriefings, Curveball was "not a biological weapons expert nor is he a life science expert. Source simply designed [one word redacted] production facilities. He never claimed that the project he was involved in was used to produce biological agents."[191] Hamish Killip, a former UNSCOM inspector who returned to Iraq with the ISG to investigate Iraq's BW program, was surprised by how vague the Curveball reports were. He concluded that the most dire aspects of Iraq's putative mobile BW production program were the product of the imagination of intelligence officials, not Curveball.[192] David Kay, the first leader of the ISG, has accused the BND of being "dishonest, unprofessional and irresponsible" in its handling of Curveball.[193] As Bob Drogin has observed, "whether the distortions in the intelligence file flowed from poor translations, analytic sloppiness, or willful deception, the outcome was the same."[194]

Despite the lack of direct access to Curveball, between 2000 and 2003 CIA analysts and managers received a number of warnings from their own personnel, from SIS, and from the BND itself about Curveball's unreliability. These

188. SSCI Report, 152; and Drogin, *Curveball,* 26, 65–67.
189. Bob Drogin and John Goetz, "How U.S. Fell under the Spell of Curveball," *Los Angeles Times,* November 20, 2005.
190. Drogin and Goetz, "How U.S. Fell under the Spell of Curveball."
191. SSCI Report, 156–57.
192. Drogin, *Curveball,* 245.
193. John Goetz and Marcel Rosenbach, "German Intelligence Was 'Dishonest, Unprofessional and Irresponsible'," *Der Spiegel,* March 22, 2008, http://www.spiegel.de/international/world/0,1518,542888,00.html.
194. Drogin, *Curveball,* 246.

warnings reached the top leadership of the Directorate of Operations and the office of the deputy director of the CIA but were never acted on.[195] These warnings were not shared with other agencies in the intelligence community.

In May 2000 a Department of Defense detailee working for the Directorate of Operations in the CIA met Curveball and discovered that he spoke excellent English, contrary to statements by the BND, and he also appeared hungover. In addition, the detailee reported that the BND case officer responsible for debriefing Curveball "had fallen in love with his asset and the asset could do no wrong."[196] These concerns were shared by the detailee with CIA officials but not with other BW analysts in the intelligence community.[197]

In April 2002 the SIS informed the CIA that it was "not convinced that Curveball is a wholly reliable source." The SIS believed that Curveball's detailed technical descriptions meant that a significant part of his reporting was probably true, but they noted that some of his behaviors "strike us as typical of individuals we would normally assess as fabricators" and identified inconsistencies that raised doubts about his reliability.[198]

Curveball began acting erratically in 2001, including contradicting himself during debriefings and recanting previous statements about his firsthand knowledge of BW activities. Instead of reevaluating the source's reliability and perhaps recalling reports based on his information, the BND informed U.S. intelligence officials through other channels of the problems they were having with their source.[199] BND officials warned CIA officials on multiple occasions in 2001 and 2002 that Curveball appeared to have personal and/or mental problems and that the BND could not confirm his information. While these concerns were shared with CIA analysts and managers, there is no record of them being shared with other intelligence agencies.[200] In late January 2003, a CIA station in Germany repeated the BND's concerns to Langley and advised headquarters that, given the importance of the subject matter, it should "take the most serious consideration" before using unconfirmed information provided by a liaison service.[201]

Despite the lack of direct access to the source and warnings from the BND, the SIS, and the CIA's own Directorate of Operations about Curveball's reliability,

195. Silberman-Robb Report, 95–105; and Tyler Drumheller, *On the Brink: An Insider's Account of How the White House Compromised American Intelligence* (New York: Carroll and Graf, 2006), 781–86.

196. SSCI Report, 155–56.

197. Silberman-Robb Report, 90–91; and SSCI Report, 156.

198. Silberman-Robb Report, 91; and Drogin and Goetz, "How U.S. Fell under the Spell of Curveball."

199. Drogin, *Curveball,* 85–88, 90–91, 131.

200. SSCI Report, 190; Silberman-Robb Report, 91, 95; Drogin, *Curveball,* 138; and Drumheller, *On the Brink,* 78–80.

201. Silberman-Robb Report, 102–4.

BW analysts in the CIA's Weapons Intelligence, Nonproliferation, and Arms Control (WINPAC) division believed in Curveball and viewed his reporting as highly credible. These analysts exhibited a strong confirmation bias to interpret incoming, and often ambiguous or fragmentary, information—or even the lack of information—as supporting this consensus and to ignore contradictory information.[202] In addition, analysts committed a number of errors due to cognitive biases, sloppy methodology, and poor analysis that portrayed Iraqi BW capabilities and intentions as more threatening and with a higher degree of certainty than the evidence allowed.

An underlying factor, which influenced the entire intelligence cycle, was the overriding presumption within the intelligence community that Iraq had retained elements of its pre-1991 WMD programs and would reconstitute them once inspections ended or sanctions were lifted.[203] This belief was valid up to a certain point. Iraq's history of "cheat and retreat" with UNSCOM in the 1990s, and its 1995 revelations about its past BW program, ruined Iraq's credibility on this issue. UNSCOM's withdrawal from Iraq in December 1998 deprived the intelligence community of a key source of information on Iraq's WMD-related activities. According to a senior intelligence official responsible for collection, "it's very difficult to overstate the degree to which we were focused on and using the output from the U.N. inspectors."[204]

Paradoxically, the reaction of analysts to the loss of UNSCOM was not greater uncertainty but greater certainty about Iraq's BW intentions. UNSCOM's withdrawal triggered a series of increasingly bleak assessments of the status of Iraq's BW program. In less than a year, and in the absence of any new information, the intelligence community changed its assessment of Iraqi BW activities from hypothetical to projected to definitive.[205] When defectors began filling the information vacuum in 2000 with tales of mobile BW production systems, they found a receptive audience that already firmly believed that Iraq maintained a BW program but lacked the evidence to prove it.

Past experience with collecting and analyzing intelligence on the Soviet and Iraqi BW programs led analysts to be overconfident about the value of defectors from such programs. The defections of Pasechnik and Alibek had been crucial to the intelligence community's gaining a broad and deep understanding of the

202. SSCI Report, 18–22; and Robert Jervis, "Reports, Politics, and Intelligence Failures: The Case of Iraq," *Journal of Strategic Studies* 29, no. 1 (2006): 20–27.

203. SSCI Report, 18; and Silberman-Robb Report, 110.

204. SSCI Report, 258.

205. NIC, *Iraq: WMD and Delivery Capabilities after Operation Desert Fox,* February 1999, cited in SSCI Report, 143; NIC, *Iraq: Post-Desert Fox Activities and Estimated Status of WMD Programs,* July 1999, cited in Silberman-Robb Report, 82; and NIC, *Worldwide BW Programs: Trends and Prospects,* NIE 2000–12HCX, cited in SSCI Report, 144.

Soviet BW program. In addition, immediately after the 1991 Persian Gulf War, the United States obtained valuable information from Iraqi defectors that indicated that the intelligence community had underestimated or completely missed several key aspects of the Iraqi BW program. These sources provided information about the locations where BW agents had been produced, the types of agents produced, their code names, the type of containers the agents were stored in, and locations where this bulk agent was hidden during the Gulf War. In addition, these sources provided details about Iraq's weaponization of BW agents, including the types of dissemination devices tested, the numbers and types of munitions filled with a BW agent, and the sites where Iraq had deployed these munitions during the war.[206] The value of these sources was validated when Iraq later provided details to UNSCOM on its pre-1991 BW program that matched the reporting of these defectors. Focusing on these successes, however, overlooks the fact that the information provided by most defectors on Iraq's WMD programs after the 1991 Gulf War was worthless.[207]

Curveball's information on Iraq's development of mobile BW production facilities was also embraced because it appeared to confirm what analysts had long suspected. The intelligence community already knew from UNSCOM that Iraq had considered the development of mobile BW facilities in the late 1980s, although this proposal was rejected as impractical at the time. The CIA had also obtained Military Industrialization Commission documents discovered by UNSCOM in 1995 that referred to the planned acquisition of a "mobile fermentation" capability.[208] In addition, UNSCOM had shared with the CIA its long-time suspicions that Iraq might have developed mobile BW agent production facilities, although it had no direct evidence.[209] Iraq's development of a mobile BW agent production capability was seen as a logical way for Iraq to retain a BW production capability once it was forced to reveal and destroy its primary production facility at Al Hakam. Indeed, CIA analysts believed that Iraq's initiation of the mobile BW production program in May 1995 allowed it to make its first disclosure about its offensive BW program to UNSCOM in July 1995.[210] An Iraqi shift from large, fixed facilities capable of producing large quantities

206. CIA, *BW Missile Programs,* June 1991, Gulflink website; CIA, *Status of BW,* August 1991, Gulflink website; and CIA, *Intelligence Related to Possible Sources of Biological Agent Exposure.*

207. Jean Krasno and James Sutterlin, *The United Nations and Iraq: Defanging the Viper* (Westport, CT: Praeger, 2003), 92.

208. Silberman-Robb Report, 98; and SSCI Report, 150.

209. Ritter, *Endgame,* 153, 219–20; Scott Ritter, *Iraq Confidential: The Untold Story of the Intelligence Conspiracy to Undermine the UN and Overthrow Saddam Hussein* (New York: Nation Books, 2005), 213–15, 248; and Bob Drogin and Greg Miller, "Iraqi Defector's Tales Bolstered U.S. Case for War," *Los Angeles Times,* March 28, 2004.

210. CIA, *Iraq: Mobile Biological Warfare Agent Production Capability,* October 10, 2001, 5, cited in Silberman-Robb Report, 218 n. 282.

of BW agents for stockpiling to smaller, mobile facilities that could produce BW agents at short notice was seen by intelligence analysts as a general trend in the BW field. The Soviet Union reportedly adopted a similar strategy in the late 1980s to avoid anticipated inspections.[211] In the words of a BW analyst with the State Department, "it's very appealing to the analysts to learn about a mobile BW program. It fits with what we think the state of the BW program world-wide are heading toward. It's kind of like a built-in bias."[212]

Analysts also failed to realize before the war that some evidence consistent with their assessments of Iraq's BW program were also consistent with other inter-pretations. As Robert Jervis has noted, "analysts often seemed to think that the latter was not the case, which meant that they saw the evidence as not only fit-ting with their explanation, but as giving independent support to it and there-fore as justifying greater confidence in the overall judgment."[213] This problem was particularly acute in assessments of dual-use facilities and procurement. The technical intelligence systems that provided the bulk of U.S. collection capabili-ties were able to detect activities at dual-use facilities and monitor procurement of dual-use materials, but they were unable to provide insight into the intent behind these activities. Satellite imagery of several nominally civilian dual-use facilities that had been associated with the Iraqi BW program prior to 1991 indi-cated that the sites were undergoing improvement or expansion.[214] In addition, the intelligence community had received multiple reports, most likely derived from communication intercepts, of Iraq's attempted procurement of dual-use biotechnology equipment through front companies and intermediaries in viola-tion of United Nations sanctions.[215] At the time, analysts were aware of plausi-ble peaceful explanations for these activities unrelated to biological weapons, but these alternative explanations were dismissed out of hand and not included in the NIE.[216] The prevailing mindset that Iraq had a BW program, and the pre-sumed efficacy of Iraqi denial-and-deception measures, led analysts to consis-tently assess that these dual-use activities had a sinister purpose.

Analysts used Iraq's history of successful denial and deception as a crutch to explain the presence of contradictory information and the absence of confirm-ing evidence. This belief in the efficacy of Iraqi denial-and-deception techniques made it impossible to disprove defector reports of mobile BW facilities. The lack of confirming evidence, such as the absence of mobile BW production units at

211. Alibek, *Biohazard,* 145, 191, 205.
212. SSCI Report, 161–62.
213. Jervis, "Reports, Politics, and Intelligence Failures," 16.
214. DCI, *Iraq's Weapons of Mass Destruction Programs,* 15–16; and SSCI Report, 162–66.
215. SSCI Report, 145, 179–81.
216. SSCI Report, 161, 181.

reported sites, was seen as a successful example of Iraqi denial measures.[217] In contrast, the importance of contradictory information, such as the presence of a wall at the Djerf al-Naddaf hide site that would have prevented vehicles from entering and leaving the facility as described by Curveball, was discounted as being an Iraqi deception measure. Since Djerf al-Naddaf was the only site linked to the mobile BW program that Curveball claimed to have visited himself, the discrepancy between his description of the site and the overhead imagery should not have been dismissed so quickly.[218]

Analysts and managers were also guilty of cherry-picking intelligence that fit their belief that Iraq had a BW program and a mobile BW production capability. The NIE included information from three different human sources that were portrayed as corroborating Curveball's account.[219] The information provided by all of these sources, however, was highly problematic. None of the sources provided firsthand confirmation of the mobile BW production facilities; instead, they were only reporting what they had heard.[220] In addition, since none of their reporting matched Curveball's reporting, such sources should have been considered at best complementary, not confirmatory.[221] The inclusion of these sources in the NIE and in Secretary Powell's speech appears to be the result of a desire by analysts and managers to build the strongest possible case for Iraq's mobile BW production program.

The first source was an Iraqi civil engineer who reported in June 2001 on the presence of at least one truck-transportable biological production facility at the Karbala ammunition depot in December 2000. This information was interpreted as corroborating Curveball's account despite two major problems. First, satellite imagery was unable to locate the transportable BW system at the reported location and time. Analysts attributed this failure to successful Iraqi denial-and-deception efforts instead of the unreliability of the source. Second, Curveball had never implicated the Karbala ammunition depot as part of the mobile BW program. This source recanted in October 2003.[222]

In September 2002 the United States received information from a source run by the SIS, code-named Red River, about the existence of mobile fermentation

217. SSCI Report, 149–50; and Silberman-Robb Report, 92, 98.

218. Drogin and Goetz, "How U.S. Fell under the Spell of Curveball"; Silberman-Robb Report, 92, 224 n. 399; and SSCI Report, 149–50.

219. CIA and DIA, *Iraqi Mobile Biological Warfare Agent Production Plants,* 1–2; SSCI Report, 151–52, 160; and Silberman-Robb Report, 84–85.

220. Drogin and Miller, "Iraqi Defector's Tales Bolstered U.S. Case for War."

221. Butler Report, 10.

222. Silberman-Robb Report, 84, 92; SSCI Report, 161, 248; and Douglas Jehl, "Doubts on Informant Deleted in Senate Text," *New York Times,* July 13, 2004, A9.

systems.[223] The stated purpose of these systems was for the manufacture of single-cell protein, but the source claimed that they could also be used for BW agent production.[224] This source was problematic for two reasons. First, Red River was not the direct source of the reporting attributed to him by the SIS, but rather he was passing on information from a new subsource. The SIS refused to share with the CIA the identity of the subsource for fear of leaks, which made it impossible for the CIA to determine if the source was linked to any Iraqi opposition groups. The source reportedly failed a polygraph exam administered by the United States, and the source's reporting is now viewed by U.S. officials as inaccurate and possibly fabricated.[225] Second, it appears that U.S. intelligence analysts stretched the source's reporting to provide additional support to Curveball's reports of Iraq's mobile BW production capability. On reviewing the original report of the source's debriefing, Senate investigators discovered that analysts had been overly assertive in linking the source's information to Iraq's BW program. The informant reported that he was working on a mobile fermentation system to produce single-cell protein, that his work was unrelated to biological warfare, and that he did not know of any BW-related activity in Iraq.[226]

The third source, a former major in the Iraqi intelligence service, had already been discredited as a fabricator when his report of Iraqi mobile BW labs was incorporated into the October 2002 NIE. In a February 2002 debriefing by the DIA, the major stated that in 1996 Iraq decided to create a fleet of mobile laboratories for biological research to evade UNSCOM inspectors under a program managed by Rihab Taha (nicknamed Dr. Germ by weapons inspectors). He admitted, however, that he was not aware of the exact nature of the research conducted in the labs.[227] Shortly thereafter, the Iraqi National Congress, a government opposition group, arranged for the major to give media interviews in which he described a wide range of illicit WMD activities in Iraq.[228] In response,

---

223. Jehl, "Doubts on Informant Deleted in Senate Text."

224. CIA and DIA, *Iraqi Mobile Biological Warfare Agent Production Plants,* 1–2.

225. Butler Report, 128; Silberman-Robb Report, 180, 216 n. 242, 225 n. 407; Jehl, "Doubts on Informant Deleted in Senate Text"; and Bob Drogin, "Spy Work in Iraq Riddled by Failures," *Los Angeles Times,* June 17, 2004.

226. James Risen, "CIA Held Back Iraqi Arms Data, U.S. Officials Say," *New York Times,* July 6, 2004, A1; and Douglas Jehl, "U.S., Certain That Iraq Had Illicit Arms, Reportedly Ignored Contrary Reports," *New York Times,* March 6, 2004, A6; and Butler Report, 128.

227. Secretary of State Colin Powell, "Remarks to the United Nations Security Council," New York City, February 5, 2003, http://www.state.gov/secretary/former/powell/remarks/2003/17300.htm.; CIA and DIA, *Iraqi Mobile Biological Warfare Agent Production Plants,* 1–2; SSCI Report, 151–52, 160; Silberman-Robb Report, 84–85; Butler Report, 128; Jehl, "Doubts on Informant Deleted in Senate Text,"; and Jim Dwyer, "Defectors' Reports on Iraq Arms Were Embellished, Exile Asserts," *New York Times,* July 9, 2004, A1.

228. David Rose, "Iraq's Arsenal of Terror," *Vanity Fair,* May 2002, 120–31; and CBS News, *60 Minutes,* March 3, 2002.

the DIA, the SIS, and the CIA's Directorate of Operations judged the source to be a fabricator, and the DIA issued an official "fabrication notice."[229] Although the DIA did not recall the original reports from the defector, BW analysts received five warnings over the next five months about the unreliability of this source. Despite these warnings, reporting from this source was included in five intelligence reports in 2002, including the NIE. Although analysts acknowledged that they were aware of the source's questionable reliability at the time, they believed that the reporting on the mobile labs remained plausible and that even fabricators will usually have some truth to their stories.[230]

Analysts also fell victim to the trap of "layering" by building one uncertain assessment on top of another. The primary basis for the prewar judgment that Iraq had a stockpile of BW agents was a single report from Curveball that Iraq had the ability to produce BW agents in a dry powder form using mobile production facilities.[231] Dry BW agent is more suitable for stockpiling than wet agent since it is more stable and has a longer shelf-life. A senior U.S. intelligence official said, "We took that [report of mobile BW production plants from Curveball] seriously as a biological weapon capability that exists. . . . In our view what that means was we thought they had probably produced agent and weapons and had them sitting around."[232] The presumed efficacy of Iraqi denial-and-deception measures led analysts to equate a mobilization capability with a weapons stockpile since the intelligence community believed that it would be unable to detect the activation of such a production capability.[233] The assumptions underlying this chain of reasoning were not clearly stated in intelligence assessments.

Analysts also exaggerated the production capacities of the mobile BW production units described by Curveball. The NIE stated that the seven mobile BW units described by Curveball could produce in three to six months as much BW agent as Iraq had produced prior to the 1991 Gulf War.[234] This estimate was unrealistic and irresponsible. Even under a worst-case assessment assuming that Iraq's mobile production units ran constantly, that they did not require

229. SSCI Report, 161; and SSCI, Report on *Whether Public Statements Regarding Iraq by U.S. Government Officials Were Substantiated by Intelligence Information* (Washington, DC: GPO, 2008), 20.

230. SSCI, INC Report, 58–65.

231. Butler Report, 130; Silberman-Robb Report, 83; and Drogin, *Curveball*, 53. Analysts judged that the most likely BW agents being produced by Iraq were *B. anthracis,* botulinum toxin, and *Staphylococcus* spp. DOD, *Briefing on Weapons of Mass Destruction Exploitation in Iraq,* May 7, 2003, http://www.defenselink.mil/transcripts/transcript.aspx?transcriptid=2583.

232. Douglas Jehl and David E. Sanger, "Powell's Case, a Year Later: Gaps in Picture of Iraq Arms," *New York Times,* February 1, 2004, A1.

233. Stuart A. Cohen, *Iraq's WMD Programs: Culling Hard Facts from Soft Myths,* November 28, 2003, http://www.dni.gov/nic/articles_iraq_wmd.htm.

234. NIC, *Iraq's Continuing Program for Weapons of Mass Destruction,* 7; and SSCI, Whether *Public Statements Regarding Iraq,* 25.

maintenance, and that every batch of agent was of high quality—a truly heroic set of assumptions—it would have taken at least seven months to achieve pre-1991 production figures.[235] A more realistic estimate would have been closer to a year. As a result of these errors, the threat posed by Iraq's BW capability was portrayed with greater certainty as being larger and more advanced than the evidence allowed.

Analysts also discounted HUMINT that contradicted this assessment. Prior to the war, the CIA approached thirty family members of key Iraqi weapons scientists to try to find out information about the status of Iraq's WMD programs. All of these relatives reported to the CIA that the scientists said that Iraq's WMD programs had been abandoned. This information was not used by the Directorate of Intelligence or distributed outside the CIA. According to David Kay, the CIA had also interviewed an Iraqi defector, an engineer who had worked with Curveball, who specifically denied that they had worked on mobile biological production facilities. This defector, or a separate one, also reported that the trailers said by other defectors to be for weapons had a benign purpose.[236]

The management and leadership of the intelligence community also performed poorly and made two significant contributions to the flawed assessments of Iraq's BW capabilities and intentions. First, the failure of managers to share information within and between intelligence agencies hindered efforts to validate the credibility and reliability of reports that Iraq had a mobile BW production program. Second, for bureaucratic and political reasons, the management and leadership of the CIA created an environment that favored analysis supporting the existing consensus and stifled dissenting voices.

---

235. Each mobile unit was reportedly able to produce enough agent to fill seven R-400 bombs (which contain 90 liters of ten-times concentrated agent) a month. Duelfer Report, 3:89. Thus, the seven reported mobile units would have been able to produce a total of 4,410 liters of ten-times concentrated BW agent a month.

Iraq declared having produced about 31,000 liters of BW agent prior to 1991. Therefore, it would have taken the entire fleet of mobile BW production units about seven months of around-the-clock operation to produce this much agent. This does not take into account the 12–20% batch failure rate experienced by Iraq in the past, the need to take fermenters off-line 10% of the time for minor maintenance and for two weeks for major maintenance, and special challenges associated with operating mobile fermentation systems. On Iraqi BW production practices, see UNMOVIC, *Compendium,* 903.

236. James Risen, *State of War: The Secret History of the CIA and the Bush Administration* (New York: Free Press, 2006), 90–91, 106; Drogin and Miller, "Iraqi Defector's Tales Bolstered U.S. Case for War,"; Douglas Jehl, "U.S., Certain That Iraq Had Illicit Arms, Reportedly Ignored Contrary Reports," *New York Times,* March 6, 2004, A6; James Risen, "CIA Held Back Iraqi Arms Data, U.S. Officials Say," *New York Times,* July 6, 2004, A1; Erich Follath, John Goetz, Marcel Rosenbach, and Holger Stark, "How German Intelligence Helped Justify the U.S. Invasion of Iraq," *Der Spiegel,* March 22, 2008; and John Goetz and Bob Drogin, "'Curveball' Speaks, and a Reputation as a Disinformation Agent Remains Intact," *Los Angeles Times,* June 18, 2008.

On multiple occasions, important information was not shared within the CIA between collectors and analysts or passed up the chain of command. The CIA also withheld information from the rest of the intelligence community that cast doubt on Curveball's reliability. Policymakers were not adequately informed about the basis for analytical judgments about Iraq's BW program or doubts about the reliability of human sources reporting on Iraq's mobile BW production units. Finally, foreign intelligence services refused to provide access to or share information about human sources necessary to validate their reliability.

When Iraq's WMD programs became a political issue in 2002, the pressure to conform to the view that Iraq had a large and active BW program and to find evidence to support this assessment grew stronger. As a result, the standard of evidence required to support this viewpoint was lowered while analytical judgments became more expansive and bolder than was warranted by the available intelligence. The major inquiries into the prewar intelligence found that some of this pressure was self-imposed by analysts who believed that war with Iraq was inevitable. Their desire to ensure that the military was properly prepared for a possible CBW attack may have contributed to their tendencies to make worst-case assessments about Iraq's capabilities.[237] This explanation, however, does not account for the most important flaws in prewar intelligence. The intelligence community began revising upward its assessment of the threat posed by Iraq's BW program in 2000 based on Curveball's reporting, and by 2001 they had concluded that Iraq had a stockpile of recently produced BW agent, well before the drumbeat of war with Iraq started.[238] The U.S. Air Force, the military service most likely to make worst-case assessments of the threat posed by Iraq's airborne CBW delivery capabilities, disagreed with the rest of the intelligence community that Iraq's unmanned aerial vehicles were designed to deliver CBW.[239] While similar pressure to protect the military by warning them of the full range of potential threats was no doubt felt by intelligence analysts during the run-up to Operation Desert Storm in 1991, WMD-related analyses in 2002 were fundamentally different because they were being used as the primary justification for war and were being used publicly for that purpose.

Efforts by CIA managers and leaders to squelch internal dissent, and their refusal to acknowledge mistakes after the war, strongly suggests that prewar anxiety was not a major factor in the flawed intelligence assessments. A BW analyst

---

237. Silberman-Robb Report, 176; SSCI Report, 250, 505; and Jane Harman, "Serious Intelligence Reform," (speech, American Enterprise Institute, Washington, DC, March 5, 2004, http://www.aei.org/news20058).

238. Silberman-Robb Report, 83.

239. "Air Force Assessment before War Said Iraqi Drones Were Minor Threat," Associated Press, August 25, 2003; Bradley Graham, "Air Force Analysts Feel Vindicated on Iraqi Drones," *Washington Post,* September 26, 2003, A23; and Silberman-Robb Report, 136–37.

who traveled to Iraq after the war to investigate Curveball was forced to leave WINPAC after reporting back to headquarters that he believed the source was a fabricator.[240] The CIA also disregarded the finding of a DIA-led investigation into the two trailers discovered in Iraq in mid-2003 that resembled the mobile BW production units described by the United States before the war that the trailers were designed to produce hydrogen for weather balloons, not BW agents.[241] This finding was later reaffirmed by the ISG.[242] Rod Barton, who led the ISG's investigation into Iraq's BW program, also experienced pressure to tailor his findings so that they would not contradict the CIA's prewar assessments.[243] WINPAC's resistance to reassessing prewar intelligence on Iraq's BW program led the Silberman-Robb Commission to criticize the organization for fostering a "culture of enforced consensus."[244]

Although none of the major inquiries into prewar intelligence on Iraqi WMD found direct evidence that analysts had been pressured to change their findings, the Silberman-Robb Commission and an internal CIA review found that the environment created by the Bush administration's public justification for war based on Iraq's development of WMD may have influenced analysts and managers working on these issues.[245] The extent to which this environment was cultivated within the intelligence community has been revealed by the so-called Downing Street memo. After meeting with Director of Central Intelligence George Tenet at an annual CIA-SIS conference in July 2002, SIS chief Sir Richard Dearlove reported to a British cabinet meeting on Iraq that "there was a perceptible shift in attitude [in Washington]. Military action was now seen as inevitable. Bush wanted to remove Saddam, through military action, justified by the conjunction of terrorism and WMD. But the intelligence and facts were being fixed around the policy."[246] This sentiment was encapsulated by the deputy chief of the CIA's Iraq WMD Task Force, who told a subordinate who had expressed serious reservations about the BW-related HUMINT being used by Secretary Powell, "Let's keep in mind the fact that this war's going to happen regardless of what Curve

---

240. Silberman-Robb Report, 192–94.

241. Joby Warrick, "Lacking Biolabs, Trailers Carried the Case for War," *Washington Post*, April 12, 2006, A1.

242. Duelfer Report, 3:79, 91.

243. Barton, *Weapons Detective*, 249–50.

244. Silberman-Robb Report, 196.

245. SSCI Report, 272–88; Richard Kerr, et al., "Collection and Analysis on Iraq: Issues for the U.S. Intelligence Community," *Studies in Intelligence* 49, no. 3 (2005): 47–54; and Silberman-Robb Report, 188–91.

246. Memorandum from Matthew Rycroft to David Manning, subject: "Iraq: Prime Minister's Meeting, 23 July, S 195/02," July 23, 2002, http://www.timesonline.co.uk/tol/news/uk/article387374.ece; and Risen, *State of War*, 113–14.

Ball said or didn't say, and that the Powers That Be probably aren't terribly interested in whether Curve Ball knows what he is talking about."[247]

Politicalization can take many forms. When a strong wind is blowing in one direction and there are multiple opportunities for biases to be introduced into analyses, the cumulative effect of such pressure can be significant, especially when managers are predisposed to promote intelligence that they believe political leaders will find favorable.[248] The fight over Curveball between the Directorate of Operations and WINPAC illustrates the organizational and political pressures that influenced intelligence on Iraq's WMD programs. Analysts who believed that Curveball was credible had the political wind to their backs while skeptics in the Directorate of Operations who questioned the source's reliability had to swim against the tide. These skeptics were further hampered by the unwillingness of their superiors to press the issue at the highest levels of the intelligence community.

BW Intelligence: Lessons Learned and Implications

Biological weapons programs represent one of the most difficult targets for intelligence agencies. The multiuse nature of biotechnology; the difficulty in distinguishing between offensive, defensive, and civilian biological activities; the importance and opacity of intentions for assessing BW programs; and the extensive secrecy that shrouds these programs pose unique challenges for intelligence collection and analysis.

HUMINT has been responsible for the most significant breakthroughs in biological threat assessments. The Hirsch report, the sources that provided information on the outbreak of anthrax at Sverdlovsk in 1979, and the defections of Pasechnik and Alibek were crucial to piercing the veil of secrecy surrounding the Soviet BW program. The Iraqi defectors who emerged in 1991 and the defection of Hussein Kamel in August 1995 provided invaluable information on the organization and status of the Iraqi BW program. Only such knowledgeable insiders can provide the required insights into intent and activities that is required for a comprehensive understanding of an adversary's BW program.

HUMINT, however, can be a double-edged sword. The information provided by defectors can be difficult to corroborate, and such sources may be purposefully or inadvertently transmitting false information, thus contributing to

---

247. SSCI Report, 249.
248. Paul R. Pillar, "Intelligence, Policy, and the War in Iraq," *Foreign Affairs* 85, no. 2 (2006): 15–27.

flawed assessments. The success of HUMINT with regard to the Soviet BW program and the early Iraqi program may have contributed to the laxity with which the accounts of more recent Iraqi defectors were analyzed.

Unlike humans, pictures don't lie. But they also don't tell the whole truth. Overhead reconnaissance, one of the mainstays of U.S. intelligence collection, can identify suspicious features of some biological facilities, but they cannot determine the types or purposes of activities being conducted inside. Analysts misinterpreted imagery of the Soviet BW test site at Vozrozhdeniya Island in the 1960s, which led them to completely reevaluate the nature of the Soviet BW program. While storage bunkers provided a useful indicator of which facilities in the Soviet Union were associated with the BW program, similar structures in Iraq were not linked to the BW program. In the case of Iraq, analysis of satellite imagery prior to the 1991 Gulf War failed to detect the locations where Iraq was producing BW agents or that Iraq was testing and deploying biological weapons. In 2002 the misinterpretation of imagery of dual-use sites in Iraq led to sinister conclusions about benign civilian facilities.

Signal intelligence has played an important but indirect role in BW intelligence collection. The dependence of the pre-1991 Iraqi BW program on imported equipment and materials made it particularly vulnerable to communication intercepts. Iraq's foreign procurement efforts were one of the early indicators of their interest in biological weapons, allowing intelligence agencies to track the program's progress and providing UNSCOM with the means of uncovering their offensive program. Iraq's procurement networks were also targeted in 1990s by communication intercepts, but these efforts did not provide good insight into Iraq's weapons programs.[249] Indeed, analysts consistently misinterpreted the acquisition of dual-use equipment as being destined for a BW program. U.S. intelligence agencies are known to have kept a close tab on Soviet procurement of Western technology during the cold war.[250] It is not known to what extent Soviet acquisition of Western biotech-related equipment provided useful intelligence on the Soviet BW program. By analyzing personal communications, orders for equipment and matériel from Soviet factories, and the nature of communications between facilities, analysts were able to establish links between civilian and military scientists and facilities in the Soviet Union.[251] Such information was not conclusive on its own but provided a possible means for cross-checking intelligence collected through other means.

---

249. Silberman-Robb Report, 163.

250. DCI, *The Technology Acquisition Efforts of the Soviet Intelligence Services,* Interagency Intelligence Memorandum, June 1982, FOIA; and CIA, *Soviet Acquisition of Militarily Significant Western Technology: An Update,* September 1985, FOIA.

251. Interview with former National Security Agency CBW analyst, 2008.

Open-source intelligence can be particularly useful in the field of BW intelligence. Scientific publications were the primary source of information on Soviet activities in BW-related disciplines through the 1960s. While such publications may provide evidence of a nation's scientific and technical capabilities, they rarely provide insight into a nation's intent. Open-source intelligence can also be used to gauge the level of transparency exercised by a facility and determine if that level of transparency is consistent with its stated purpose. Lack of local media coverage of an ostensibly civilian site or activity might raise suspicion, while conspicuous media attention focused on a suspected BW facility might indicate that it is engaged in legitimate activities. For example, news of major public health and veterinary immunization campaigns in Iraq between 1998 and 2002 provided a plausible peaceful explanation for the increased level of activity observed at dual-use biological sites during this time.[252]

These cases also demonstrate the importance and pitfalls of liaison intelligence. The United States and United Kingdom engaged in a productive exchange of intelligence on the Soviet BW program throughout the cold war.[253] The United States also exchanged intelligence on the Iraqi BW program with the British and Israeli intelligence services prior to the 1991 Gulf War. In contrast, while the CIA received reports from the SIS and BND on Iraqi BW activities between 2000 and 2002, the agency was never given access to these sources or information about their identities that would have enabled it to verify their reliability. The lack of direct access to Curveball was a major contributing factor to the flawed assessments of Iraq's BW capabilities and intentions.

Denial-and-deception measures adopted by the Soviet Union and Iraq not only interfered with the collection of intelligence on their BW programs but also with its analysis. The success of Soviet denial-and-deception measures was such that even the most alarmist U.S. intelligence analysts underestimated the Soviet BW program. Iraq successfully hid the existence of its primary BW production plant at Al Hakam, which led the United State to bomb the wrong targets during the 1991 Gulf War. Iraq's denial-and-deception measures were so good in the 1980s and early 1990s that intelligence analysts began assuming that the absence of confirming evidence was an indication of a successful denial operation and that the presence of contradictory evidence was the result of deception.

---

252. SSCI Report, 163–66.
253. The British not only shared all of the debriefing information from Vladimir Pasechnik with the CIA, but they also allowed CIA experts to debrief him themselves. Mangold and Goldberg, *Plague Wars,* 101. The only major exception to this relationship was a cache of top-secret information on the Soviet BW program put together by the United States in 1989 code-named Juniper. Ibid., 87; and interview with former British intelligence officer, 2004.

States developing biological weapons have a strong incentive to embed their BW activities in legitimate civilian enterprises, which greatly complicates the collection and analysis of intelligence. As advanced multiuse biotechnologies diffuse globally and become more central to economic growth, a growing number of states will have the option of adopting this strategy to shield offensive activities and facilities from intelligence agencies. Given these trends, it will become increasingly untenable to associate capability with intent. This will place a premium on developing innovative new methods for assessing a nation's intentions in regard to biological warfare.

The analysis of BW intelligence can be likened to creating a mosaic that is built piece by piece over time. This type of intelligence work requires all-source analysis that synthesizes the information gathered by all of the different collection methods and integrates both regional and technical expertise. Given the dearth of direct hard evidence on Soviet and Iraqi BW activities, analysts working with ambiguous, fragmentary, and contradictory information frequently fell prey to a range of cognitive biases including groupthink, mirror-imaging, and resistance to inconsistent data. These types of biases cannot be eliminated, but they can be ameliorated through more rigorous training of analysts and a stronger focus on the nontechnical factors that may influence a nation's BW intentions and capabilities.

These difficulties have been exacerbated by the limited resources devoted to solving these collection and analysis problems. A former CBW analyst with the National Security Agency estimates that there were perhaps a hundred CBW analysts in the entire intelligence community in the mid-80s, with about one-third dedicated to BW issues and around ten of these devoted to the Soviet BW program. In comparison, the National Security Agency alone typically had a hundred analysts assigned to monitor each Soviet strategic missile army.[254] After the 1991 Gulf War, a CIA review of CBW intelligence found that the number of analysts devoted to CBW issues was inadequate and that this had a direct impact on the level of support for policymakers and military commanders.[255] At the time, there were roughly one hundred nuclear proliferation analysts for every one CBW analyst.[256]

The failure of the intelligence community and policymakers to devote more resources to BW intelligence may reflect what Christopher Davis has termed "nuclear blindness."[257] During the cold war, nuclear weapons were the currency

---

254. Interview with former National Security Agency CBW analyst, 2008.

255. Persian Gulf War Illnesses Task Force, *Lessons Learned*.

256. Albert J. Mauroni, *Chemical-Biological Defense: U.S. Military Policies and Decisions in the Gulf War* (Westport, CT: Praeger, 1998), 136.

257. Christopher J. Davis, "Nuclear Blindness: An Overview of the Biological Weapons Programs of the Former Soviet Union and Iraq," *Emerging Infectious Diseases* 5, no. 4 (1999): 509.

of superpower politics, and their capacity for mass destruction had been amply demonstrated. Biological weapons, in contrast, remained on the margins of national security planning and threat assessment. As a result, the United States failed to devote the resources necessary to properly assess the size, scope, and sophistication of foreign BW programs.

Despite a number of reorganizations of the intelligence community's WMD portfolio since the early 1990s, the number of BW analysts remains inadequate. Of the seven hundred analysts working on WMD at the CIA in 2003 only six specialized in BW.[258] As a result, analysts are responsible for monitoring BW programs in multiple countries and often in more than one region. This cross-coverage limits their ability to conduct strategic research on BW issues and develop an understanding of how political, economic, technical, and military factors might affect a specific nation's BW intentions and capabilities.

High-quality intelligence will not negate the threat posed by biological weapons, but it would help states calibrate defensive and diplomatic responses to these threats and reduce the likelihood of counterproductive actions. The difficulty in conducting accurate biological threat assessments has several implications for reducing the danger posed by biological weapons.

First, without adequate intelligence, it is more difficult to develop and deploy effective defenses. The agent-specific nature of most medical countermeasures and diagnostic and detection systems requires advance knowledge of which agents an adversary is developing. Although this factor is partially mitigated by the short list of the most dangerous agents, novel, obscure, or genetically engineered pathogens may allow the attacker to attain an element of surprise. In addition, without credible intelligence indicating that an adversary's BW program poses a significant threat, it may not be possible to mobilize the resources for researching and fielding defenses against the threat.

Second, without credible intelligence, it is much more difficult to rally domestic and international support for diplomatic efforts to bring states into compliance with their biological arms control obligations. Paradoxically, the reluctance to share sensitive information may limit the utility of the most useful types of intelligence on foreign BW programs, such as that provided by spies and defectors. On the other hand, allegations of BW development or use that prove to be false are likely to cause long-term credibility problems for the accuser. This loss of credibility may complicate future efforts to obtain public and international support for measures to combat the threat of biological weapons.

Third, poor intelligence hampers efforts to use inspectors to verify a state's compliance with biological arms control agreements. As demonstrated by the experiences of the United States and United Kingdom in the Soviet Union and

---

258. Drogin, *Curveball*, 64.

Russia and of UNSCOM in Iraq, accurate intelligence is crucial for planning, conducting, and analyzing inspections.[259] The poor record of U.S. intelligence on assessing foreign BW programs, however, should give pause to those who take comfort in the intelligence community's successfully having predicted every Soviet intercontinental ballistic missile *before* it was tested.[260] The performance of the U.S. intelligence community in monitoring Soviet strategic nuclear forces is not an appropriate indicator of their ability to obtain accurate intelligence on BW programs. Indeed, the low-quality U.S. intelligence provided to UNMOVIC on Iraq's WMD programs in 2002–3 was more of a hindrance than a help.

The fourth implication is that poor intelligence hinders effective military action. Accurate intelligence is necessary for planning and conducting attacks on BW facilities as part of a broader military conflict, a preventive or preemptive action, or as a retaliatory strike. The failure of the United States to identify Iraq's main BW production plants prior to the 1991 Gulf War allowed Iraq's BW program to emerge from the war virtually unscathed. In modern conflicts it is important not only to strike the right target but also to avoid destroying the wrong one. During the 1991 Gulf War, the United States destroyed an infant-formula production plant in the mistaken belief that it was involved in BW production. The destruction of the "baby-milk factory" was a propaganda coup for Baghdad. In 1998 the United States attacked the Al Shifa pharmaceutical plant in Sudan, which it mistakenly believed was involved in the production of a chemical weapon precursor.[261] The controversies engendered by these strikes highlight the need for accurate intelligence on dual-use facilities believed to be engaged in CBW activities.

Fifth, in the absence of firm and reliable intelligence, governments may engage in worst-case planning and undertake an exaggerated reaction to perceived threats.[262] Especially during a crisis or wartime, the tendency of government officials will be to assume the worst about their adversaries. Since intentions are the key to determining the purpose and significance of multiuse biotechnology capabilities, even peaceful and defensive activities of a state viewed as hostile are likely to be considered suspicious. As Undersecretary of State John Bolton put it,

---

259. David C. Kelly, "The Trilateral Agreement: Lessons for Biological Weapons Verification," in *Verification Yearbook, 2002,* ed. Trevor Findlay and Oliver Meier (London: VERTIC, 2002), 104; and Tim Trevan, "Exploiting Intelligence in International Organizations," in *Biological Warfare: Modern Offense and Defense,* ed. Raymond Zilinskas *(Boulder, CO: Lynne Reinner, 2000),* 207–24.

260. Barbara Hatch Rosenberg and Gordon Burck, "Verification of Compliance with the Biological Weapons Convention," in *Preventing a Biological Arms Race,* ed. Susan Wright (Cambridge: MIT Press, 1990), 305 (italics in original).

261. For details on these incidents, see Koblentz, "Countering Dual-Use Facilities," 48–53.

262. Robert Jervis, *Perception and Misperception in International Politics* (Princeton: Princeton University Press, 1976), 64–66.

"once a rogue state's intentions become apparent, we should assume that the dual-use technologies it acquires will be used for illegitimate purposes."[263] This tendency toward worst-case assessments of the capabilities of hostile states may account for U.S. overestimation of the BW capabilities of the so-called rogue states—Iraq, Libya, and Cuba—during the 1990s.[264]

The interpretation of uncertain intelligence in this way could lead to a security dilemma in which states take actions to improve their own defense that inadvertently threatens other states. As the number and size of national biological defense programs around the world increases, other states may perceive these activities as threatening, thereby providing a justification for initiating or continuing a BW program. The shift from threat-based to science-based defensive research exacerbates this dilemma by increasing the scope of potential agents that require investigation and the necessity of inventing new agents to develop defenses against them.[265] Worst-case assessments of an adversary's BW capabilities and intentions are especially likely if the adversary is viewed as particularly difficult to deter. The logic of preventive action reduces the threshold of evidence required to justify action because an attack is viewed as inevitable and the consequences of such an attack are perceived as being large. The application of this logic to counterproliferation was observed in both the Clinton administration's decision to strike the Al Shifa pharmaceutical plant in Sudan in 1998 and the George W. Bush administration's decision to invade Iraq in 2003.

263. John R. Bolton, Undersecretary of State for Arms Control and International Security, "The International Aspects of Terrorism and Weapons of Mass Destruction," *Second Global Conference on Nuclear, Bio/Chem Terrorism.* Hudson Institute, Washington, DC, November 1, 2002. http://www.state.gov/t/us/rm/14848.htm.

264. On the intelligence community's revised assessment of Cuban BW intentions, see Steven R. Weisman, "In Stricter Study, U.S. Scales Back Claim on Cuba Arms," *New York Times,* September 18, 2004, A7. The Silberman-Robb Commission also found that U.S. intelligence on Libya's BW program could not be confirmed. Silberman-Robb Report, 255–56.

265. Jonathan B. Tucker, "Biological Threat Assessment: Is the Cure Worse Than the Disease?" *Arms Control Today,* October 2004, 13–19.

5

BIOLOGICAL TERRORISM

The prospect of a terrorist group acquiring and using biological weapons has become one of the most feared threats to international security. According to then UN Secretary-General Kofi Annan, "the most important under-addressed threat relating to terrorism, and one which acutely requires new thinking on the part of the international community, is that of terrorists using a biological weapon."[1] In 2008, the Commission on the Prevention of Weapons of Mass Destruction Proliferation and Terrorism judged that it was more likely than not that a biological terrorist attack would take place within five years.[2] The intelligence community estimates that of the fifteen terrorist groups that have expressed an interest in acquiring biological weapons, only three of these groups have demonstrated a commitment to acquiring the capability to use them to cause mass casualties.[3] This chapter provides a brief history of biological terrorism, a framework for assessing

---

1. Kofi Annan, *Uniting against Terrorism,* Report of the Secretary-General, United Nations General Assembly A/60/825, April 27, 2006, 11, http://www.un.org/unitingagainstterrorism.

2. Bob Graham and Jim Talent, *World at Risk: Report of the Commission on the Prevention of Weapons of Mass Destruction Proliferation and Terrorism* (New York: Vintage Books, 2008), xv.

3. Interview with senior U.S. intelligence official, Washington, DC, May 2008.

the threat posed by biological weapons in the hands of nonstate actors, and an assessment of the current threat of biological terrorism.

Biological terrorism first emerged as a major security issue in the mid-1990s due to three factors. First, and most important, were reports that Aum Shinrikyo, the Japanese cult responsible for the nerve gas attack in the Tokyo subway system in 1995, had also developed biological weapons. Aum Shinrikyo was widely viewed as the harbinger for other nonstate actors interested in causing mass casualties and capable of acquiring nuclear, biological, chemical, or radiological weapons.[4] The second factor was the nexus between states that were developing biological weapons and states that were linked to international terrorist groups. All seven nations on the State Department's list of state sponsors of terrorism in the 1990s were believed to have BW programs at the time.[5] The third factor was the social and economic upheaval in Russia that increased the risk that terrorist groups might obtain expertise or materials from the former Soviet BW program that could facilitate their development of biological weapons.[6]

The terrorist attacks on the United States on September 11, 2001, and the subsequent anthrax letter attacks brought together the twin dangers of mass casualty terrorism and biological weapons in a frightening new way. The combination of these two events propelled biological terrorism to the forefront of public health, homeland security, and national security planning. Groups such as Aum Shinrikyo and al Qaeda have demonstrated their desire and ability to cause mass casualties and an interest in using disease as a weapon. Despite concerted efforts by both groups to produce deadly pathogens and toxins, however, neither has successfully caused any casualties with such weapons, let alone developed a mass casualty-producing biological weapon. The difficulties these groups failed to overcome illustrate the significant hurdles that terrorists face in progressing beyond crude weapons suitable for assassination and the contamination of food

---

4. Richard Falkenrath, Robert Newman, and Bradley Thayer, *America's Achilles' Heel: Nuclear, Biological, and Chemical Terrorism and Covert Attack* (Cambridge: MIT Press, 1998); and Jessica Stern, *The Ultimate Terrorists* (Cambridge: Harvard University Press, 1999).

5. The seven state sponsors of terrorism were Cuba, Iran, Iraq, Libya, North Korea, Sudan, and Syria. Department of State, *Patterns of Global Terrorism 2001* (Washington, DC: GPO, 2002). On the BW programs of these states, see Department of Defense, *Proliferation: Threat and Response* (Washington, DC: GPO, 2001); and Central Intelligence Agency (CIA), *Unclassified Report to Congress on the Acquisition of Technology Relating to Weapons of Mass Destruction and Advanced Conventional Munitions, 1 January through 30 June 2001,* January 30, 2002, https://www.cia.gov/library/reports/archived-reports-1/jan_jun2001.htm.

6. Jonathan B. Tucker and Kathleen M. Vogel, "Preventing the Proliferation of Chemical and Biological Weapons Materials and Know-How," *Nonproliferation Review* 7, no. 1 (2000): 88–96.

or water to biological weapons based on aerosol dissemination technology capable of causing mass casualties.[7]

This chapter is divided into four sections. The first provides a brief history of biological terrorism and traces the evolution of bioterrorism capabilities. The next two assess the threats posed by state-sponsored biological terrorism and by al Qaeda. The final section discusses the challenges faced by law enforcement and intelligence agencies in detecting preparations by nonstate actors for acquiring and using biological weapons.

History of Biological Terrorism

Biological terrorism has been exceedingly rare. Milton Leitenberg's review of five public databases on nuclear, biological, chemical, and radiological terrorism found an "extremely low" incidence of confirmed biological terrorism cases compared to reports of hoaxes, threats, and criminal acts involving biological agents.[8] Of the 180 confirmed cases of illicit biological agent activity by nonstate actors during the twentieth century compiled by Seth Carus, only 27 involved terrorist groups and in only 8 of those cases did the terrorist group actually acquire a biological agent.[9] Prior to the anthrax letter attacks in 2001, only one group, the disciples of guru Bhagwan Shree Rajneesh in Oregon, managed to cause any casualties with a biological agent.

The framework for examining the evolution of state-based BW capabilities described in chapter 1 is also applicable to terrorist efforts to develop biological weapons. Although terrorists have fewer resources to develop BW compared to states, their needs are more limited. Unlike states, terrorists can achieve their objectives without developing BW agents that can be produced in large quantities, stored for significant periods of time, disseminated by highly efficient and reliable devices, and delivered by systems designed for use under battlefield conditions. Nevertheless, terrorists who seek to inflict mass casualties still face significant hurdles in acquiring and producing virulent agents and designing effective dissemination devices. Terrorists whose interest is limited to causing a small number of casualties or mass disruption face fewer obstacles. As the proliferation of

---

7. On the difficulties of developing biological weapons outside of a state-run program, see General Accounting Office, *Need for Comprehensive Threat and Risk Assessments of Chemical and Biological Attacks*, GAO-NSIAD-99-163 (Washington, DC: GAO, September 1999).

8. Milton Leitenberg, *The Problem of Biological Weapons* (Stockholm: Swedish National Defence College, 2004), 25–27.

9. W. Seth Carus, *Bioterrorism and Biocrimes: The Illicit Use of Biological Agents since 1900* (Washington, DC: National Defense University, February 2001), 8.

anthrax hoax letters since 2001 has demonstrated, individuals interested in caus-ing terror and disruption at a local level can achieve their objectives with noth-ing more than a powdery substance and a threatening note.

First-Generation Biological Terrorism

First-generation biological terrorism uses materials naturally infected with a pathogen or toxin. In the 1950s the Mau Mau national liberation movement in Kenya used the sap of the African milk bush to poison cattle belonging to British settlers.[10] In the 1960s Vietcong guerilla in South Vietnam designed booby traps containing sharpened bamboo stakes, called punji sticks, smeared with feces to promote bacterial infections in the wound.[11] These simple but effective weap-ons caused 2 percent of American deaths and injuries during the Vietnam War.[12] There have also been a number of domestic cases where individuals have been intentionally injected with blood contaminated with HIV, but all of the per-petrators had criminal, not terrorist, motivations.[13]

Second-Generation Biological Terrorism

Second-generation biological terrorism requires the ability to produce small quantities of biological agents, although dissemination remains limited to the use of fomites, vectors, the contamination of food or water, or direct injection into the victim. These types of capabilities are best suited for small-scale attacks, al-though under the right conditions they could cause mass disruption or even mass casualties. Most attempts by terrorists to acquire biological weapons fall into this category.

The most successful example of second-generation biological terrorism was the use of *Salmonella* Typhimurium by members of the Rajneeshee cult to poi-son salad bars in The Dalles, Oregon, in 1984. From the establishment of their ranch in The Dalles in 1981, the Rajneeshee found themselves in a series of dis-putes with state and local authorities. As part of a strategy to influence a local election, the cult contaminated ten salad bars in the town with *Salmonella* Typhi-murium that they had produced in their medical clinic. This contamination re-sulted in 751 townspeople becoming victims of food poisoning. The state public

---

10. Carus, *Bioterrorism and Biocrimes,* 63–64.

11. George Christopher, et al., "Biological Warfare: A Historical Perspective," *Journal of the American Medical Association* 278, no. 5 (1997): 412.

12. Spurgeon Neel, *Medical Support of the U.S. Army in Vietnam, 1965–1970* (Washington, DC: Department of the Army, 1991), 54.

13. Carus, *Bioterrorism and Biocrimes,* 47–48.

health department and CDC believed that the cause of the mass food poisoning was unsanitary practices by food handlers at the restaurants. The identity of the perpetrators wasn't revealed until the mastermind of the attack had a falling out with other members of the cult and the group's leader publicly accused her of poisoning local officials and the townspeople.[14]

The most common example of a second-generation biological terrorism capability is the toxin ricin, derived from the castor bean plant (*Ricinus communis*). Ricin's popularity is primarily due to the ease with which it can be produced. Ricin's "cloak and dagger" mystique also adds to its attractiveness. The materials needed to produce ricin are readily available, instructions for producing the toxin can be found using the Internet, and the production process does not require any specialized skills.[15] Ricin, however, generally does not cause mass casualties since it is difficult to produce the toxin in a sufficiently pure and easily aerosolized form.[16] Crude ricin preparations are suitable only for contaminating food or beverages or injecting directly into a victim. In 1978 Bulgarian dissident Georgi Markov was assassinated by an agent of the Bulgarian secret police in London by a ricin-filled pellet, fired from a pen-shaped device, not a modified umbrella as commonly believed.[17] A number of individuals in the United States have acquired or attempted to acquire ricin for criminal and terrorist purposes.[18] During fall 2003, letters containing ricin were intercepted at a South Carolina post office and at the White House's off-site mail sorting facility. In February 2004, ricin was discovered in the mailroom of Senate Majority Leader Bill Frist.[19] The individual(s) responsible for sending these letters has not been identified.

---

14. W. Seth Carus, "The Rajneeshees (1984)," in *Toxic Terror: Assessing Terrorist Use of Chemical and Biological Weapons,* ed. Jonathan B. Tucker (Cambridge: MIT Press, 2000), 115–37; and Thomas J. Torok, et al., "A Large Community Outbreak of Salmonellosis Caused by Intentional Contamination of Restaurant Salad Bars," in *Biological Weapons: Limiting the Threat,* ed. Joshua Lederberg (Cambridge: MIT Press, 1999), 167–84.

15. Susanne Lundberg, Lena Melin, Calle Nilsson, and Pontus von Schoenberg, *Ricin: Threat, Effects and Protection* (Umea: Swedish Defence Research Agency, June 2004); and Dana Shea and Frank Gottron, *Ricin: Technical Background and Potential Role in Terrorism* (Washington, DC: Congressional Research Service, February 4, 2004).

16. The United States, United Kingdom, and Iraq experimented with, and then abandoned, biological weapons based on ricin.

17. Hristo Hristov, *The Double Life of Agent Picadilly,* trans. David Mossop (2008), available online at http://hristo-hristov.com/content/view/1/2/lang,english/.

18. For a list of ricin-related incidents, see Lundberg, et al., *Ricin,* 28–29; and Center for Nonproliferation Studies, *Special Report on Ricin,* February 29, 2008, http://www.cns.miis.edu/pubs/week/pdf/080229_ricin.pdf.

19. Judith Miller, "Poison Found at Post Office," *New York Times,* October 23, 2003, A14; David Johnston and Carl Hulse, "Finding of Deadly Poison in Office Disrupts the Senate," *New York Times,* February 3, 2004, A1; and Dan Eggen, "Letter with Ricin Vial Sent to White House," *Washington Post,* February 4, 2004, A7.

Aside from the Markov assassination, there have been no known fatalities linked to the use of ricin as a weapon.

Third-Generation Biological Terrorism

Third-generation biological terrorism capabilities require the ability to disseminate pathogens or toxins in an aerosol of particles in the 1–10 micron range. The only successful example of this form of biological terrorism was the 2001 anthrax letter attacks. Although this attack did not utilize a dissemination device such as a bomblet or spray device, the high quality of the powder in some of the letters made them a potent aerosolization hazard in their own right. The Federal Bureau of Investigation alleges that a microbiologist at Fort Detrick who specialized in *B. anthracis* was responsible for the anthrax letter attacks. The only other known attempt by terrorists to intentionally create an aerosolized biological weapon was by the Japanese cult Aum Shinrikyo. Aum tried and failed on multiple occasions to disseminate aerosols of *B. anthracis* and botulinum toxin. Both of these cases highlight the difficulties that a terrorist group faces in perfecting a third-generation biological weapon based on an aerosolized BW agent.

2001 Anthrax Letter Attacks   In September and October 2001, seven envelopes containing a dry powder of *B. anthracis* spores were mailed to Senators Thomas Daschle (D-SD) and Patrick Leahy (D-VT) and five media outlets: American Media International (AMI) in Boca Raton, Florida, the editor of the *New York Post,* Tom Brokaw at NBC, Dan Rather at CBS, and ABC News.[20] The letters caused twenty-two cases of anthrax, including eleven cases of cutaneous anthrax and eleven cases of inhalation anthrax. Five of the cases of inhalation anthrax were fatal. The letters also contaminated over thirty postal facilities, government buildings, and media offices with *B. anthracis.* The cost of decontaminating these sites was at least $250 million.[21] The total cost of the anthrax letter attacks has been estimated at $6 billion.[22] The anthrax letter attacks were dubbed Amerithrax by the FBI.

The anthrax letter attacks qualify as third-generation bioterrorism because the powder of *B. anthracis* spores contained in the letters sent to the senators was

20. Of the five letters that are believed to have been sent to the media outlets, only those sent to the *New York Post* and Tom Brokaw, postmarked September 18, have been recovered. Both Senate letters, postmarked October 9, were recovered by the FBI.

21. Dorothy A. Canter, "Remediating Anthrax-Contaminated Sites: Learning from the Past to Protect the Future," *Chemical Health and Safety,* July/August 2005, 16.

22. Leonard A. Cole, "WMD and Lessons from the Anthrax Attacks," in *The McGraw-Hill Homeland Security Handbook,* ed. David G. Kamien (New York: McGraw-Hill, 2006), 170.

of such high quality that it was easily aerosolized and capable of causing inhalation anthrax.[23] The letters that were recovered from the *New York Post* and NBC contained a much less refined powder.[24] The Senate letters contained a dry powder of highly concentrated *B. anthracis* spores with no debris or vegetative cells.[25] Contrary to press reports, the powder in these letters was not coated with silica or other additives to enhance their aerosolization.[26] Nonetheless, the simple act of cutting open the taped anthrax letter sent to Senator Daschle was sufficient to release enough *B. anthracis* spores to expose twenty-eight office workers and first responders to the bacteria.[27] The powder in the Daschle letter also demonstrated good secondary aerosolization properties.[28]

Due to the high quality of the dried *B. anthracis* spores in the Senate letters, the United States Postal Service unintentionally served as the primary means of dissemination. The mail sorting machines pinched and twisted the anthrax letters, squeezing large quantities of spores out of the envelopes, which contaminated the mail-sorting machines and other pieces of mail flowing through them. The use of high-pressure air to clean these machines at the end of each shift re-aerosolized the spores and presented a further inhalation hazard. As a result, postal workers accounted for seven of the eleven cases of inhalation anthrax, and two other victims of inhalation anthrax are believed to have contracted the disease from mail cross-contaminated by one of the Senate letters.[29]

In August 2008 the FBI announced that its sole suspect in the Amerithrax case was Bruce E. Ivins, a microbiologist and anthrax vaccine researcher with the United States Army Medical Research Institute for Infectious Diseases (USAMRIID) at Fort Detrick, Maryland.[30] Ivins, who had been under

---

23. The letters sent to the senators caused nine of the eleven cases of inhalation anthrax. In contrast, the four letters sent to the New York media outlets on September 18 caused nine cases of cutaneous anthrax, none of which was fatal. Daniel B. Jernigan, et al., "Investigation of Bioterrorism-Related Anthrax, United States, 2001: Epidemiologic Findings," *Emerging Infectious Diseases* 8, no. 10 (2002): 1019–28.

24. Thomas F. Dellafera, "Affidavit in Support of Search Warrant," Document 07-524-M-01, October 31, 2007, 4, http://www.usdoj.gov/amerithrax.

25. Lois Ember, "Anthrax Sleuthing," *Chemical and Engineering News* 84, no. 49 (2006): 47–54.

26. Douglas J. Beecher, "Forensic Application of Microbiological Culture Analysis to Identify Mail Intentionally Contaminated with *Bacillus anthracis* Spores," *Applied and Environmental Microbiology* 72, no. 8 (2006): 5309; and Matthew Meselson and Ken Alibek, "Anthrax under the Microscope," *Washington Post,* November 5, 2002, A24.

27. Vincent P. Hsu, et al., "Opening a *Bacillus anthracis*–Containing Envelope, Capitol Hill, Washington, DC: The Public Health Response," *Emerging Infectious Diseases* 8, no. 10 (2002): 1039–43.

28. Christopher P. Weiss, et al., "Secondary Aerosolization of Viable *Bacillus Anthracis* Spores in a Contaminated U.S. Senate Office," *Journal of the American Medical Association* 288, no. 22 (2002): 2853–58.

29. Rick Weiss and Ellen Nakashima, "More Mail Believed to Be Tainted," *Washington Post,* December 4, 2001.

30. Department of Justice (DOJ), *Transcript of Amerithrax Investigation Press Conference* (Washington, DC: DOJ, August 6, 2008), http://www.usdoj.gov/opa/pr/2008/August/08-opa-697.html.

investigation for over a year and knew he was about to be indicted for the anthrax letter attacks, died on July 29 from an intentional drug overdose. From the publicly available evidence, the FBI's case against Ivins appears to be based on circumstantial evidence, since the bureau does not have eyewitnesses, surveillance camera footage, handwriting analysis, or analysis of trace evidence that directly link Ivins to the production and mailing of the anthrax letters. In addition, the FBI investigated former USAMRIID researcher Steven J. Hatfill as a "person of interest" for six years before settling a multimillion-dollar lawsuit with him and clearing his name.[31] Nonetheless, the Department of Justice has expressed confidence that if the Amerithrax case had gone to trial it would have been able to prove beyond a reasonable doubt that Ivins was the anthrax letter mailer. Since the suicide of Ivins precludes the case against him from going to trial, the FBI has taken the unusual step of releasing some, but not all, of the evidence collected by investigators regarding his responsibility for committing the anthrax letter attacks. The strongest evidence presented by the FBI links the *B. anthracis* used in the attacks to a flask of *B. anthracis* in Ivins's lab at USAMRIID. The FBI has presented little information about how it eliminated other suspects who also had access to this flask and determined that Ivins was the sole perpetrator of the attacks.

The FBI's investigation of the anthrax letter attacks was the most scientifically complex case the agency has ever undertaken.[32] It contracted with nineteen outside laboratories to conduct microbiological, genomic, chemical, isotopic, and other analyses of the *B. anthracis* spores used in the attacks.[33] Based on these analyses, the FBI concluded that the source of the *B. anthracis* spores used in the anthrax letter attacks was a laboratory at USAMRIID at Fort Detrick. Although *B. anthracis* is one of the most genetically uniform bacterial species known, the FBI and its scientific partners found that the *B. anthracis* in the letters possessed a number of genetic mutations that provided a distinctive signature. Scientists developed assays to detect four of these mutations and used them to screen 1,070 samples of the Ames strain of *B. anthracis* collected by the FBI from nineteen domestic and foreign laboratories. Screening of this collection revealed that only eight samples, from USAMRIID and one other facility, had all four genetic markers. All of these samples could be traced back to a flask of Ames strain *B. anthracis* spores, known as RMR-1029, stored at USAMRIID. The flask did not contain a single

---

31. Carrie Johnson, "U.S. Settles with Scientist Named in Anthrax Cases," *Washington Post,* June 28, 2008, A1; and Carrie Johnson and Joby Warrick, "Prosecutors Clear Hatfill in Anthrax Case," *Washington Post,* August 9, 2008, A3.

32. In August 2008, the FBI requested that the National Academy of Sciences conduct an independent review of the scientific aspects of the FBI's Amerithrax investigation.

33. Marilyn W. Thompson, Carrie Johnson, and Rob Stein, "FBI to Show How Genetics Led to Anthrax Researcher," *Washington Post,* August 6, 2008, A3.

culture of *B. anthracis* but instead an unusual combination of spores produced at USAMRIID and the Army's Dugway Proving Ground in thirty-five separate production runs. Each production run created the opportunity for genetic mutations to arise in the bacteria, and the pooling of spores from multiple production runs gave the RMR-1029 flask the "genetic fingerprint" that investigators were able to match to the material in the anthrax letters.[34] In addition, isotopic analyses enabled the FBI to determine that the *B. anthracis* spores used in the letters were grown no more than two years before they were mailed and that they were produced using water from the northeastern region of the United States.[35]

The RMR-1029 flask was created by Ivins in 1997 and used for aerosol challenge experiments to test the efficacy of anthrax vaccines and therapeutics. Although the FBI described Ivins as being the sole custodian of the flask in 2001, as many as one hundred or more other individuals also had access to the flask or this particular version of the Ames strain. By 2007 the FBI had excluded these other individuals as suspects and concluded that Ivins was the sole perpetrator of the anthrax letter attacks.[36] Contributing to this conclusion was a number of Ivins's activities at USAMRIID in 2001 and 2002 that were viewed with suspicion by the FBI. For example, before both waves of anthrax letter mailings, Ivins spent several evenings working alone in his laboratory where the RMR-1029 flask was stored and where he had access to equipment necessary to produce and dry the spores. Ivins acknowledged that his research at the time could not justify these unusual work hours, and he claimed that he went to the lab after hours to escape from stress at home.[37] In addition, Ivins engaged in unauthorized sampling of his office area on two occasions, which revealed contamination with *B. anthracis.* In December 2001 Ivins decontaminated the affected areas without informing his superiors that there had been a biocontainment breach. In April 2002, after discovering further contamination in his office and other nonlaboratory areas, Ivins reported this finding to his superiors, which triggered a broader investigation into biosafety practices at USAMRIID.[38]

According to the FBI, Ivins's possible motive for sending the anthrax letters was his frustration with the slow pace of anthrax vaccine development and

34. Dellafera, "Affidavit in Support of Search Warrant," 4–5; and FBI, *FBI Roundtable Discussion Regarding the Anthrax Investigation,* August 18, 2008, http://www.fredericknewspost.com/media/pdfs/FBI_0818_morning_bfg.pdfl.

35. Scott Shane and Nicholas Wade, "Pressure Grows for FBI's Anthrax Evidence," *New York Times,* August 5, 2008; and Brian Williams, "Five Year Anniversary of First US Anthrax Terrorist Death," *NBC Nightly News,* October 5, 2006.

36. DOJ, *Transcript of Amerithrax Investigation Press Conference.*

37. Dellafera, "Affidavit in Support of Search Warrant," 8–9.

38. United States Army Medical Research Command, *AR 15–6 Investigation into Anthrax Contamination at USAMRIID,* May 16, 2002.

criticisms of the anthrax vaccine.[39] Since beginning his career at USAMRIID in 1980, Ivins's research had focused on studying the efficacy of the licensed human anthrax vaccine and developing an improved vaccine based on recombinant protective antigen. By the fall of 2001, both of these efforts had virtually ground to a halt due to technical, bureaucratic, political, and financial problems. According to the FBI, Ivins was also suffering at this time from serious mental health problems requiring the prescription of psychotropic medications.[40]

In April 2000 Ivins was assigned to the Anthrax Potency Integrated Product Team, which was charged with assisting the private firm BioPort to gain Food and Drug Administration approval to resume shipments of anthrax vaccine to the Department of Defense.[41] By fall 2001, BioPort's continued inability to gain FDA approval left the military with only ten thousand doses of anthrax vaccine and forced the Pentagon to drastically limit the anthrax vaccine immunization program.[42] Based on e-mail letters released by the FBI, Ivins felt under tremendous pressure during 2000 and 2001 to help BioPort gain FDA licensure and allow DOD to resume its troubled anthrax immunization program. Ivins's other major research interest, a second-generation anthrax vaccine based on recombinant protective antigen, was also suffering problems during fall 2001. According to an e-mail letter sent by Ivins on September 7, 2001, the program was "in limbo" due to the army's refusal to accede to a subcontractor's demand that it be paid $200,000 a year for lawsuit indemnification before turning over a batch of the new vaccine to army researchers.[43]

If Ivins did mail the anthrax letters, his suicide precludes a definitive understanding of his motivation and objective. Nonetheless, it is possible to make some inferences based on the timing, content, and targets of the anthrax letters. In the aftermath of the terrorist attacks on September 11, 2001, Ivins may have feared that the next terrorist attack could involve biological weapons that could cause even more harm than 9/11 had. Ivins may have intended the anthrax letters as a warning to the nation about the dangers posed by biological weapons and the need for stronger defenses against these weapons. The number of deaths caused by the anthrax letters was most likely not an intended result. All of the envelopes were sealed shut with tape, ostensibly to prevent the leakage of

---

39. Dellafera, "Affidavit in Support of Search Warrant," 2, 12–14.

40. Dellafera, "Affidavit in Support of Search Warrant," 11–14.

41. Caree Vander Linden, "USAMRIID Employees Earn Top Civilian Award," *Fort Detrick (MD) Standard,* March 19, 2003.

42. Jim Garamore, "DOD Slows Anthrax Vaccination Program Again," American Forces Press Service, June 11, 2001; and Nicholas Wade, "U.S. Moves toward Making Anthrax Vaccine Available," *New York Times,* October 27, 2001, B7.

43. Dellafera, "Affidavit in Support of Search Warrant," 12.

spores.[44] All of the recovered letters included notes warning the recipient that they had just been exposed to *B. anthracis* or advising them to take penicillin, an FDA-approved antibiotic for treating inhalation anthrax. As noted in chapter 1, surprise is crucial to the success of a BW attack, and the anthrax letter mailer purposefully sacrificed this advantage. All of the victims of inhalation anthrax were infected unknowingly, either at postal processing centers or through cross-contaminated mail. If the anthrax letter mailer intended to cause mass casualties, he could have conducted a single covert attack in a crowded building or subway. An attack of this type could have exposed hundreds or thousands of people to lethal doses of *B. anthracis*.[45]

The first wave of letters, sent to five prominent TV and print media outlets one week after September 11, may have been intended to generate intense media coverage of, and public anxiety about, the threat posed by biological terrorism. The choice of targets and the language used in the notes inside the letters indicate that the mailer sought to capitalize on the nation's sense of vulnerability following the September 11 attacks by al Qaeda. Four of the five targets in the first wave of letters were located in New York City, the recent target of the worst terrorist attack in history. In addition, the notes were all dated 9-11-01, warned *"This is next,"* and used language associated with radical Islamist movements.[46]

The second wave of letters was sent three weeks later to Senator Daschle, the Senate Majority leader, and Senator Leahy, chairman of the Senate Judiciary Committee. The purpose of these letters may have been to galvanize a political response to the threat of bioterrorism by capitalizing on the nationwide anxiety generated by the first wave of letters. According to the FBI, Daschle and Leahy may also have been targeted due to their status as pro-life Catholic politicians and their perceived opposition to the USA PATRIOT Act passed in late October 2001.[47] In addition, Daschle had cosigned a letter to Secretary of Defense Donald Rumsfeld in June 2001 questioning the safety and efficacy of the anthrax vaccine and calling on the Pentagon to suspend its anthrax vaccine immunization program.[48] By targeting Congress, the anthrax letter mailer may have hoped to make biodefense a top national priority, which would increase funding

---

44. Prior to the anthrax letter attacks, it was not well appreciated that spores of *B. anthracis* could escape from a sealed envelope. An exception is B. Kournikakis, et al., *Risk Assessment of Anthrax Threat Letters,* DRES TR-2001-048 (Suffield, Canada: Defense Research Establishment Suffield, September 2001).

45. William C. Patrick III "Potential Incident Scenarios," in U.S. Public Health Service, *Proceedings of the Seminar on Responding to the Consequences of Chemical and Biological Terrorism, July 11–14, 1995* (Washington, DC: GPO, 1996), chapter 1.

46. All of the recovered notes ended with the lines *"Death to Israel/Death to America/Allah is great."*

47. Dellafera, "Affidavit in Support of Search Warrant," 18–19.

48. David Altimari, "Anthrax Vaccine Safety Complaints Part of Ivins Case," *Hartford Courant,* August 6, 2008.

to biodefense programs and overcome political and bureaucratic obstacles to developing new medical countermeasures.

Notwithstanding the important unanswered questions regarding whether, how, and why Bruce Ivins conducted the anthrax letter attacks, it is possible to make several observations about the implications of this case for assessing the threat posed by bioterrorism. In terms of the threat posed by terrorist groups, the Amerithrax case indicates that the current level of concern about the capabilities of nonstate actors to develop sophisticated biological weapons on their own is overstated. In contrast, the recent biodefense research boom might be increasing the risk of biological terrorism by increasing the accessibility of dangerous pathogens and providing training to a new generation of scientists on the safe handling, production, and aerosolization of such pathogens.[49]

If Ivins was in fact the perpetrator of the anthrax letter attacks, he possessed a level of experience, set of skills, and extensive tacit knowledge that could only be found in an individual affiliated with a state-run biodefense program. Ivins was a PhD microbiologist with over twenty years of experience working with *B. anthracis* and was considered an expert in the growth, sporulation, and purification of the bacteria. According to the FBI, "at the time of the anthrax mailings, Dr. Ivins possessed extensive knowledge of various anthrax production protocols. Dr. Ivins was adept at manipulating anthrax production and purification variables to maximize sporulation and improve the quality of anthrax spore preparations. He also understood anthrax aerosolization dosage rates and the importance of purity, consistency, and spore particle size due to his responsibility for providing liquid anthrax spore preparations for animal aerosol challenges."[50] Ivins's employment at USAMRIID also afforded him advantages such as access to a highly virulent strain of *B. anthracis,* access to a well-equipped biocontainment laboratory, experience working in such a lab, immunization against anthrax, and knowledge of decontamination procedures.[51] These are resources that a terrorist group would find difficult to acquire on its own.

The high concentration and very good aerosolization properties of the *B. anthracis* spores sent to Senators Daschle and Leahy led many to assume that the powder was produced using sophisticated equipment and/or the use of special additives or coatings. Initial reports of high levels of silicon in the spores led to speculation that silica had been added to the spores to improve their

49. Eileen Choffnes, "Bioweapons: New Labs, More Terror?" *Bulletin of the Atomic Scientists* 58, no. 5 (2002): 28–32; and Nick Shwellenbach, "Biodefense: A Plague of Researchers," *Bulletin of the Atomic Scientists* 61, no. 3 (2005): 14–16.

50. Dellafera, "Affidavit in Support of Search Warrant," 7.

51. Dellafera, "Affidavit in Support of Search Warrant," 3, 7, 9.

aerosolizability.[52] Subsequent tests commissioned by the FBI found that there was no sign of any additives or coatings on the spores that would make them more dispersible.[53] Although the FBI does not know how the powder of *B. anthracis* spores was produced, it believes that Ivins used a lyophilizer, a standard piece of laboratory equipment used to dry small amounts of biological material.[54] According to the FBI, scientific literature from the 1950s illustrates the dangers posed by the aerosolization of lyophilized cultures of infectious diseases.[55] The FBI's contention that Ivins was able to produce such high-quality powder of *B. anthracis* spores as seen in the letters to the senators with standard laboratory equipment and without the use of any special additives has raised concern that the technical threshold for sophisticated biological weapons is lower than commonly assumed. This inference, however, ignores the high level of tacit knowledge that Ivins possessed about *B. anthracis* and the difficulty he nonetheless faced in producing the high-quality powder found in the letters to the senators.[56] According to the FBI, Ivins spent 6 hours and 45 minutes over the course of three evenings preparing the approximately ten grams of cruder *B. anthracis* powder sent to the five media outlets in mid-September 2001. In contrast, he logged over 15 hours in his lab for eight consecutive nights to prepare approximately four grams of the more refined powder enclosed in the two letters sent to the senators.[57] Thus, even if Ivins employed a low-tech method to produce the powder in the anthrax letters, it does not mean that this method did not require a high level of skill to apply successfully.

Aum Shinrikyo   The Japanese cult Aum Shinrikyo is the only group that has tried to create an aerosolized biological weapon to cause mass casualties. Aum's efforts, however, were unsuccessful due to scientific, technical, operational, and organizational deficiencies. Aum, led by its guru Shoko Asahara, was characterized by an apocalyptic ideology that justified the murder of nonbelievers. Although Aum was motivated by a mix of religious beliefs, it also had an extremely ambitious political objective: the overthrow of the Japanese government. Aum began developing biological weapons in 1990 after it failed to get any

52. Gary Matsumoto, "Anthrax Powder: State of the Art?" *Science* 302 (November 28, 2003): 1492–96.
53. FBI, *FBI Roundtable Discussion Regarding the Anthrax Investigation.*
54. Carrie Johnson, Joby Warrick, and Marilyn W. Thompson, "Anthrax Dryer a Key to Probe," *Washington Post,* August 5, 2008, A1.
55. Beecher, "Forensic Application of Microbiological Culture Analysis to Identify Mail Intentionally Contaminated with *Bacillus anthracis* Spores," 5309.
56. On the role of tacit knowledge in the development of biological weapons, see Kathleen Vogel, "Bioweapons Proliferation: Where Science Studies and Public Policy Collide," *Social Studies of Science* 36, no. 5 (2006): 659–90.
57. Dellafera, "Affidavit in Support of Search Warrant," 8–9.

of its candidates elected to parliament. Despite its significant financial resources, the scientific backgrounds of many of its members, and its ability to operate un-molested by Japanese authorities, none of Aum's ten attempted BW attacks con-ducted between 1990 and 1995 resulted in any casualties.[58] Aum's inability to develop an effective aerosolized biological weapon led the cult to turn to chemi-cal weapons. The group released the nerve gas sarin in Matsumoto in June 1994 and on the Tokyo subway system in March 1995 killing a total of nineteen and injuring over one thousand.

Aum's experience sheds some light on the difficulties that terrorists face in developing biological weapons, especially third-generation weapons based on aerosol dissemination. Although Aum was well funded and well equipped, their BW effort suffered several handicaps.[59] At the scientific level, Aum did not have the appropriate expertise. The head of the BW program, Seiicho Endo, had lim-ited training in virology and veterinary medicine, but he was not a microbiol-ogist who knew how to work with bacteria. As a result, Endo was unable to cultivate a lethal strain of botulinum toxin from the wild, and the only strain of *B. anthracis* he could acquire was a vaccine strain used for animals.[60] At the tech-nical level, the slurry of *B. anthracis* that was produced was very low quality. A sample obtained from Aum's 1993 attempt to disseminate aerosolized *B. anthra-cis* from a rooftop sprayer had a large amount of debris and vegetative cells, a low concentration of spores, and was too viscous to be easily aerosolized. Aum also lacked the technical engineering capability to disseminate a liquid slurry of *B. anthracis.* Their rooftop sprayer was prone to breaking down, leaking, getting clogged, and apparently was either incapable or highly inefficient at producing particles in the 1–5 micron size. At the operational level, Aum did not demon-strate an understanding of the proper environmental conditions conducive to a BW attack. Aum attempted to disseminate its biological agents during the day, which exposed the agents to UV radiation and thermal updrafts, reducing the viability of the agents and the area covered by the aerosol.

---

58. Masaki Sugishima, "Biocrimes in Japan," in *A Comprehensive Study on Bioterrorism,* ed. Masaki Sugishima (Gifu, Japan: Asahi University, 2003), 98–101; and David E. Kaplan, "Aum Shinrikyo (1995)," in *Toxic Terror,* ed. Tucker, 220.

59. This section is based on William Rosenau, "Aum Shinrikyo's Biological Weapons Program: Why Did it Fail?" *Studies in Conflict and Terrorism* 24 (2001): 289–301; Hiroshi Takahashi, et al., *"Bacillus an-thracis* Incident, Kameido, Tokyo, 1993," *Emerging Infectious Diseases* 10, no. 1 (2004): 117–20; Amy E. Smithson and Leslie-Anne Levy, *Ataxia: The Chemical and Biological Terrorism Threat and the U.S. Re-sponse* (Washington, DC: Henry L. Stimson Center, 2000), 71–111; and Milton Leitenberg, "Aum Shin-rikyo's Effort to Produce Biological Weapons: A Case Study of the Serial Propagation of Misinformation," *Terrorism and Political Violence* 11, no. 4 (1999): 149–58.

60. Of the seven types of botulinum neurotoxins produced by *C. botulinum* (types A–G), only A, B, and E are lethal for humans.

Many of these problems can be attributed to the nature of Aum's organization. Aum was a fanatical religious cult that viewed Shoko Asahara as a god. As a result of the harsh regimen expected of the cult's members, Asahara's inconsistent and unrealistic demands, and the desire of cult members to curry favor with him, Aum's weapons programs were erratic. Asahara and his underlings were fascinated with acquiring high-tech weapons such as lasers and nuclear weapons, but they were unable to solve the technical problems required to make even simpler weapon technologies work. For example, Aum imported a factory to mass-produce assault rifles, a helicopter from Russia, and drone aircraft, but they were unable to make any of these things operational.[61] Aum's unconventional weapons programs were also hampered by personal rivalries between key members responsible for developing chemical and biological weapons.[62]

Aum's failure indicates that biological terrorism capable of causing mass casualties through an aerosolized agent is not as easy as commonly portrayed. Developing biological weapons requires the right strain of a pathogen, the ability to produce the organism in a form suitable for dissemination, and a means of effectively disseminating the agent at the desired location. Aum failed on all of these levels. Aum's experience demonstrates that money, equipment, and educated personnel alone are not sufficient to produce BW; skill and organization are needed as well.

Fourth-Generation Biological Terrorism

Advances in the life sciences have raised concerns that a terrorist group might be able to genetically modify a pathogen for use as a weapon.[63] There is no known case of a terrorist group developing such a capability. Assessments of the threat posed by genetically engineered weapons in the hands of terrorists frequently make two mistakes that serve to exaggerate the severity of this threat. First, they conflate the ability of states to conduct such research with those of terrorist groups that have much more limited scientific, technical, and financial resources. Given the difficulty that terrorists have faced in successfully carrying out even crude biological attacks with toxins, let alone developing a sophisticated capability based on an aerosolized weapon, it is unlikely that they would

61. Kaplan, "Aum Shinrikyo (1995)," 212, 216.

62. Robert Jay Lifton, *Destroying the World to Save It: Aum Shinrikyo, Apocalyptic Violence and the New Global Terrorism* (New York: Metropolitan Books, 1999), 157–59; and Anthony T. Tu, *Chemical Terrorism: Horrors in Tokyo Subway and Matsumoto City* (Fort Collins, CO: Alaken, 2002), 190.

63. Raymond Zilinskas, "Possible Terrorist Use of Modern Biotechnology Techniques" (paper presented at Conference on Biosecurity, Istituto Diplomatico, Rome, Italy, September 18–19, 2000); and Christopher F. Chyba and Alexander L. Greninger, "Biotechnology and Bioterrorism: An Unprecedented World," *Survival* 46, no. 2 (2004): 143–62.

be able or willing to devote the additional resources to develop a genetically engineered pathogen. Second, assessments that focus on the scientific and technical aspects of biological terrorism typically ignore the issue of motivation. Terrorists have little incentive to develop this type of capability since natural pathogens are lethal and terrifying enough for their purposes. As the anthrax letter attacks showed, even small-scale attacks can have dramatic effects. According to Charles Allen, head of intelligence for the Department of Homeland Security, "in general, we see terrorists in the early stages of biological capabilities, and we do not anticipate a rapid evolution to include sophisticated methods that will enable the creation of new organisms or genetic modification to enhance virulence."[64]

State-Sponsored Biological Terrorism

One potential avenue for a terrorist group to overcome the obstacles to developing a biological weapon capable of causing mass casualties would be to obtain these weapons from a state with a BW program. Concern over this type of proliferation has been fueled by the emergence of so-called rogue states that sponsor terrorism and pursue WMD programs. In December 2001, President George W. Bush warned, "Rogue states are clearly the most likely sources of chemical and biological and nuclear weapons for terrorists."[65] The transfer of a nuclear, biological, or chemical weapon to a terrorist group would allow a state to remain anonymous and avoid retaliation.[66] The prospect that Iraq would transfer such weapons to al Qaeda was one of the primary reasons put forward by the Bush administration to justify the use of force to disarm Iraq.

State-sponsored biological terrorism, however, is unlikely. Although there is a long history of states supporting terrorist groups, there is no evidence that any state has provided a terrorist group with nuclear, biological, or chemical weapons. There are two major restraints on states that discourage them from engaging in such behavior. First, transferring biological weapons to a terrorist group would mean ceding control over a powerful weapon to a potentially unreliable proxy. Authoritarian states, a category that includes "rogue" states, typically place a premium on maintaining tight control over their military and security

---

64. House Homeland Security Committee, *Bioscience and the Intelligence Community,* 109th Cong., 1st and 2nd sess., November 3, 2005, and May 4, 2006, 47.

65. President George W. Bush, "President Speaks on War Effort to Citadel Cadets," December 11, 2001, http://www.whitehouse.gov/news/releases/2001/12/20011211-6.html.

66. Steven Simon and Daniel Benjamin, "America and the New Terrorism," *Survival* 42, no. 1 (2000): 59–75.

forces for fear of a coup. One of the main mechanisms for achieving rigid control is by appointing loyal military and internal security leaders based on family, ethnic, or religious ties. This desire for coup-proofing is so strong that state leaders will maintain these strategies even at the expense of military effectiveness on the battlefield against foreign enemies.[67]

The widespread adoption of these coup-proofing strategies among authoritarian states suggests that leaders of such states will not entrust a weapon of mass destruction to a terrorist group. Doing so would expose the state sponsor to several dangers. The sponsor would have to worry that the terrorist group might botch an attack or that its operatives might be arrested before or after an attack and reveal the source of the weapon. The government would also have to worry about the principal-agent problem: the group might use its new capability to promote its own political interests and not those of its sponsor. Finally, the government would also have to consider the potential for blackmail, or even a boomerang effect, if the terrorists decided to turn against their erstwhile sponsor.

The second restraint is the fear of retaliation. Although terrorist groups may not care if they are targeted for retaliation (they may even welcome it) or they may feel immune from attack, states have capitals that are vulnerable to attack and leaders that care predominantly about their own survival. States that sponsor terrorism typically do so from a position of military weakness that also limits their willingness to risk direct confrontation with their opponents. As a result, states calibrate their use of terrorism to achieve specific policy objectives when the benefits are clear and the costs appear manageable, and they rein in such activities when the costs outweigh the potential gains and the risk of retaliation is high.[68] Although it may be difficult for a state to assess the benefits of sponsoring a biological terrorist attack, the potential costs would be more tangible. The severity of retaliation for an act of state-sponsored biological terrorism depends on several factors such as the number of casualties caused by the attack, the victim's perceived vulnerability to future attacks, the importance of national interests threatened by the attack, and the domestic and international political environments.[69] Since the mid-1990s, the United States has threatened to retaliate with overwhelming force, including nuclear weapons, against a nuclear, biological,

---

67. James T. Quinlivan, "Coup Proofing: Its Practice and Consequences in the Middle East," *International Security* 24, no. 2 (1999): 131–65.

68. Daniel Byman, *Deadly Connections: States That Sponsor Terrorism* (New York: Cambridge University Press, 2005), 1–78; and Bruce Hoffman, *Inside Terrorism* (New York: Columbia University Press, 2006), 258–67.

69. Brad Roberts, "Rethinking How Wars Must End: NBC War Termination Issues in the Post-Cold War Era," in *The Coming Crisis: Nuclear Proliferation, U.S. Interests, and World Order,* ed. Victor A. Utgoff (Cambridge: MIT Press, 2000), 245–77.

or chemical attack.[70] The United States invasion of Afghanistan to overthrow the Taliban regime in response to the September 11 attacks, which claimed three thousand lives, and the 2003 invasion of Iraq due to the perceived threat posed by its WMD programs demonstrated to the world that the United States would retaliate severely against any state that supported, or appeared to support, mass-casualty terrorism against the United States.

There are three counterarguments for why these restraints on state-sponsored biological terrorism are not sufficiently strong to completely preclude such behavior. The first counterargument is that a state could minimize the principal-agent problem and other dangers of working with a proxy group by entrusting weapons only to a terrorist group that has strong ties to the state.[71] While this tactic might increase the state's confidence that the group will carry out its mission faithfully and successfully, it also raises the risk that the state sponsor will be identified as the source of the weapon and suffer retaliation. A state's confidence in a terrorist group's loyalty is probably correlated to the duration of their relationship, the level of overall support provided by the state to the group, and the degree of dependency of the group on the state. The stronger the ties between the state and terrorist group, the more likely that this relationship will be known to foreign intelligence agencies and place the state sponsor at the top of the list of potential suppliers of biological weapons after a BW attack by that group.

The second counterargument is that a state may be emboldened to provide biological weapons to terrorists if it believes that the victim will be unable to trace the weapons back to the source. If the state can remain anonymous it can avoid retaliation. The ability to deliver biological weapons covertly, the delayed effects of these weapons, and the difficulty of differentiating between natural and man-made disease outbreaks could provide terrorists with enough time to cover their tracks before the victim even realizes that there has been an attack.

Compared to the ability of the United States to determine the source of a nuclear or missile attack, its ability to identify the perpetrator of a biological attack is much more limited. Nuclear forensics can derive a large amount of information about the history and composition of the fissile material used in a nuclear weapon.[72] Likewise, the United States can determine the launch point of a ballistic missile fired from anywhere in the world using space-based sensors.[73]

---

70. Scott Sagan, "The Commitment Trap: Why the United States Should Not Use Nuclear Threats to Deter Biological and Chemical Weapon Attacks," *International Security* 24, no. 4 (2000): 85–115.

71. Jasen J. Castillo, "Nuclear Terrorism: Why Deterrence Still Matters," *Current History* 102, no. 668 (2003): 426–31.

72. *Nuclear Forensics: Role, State of the Art, Program Needs* (Washington, DC: American Physical Society and American Association for the Advancement of Science, 2008).

73. Jeffrey Richelson, *America's Space Sentinels: DSP Satellites and National Security* (Lawrence: University of Kansas Press, 1999).

Determining the origins of a BW agent used in an attack is complicated by the availability of most pathogens from multiple sources, including laboratories, culture collections, and nature, and the inability to fully characterize this availability. Determining the source of an attack is also complicated by the lack of unique genetic "fingerprints" for many pathogens and toxins.[74] The goal of the emerging discipline of microbial forensics is to pinpoint the source of a pathogen used as a weapon and assist in the identification of the perpetrator of a biological attack.[75] Although microbial forensics still faces important limitations, it has made impressive gains in just a few years.[76] To compensate for the limitations of genetic analysis, investigators have also developed a growing array of increasingly sophisticated non-DNA techniques to characterize biological agents.[77]

The progress in understanding the genomics of *B. anthracis* and its impact on the investigation of the 2001 anthrax letter attacks provides a case in point. *B. anthracis* has been described as the "most genetically uniform bacterial species known."[78] Nonetheless, between 1997 and 2002, scientists perfected techniques that allowed them to reliably identify isolates of *B. anthracis* at the strain level. These techniques allowed investigators to determine that the strain of *B. anthracis* used in the anthrax letter attacks was the Ames strain and that it most likely originated from a laboratory, but they could not pinpoint which lab was the source of the material used in the letters.[79] Beginning in 2002, scientists used whole-genome sequencing and comparative genomic tools to identify four genetic mutations in the *B. anthracis* from the anthrax letters and develop assays that could be used to test samples of *B. anthracis* for the presence of these mutations. By 2005 scientists were able to match this distinctive signature to a specific flask of *B. anthracis* stored at USAMRIID.[80] This breakthrough enabled the FBI to focus its investigation on those individuals who had access to this flask or particular strain of *B. anthracis* and exclude suspects who did not have access to this material.

---

74. Bruce Budowle, et al., "Microbial Forensics," in *Microbial Forensics,* ed. Roger G. Breeze, Bruce Budowle, and Steven E. Schutzer (Boston: Elsevier Press, 2005), 9.

75. Bruce Budowle, et al., "Building Microbial Forensics as a Response to Bioterrorism," *Science* 301 (September 26, 2003): 1852.

76. American Academy of Microbiology, *Microbial Forensics: A Scientific Assessment* (Washington, DC: American Academy of Microbiology, 2003); and Breeze, Budowle, and Schutzer, *Microbial Forensics.*

77. Charlene M. Schaldach, "Non-DNA Methods for Biological Signatures," in *Microbial Forensics,* ed. Breeze, Budowle, and Schutzer, 251–94.

78. Paul Keim, et al., "Molecular Evolution and Diversity in *Bacillus anthracis* as Detected by Amplified Fragment Length Polymorphism Markers," *Journal of Bacteriology* 179, no. 3 (1997): 818–24.

79. Lindler, et al., "Genetic Fingerprinting of Biodefense Pathogens for Epidemiology and Forensic Investigation," in *Biological Weapons Defense: Infectious Diseases and Counterbioterrorism,* ed. Luther E. Lindler, Frank J. Lebeda, and George W. Korch (Totowa, NJ: Humana Press, 2005), 457–59.

80. Martin Enserink, "Full-Genome Sequencing Paved the Way from Spores to a Suspect," *Science* 321 (August 15, 2008): 898–99; and FBI, *FBI Roundtable Discussion Regarding the Anthrax Investigation.*

It is important to keep in mind that the discipline of microbial forensics is just one source of information that would be used by law enforcement and intelligence agencies to determine the source of an attack. As advances in microbial forensics provide intelligence and law enforcement agencies with increasingly powerful tools to complement their traditional sources and methods for investigation and attribution, the confidence of states that they will be able to hide their role in providing BW capabilities to a terrorist group should decline significantly.

The third counterargument is that if a regime with biological weapons believes that its existence is threatened, then its fear of retaliation and its reluctance to rely on a proxy might be greatly diminished. If a state feared that a decapitating strike was imminent or that it was about to be overthrown, it might have few disincentives to transfer these weapons to a terrorist group in the hopes of gaining a last-minute reprieve or to exact revenge. This is the most likely condition under which deterrence of state-sponsored biological terrorism would fail.

Indirect state support of bioterrorism is a greater worry than direct support. As discussed in chapter 3, organizations that develop biological weapons tend to be endowed with a high level of autonomy that complicates civilian efforts to exercise effective oversight. This autonomy can lead to corruption and heightens the risk of proliferation of BW-related materials and expertise. Two scenarios are particularly worrisome. The potential for unauthorized transfer of biological weapons to terrorists is heightened if a government agency is responsible for both developing biological weapons and providing assistance to terrorist groups. For example, in Iran the Islamic Revolutionary Guard Corps is in charge of Iran's WMD programs and also provides support to Hezbollah in Lebanon, Palestinian terrorist groups, insurgents in Iraq, and the Taliban in Afghanistan.[81] Another worrisome possibility is that an individual scientist working within a BW program might provide materials or expertise to a terrorist group for ideological or financial reasons. In both Russia and South Africa, former BW scientists have offered such resources on the international market or to states known to be pursuing biological weapons. So far there is no indication that al Qaeda has succeeded in recruiting any scientists affiliated with Pakistan's CBW programs.[82]

---

81. Gregory F. Giles, "The Islamic Republic of Iran and Nuclear, Biological, and Chemical Weapons," in *Planning the Unthinkable: How New Powers Will Use Nuclear, Biological and Chemical Weapons,* ed. Peter Lavoy, Scott Sagan, and James Wirtz (Ithaca: Cornell University Press, 2000), 79–80; and Department of State, *Designation of Iranian Entities and Individuals for Proliferation Activities and Support for Terrorism,* October 27, 2007, http://www.state.gov/r/pa/prs/ps/2007/oct/94193.htm.

82. For reports of a Pakistani CBW program, see Defense Intelligence Agency, *A Primer on the Future Threat: The Decades Ahead, 1999–2020,* July 1999, 36, in Rowan Scarborough, *Rumsfeld's War: The Untold Story of America's Anti-Terrorist Commander* (Washington, DC: Regnery, 2004), 196; Douglas Jehl, "U.S. Intelligence Review Is Softening Some Judgments about Illicit Arms Abroad," *New York Times,*

Al Qaeda and Biological Terrorism

Al Qaeda is commonly viewed as the terrorist group most likely to develop both the motivation and the capability to cause mass casualties with biological weapons. Al Qaeda has amply demonstrated its desire to inflict as much death, destruction, and economic disruption as possible against its enemies. Al Qaeda has also made clear that it intends to acquire weapons of mass destruction. In December 1998 Osama bin Laden declared it a "religious duty" to acquire nuclear, biological, and chemical weapons.[83] In May 2003 a Saudi cleric issued a fatwa legitimating the use of nuclear, biological, and chemical weapons against infidels.[84] This section provides an overview of al Qaeda's efforts to develop biological weapons and assesses the bioterrorist threat posed by al Qaeda and its affiliates.

Al Qaeda began pursuing a BW capability in 1999. By 2001 the group had established two laboratories in Afghanistan, obtained scientific literature on several bacterial pathogens, procured dual-use production equipment, recruited microbiologists, and had a small cell dedicated to producing *B. anthracis*. Al Qaeda's effort has been stymied by its inability to obtain a virulent strain of *B. anthracis* or to master the techniques necessary to aerosolize a biological agent. According to captured al Qaeda operatives, the group's BW efforts were in the early "conceptual stage" when it was disrupted by the United States invasion of Afghanistan.[85] Al Qaeda's BW ambitions were set back further by the death or arrest of many of the key participants in the program. Although al Qaeda's aspirations in this area far outstrip its capabilities, the fact that this group has been as interested in these weapons for as long as it has sets them apart from other terrorist organizations.

Al Qaeda's CBW program, code-named Project al-Zabadi (Arabic for yogurt), was headed by Ayman al-Zawahiri, the second-ranking official in al Qaeda, and Mohammed Atef (Abu Hafs al-Masri), al Qaeda's military commander and Osama bin Laden's designated successor. Zawahiri was attracted to biological weapons because he believed that these weapons were as lethal as nuclear weapons, that they could be produced simply, that the delayed effects of a biological attack would increase the number of casualties, and that defending

---

November 18, 2003, A6; and Department of Commerce, "India and Pakistan Sanctions and Other Measures," *Federal Register* 63, no. 23 (1998): 64337–41.

83. "Conversation with Terror," *Time,* January 11, 1999.

84. Nasir Bin Hamd al-Fahl, *A Treatise on the Legal Status of Using Weapons of Mass Destruction against the Infidels,* May 2003, http://www.marisaurgo.com/msj/Ulema_files/Treatise.pdf.

85. "Al-Qaeda Program to Make WMD Halted by Afghan War," *USA Today,* January 26, 2004.

against these weapons was very difficult.[86] Mohammed Atef led a hard-line faction within al Qaeda's governing council that advocated the acquisition and use of weapons of mass destruction.[87]

From its inception, al Qaeda sought expert assistance as the "fastest, safest, and cheapest" means of developing these weapons.[88] In 1999 Zawahiri reportedly recruited a Pakistani microbiologist, Abdur Rauf, to set up a small lab in Kandahar to work on biological weapons.[89] Rauf worked at the Pakistan Council of Scientific and Industrial Research in Lahore, which houses a center for food microbiology and biotechnology that is equipped with laboratory equipment, fermenters, centrifuges, freeze-drying equipment, and a culture collection including a hundred strains of different bacteria.[90] Rauf traveled to Europe in an unsuccessful attempt to obtain a virulent strain of *B. anthracis*. He also helped al Qaeda procure equipment and plan BW research and production. He was detained by Pakistani authorities in 2001 but released in 2003.[91]

In 2000 Zawahiri started a parallel BW effort run by Yazid Sufaat, a former Malaysian army captain, U.S.-trained biochemist, and member of the al Qaeda–affiliated terrorist group Jemaah Islamiya. Sufaat ran a laboratory in Kandahar with two assistants.[92] Sufaat unsuccessfully sought to acquire a virulent strain of *B. anthracis* through his front company Green Laboratory Medicine Company.[93] During summer 2001 Sufaat "wrapped up" his research and briefed Zawahiri and Riduan Isamuddin (also known as Hambali), the leader of Jemaah Islamiya, on his progress in isolating *B. anthracis*.[94] Sufaat fled Afghanistan after the U.S. invasion, possibly with the objective of restarting his BW work in Indonesia, but he was arrested in Malaysia at the end of 2001.

---

86. Alan Cullison and Andrew Higgins, "Files Found: A Computer in Kabul Yields a Chilling Array of al Qaeda Memos," *Wall Street Journal,* December 31, 2001; and Alan Cullison, "Inside Al-Qaeda's Hard Drive," *Atlantic Monthly* 294, no. 4 (2004): 55–70.

87. Abu Walid al-Misri, *The History of the Arab Afghans from the Time of Their Arrival in Afghanistan until Their Departure with the Taliban,* serialized in *Asharq Al-Awsat,* December 8–14, 2004.

88. Cullison and Higgins, "Files Found."

89. George Tenet, *At the Center of the Storm: My Years at the CIA,* with Bill Harlow (New York: HarperCollins, 2007), 278.

90. *Pakistan Council of Scientific and Industrial Research,* http://www.brain.net.pk/~pcsir/lhr.htm; and *Pakistan Type Culture Collection, Biotechnology and Food Research Center,* Pakistan Council of Scientific and Industrial Research, http://wdcm.nig.ac.jp/CCINFO/CCINFO.xml?753#ch3.

91. Eric Lipton, "Qaeda Letters Are Said to Show Pre-9/11 Anthrax Plans," *New York Times,* May 21, 2005, A9; and Joby Warrick, "Suspect and A Setback in Al-Qaeda Anthrax Case," *Washington Post,* October 31, 2006, A1.

92. White House, "President Discusses Creation of Military Commissions to Try Suspected Terrorists," September 6, 2006, http://www.whitehouse.gov/news/releases/2006/09/print/20060906-3.html.

93. Maria Ressa, "Al Qaeda Operative Sought Anthrax," *CNN.com,* October 10, 2003.

94. Tenet, *Center of the Storm,* 278–79.

After invading Afghanistan, the United States discovered documents and equipment associated with al Qaeda's BW program. Al Qaeda's BW laboratory near Kandahar reportedly contained medical supplies and lab equipment, including a centrifuge and drying oven. At the time it was believed that the laboratory was still under construction, but information gathered later from captured al Qaeda operatives and documents led some analysts to believe that it had been completed before the invasion and was partially disassembled prior to its discovery. No evidence of BW production was found at this site.[95] U.S. forces also found scientific articles on the isolation, purification, and production of bacterial pathogens including *B. anthracis, C. botulinum,* and *Y. pestis* at an al Qaeda training camp near the laboratory.[96] Based on these discoveries, the intelligence community assessed that al Qaeda's BW effort was "extensive, [and] well-organized" and had made greater-than-expected progress on *B. anthracis.*[97]

The capture of Khalid Sheikh Mohammed in March 2003 shed new light on al Qaeda's BW activities and dealt another blow to these efforts. Mohammed, one of al Qaeda's principal operational planners, took charge of managing the BW program after Atef was killed in a U.S. airstrike in November 2001.[98] Information obtained from his interrogation and from his computer indicates that al Qaeda had completed plans and obtained the materials necessary to produce botulinum toxin and salmonella and were close to a feasible production plan for *B. anthracis.* Among the documents recovered from the computer were a directive to purchase *Bacillus anthracis* (albeit not one of the more virulent strains), timelines for producing chemical and biological agents, and inventories of equipment and indicators of readiness to produce and dry biological agents into a form suitable for aerosol dissemination. These documents, however, did not reflect an

95. Five samples taken from sites suspected of being linked to al Qaeda's WMD activities tested positive for the presence of *B. anthracis* or ricin, but the agents were present in such tiny quantities that they could have been naturally occurring. David Johnston and James Risen, "U.S. Concludes Al Qaeda Lacked a Chemical or Biological Stockpile," *New York Times,* March 20, 2002, A12; Michael R. Gordon, "U.S. Says It Found Qaeda Lab Being Built to Produce Anthrax," *New York Times,* March 23, 2002; Charles Aldinger, "Troops Find Suspected Biowarfar Lab in Afghanistan," Reuters, March 23, 2002; DOD News Briefing, March 25, 2002; Judith Miller, "Lab Suggests Qaeda Planned to Build Arms, Officials Say," *New York Times,* September 14, 2002, A7; and Barton Gellman, "Al Qaeda near Biological, Chemical Arms Production," *Washington Post,* March 23, 2003, A1.

96. James Petro and David A. Relman, "Understanding Threats to Scientific Openness," *Science* 302 (December 12, 2003): 1898.

97. Commission on the Intelligence Capabilities of the United States Regarding Weapons of Mass Destruction, *Report to the President* (Washington, DC: GPO, 2005), 260–70 [hereafter Silberman-Robb Report]. This report refers to *B. anthracis* as "Agent X."

98. "Verbatim Transcript of Combatant Status Review Tribunal Hearing for ISN 10024," March 10, 2007, U.S. Naval Base Guantanamo Bay, Cuba, Enclosure (3), 17, (revised March 15, 2007), http://www.defenselink.mil/news/transcript_ISN10024.pdf; and Gellman, "Al Qaeda near Biological, Chemical Arms Production."

understanding of techniques needed to produce high-quality dry powders that are easily aerosolized.[99] Although al Qaeda operatives have expressed an interest in crop dusters, which could potentially be used to disseminate chemical or biological agents over a large area, this new information indicates that it had not yet developed the capability to deploy an aerosol-based biological weapon.

The United States response to 9/11 has significantly impaired al Qaeda's ability to develop a BW capability. The invasion of Afghanistan robbed al Qaeda of a sanctuary where it was able to plan, recruit, establish laboratories, and conduct research without interference. The United States has also captured or killed most of the known participants in al Qaeda's BW program. Information from Mohammed and Sufaat led to the arrest of Sufaat's two principal assistants in his BW cell.[100] Without this expertise and, perhaps more important, senior operatives who are willing to invest the organization's limited resources in developing this type of weapon, al Qaeda's BW program may not be able to recover from this major setback. Although Zawahiri remains at large, the death of Atef and the capture of Mohammed and Hambali may have robbed al Qaeda of its strongest advocates for developing biological weapons. Indeed, the intelligence community has reported that it did not receive any reliable evidence of an active al Qaeda BW effort in 2004, 2005, and 2006.[101] Nonetheless, al Qaeda has demonstrated persistence and patience in planning terrorist operations, enjoys sanctuary in the tribal areas of Pakistan, and continues to recruit new members, including those with scientific training.[102]

In addition to the bioterrorist threat posed directly by al Qaeda, there is concern that al Qaeda–trained or inspired cells could also launch bioterrorist attacks. In 2002 and 2003, al Qaeda–affiliated cells were linked to plots to use ricin in attacks in the United Kingdom, France, and Spain. Subsequent analyses, however, demonstrated that none of these groups actually possessed the toxin.[103]

99. Gellman, "Al Qaeda near Biological, Chemical Arms Production."

100. White House, "President Discusses Creation of Military Commissions."

101. Director of National Intelligence (DNI), *Unclassified Report to Congress on the Acquisition of Technology Relating to Weapons of Mass Destruction and Advanced Conventional Munitions, 1 January–31 December 2004,* n.d., 5–7; DNI, *Unclassified Report to Congress on the Acquisition of Technology Relating to Weapons of Mass Destruction and Advanced Conventional Munitions, 1 January–31 December 2005,* n.d., 4–5; and DNI, *Unclassified Report to Congress on the Acquisition of Technology Relating to Weapons of Mass Destruction and Advanced Conventional Munitions, 1 January–31 December 2006,* n.d., 7.

102. Mohammed was arrested in March 2003 in a house owned by a Pakistani bacteriologist who has since disappeared. Gellman, "Al Qaeda near Biological, Chemical Arms Production."

103. Lundberg, et al., *Ricin,* 18; Senate Select Committee on Intelligence, *Report on the U.S. Intelligence Community's Prewar Intelligence Assessments on Iraq* (Washington, DC: GPO, 2004), 14, 93–94; and Andrew McGregor, "Ricin Fever: Abu Musab al-Zarqawi in the Pankisi Gorge," *Terrorism Monitor* 2, no. 24 (2004): 10–12.

In the London case, the authorities did discover castor beans and a recipe for producing ricin. Duncan Campbell, "The Ricin Ring That Never Was," *Guardian,* April 15, 2005; and George Smith, "UK

Two factors have contributed to an exaggerated perception of the threat posed by do-it-yourself jihadi bioterrorism. The first is the wide availability of recipes in al Qaeda training manuals and online jihadist chat rooms that purportedly describe how to produce biological weapons.[104] These recipes on how to produce *C. botulinum, Y. pestis,* and ricin are rudimentary, lack important details or include incorrect information, and are unsuited for producing pathogens or toxins of sufficient quantity or quality to cause mass casualties. At best, the recipes for botulinum toxin and ricin might be suitable for producing small, crude quantities of the agent. None of these recipes describes techniques for weaponizing these agents or disseminating them as an aerosol, thereby limiting their utility to assassinations or the contamination of food or beverages.[105] Based on these recipes, al Qaeda is still seeking second-generation bioterrorist capabilities.

The second factor is the emergence of a new generation of terrorists who are inspired by al Qaeda's narrative that the West is waging a war against Islam. These self-radicalized jihadists form small cells or loose networks that do not receive support from or commands from al Qaeda or its affiliates.[106] The phenomenon of "leaderless jihad," with its fluid networks and lack of connections to existing terrorist groups, increases the difficulty for intelligence and law enforcement agencies to prevent attacks. The al Qaeda veteran Mustafa Setmariam Nasar (also known as Abu Mus'ab al-Suri), who was one of the first jihadi strategists to advocate this type of decentralized global jihad movement, has also championed the use of weapons of mass destruction.[107] The small size and limited resources of most such cells, however, will limit their ability to engage in the long-term, expensive, technically demanding, and multidisciplinary work needed to develop a biological weapon capable of causing mass casualties. A key feature of "leaderless jihad" with important implications for the prospect of bioterrorism is the role of social networks based on friendship and kinship in the radicalization process.[108] Thus, the risk remains that scientifically trained

Terror Trial Finds No Terror," *National Security Notes,* April 11, 2005, http://www.globalsecurity.org/org/nsn/index.html.

104. Steve Coll and Susan B. Glasser, "Terrorists Turn to the Web as Base of Operations," *Washington Post,* August 7, 2005, A1.

105. Sammy Salama and Lydia Hansell, "Does Intent Equal Capability? Al-Qaeda and Weapons of Mass Destruction," *Nonproliferation Review* 12, no. 3 (2005): 615–53; Anne Stenersen, "Chem-Bio Cyber-Class," *Jane's Intelligence Review,* September 2007, 8–13; and Adam Dolnik and Rohan Gunaratna, "Jemaah Islamiyah and the Threat of Chemical and Biological Terrorism," in *Weapons of Mass Destruction and Terrorism,* ed. Russell D. Howard and James J. F. Forest (McGraw-Hill, 2008), 280–94.

106. Marc Sageman, *Leaderless Jihad: Terror Network in the Twenty-first Century* (Philadelphia: University of Pennsylvania Press, 2008).

107. Brynjar Lia, *Architect of Global Jihad: The Life of Al-Qaida Strategist Abu Mus'ab al-Suri* (New York: Columbia University Press, 2008), 1–28, 299–313.

108. Sageman, *Leaderless Jihad,* 66–69, 84–89.

individuals who work, play, or pray together, and have access to the necessary equipment and materials, could form the nucleus of a group attempting to develop biological weapons for use in a terrorist attack. While many of these jihadists tend to be young and poorly educated, the involvement of three medical doctors in the failed car bomb attacks in the United Kingdom in July 2007 indicates that highly educated individuals are also susceptible to jihadist ideology and self-radicalization.

Intelligence and Biological Terrorism

Detecting efforts by terrorists to develop biological weapons is even more challenging than collecting intelligence on state-based BW programs. Terrorist groups require smaller quantities of agent, less sophisticated dissemination devices, and much simpler delivery systems than military programs. As a result, the footprint of a bioterrorism program, in terms of the number of personnel, physical infrastructure, and the need for specialized materials and equipment, would be much smaller than a military program. Terrorist groups are also naturally highly secretive in order to ensure their survival against their much stronger adversaries. According to an exhaustive review of bioterrorism cases in the twentieth century, "the available evidence suggests that intelligence and law enforcement agencies are unlikely to learn that a particular terrorist group is interested in acquiring and using biological agents."[109] The Silberman-Robb Commission found that the intelligence community had "limited" knowledge of al Qaeda's BW effort before September 11, 2001.[110] According to a CIA analyst, "if it hadn't been for finding a couple key pieces of paper [in Afghanistan]... we still might not have an appreciation for it [al Qaeda's work on *B. anthracis*]. We just missed it because we did not have the data."[111] The difficulty of gathering accurate and useful information on bioterrorists is illustrated by the FBI's seven-year effort to identify the perpetrator of the 2001 anthrax letter attacks.

As with gathering intelligence on national BW programs, human intelligence has been crucial to detecting the efforts of terrorist groups to develop and use biological weapons. Most of the BW activities of terrorist groups that have been uncovered by law enforcement and intelligence agencies were only made possible by the assistance of insiders who provided evidence against other group

---

109. Carus, *Bioterrorism and Biocrimes,* 31–32.
110. Silberman-Robb Report, 270.
111. Ibid., 274.

members. Prior to Aum Shinrikyo's nerve gas attack in the Tokyo subway system, neither the CIA nor the FBI were aware of the cult, its preparations to use chemical and biological weapons, or its virulent anti-Americanism. The Japanese and U.S. governments did not learn of the cult's multiple attempts to disseminate *B. anthracis* and botulinum toxin against Japanese and U.S. Navy targets in Japan until captured cult members disclosed these activities to the police.[112] The use of *Salmonella* Typhimurium by members of the Rajneesh cult to contaminate salad bars in a small Oregon town in 1984 went undiscovered for over a year until investigators were tipped off by feuding cult members.[113] The BW aspirations of the ecoterrorist group R.I.S.E. and the right-wing antigovernment group Minnesota Patriots Council were also foiled by police who were alerted by informants.[114]

Biological Terrorism: Gauging the Threat

Very few terrorist groups have attempted to develop a biological weapon capability, and even fewer have succeeded. While this history is reassuring, the events of September 11, 2001, are a reminder that past experience is not always a reliable predictor of future threats. The disquieting reality is that intelligence and law enforcement agencies will be hard-pressed to detect the emergence of a terrorist group capable of developing and using biological weapons. Given the difficulty in gauging the capability of terrorist groups to engage in biological terrorism, it is not unrealistic to focus preventive and preemptive measures on the small number of groups that have demonstrated an interest in developing these weapons.

It is important to keep the threat posed by terrorists using biological weapons in context. Terrorists still overwhelmingly prefer to use guns and bombs to wreak havoc. The next bioterrorist attack—whether by al Qaeda, self-radicalized jihadists, or homegrown extremists—will most likely be based on second-generation capabilities involving the production or acquisition of small quantities of low-quality biological agents and a crude means of dissemination. Such weapons would be effective only for assassination, contaminating food or drinks, or for use in a small enclosed space.[115] These weapons would be capable of inducing mass anxiety, possibly causing mass disruption for a limited time, and

112. Carus, *Bioterrorism and Biocrimes,* 31–32.

113. Carus, "The Rajneeshees (1984)," 115–37.

114. W. Seth Carus, "R.I.S.E. (1972)," in *Toxic Terror,* ed. Tucker, 55–70; and Jonathan B. Tucker and Jason Pate, "The Minnesota Patriots Council (1991)," in *Toxic Terror,* ed. Tucker, 159–83.

115. CIA, *Terrorist CBRN: Materials and Effects* (Langley, VA: CIA, May 2003).

maybe even mass casualties if the public health and medical responses to the attack are lacking.

The longer-term prospects of biological terrorism, however, are more worrisome. Despite the significant hurdles that terrorists face in developing biological weapons and the improbability that they will be able to obtain such weapons directly from a state, several trends raise the risk of biological terrorism. First, globalization is making the multiuse ingredients necessary for biological terrorism—information, expertise, equipment, and materials—more widely available.[116] Second, advances in the life sciences are not only generating new knowledge and techniques that can be misused for hostile purposes, but, more important from a counterterrorism perspective, they may be reducing the level of expertise required to utilize previously developed techniques.[117] Both of these trends may increase the pool of individuals who can exploit biotechnology for hostile purposes. The third trend is the continuing increase in the lethality of terrorist organizations. The first ten years of the twenty-first century have seen more terrorist attacks that have killed over one hundred people than there were in the entire twentieth century.[118] Although these attacks reaffirm the long-standing interest of terrorist groups in using guns and bombs to obtain their objectives, the pursuit of ever-higher casualty counts may lead more such groups to explore the use of nuclear, biological, or chemical weapons to inflict mass casualties.

---

116. Institute of Medicine and National Research Council, *Globalization, Biosecurity, and the Future of the Life Sciences* (Washington, DC: National Academies Press, 2006).

117. Robert Carlson, "The Pace and Proliferation of Biological Technologies," *Biosecurity and Bioterrorism* 1, no. 3 (2003): 1–12.

118. The twentieth century experienced fourteen such attacks, while twenty such attacks occurred between 2000 and 2009. Author's data.

Conclusion

Reducing the Danger Posed by Biological Weapons

Biological weapons present a number of paradoxes and dilemmas. They are widely feared, yet rarely used. They were the first weapon prohibited by an international treaty, yet the proliferation of these weapons increased after the ban. They are frequently called the poor man's atomic bomb, yet they cannot provide the same deterrent value as nuclear weapons. In addition, the technology needed to produce these weapons is also a source of huge benefits to global society. Finally, those who use this technology whether for good or for evil shroud their activities in secrecy.

These findings bode ill for a world where biotechnology is exploited for military purposes.[1] Since biological weapons are more effective as a means of attack than as a means of deterrence, states will likely view the development of BW programs among adversaries with alarm. The security dilemma will provide incentives for even status quo states to engage in competition and hinder arms control efforts. With the latent capabilities for biological weapons already

---

1. Matthew Meselson, "Averting the Hostile Exploitation of Biotechnology," *CBW Conventions Bulletin* 48 (June 2000): 16–19.

widespread, the future proliferation of these weapons will depend heavily on a nation's intentions. Since intentions are notoriously hard to gauge, misperceptions and miscalculations are likely. In sum, the proliferation of biological weapons and their enabling technologies will have a destabilizing influence on international security.

Forecasting Future Biological Threats

The magnitude of the future threat posed by biological weapons will be determined by two poorly understood and difficult to influence variables. The first variable is the net impact of the biotechnology revolution and genetic engineering on the offensive, defensive, and deterrent aspects of biological warfare and the ability to detect offensive BW activities. Will advances in the life sciences strengthen the defender and provide new capabilities to verify biological arms control agreements or enable attackers to develop more sophisticated weapons and the means of concealing them? This assessment is complicated by the accelerating rate of innovation in the life sciences, the inevitable global diffusion of these technologies, and the intrinsic value of scientific and commercial research for the development of new and improved weapons. Many nations, particularly the United States and its allies, are investing heavily in biodefense research in a bid to alter the balance between offense and defense. It must be recognized, however, that the dramatic increases in defensive research may also generate knowledge that could be used to develop advanced biological weapons. Biodefense programs may also be perceived as being offensive in nature. The national security community needs to remain sensitive to the potential risks associated with a robust biological defense program and ensure that appropriate transparency and oversight measures are in place to mitigate these risks.

The second key variable is the level of interest of states and nonstate actors in pursuing BW capabilities. Will the norm against BW continue to limit the appeal of these weapons? Or will security concerns and the bureaucratic ambitions of scientific and military leaders overwhelm this inhibition? The growth in biodefense programs provides a foundation for the development of offensive capabilities due to the security dilemma or the parochial interests of scientists and military organizations. Secretive biodefense programs are more likely to provide such a stepping stone to an offensive program than transparent programs. What is the likelihood that nonstate actors will emerge that combine technical acumen, a desire to cause mass casualties, and an interest in biological weapons? Thus far, no terrorist group has combined both the capability and motivation to use biological weapons to cause mass death. Given the difficulty in tracking terrorist groups and detecting activities to develop biological weapons, it is possible that such a group will arise with little or no warning. Preventing the emergence of such groups and the misuse of the biotechnology revolution will be major security challenges for the twenty-first century.

Reducing the Dangers Posed By Biological Weapons

Based on this analysis I offer six policy prescriptions for countering the growing danger posed by biological weapons: (1) strengthen defenses against biological weapons, (2) increase the transparency and oversight of defensive and civilian biological activities, (3) improve intelligence and forensic capabilities, (4) revitalize the Biological Weapons Convention, (5) enhance cooperative nonproliferation programs, and (6) reinforce the norm against the development and use of these weapons. These prescriptions are mutually reinforcing: robust defenses reduce the attractiveness of these weapons and force an actor to acquire a larger or more sophisticated capability that is harder to accomplish and more easily detectable, while strong norms deter actors from pursuing these weapons and make it easier to rally international cooperation for these measures.

Strengthen Defenses

Defenses against biological weapons should be strengthened to make these weapons less effective and less likely to be used in future conflicts. This can be accomplished by fundamentally shifting the offense-defense balance toward defense, investing sufficient resources in defense to offset the advantage held by the offense, or a combination of both of these measures. Even if it is not possible to dramatically reduce the advantage of the offense in biological warfare, the United States and its allies are wealthy enough to invest the resources necessary to minimize that advantage. The United States has already committed substantial funding to improving defenses against biological weapons, more than $50 billion since 2001.[2] What is required now is channeling these resources to the most effective programs, improving their integration, and ensuring their sustainability.

In order to shift the offense-defense balance in biological warfare more toward defense, the United States and its allies must engage in an intensive effort to develop new detection, protection, and treatment technologies to defend against biological weapons. Robust defenses against the most threatening agents

---

2. Alan Pearson, *Federal Funding for Biological Weapons Prevention and Defense, Fiscal Years 2001 to 2009* (Washington, DC: Center for Arms Control and Non-Proliferation, 2008).

and further improvements in vaccines, sensors, physical defenses, surveillance systems, diagnostic tools, and treatments could create sufficient uncertainty about the likelihood of success to deter such attacks. Given the diversity of threat agents and the difficulty in accurately gauging biological threats, defensive preparations should emphasize measures that provide broad-spectrum protection against a range of man-made and naturally occurring pathogens and outbreaks.

Genome sequencing is a particularly rewarding field, since the results can be used to develop improved versions of the full range of countermeasures: sensors, diagnostic devices, vaccines, medical treatments, and forensic tools.[3] The ability to conduct rapid sequencing and comparative analysis is especially important to counter the threat of novel infectious diseases or modified BW agents. In 2003 scientists were able to sequence the entire genome of the virus that causes Severe Acute Respiratory Syndrome (SARS) in less than six weeks. This information was immediately utilized by researchers around the world to begin the development of vaccines, antiviral drugs, and diagnostic tests.[4]

Although the United States has devoted significant funding to research on new biodefense drugs, its return on investment has been meager so far.[5] The development of medical biodefense countermeasures is fraught not only with scientific and technical challenges but also political, economic, and regulatory problems. Given the limited market and low margins for new biodefense-related products compared to the mass market and potential profits for blockbuster drugs, uncertainties about long-term government commitments to procure biodefense drugs as well as unresolved patent and liability issues, major pharmaceutical firms have been reluctant to enter this field. Instead, smaller biotechnology firms have become the primary players, but these firms lack the capital and experience to shepherd new drugs through the expensive safety and efficacy review process or engage in large-scale production of approved drugs.[6] As a result, government agencies may have to take a stronger role in developing and producing biodefense pharmaceuticals that the private sector views as too risky or not profitable enough. The biodefense countermeasure strategy should shift its focus from the "one bug, one drug" paradigm to the development of broad-spectrum drugs, diagnostics, platforms, and technologies that are useful against both BW and naturally occurring disease threats. Such capabilities are not only more likely to

3. Clare Fraser, "A Genomics-Based Approach to Biodefense Preparedness," *Nature Reviews Genetics* 5 (2004): 23–33.

4. National Research Council, *Seeking Security: Pathogens, Open Access, and Genome Databases* (Washington, DC: National Academies Press, 2004), 31–33.

5. Renae Merle, "Bioterror Antidote: Unfulfilled Prescription," *Washington Post,* January 16, 2007, D1; "U.S. Biodefense—Shocking and Awful," *Nature Biotechnology* 25, no. 6 (2007): 603.

6. Kendall Hoyt, "The Role of Military-Industrial Relations in the History of Vaccine Innovation" (PhD diss., Massachusetts Institute of Technology, 2002), chap. 5.

attract and sustain the interest of the private sector, but they also provide greater benefits for the public's health in the absence of a BW attack.

Because the biological warfare threat to civilians during peacetime is relatively small and all vaccines have some adverse side effects, protection of the civilian population will have to rely on a combination of public health surveillance and medical treatment to rapidly detect and respond to a BW attack. Such defensive preparations need to be more fully integrated into all-hazard public health emergency preparedness to ensure that they will have the beneficial effect of enhancing preparedness for natural outbreaks of infectious diseases.

Early detection of a biological weapon attack—either on the battlefield or the home front—is the key to mitigating its consequences. An effective defensive system should employ a layered system to provide defense in depth: aerosol detection for open-air releases or indoor releases at critical facilities or likely targets; public health surveillance of the general population; and diagnostic tests in clinical settings. Each of the detection technologies currently in use has its strengths and weaknesses. Aerosol detection systems have the potential to provide the earliest warning of an attack, but the current generation of sensors are too slow, unreliable, expensive, and limited in the number of agents they can detect.[7] In addition, these systems are of little use for detecting naturally occurring outbreaks or nonaerosolized biological attacks. Public health agencies are improving the timeliness with which they can detect both natural and manmade outbreaks, regardless of the identity of the agent, by using syndromic surveillance systems that detect unusual patterns in data collected from hospitals, pharmacies, emergency medical services, and other sources. The value of these systems is limited by their low sensitivity and reliance on data generated after people fall ill and seek medical treatment. As a result, they are best suited to detecting large outbreaks that will likely come to the attention of public health officials through clinical channels.[8] Public health surveillance can be further enhanced through the integration of traditional surveillance methods, syndromic surveillance systems, biological sensors, and new sources of information, such as veterinarians. Medical diagnostic kits and laboratory tests for BW agents need to be more rapid, accurate, reliable, and affordable. The widespread adoption of an affordable point-of-care diagnostic system that could quickly screen samples for the presence of hundreds of pathogens would enable physicians to accurately diagnose diseases ranging from the common cold to anthrax.

---

7. Office of the Secretary of Defense, *Proliferation: Threat and Response* (Washington, DC: Department of Defense, 2001), 92–94, 199–20.

8. James W. Buehler, et al., "Syndromic Surveillance and Bioterrorism-Related Epidemics," *Emerging Infectious Diseases* 9, no. 10 (2003): 1197–1204; and Michael A. Stoto, Matthias Schonlau, and Louis T. Mariano, "Syndromic Surveillance: Is It Worth the Effort?" *Chance* 17, no. 1 (2004): 19–24.

The United States should also make a stronger effort to engage in international biodefense cooperation. The United States already encourages its allies to enhance their biological defenses through bilateral mechanisms and on a multilateral basis through NATO and the Group of Eight (Canada, France, Germany, Italy, Japan, Russia, United Kingdom, United States). This international cooperation should be strengthened in two ways. First, the United States and its allies should develop the capability to deploy biological defenses such as sensors, specially trained public health and medical teams, and pharmaceutical stockpiles to states that are threatened or attacked with biological weapons. The deployment of such capabilities may be necessary to maintain coalition solidarity in the face of explicit or suspected BW threats. This capability would also fulfill the commitment of parties to the BWC under Article VII to assist states threatened by BW. Second, the United States should lead an international effort to enhance the global public health surveillance system. Under the World Health Organization's 2005 International Health Regulations, states are required to develop and maintain core national surveillance capabilities by 2012.[9] This is an ambitious initiative that can only succeed with strong support and leadership from the United States. Assisting developing nations in improving their disease surveillance capabilities, which would be useful for combating both BW threats and naturally occurring infectious diseases, would yield both humanitarian and security benefits. As the AIDS pandemic, 2003 SARS outbreak, and ongoing H5N1 avian influenza outbreaks have shown, naturally occurring diseases can have significant political, economic, and even security implications.[10] Stronger international surveillance and response capabilities may deter the use of BW by reducing the likelihood that a BW attack would achieve its objectives. Preventing the successful use of BW is also important for denying the attacker valuable operational experience and demonstrating the military utility of these weapons. The use of biological weapons anywhere by anyone would also erode the norm against these weapons everywhere.

Increase Transparency and Oversight

The transparency and oversight of defensive and civilian activities in the fields of biology and biotechnology need to be increased to ensure that advances in these fields are not misused, or perceived as being misused, for hostile purposes.

---

9. Michael G. Baker and David P. Fidler, "Global Public Health Surveillance under New International Health Regulations," *Emerging Infectious Diseases* 12, no. 7 (2006): 1058–65.

10. Stefan Elbe, *Strategic Implications of HIV/AIDS,* Adelphi Paper No. 357 (Oxford: Oxford University Press, 2003); and Christian Enemark, *Disease and Security: Natural Plagues and Biological Weapons in East Asia* (New York: Routledge, 2007).

The three areas that are in greatest need of attention are international standards for the security of pathogens and toxins, mechanisms for national and international oversight over dual-use research, and domestic oversight of biodefense programs.

Enhancing the security of pathogens and toxins took on new urgency after the anthrax letter attacks in fall 2001. The United States has taken the lead in imposing stricter regulations on the handling of dangerous biological materials, although other developed nations have followed suit. In contrast, relatively little has been done on the international level.[11] In April 2004 the United Nations Security Council passed Resolution 1540, which requires states to ensure that WMD-related materials are properly secured.[12] The resolution, however, provided no guidance on how to achieve that objective. The United States has a strong incentive to internationalize its domestic pathogen security measures to level the playing field for domestic industry and academia and to cut off foreign sources of pathogens for terrorists.[13]

To foster greater international collaboration on pathogen security and provide the foundation for a global regime, the mandate of the Australia Group should be extended to govern domestic controls on the safety and security of pathogens and toxins. The Australia Group is an informal multilateral arrangement used by forty-one states to harmonize national export control policies regarding dual-use materials that could be used to produce chemical and biological weapons. This initiative would take advantage of the mechanisms already developed by the Australia Group to share information among its members and increase the relevance of the group for addressing the threat of biological terrorism. The Australia Group could provide a forum for member and nonmember states to discuss models of pathogen security measures as well as technical assistance to states for developing and implementing relevant legislation. Although the Australia Group has been viewed by some developing nations as a discriminatory organization that impedes peaceful development in the chemical and biological fields, the requirement enshrined in Resolution 1540, that all nations are responsible for exercising effective domestic and export controls, should lessen the stigma attached to this group.

Oversight of dual-use research by the life sciences community needs to be enhanced to prevent accidents and reduce the risk that such research could be used for malevolent purposes. The United States has taken the lead in increasing

11. Jonathan B. Tucker, "Preventing the Misuse of Pathogens: The Need for Global Biosecurity Standards," *Arms Control Today* (June 2003): 3–10.

12. United Nations Security Council, *Resolution 1540,* S/RES/1540 (2004), April 28, 2004.

13. Kendall Hoyt and Stephen G. Brooks, "A Double-Edged Sword: Globalization and Biosecurity," *International Security* 28, no. 3 (2003/4): 123–48.

the awareness of the life sciences community about the need to apply additional scrutiny to research that could be misused for hostile purposes.[14] In 2004 the United States created the National Science Advisory Board for Biosecurity (NSABB) at the National Institutes of Health (NIH) to develop guidelines for reviewing dual-use research. In June 2007, NSABB proposed a framework for dual-use research oversight for all federal agencies and private entities that receive federal research funding.[15] This proposal has several weaknesses. First, the NSABB's definition of "dual-use research of concern" sets a very high threshold for an experiment to be considered at risk for misuse. The NSABB's criterion for identifying "dual-use research of concern" is "research that, based on current understanding, can be reasonably anticipated to provide knowledge, products, or technologies that could be directly misapplied by others to pose a threat to public health and safety, agriculture, plants, animals, the environment, or materiel."[16] The use of the qualifiers "current understanding", "reasonably anticipated," and "directly misapplied" will exclude large swathes of basic and applied research from review. In addition, NSABB proposes that the potential consequences of the research must pose a broad threat to public health or national security. This combination of criterion imposes a high burden of proof on those who would designate a specific research project as being "dual-use research of concern." The risk assessment process under this framework may be biased by the view of the scientific and health benefits of life sciences research as being immediate, tangible, and direct and the perception of the risks of misuse being distant, theoretical, and uncertain.

Second, the institutional biosafety committees, which every biological research facility must have in order to receive NIH funding and which will implement NSABB's guidelines at the local level, are weak, nonexistent, or opaque.[17] The institutional biosafety committee system needs to be thoroughly overhauled before it can be entrusted with overseeing any new biosecurity measures. Third, the proposed framework relies heavily on the principal investigator to evaluate his or her own research for dual-use implications. Most researchers in the life sciences, however, are not familiar with the security implications of dual-use research, how to review such research, and their responsibilities for preventing

---

14. National Research Council, *Biotechnology Research in an Age of Terrorism: Confronting the Dual Use Dilemma* (Washington, DC: National Academies Press, 2004).

15. NSABB, *Proposed Framework for the Oversight of Dual Use Life Sciences Research: Strategies for Minimizing the Potential Misuse of Research Information* (Washington, DC: NSABB, June 2007).

16. NSABB, *Proposed Framework for the Oversight of Dual Use Life Sciences Research,* 17.

17. Margaret S. Race and Edward Hammond, "An Evaluation of the Role and Effectiveness of Institutional Biosafety Committees in Providing Oversight and Security of Biocontainment Laboratories," *Biosecurity and Bioterrorism* 6, no. 1 (2008): 19–35.

the misuse of biotechnology.[18] The development of a code of conduct for life scientists is a first step to achieving a broader awareness among and active participation by researchers in dual-use research oversight.[19] To be meaningful, such a code must be accompanied by an intensive outreach-and-education program for scientists in academia, industry, and the government. As a means of jump-starting and sustaining such a program, federal agencies that fund biodefense research should devote a percentage of their budget to outreach and education. This effort could be modeled on the Human Genome Project, which devoted 3–5 percent of its budget to studying the ethical, legal, and social implications of the growing availability of genetic information.[20]

In this age of globalization, when life scientists, scientific articles, infectious diseases, and terrorist groups do not recognize national borders, national biosecurity initiatives are not sufficient. The diffusion of multiuse expertise around the world, the transnational nature of modern life sciences research and communication, and the growing economic importance of biotechnology for developed and developing states requires an international approach to this problem.[21] The self-interest of scientists in preserving their autonomy, the lack of international consensus on the scope and importance of the dual-use problem, and the inability or unwillingness of many governments to oversee the research activities of their own scientists are formidable obstacles to a global dual-use research oversight regime. Instead, international oversight should focus on research on the pathogens that pose the greatest degree of danger to global public health. A model for this type of international oversight is provided by the WHO experience in overseeing research conducted on variola virus in the United States and Russia.[22] The WHO ensures that research on this virus is being conducted by the right people under the right conditions for the right purposes. This oversight mechanism should be extended to include research on organisms that pose a special danger of global pandemic due to their combination of transmissibility and pathogenicity.

---

18. Brian Rappert, *Biotechnology, Security and the Search for Limits: An Inquiry into Research and Methods* (New York: Palgrave Macmillan, 2007); and Malcom Dando, "Raising Life Scientists' Awareness," *Bulletin of the Atomic Scientists* (June 9, 2008), http://www.thebulletin.org/node/3122.

19. Margaret A. Somerville and Ronald M. Atlas, "Ethics: A Weapon to Counter Bioterrorism," *Science* 307 (March 25, 2005): 1881–82.

20. Shane K. Green, "E³LSI Research: An Essential Element of Biodefense," *Biosecurity and Bioterrorism* 3, no. 2 (2005): 128–37.

21. Institute of Medicine and National Research Council, *Globalization, Biosecurity, and the Future of the Life Sciences;* and John Steinbruner, Elisa D. Harris, Nancy Gallagher, and Stacy M. Okutani, *Controlling Dangerous Pathogens: A Prototype Protective Oversight System* (College Park: Center for International and Security Studies at Maryland, March 2007).

22. Jonathan B. Tucker and Stacy M. Okutani, *Global Governance of "Contentious" Science: The Case of the World Health Organization's Oversight of Smallpox Virus Research,* paper no. 18, (Stockholm: Weapons of Mass Destruction Commission, n.d.).

Current candidates include the "resurrected" 1918 influenza virus and hybrids of highly pathogenic avian influenza and human influenza viruses. The purpose of this oversight is not to ban research on such viruses but to ensure that it is conducted under safe and secure conditions by competent researchers and that it will yield knowledge whose value is commensurate with the risks created by such research. Once the life sciences community develops a greater appreciation of the security implications of their research and gains more experience reviewing high-risk dual-use research, it may be possible to expand international oversight into a global regime.

The growth of biological defense programs around the world, especially in the United States, requires a greater level of transparency to ensure that these activities are subject to appropriate domestic oversight and are not being used, or perceived as being used, to mask an offensive program.[23] Although it is unlikely that any state not already developing biological weapons would begin to do so now out of fear of a secret offensive program underway in the United States, the lack of transparency in one state regarding defensive activities provides other states with a convenient excuse for resisting greater transparency in their own ostensibly defensive programs. The United States should take the lead in promoting transparency in biodefense programs by serving as a role model. There is, of course, a tension between transparency and the need to safeguard sensitive information on vulnerabilities that could be exploited by another nation.[24] Full disclosure of all facets of defensive activities and countermeasures, however, is unlikely to be required to reassure other states that no offensive program is underway. The U.S. military's program to develop biodefense detection and diagnostic systems and medical countermeasures is unclassified and is already subject to extensive reporting requirements from Congress.[25] Indeed, the regulatory process in advanced industrialized nations required to field a medical countermeasure makes it impossible to develop and produce such a countermeasure in secret.

The most problematic types of biodefense research are those related to threat assessment such as research on offensive BW capabilities to gauge their feasibility, ability to exploit vulnerabilities in defenses, and potential to develop

---

23. Between 1993 and 2003, the number of countries with declared biodefense programs grew from eleven to twenty-one. Iris Hunger, *Confidence Building Needs Transparency: A Summary of Data Submitted under the Bioweapons Convention's Confidence Building Measures, 1987–2003* (San Antonio, TX: Sunshine Project, 2005), 10–15.

24. Although an adversary might use such knowledge to develop different agents for which no defenses are available, such agents are unlikely to be as well studied and may not be as suitable for use as mass casualty–producing weapons.

25. The Pentagon's 2006 annual report to Congress on chemical and biological defense programs is 334 pages long.

new countermeasures against them. Revelations since September 2001 have il-
luminated significant shortfalls in oversight over classified biodefense threat-
assessment projects in the United States, especially those conducted by intelligence
agencies.[26] Traditional BW threat assessments were guided by intelligence indicating the offensive capabilities of adversaries. Since 2001 the United States
has shifted to science-based assessments that focus on anticipated future threats
driven by advances in the life sciences. Concern over the legal and security
implications of this type of research has been heightened by the creation of a
specialized facility, the National Biodefense Analysis and Countermeasures
Center under the Department of Homeland Security dedicated to this type of
research.[27]

Oversight of classified biodefense projects, especially those engaged in threat
assessment, should be vested in an interagency review group capable of balanc-
ing the competing needs of secrecy and transparency. This group would be required to submit annual reports to the appropriate Congressional committees to
ensure accountability. Given the inherent secretiveness of intelligence agencies
and the research capabilities already available within military and civilian institutes, the role of intelligence agencies in biodefense research should be strictly
limited. Transparency of biodefense programs would not only promote accountability, reduce suspicion, and build confidence in compliance with the BWC, but
it could also serve a deterrent function by demonstrating the availability of defenses against a range of biological threats.

Improve Intelligence and Forensics

Intelligence is the first line of defense against biological weapons. The capability
to reliably detect clandestine offensive biological activities, especially by nonstate
actors, and to distinguish them from defensive and civilian activities is in need
of drastic improvement. This capability is needed for four reasons: (1) to establish a foundation for verification, (2) to provide policymakers with insight into
the capabilities and intentions of other actors, (3) to improve the effectiveness
of defenses, and (4) to identify the perpetrator(s) of a BW attack. Accurate and
timely intelligence is crucial to achieving these objectives. Improved intelligence

---

26. The Department of State and National Security Council were not informed of certain classified
biodefense activities that should have been declared to the United Nations as part of a BWC confidence-
building measure.

27. Milton Leitenberg, James Leonard, and Richard Spertzel, "Biodefense Crossing the Line," *Politics and the Life Sciences* 22, no. 4 (2004): 1–2; Jonathan B. Tucker, "Biological Threat Assessment: Is
the Cure Worse Than the Disease?" *Arms Control Today* (October 2004): 13–19; and James B. Petro and
W. Seth Carus, "Biological Threat Characterization Research: A Critical Component of National Biodefense," *Biosecurity and Bioterrorism* 3, no. 4 (2005): 295–308.

on bioterrorist threats and foreign BW programs is necessary to provide national security and public health officials with information on which agents and modes of delivery are being developed by adversaries as well as to provide warning of an impending attack. Intelligence is the antidote to secrecy. Without secrecy, surprise is more difficult, and without surprise, biological weapons lose much of their effectiveness. Intelligence can also enhance the effectiveness of the other lines of defense by providing information useful for cuing sensors, prepositioning pharmaceuticals in anticipation of an attack, and heightening the readiness of the public health and medical systems. However, the proper standard of assessing how much protection the other lines of defense provide is their effectiveness absent any prior intelligence.

The deeply flawed intelligence on Iraq's BW capabilities and intentions before Operation Iraqi Freedom in 2003 highlights the urgent need for improvements in this field. Subsequent reassessments have also called into question earlier intelligence estimates about BW programs in other countries such as Cuba and Libya.[28] The United States and its allies should engage in a concerted effort to enhance the collection and analysis of intelligence regarding BW programs.

First, new technical means of collecting intelligence on BW-related activities must be developed to supplement traditional imagery and signals intelligence systems, which are not well suited to this task. The most promising new technologies, such as on-site and standoff biological sampling and analysis, fall under the category of measurement and signature intelligence.[29] These technical means should be complemented by greater exploitation of open-source information, especially the biomedical literature and commercial databases.[30] Despite the disastrous experience with defectors such as Curveball, human sources remain the best way to gain insight into an adversary's BW intentions and capabilities. Such sources need to be aggressively recruited, thoroughly validated, and shared with foreign partners as necessary. In order to properly collect and analyze information from these sources, the intelligence community needs to build a cadre of experienced collectors and all-source analysts with strong backgrounds in biology and related disciplines. Mechanisms should also be developed to provide these

---

28. See Steven R. Weisman, "In Stricter Study, U.S. Scales Back Claim on Cuba Arms," *New York Times,* September 18, 2004, A5; Department of State, *Adherence to and Compliance with Arms Control, Nonproliferation and Disarmament Agreements and Commitments* (Washington, DC: Department of State, 2005), 19–20, 24–25; and Commission on the Intelligence Capabilities of the United States Regarding Weapons of Mass Destruction, *Report to the President* (Washington, DC: GPO, 2005), 252–58.

29. Jeffrey T. Richelson, "MASINT: The New Kid in Town," *International Journal of Intelligence and Counterintelligence* 14 (2001): 149–92.

30. Amy Sands, "Integrating Open Sources into Transnational Threat Assessments," in *Transforming U.S. Intelligence,* ed. Jennifer E. Sims and Burton Gerber (Washington, DC: Georgetown University Press, 2005), 63–78.

collectors and analysts with access to outside scientists with expertise in esoteric or cutting-edge fields of the life sciences. Assessments of foreign BW programs should also integrate not only scientific and technical analyses but also an understanding of the political, cultural, economic, and military factors that may influence a state's BW capabilities and intentions. Finally, the intelligence community must learn to provide useful intelligence products to nontraditional customers who play key roles in preventing, detecting, and responding to BW threats such as the healthcare, biomedical research, and public health communities.

A major research program is required to develop and refine techniques and technologies that could be employed to investigate criminal and terrorist acts involving pathogens and toxins. The ability of intelligence and law enforcement agencies to rapidly and accurately identify the perpetrator(s) of a biological attack, and thus pave the way for apprehension or retaliation, forms the foundation for deterrence. Equally important is the capability to exclude individuals, groups, or states from the list of suspects. The emerging field of microbial forensics can make a significant contribution to the attribution process.

The microbial forensic capabilities of the United States have improved significantly since the anthrax letters of 2001 thanks to scientific advancements and the leadership of the FBI.[31] The Amerithrax case spurred the development and validation of a wide range of microbial forensic techniques that will have utility for future bioterrorist and biocrime investigations. The creation of a dedicated microbial forensics facility within the Department of Homeland Security, the National Bioforensic Analysis Center, is another important step forward. Further development of this capability will require a national strategy that addresses the legal and policy implications of this new field, establishes a coordinated interagency research plan, and provides funds to build the relevant scientific expertise. This strategy should foster the development of capabilities that take into account the different operating conditions of criminal investigators, intelligence agents, and inspectors and the special demands required for prosecution, attribution, and verification.

Revitalize the Biological Weapons Convention

Multilateral efforts to combat the proliferation of biological weapons were dealt a major setback in 2001 when the negotiations on the BWC protocol ended in failure. The annual meetings that were begun in 2003 to exchange information

---

31. In 2002 the FBI created the Scientific Working Group on Microbial Genetics and Forensics to develop guidelines on the development and application of techniques to analyze biological agents. Bruce Budowle, et al., "Building Microbial Forensics as a Response to Bioterrorism," *Science* 301 (September 26, 2003): 1852–53.

and discuss new proposals to reduce the dangers posed by biological weapons have shown some value. The establishment of the Implementation Support Unit is a major step forward. The further development of these new measures would help revitalize the BWC regime. The annual meetings have yet to yield any tangible new developments, but they have fostered dialogue and opened up new avenues of potential international cooperation. The goal of the next BWC review conference in 2011 should be to translate the information and proposals discussed as part of these meetings into concrete plans of action.

The ISU's authority and resources should be increased significantly to enable it to play a more active role in promoting and implementing the BWC. A strengthened ISU should take on three additional responsibilities. First, the ISU should focus its efforts on boosting membership in the BWC, which has the lowest participation rate of the four multilateral nonproliferation treaties. This is a low-cost means of consolidating international support for the treaty. Second, the ISU should be charged with overseeing the implementation of new confidence-building, nonproliferation, or biosecurity measures adopted at the next review conference. Finally, the ISU should also be given the responsibility of maintaining the roster of experts and laboratories that the UN Secretary-General can call on to investigate alleged uses of biological weapons. The existence of an international investigative capability could help deter the use of biological weapons and assist in attribution if they are used.

Enhance Nonproliferation

Preventing the proliferation of advanced BW capabilities will hinder the progress of states and terrorist groups pursuing biological weapons. Export controls, although imperfect, nonetheless need to be rigorously enforced with the goal of slowing down and imposing additional costs on offensive BW programs. In addition, cooperative measures to prevent the flow of materials, equipment, or expertise from abandoned BW programs is also necessary. The end of the cold war coincided with the termination of biological warfare programs sponsored by the Soviet Union and South Africa. Iraq, Iran, and Libya have sought access to the legacies of these programs in order to expand or accelerate their own programs.[32] Some of the former Soviet republics hold unique collections of dangerous pathogens, including strains that have been genetically engineered.[33]

---

32. Judith Miller and William Broad, "Iranians, Bioweapons in Mind, Lure Needy Ex-Soviet Scientists," *New York Times,* December 8, 1998, A1; and R. Jeffrey Smith, "Russians Admit Firms Met Iraqis; Plants That Could Make Germ Weapons at Issue," *Washington Post,* February 18, 1998, A16.

33. Kathleen M. Vogel, "Pathogen Proliferation: Threats from the Former Soviet Bioweapons Complex," *Politics and the Life Sciences* 19, no. 1 (2000): 3–16.

Enhanced nonproliferation efforts would complement efforts to strengthen biological defenses by slowing the progress of offensive programs and harnessing former weapons scientists in defensive research.

Bilateral and international programs to convert former BW-related facilities to peaceful purposes, increase their security, and employ former weapons scientists should be intensified and expanded. Given the size and sophistication of the former Soviet BW program and the poor economic conditions in the newly independent states, preventing the proliferation of BW-related resources from these countries is essential.[34] The former director for Nonproliferation and Export Controls on the National Security Council Elisa Harris has estimated that a comprehensive program in the former Soviet Union to keep the estimated seven thousand critical BW scientists in Russia above the poverty line, eliminate BW infrastructure in non-Russian republics, and improve the physical security at former BW research and production facilities in Russia would require $750 million over five years, roughly 50 percent more than current funding levels.[35]

The precedent established by cooperative efforts to dismantle weapons facilities and redirect weapons scientists in the former Soviet Union has recently been expanded to Iraq and Libya. Similar programs would also be useful in other states that make the strategic decisions to terminate their offensive BW program but are unable to safely dismantle the program on their own or fully employ former weapons scientists in peaceful research.

An additional advantage of cooperative nonproliferation programs is their ability to promote transparency regarding current activities and provide insight into past activities of concern. While the formal reciprocal inspections that were the heart of the so-called trilateral process between the United States, United Kingdom, and Russia have been on hold since 1994, the United States has retained access to a significant portion of the former Soviet Union's BW program through a variety of cooperative threat reduction programs. In return for scientific cooperation and funding for research projects, the United States has been able to regularly visit and monitor the research activities at major civilian research facilities that previously were part of the Soviet BW organization

34. Amy Smithson, *Toxic Archipelago: Preventing Proliferation from the Former Soviet Chemical and Biological Weapons Complexes* (Washington, DC: Henry L. Stimson Center, 1999); and Sonia Ben Ouagrham, "Biological Weapon Threats from the Former Soviet Union," (paper presented at The Future of Russia Conference sponsored by the Liechtenstein Institute for Self-Determination, Princeton University at Triesenberg, Liechtenstein, March 15, 2002).

35. Prepared statement of Elisa D. Harris, research fellow, Center for International and Security Studies, University of Maryland, before House International Relations Committee, *Russia, Iraq, and Other Potential Sources of Anthrax, Smallpox and Other Bioterrorist Weapons,* 107th Cong., 1st sess., December 5, 2001. These biological threat–reduction programs received around $100 million a year between 2001 and 2006. Pearson, *Federal Funding for Biological Weapons Prevention and Defense, Fiscal Years 2001 to 2009.*

Biopreparat.[36] This form of cooperation serves both the United States' interest in preventing the spread of BW know-how and materials from Russia and provides assurance that at least a portion of the former Soviet offensive program is no longer active. Russia's refusal, however, to open its four military biological research facilities is a matter of great concern and should be a priority in U.S.-Russian relations.

These measures will not be able to prevent the proliferation of BW, but they can complicate terrorist access to biological weapons based on traditional pathogens and hinder the development of more sophisticated weapons by states.

Reinforce Norms

The norm against the development and use of biological weapons should be strengthened to reduce the motivation of states and terrorists to acquire and use these weapons. Since the capability to produce BW is already widespread and advances in biotechnology are diffusing globally, it is vital to focus on shaping the intentions of actors that could seek these weapons. Given the rare use of biological weapons to date, it is especially important to sustain this taboo to deter future uses of the weapons.

One valuable step in this direction would be an international agreement that the use of biological weapons represents a crime against humanity. By adding this act to the list of crimes subject to universal jurisdiction, such as piracy and hijacking, states would be allowed to arrest and prosecute violators even if their crime took place outside of their nominal jurisdiction.[37] Criminalizing biological weapons would further delegitimize these weapons and add another element of uncertainty to the calculations of political and military leaders contemplating the development and use of these weapons.

While it may be tempting to capitalize on the norm against BW to shame states into halting their programs by publicly accusing them of developing BW, this strategy does carry some risks. As discussed in chapter 3, public and private pressure on the Soviet Union, Russia, and South Africa provided moderates in those states with leverage to gain greater control over BW programs. A strategy of "naming names," however, can be counterproductive, since proving an

---

36. Judith Miller, Stephen Engelberg, and William Broad, *Germs: Biological Weapons and America's Secret War* (New York: Simon and Schuster, 2001), 228–29; Jonathan Tucker, *Scourge: The Once and Future Threat of Smallpox* (New York: Atlantic Monthly Press, 2001), 226–29.

37. For proposals along these lines, see Matthew Meselson and Julian Robinson, *A Draft Convention to Prohibit Biological and Chemical Weapons under International Criminal Law* (Cambridge: Harvard Sussex Program on CBW Armament and Arms Limitation, March 2003); and Barry Kellman, "Draft Model Convention on the Prohibition and Prevention of Biological Terrorism," *Terrorism and Political Violence* 14, no. 4 (2002): 163–208.

allegation is typically a difficult exercise given the multiuse nature of biotechnology and false accusations can destroy a state's credibility. In the aftermath of the fiasco over prewar intelligence on Iraqi WMD programs and subsequent reassessments of Cuban and Libyan BW programs, the international community will impose a higher standard of evidence before taking such accusations seriously.

One of the most worrisome threats to the norm against BW is the growing interest in nations around the world in acquiring incapacitating biochemical agents for use in law enforcement, counterterrorism, and military operations.[38] Prime candidates for such agents are bioregulators, chemicals naturally produced by the human body that are crucial for proper communication between cells and the proper functioning of the brain and nervous system. The development of such agents in the pursuit of "nonlethal" weapons would open a Pandora's box of potential manipulations of human cognition, emotion, and other physiological processes.[39] The most effective way to maintain the integrity of the norm against BW is to avoid the creation of qualifications and loopholes that exempt biochemical agents or "nonlethal" weapons from the coverage of the BWC.

In his announcement in 1969 that the United States was terminating its offensive BW program, President Nixon stated, "Mankind already carries in its own hands too many of the seeds of its own destruction." Over the past sixty years, the world has avoided the worst consequences of biological warfare. World War II ended before the United States perfected its ability to mass-produce *B. anthracis* spores and fill bombs with them for use against Japan. The revolution in biology and biotechnology blossomed in the United States free of any military interest or influence because the country had already abandoned its offensive program. The Soviet Union, which aggressively sought to apply advances in biotechnology to biological warfare, collapsed before it was able to significantly achieve this objective. Will the world be so lucky at the next turning point? Maximizing the benefits that can be derived from advances in biotechnology and biomedical research while minimizing the risk of these advances being misused for hostile purposes will be one of this century's most enduring challenges.

---

38. Alan Pearson, "Incapacitating Biochemical Weapons: Science, Technology and Policy for the 21st Century," *Nonproliferation Review* 13, no. 2 (2006): 151–81.

39. Mark Wheelis, "Will the 'New Biology' Lead to New Weapons?" *Arms Control Today* (July/August 2004): 6–13; and Mark Wheelis and Malcolm Dando, "Neurobiology: A Case Study of the Imminent Militarization of Biology," *International Review of the Red Cross* 87, no. 859 (2005): 553–68.

INDEX

Page numbers in *italics* indicate tabulated material.

terrorism, biological, 3, 8, 26, 200–227, 229–30
 al Qaeda, 8, 32, 201, 215, 219, 220–25
 anthrax postal attacks of 2001, 3, 26, 201,
  205–12, 218, 225, 234, 240
 Aum Shinrikyo, 26–27, 201, 212–14, 226
 first-generation (naturally infected
  materials), 203
 fourth-generation (genetic modification), 214–15
 hoaxes, 203
 intelligence regarding, 225–26
 Markov assassination, 204–5
 Rajneeshee cult, 27, 202, 203–4, 226
 R.I.S.E., 226
 second-generation (small scale production of
  biological agents), 203–5
 state-sponsored, 201, 215–19
 third-generation (aerosolization of biological
  agent), 205–14
 threat posed by, 202–3, 226–27
Thatcher, Margaret, 118–19
threat assessment projects, 62, 70, 237–38
tick-borne encephalitis, *155*
Tilletia indica (wheat cover smut fungus), 38–39,
  95, *96*
toxins as BW, 9–10. *See also* biological weapons,
  and specific toxins
transparency and oversight. *See* oversight
TRC (Technical Research Center), Iraq, 79, 86, 171
TRC (Truth and Reconciliation Commission),
  South Africa, 106, 127, 130, 137
trichothecene mycotoxins, 95, 172
Trilateral Agreement, 62–63, 126, 242
Technical Research Center (TRC), Iraq, 79, 86, 171
Truth and Reconciliation Commission (TRC),
  South Africa, 106, 127, 130, 137
tularemia (*Francisella tularensis*)
 casualties caused by, 24–25
 genetic engineering of, 15, 125
 properties of, *23*
 Soviet/Russian development of, 20, 24, 125, 152,
  154, *155, 167, 168*
 Soviet use during WWII, 34
 vaccine for, 28, *29,* 41
Tuter, D. John, 130
typhoid (*Salmonella Typhi*), 13, 79, 203, 226
typhus (*Rickettsia prowazekii*), *155*

unique signatures, offensive programs' lack of,
  73–74
United Kingdom
 BW program, 14, 37–38, 42
 BWC and, 55–56
 liaison intelligence, 194

 Pasechnik's defection to. *See* Pasechnik, Vladimir
 SIS, 179, 181–83, 187–89, 192, 195
 South Africa's BW program and, 134–35
 Soviet BW program and, 115–19, 122
 Trilateral Agreement, 62–63, 126, 242
United Nations Monitoring, Verification, and Inspection Commission (UNMOVIC), 25,
  75, 100, 126, 175
United Nations Security Council (UNSC), 1–2,
  58–59, 75, 76–77, 89–90, 100, 103–4, 234.
  See also United Nations Special Commission (UNSCOM) in Iraq
United Nations Special Commission (UNSCOM)
  in Iraq, 7, 45, 74–101
 assessment of, 101–2
 establishing existence of Iraqi BW program,
  77–84, *82*
 Kamel's defection, disclosures following,
  93–101, *96*
 mandate and powers, 76–77
 multiuse dilemma, 66
 OMV (ongoing monitoring and verification),
  76, 85–93
 sampling and analysis, 83, 88–89, 92, 98,
  100–101, 103
 significance of, 54–55
 U.S. intelligence's reliance on, 184–85
 verification regime under BWC, implications
  for, 102–5
United States
 BWC draft verification protocol, rejection
  of, 61–63
 CIA stockpile of toxins, 139–40
 defensive program, 66, 68–70, 71, 230, 237
 intelligence assessments. *See under* intelligence
 offensive BW program, 14–18, 32–33, 36,
  37–38, 42, 69
 oversight in, 112–13, 137, 139–40, 234–37
 Russian accusations of continued offensive
  program, 121
 smallpox research, WHO oversight of, 236
 threat assessment programs, 62, 70, 237–38
 Trilateral Agreement, 62–63, 126, 242
 unilateral renunciation of BW, 18, 42, 56, 137,
  139–40, 144
United States Army Medical Research Institute
  for Infectious Diseases (USAMRIID),
  206–9, 211, 218
UNMOVIC (United Nations Monitoring, Verification, and Inspection Commission), 25,
  75, 100, 126, 175
UNSCOM. *See* United Nations Special Commission (UNSCOM) in Iraq